Mighty Change, Tall Within

SUNY series, An American Region: Studies in the Hudson Valley

Thomas S. Wermuth, editor

Mighty Change, Tall Within

Black Identity in the Hudson Valley

Edited by

Myra B. Young Armstead

State University of New York Press, Albany

Published by
State University of New York Press, Albany

Printed in the United States of America

For information, address State University of New York Press, Albany, NY
www.sunypress.edu

Production by Marilyn P. Semerad
Marketing by Fran Keneston

Library of Congress Cataloging-in-Publication Data

Mighty change, tall within : Black identity in the Hudson Valley / edited by Myra B. Young Armstead.
p.cm. — (SUNY series, an American region)
Includes bibliographical references and index.
ISBN 0-7914-5671-4 (alk. paper) — ISBN 0-7914-5672-2 (pbk.: alk. paper)
1. African Americans—Hudson River Valley (N.Y. and N.J.)— History. 2. African Americans— Hudson River Valley (N.Y. and N.J.)— Race identity. 3. Hudson River Valley (N.Y. and N.J.)— History. I. Armstead, Myra Beth Young, 1954- II. Series.

F127.H8 M57 2003
974.7'300496073— dc21 2002030446

10 9 8 7 6 5 4 3 2 1

To LeRoi, Matthew, and Nathan—

With thanks to God through Christ

Contents

Acknowledgments

This volume resulted from the efforts and input of many to whom I am indebted. I wish to thank the scholars whose several contributions constitute this book for their cooperation with the project. I am privileged in benefiting from the intellectual stimulation generated by all my colleagues in the history department at Bard College. Among these, Robert Culp, Tabetha Ewing, Mark Lytle, and Alice Stroup offered generous, helpful feedback when I first presented an outline and conceptual framework for the book at a departmental faculty seminar several years ago. In some casual conversations, departmental colleague Gennady Shkliarevsky also shaped my thinking. Bard College kindly underwrote some key production costs. Bibliographic research by Bard students Venetta Dent and Marcos Tejeda and one specific suggestion by fellow historian and Bard colleague, Wilmetta Toliver, aided me in the process of acquiring a list of contributors. Members of a mid-Hudson black scholar's summer workshop—Christie Achebe, Eudora Chikwendu, Tabetha Ewing, George Sherer, Margaret Wade-Lewis, and Michelle Wilkinson—provided both intellectual and moral support for me as I wrote the chapter on Isabella Van Wagenen. Tabetha Ewing and Michelle Wilkinson were again forthcoming with critical commentary during final revisions of the introduction. Poughkeepsie-area historians Lorraine Roberts, Clyde Griffen, and Lisa Thompson offered bibliographic assistance. Evelyn Krueger, faculty secretary at Bard College, supplied invaluable assistance as well; her patience, professionalism, and skill in helping me transform hundreds of rough pages into a polished, legible manuscript are much appreciated. Finally, I am grateful, as always, for my immediate and extended family whose love and concern fuel the creative impulses I possess.

Credits

Chapter 6, "The Rise and Fall of Skunk Hollow," by Joan H. Geismar, is from *The Archeology of Social Disintegration in Skunk Hollow: A Nineteenth-Century Rural Black Community,* by Joan H. Geismar. Copyright © 1982 by Academic Press, Inc. Used by permission of the author. See original volume for full bibliography.

Chapter 7, "Stepladder to Community," by Irma Watkins-Owens, is from *Blood Relations: Caribbean Immigrants and the Harlem Community, 1900–1930,* by Irma Watkins-Owens. Copyright © 1996 by Indiana University Press. Used by permission of the publisher.

Chapter 9. "Race and Class Politics in a Black Middle-Class Suburb," by Bruce D. Haynes, is from *Red Lines, Black Spaces: The Politics of Race and Space in a Middle-Class Black Suburb,* by Bruce D. Haynes. Copyright © 2001 by Yale University Press. Used by permission of the publisher.

Chapter 10, "Negotiating History and Memory: Racial Representation at Pinkster, an Annual New York Celebration," by Linda Pershing is from *New York Folklore,* Volume XXIV, Nos. 1–4, 1998, pp. 77–96. Used by permission of the New York Folklore Society.

Chapter 11, "Spaces, Places, and Fields: The Politics of West African Trading in New York City's Informal Economy," by Paul Stoller, is from *American Anthropologist* 98:4. Used by permission of the American Anthropological Association. It is not for sale or further reproduction.

Cover. Detail of black and white photograph of "Eel Spearing at Setauket," 1845 by William Sidney Mount (1807–1868), oil on canvas, H: 28 1/2, W: 36", N—395.55. Used by permission of Fenimore Art Museum, Cooperstown, New York.

Author photo (back cover) by Xaviera Simmons.

Myra B. Young Armstead

Introduction

Conceptualizing Black Identity in the Hudson Valley

This collection offers a special regional perspective on black identity. Such a claim undoubtedly will prompt in many minds the following kinds of questions: What is black identity? How does it differ from other social identities? What does one hope to convey by choosing black identity as a way of capturing the myriad dimensions of black life? Why not study black community instead? Or why not target a more general topic like black experience?

Black identity in the United States may be defined as the *generic* character of experience shared by *different* people of discernible African descent.[1] It is a double-faceted, seemingly self-contradictory concept meant to simultaneously convey the universal and variable aspects of black experience. The generic side of black identity unites all black people in a common experience of racialization. Yet also imbedded in this notion are the several ways in which such factors as ethnicity, region, gender, class, and time itself can account for variety in how such racialization is experienced by blacks. The employment of the term black identity is intended to capture the fluid, socially constructed quality of black experience, the power of black subjects to shape that experience, and the existence of these historical dynamics despite and alongside the historically relentless fact of black subjugation.

My deliberate choice to apply the adjective "black" rather than "African American" as a modifier is critical in describing the kind of identity and the kind of American residents and citizens studied in these pages. This linguistic decision presupposes an open approach to the range of ethnic and/or national identities that may be subsumed, masked, or reconfigured under any general race label applied to the African-descended. In contrast, "African American" here is understood to reflect its contemporary usage—that pertaining to those of African descent born in this country into families with a history as American slaves. This terminology therefore insufficiently comprehends the scope of racialized experience explored in this collection of essays. Black identity, in contrast to African American identity, may be claimed by African American blacks, non-American blacks, and ethnic blacks.

"Identity" was first utilized by scholars as a social psychological concept, but in recent years, it has been taken up by cultural theorists in the study of "difference." At the individual level, identity refers to the unique set of personality, physical, and/or social traits distinguishing one human being from another. The distinctions constituting an identity may be imposed by those outside that identity and/or claimed by those inside that identity. At the collective level, patterned clusters of traits may be applied to and/or appropriated by individuals to mark various social groups.[2] For example, age and age-linked physical and behavioral characteristics may be used to define a "childhood identity." When applied to race, identity can then become a trope employed to capture the distinctive or exclusive characteristics of *all* black experience. In this sense, black identity and black community are coterminous.

At the same time, however, it is generally acknowledged that human beings assume multiple identities both simultaneously—sometimes complementing each other, sometimes in conflict with each other—and over the course of their lives. It is also recognized that these identities can vary from those of other individuals within the same identity group at any one time and across time. Thus, one can imagine the individual who maintains a "female identity" as a mother and wife along with a "professional identity" as a lawyer at one point in her life. In later years, this same attorney may have acquired a different "female identity" as a grandmother and widow while shifting to a new "professional identity" as a writer. Another woman of the same age may never have married, borne children, or worked for wages; the latter's identity path may have diverged from her counterpart's in every manner while also claiming a "female identity." Relating these ideas to the scholarly investigation of race means that, in the study of black people, one expects to find *plural* experiences within any given moment and *change* across time among a people subjugated *as a whole* by prejudice and discrimination. When viewed from this perspective, black identity and black community are not synonymous terms. The former concept intrinsically gives way at its edges, allowing for diversity, while the latter concept collects all within its borders.

A focus on black identity reflects the intervention of cultural studies perspectives on the study of black experience throughout an ever-changing African diaspora. Within the past decade or so, such leading black cultural and race theorists as Stuart Hall, Paul Gilroy, Hazel Carby, bell hooks, Tricia Rose, Gerald Early, Robin Kelly, and Toni Morrison have dissected assorted dimensions of black life in ways that emphasize subjectivity, choice, strategizing, negotiation, and agency among black people.[3] In an effort "to demonstrate that

Black culture is complex, dynamic, and syncretic," these notions are counterpoised against any monolithic, hegemonic, and/or stereotypical understandings of race and ethnicity that simplistically reduce subjects to a victimized, undifferentiated mass.[4] Plurality, agency, and malleability—these are the aspects of black experience especially highlighted by a focus on identity.

The theorists who inform my thinking on black identity here are mostly trained in literary studies and emphasize that language is the medium through which social identities like blackness obtain vitality. Their writings, while diverse, can be characterized as focusing chiefly or exclusively on an analysis of black cultural representation through such signifiers as language, discourse, music, and style. Using these methods, they have convincingly demonstrated the power of language, broadly understood, for hegemonic and subordinate groups, black and white. For the former, dehumanization of black people is achieved through the power of language to define, communicate, and regulate subjugated identities. For the latter, liberation is realized by the power of language to deliver alternative, hidden, and subverted "texts." Speaking early on for this cohort of thinkers, for example, bell hooks criticized the patriarchal assumptions inherent in the old black power movement as a type of "master narrative" that did not consider black female experiences in shaping black identity.[5]

While such perspectives are most enlightening, as one trained in social history I find them insufficient on their own in any discussion of black identity. They lack both a temporal and material dimension. Thus whereas they often render sharp snapshots of racialization at various moments, they fail to systematically describe the *historical process* of such racialization. While they can tell us how black identities work in various black–white and black-on-black encounters, they rarely tell us how such identities came to be. Moreover, while paying lip service to material reality, they nonetheless fail to delineate that reality in careful terms. Overlooking the numerical size of the black population, for example, cultural theorists cannot inform us how or when demographic patterns make, break, or forestall certain forms of black identity. Or, failing to locate black populations precisely in the occupational structures of society, they are sloppy in their use and understanding of terms like "black elites" or "black working people" in their discussions of black identity; in many historical cases, in fact, to assume such distinctions is simplistic or dead wrong.[6] In other words, to talk about the representational side of black identity, one needs a clear picture of the referent. The representation depends upon the referent, and the referent acquires meaning only insofar as it is represented.

Furthermore, one need not look only to studies of race and representation for hidden evidence of black agency and subjectivity. Both can be revealed in materialist studies that uncover "unnoticed" material gains negotiated by the racially subordinated against the racially privileged. As Robin Kelley demonstrated, for example, black subjectivity can be observed in the cooking "mistakes" of youthful black McDonald's employees (they supplement their meager pay with food whenever they ruin an order) just as well as it can in the lyrics of gangsta' rap.[7] Thus an understanding of black agency is enhanced by social historical work. The dialectic between the cultural forms of racial subjugators and the racially subjugated is readily highlighted and interpreted by cultural theorists. But there is also a dialogue between these cultural forms and material reality in the formation of black identity that must be noted and, more to the point, undertaken.

The chapters in this interdisciplinary volume therefore mainly explore the materialist side of this rich and necessary conversation about black identity. Such standard topics as black settlements, black religion, black economic behavior, and black formal political activity figure more prominently in this collection than do issues of discourse and representation per se. With the exceptions of Linda Pershing, Sherri-Ann Butterfield, and myself, none of the contributors to this volume are explicitly concerned with questions of black identity as this concept has developed in the recent cultural studies literature. Yet from my perspective, their findings provide depth and extension to the multilayered concept of black identity that has emerged in contemporary scholarship. In prefatory comments before each chapter, therefore, I underscore the connections between the material developments informing each contribution and the larger issue of black identity as set forth by cultural theorists.

Black identity, as a social identity, is relational. That is to say that black identity, as a social identity, has "no social relevance when it is not named; it simply does not exist when it has not been conceived and elevated to public consciousness."[8] Only in the aftermath of the European-African encounter did black identity acquire significance. In U.S. history, Europeans initiated this process. First, they began to see Africans as an undifferentiated source of potential laborers in the New World plantation complex. Early in the trans-Atlantic trade, white slave traders made some ethnic distinctions among the captives on behalf of buyers who believed certain African groups to be more suitable than others for specific tasks.[9] But as the African population in America became self-reproducing, whites assumed an indiscriminate gaze upon the African-descended. From the African side of this process, it is clear that captives brought to the shores of British North America did not identify themselves as black.[10] While they were aware that their pigmentation and habits differed from their captors who they viewed initially as frightening, "bad spirits," "savage," and "ugly," the newly enslaved—distinguished from each other by plural ethnic backgrounds—did not completely "identify" with all others sharing their fate.[11] The Middle Passage certainly forged bonds among them, especially among those who shared dialects and other cultural characteristics. But it was in the crucible of New World slavery after the international trade ceased, i.e., once new infusions of ethnic variation largely ended for a long period, that black identity in America emerged from "the movement toward race and away from ethnicity."[12]

Clearly then, black identity acquires meaning only in specific contexts. Recently, historian Ira Berlin demonstrated how changes in space and time, "the usual boundaries of historical inquiry," informed the shape of black identity in British North America. He delineated four distinct, regionally-based slave systems—a northern system; a Chesapeake Bay system; a Carolina/Georgia low country system; and a lower Mississippi system—and found that each produced a different culture in which black identity took on a different sense. Berlin furthermore charted the generational evolution of all four systems in three separate periods spanning the two centuries between 1607 and 1807 to show how the contours of black identity shifted over time, even within regions. Within the grid of geography and chronology, he enumerated a number of factors—slave mortality rates, black-white population ratios, sex ratios, rural versus urban residential patterns, work regimes, physical isolation from and proximity to whites, African importation levels, to name just some—as sculptors of black identity. As these factors changed, black identity changed.[13]

The particular spatial context in which this volume explores black identity is that of the Hudson River Valley of New York State. While in the popular mind the Hudson Valley may refer to those bucolic stretches of land sandwiched between New York City and Albany or simply north of New York City, by the standards of geography, economic history, and urban history, the Hudson Valley properly refers to New York City and its riverine hinterland. The full sweep of this terrain surpasses 300 miles and stretches from the mouth of the river in the New York City-area all the way north practically to Canada. However, for the purposes of this book, the Hudson Valley is limited to those counties abutting the wider, relatively navigable southern course of the river. This area, just over 150 miles, extends in its southern reaches into both northeastern New Jersey and Manhattan Island and just beyond Albany, New York, at its northern end.[14]

Colonial policies assured an early black presence in the Hudson River Valley. By monopolizing the valley's lucrative fur trade and later distributing huge landholdings called patroonships to favored parties (Kiliaen van Renssalaer's Renssalaerwyck, for example, contained 1 million acres), the Dutch West India Company hindered early seventeenth-century European settlement in the region. The company therefore relied heavily on imports of African captives as slaves to perform labor for its enterprises. When the British wrested control of the colony of New York from the Dutch in 1664, they granted large tracts of valley land in the form of manors and patents—ranging on the modest side from Henry Beekman's 21,766 acres to Robert Livingston's extravagant 1,500,000 acres—to individuals in order to attract settlement and encourage financial viability. The valley's fur trade, however, declined in importance in the late seventeenth and early eighteenth centuries as sources further north and west were tapped. Furthermore, the institutionalization of a semi-feudal manorial system in the region impeded free holding opportunities and therefore white settlement. The new large landowners consequently devoted their estates to diversified commercial pursuits—iron manufacturing, flour and lumber production, dairy husbandry, the raising of livestock—and relied even more heavily on slave labor in the eighteenth century. Thus, in the seven decades before the American Revolution, the black, and especially the slave, population throughout the Hudson River Valley grew tremendously from heightened African importation rates and natural reproduction. In Bergen County, for example, by the 1750s the ratio of slave men to unpropertied, single white men was 306 to 8. In fact, during most of this period, only Charleston, South Carolina, outstripped New York City among American cities in numbers of slaves.[15] In the period after 1790, a black presence in the valley continued. The appendix by sociologists Andrew Beveridge and Michael McMenemy confirms this and charts intraregional fluctuations in the valley's black population to the present day.

Black identity in the Hudson Valley is distinct in several ways. First, the establishment of the Dutch Reformed Church in the area as a result of Dutch claims to New Amsterdam meant that the valley's early black population initially encountered Christianity through a unique denominational venue and reacted in singular ways to develop regionally distinct forms of religious identity. Whitsuntide, the Reformed celebration of Pentecost, was transformed throughout the valley to become a multicultural festival in which blacks figured significantly as participants.[16] This Pinkster celebration, revived and reconfigured in the 1990s as a forum for the expression of a black nationalist identity, is the topic of Linda Pershing's chapter. Also, the resistance of the Dutch Reformed Church to slave baptisms for fear of subsequent slave manumissions meant that slave conversions to Christianity proceeded slowly; they occurred more easily in friendlier and/or more aggressively proselytizing denominations like the Episcopal Church and the new evangelical Methodist Episcopal Church—a process charted by Graham Hodges in this volume's chapter on black Christianity in early New York. Evidence that the transport of African captives, fully equipped with their own ethnic cosmologies, to New York increased steadily throughout the eighteenth century also helps explain the initial reticence of the region's black population to embrace Christianity. At the same time, the argument can be made that the Americanization of Pinkster and the appearance of an independent New York-based African Methodist Episcopal Zion Church in 1796 reflected the influence of the African-born within the region's slave population.[17] Later on, in the years prior to the Civil War, New York State, and rural upstate in particular, proved especially responsive to the new religious formations occasioned by the Second Great Awakening. Conversions to evangelical Methodism, the Baptist Church, and perfectionist cults abounded.[18] The religion-inspired metamorphosis of Isabella Van Wagenen, later known as Sojourner Truth, and more specifically her involvement in Methodism, African Methodism, and a perfectionist cult located in Manhattan and Sing Sing (present-day Ossining) inform my chapter on this celebrated antebellum black resident of the Hudson Valley.

The economic identity of blacks in the Hudson Valley was also influenced by the mercantile history of the region. Unlike the South where profits from agricultural cash crops for an overseas market were the colonies' mainstay, or New England where utopian religious views provided a rationale for settlement, New Amsterdam was in its earliest stages an aquatic commercial corridor through which the Indian fur trade passed. Albany was a trading post, New York harbor was the major collection and redistribution point, while the rural hinterland supplied food for the more populous, river-based urban centers in this system. Even after farming arose as an important enterprise with the decline of the fur trade, no single staple crop emerged; rather, a diversified economy with local, regional, and international markets as targets grew in both the cities and countryside of the Hudson Valley. The region maintained and expanded this varied market economy throughout the eighteenth century. Local, regional, and international exchanges in goods and services flourished. As documented by Aileen Agnew, even slaves were active as traders in this economic network.

In the Hudson Valley, the manner in which slavery was eliminated influenced black identity. The institution disappeared painstakingly over a three-decade period following state legislation in 1799 mandating "gradual abolition."[19] Besides the emancipation provisions they contained, gradual abolition laws led to two noteworthy consequences for slaves. First, the legal context they created fueled black impatience with captivity. Formerly compliant slaves were now transformed by the legislation into vigorous lobbyists for their own early release from bondage, persistent negotiators for the liberation of their loved ones, and anxious involuntary servants more likely than ever to seize their freedom unilaterally by absconding from owners. This process is chronicled by Michael Groth in his study of Dutchess County. Second, some of the nation's earliest free black settlements in the country emerged in the valley during the period of gradual emancipation. All-black communities outside of those formed in the South as antebellum maroon enclaves or as post-Reconstruction towns for free blacks have generally escaped the notice of historians. In the Hudson Valley, land gifts to former slaves by sympathetic, abolitionist Quakers and the lack of lucrative regional economic alternatives for the manumitted explain the appearance of rural, nineteenth-century black settlements that persisted until the early twentieth century.[20] Skunk Hollow in Rockland County as researched by Joan Geismar and The Hills in Westchester County as documented by Edythe Ann Quinn are examples. When family ranks thinned and churches disappeared, black identity could not be maintained in these places.

The importance of New York City in U.S. black history is well known; Harlem's history as a mecca for southern blacks following World War I and its cultural standing during the Renaissance of the 1920s is amply documented.[21] Yet black identity in the Hudson Valley has been shaped as well in those urban areas of the region outside of that premier city. For the valley, historically these have been either residential suburbs or cities of small-to-moderate size. Black populations have always been found in these locations despite the national narrative of African American urban life, which concentrates chiefly on major metropolitan areas.[22] Many of the Hudson Valley's small cities stand among the nation's first suburbs, and their residents, including blacks, were among the nation's pioneer suburbanites, those privileged with enough wealth to lead the flight from decaying urban centers in the early twentieth century.[23] By tracing the political behavior of African Americans in Yonkers, Bruce Haynes's study reveals the middle-class identity of some of the Hudson Valley's blacks. Denise Love Johnson's essay on southern black migration modifies the standard picture of a mass physical movement towards only the large, metropolitan centers of the North. By focusing on Poughkeepsie, she demonstrates that blacks from Dixie flocking northward between 1915 and 1970 sometimes formed "additional migratory streams" that traveled "further and settled in surrounding cities and towns."[24] Moreover, southern black identities were replanted in the Hudson Valley because of the density and intimacy of the migrant pool even in communities of moderate size.

A final way in which this collection explores the distinctive aspects of black identity in the Hudson Valley is through the inclusion of three pieces that emphasize the connections between area blacks and New York City's exclusive position as the premier international reception center of the nation. Since the early nineteenth century, New York City has served the country as the major entry point for immigrant arrivals to the United States and is rightly considered one of the most cosmopolitan cities in the world.[25] Black immigrants from various points in the African diaspora, particularly sub-Saharan Africa and the former British West Indies, have increasingly figured in this polyglot since 1965, although Caribbean immigrants were noticeable in the early part of the twentieth century.[26] In her chapter, Irma Watkins-Owens notes how black Caribbean immigrants helped reshape Harlem political identities in the 1920s. Paul Stoller's research highlights diverging economic and political identities by investigating market practices and nationalist ideals among Senegalese merchants, African American entrepreneurs, African American political activists, and African American religious leaders in the mid-1990s in Harlem. Sherri-Ann Butterfield explores ethnic and racial identity formations among the city's contemporary West Indian population.

A focus on the Hudson Valley therefore permits a singular set of perspectives on transformations and continuities in black identity. When Isabella Van Wagenen shed her slave identity and her new employer refused to be called "master," she referred to her liberation as a "mighty change." By moving forward temporally from the colonial period to the present in the order in which its chapters are organized, this volume attempts to underscore the mighty change in the identity of blacks in the region over nearly a 400-year period—from captive to slave, from slave to free, from northern-born to southern-influenced, from preindustrial to postindustrial, from multiethnic to multinational. In addition, the resilient aspect of black identity, the essence and basis of black agency and resistance, is highlighted in this collection by pieces that emphasize the creative initiatives undertaken by Hudson Valley blacks in the face of racialized systemic opposition. Like Isabella, in her successful determination to reclaim her son who had been wrongfully forced into slavery, black people within the region have stood "tall within," armed within the range of their identities with "the power of a nation."[27]

Notes

1. In Britain, postcolonial subjects of Asian as well as African background claimed black identity in the 1970s and 1980s especially. On this, see, for example, Stuart Hall, "Subjects in History: Making Diasporic Identities" in Wahneema Lubiano, ed., *The House That Race Built: Black Americans, U.S. Terrain* (New York: Pantheon Books, 1997), p. 295.

2. As examples of the social psychological literature, see Michael A. Hogg and Dominic Abrams, *Intergroup Relations: Essential Readings (Key Readings in Social Psychology)* (New York: Psychology Press, 2001); Henri Tajfel, ed., *Social Identity and Intergroup Relations* (Cambridge: Cambridge University Press, 1983); and Peter W. Robinson and Henri Tajfel, eds., *Social Groups and Identities: Developing the Legacy of Henri Tajfel* (Oxford: Butterworth-Heineman, 1997).

3. See Claire Alexander, "The Art of 'Being Black': The Creation of Black British Youth Identity," Ph.D. dissertation, Oxford University, 1992; Stuart Hall, "The New Ethnicities" in J. Donald and A. Rattansi, eds., *Race, Culture, and Difference* (London: Hutchinson, 1987); Hazel Versus Carby, "'White Women Listen!' Black Feminism and the Boundaries of Sisterhood" in Centre for Contemporary Cultural Studies, ed., *The Empire Strikes Back* (London: Hutchinson, 1982); Paul Gilroy, *'There Ain't No Black in the Union Jack': The Cultural Poetics of Race and Nation* (Chicago: University of Chicago Press, 1991); bell hooks, "Postmodern Blackness," *Postmodern Culture,* Vol. 1, Issue 1 (1990); bell hooks, *Race and Representation* (Boston: South End Press, 1992); bell hooks, *Outlaw Culture: Resisting Representation* (New York: Routledge, 1994); Tricia Rose, *Black Noise: Rap Music and Black Culture in Contemporary America*

(Hanover: University Press of New England, 1994); Gerald Early, *Lure and Loathing: Essays on Race, Identity, and the Ambivalence of Assimilation* (New York: Viking Penguin Press, 1992); Robin D. G. Kelley, "House Negroes on the Loose: Malcolm X and the Black Bourgeoisie, *Callaloo,* Vol. 2, No. 2 (1998); Toni Morrison, *Playing in the Dark: Whiteness and the Literary Imagination* (Cambridge: Harvard University Press, 1992).

4. Nicole Rodriguez Toulis, *Believing Identity: Pentecostalism and the Mediation of Jamaican Ethnicity and Gender in England* (Oxford: Berg, 1997), pp. 14–15.

5. See bell hooks, *Feminist Theory from Margin to Center* (Boston: South End Press, 1984); bell hooks, *Yearning: Race, Gender, and Cultural Politics* (Boston: South End Press, 1990).

6. See, for example, Myra B. Young Armstead, *"Lord, Please Don't Take Me in August": African Americans in Newport and Saratoga Springs, 1870–1930* (Urbana: University of Illinois Press, 1999), pp. 103–109.

7. See Robin D. G. Kelley, *Race Rebels: Culture, Politics, and the Black Working Class* (New York: The Free Press, 1994).

8. Virginia R. Dominguez, *White by Definition: Social Classification in Creole Louisiana* (New Brunswick: Rutgers University Press, 1986), p. 266; Mary C. Waters, *Black Identities: West Indian Immigrant Dreams and American Realities* (Cambridge: Harvard University Press, 1999), pp. 44–93.

9. Darold D. Wax, "Preferences for Slaves in Colonial America," *Journal of Negro History* 58 (1973), pp. 391–394.

10. Michael A. Gomez, *Exchanging Our Country Marks: The Transformation of African Identities in the Colonial and Antebellum South* (Chapel Hill: The University of North Carolina Press, 1998), pp. 1–16.

11. Paul Edwards, ed., *Equiano's Travels* (1789, reprint of *The Interesting Narrative of the Life of Olaudah Equiano, or Gustavus Vassa the African, Written by Himself,* Oxford: Heineman, 1988), pp. 15–33.

12. Gomez, *Exchanging Our Country Marks,* pp. 11, 114–115, 180.

13. Ira Berlin, *Many Thousands Gone: The First Two Centuries of Slavery in North America* (Cambridge: Belknap Press of Harvard University Press, 1998), pp. 178–184, 188–193.

14. On the historical economic relationship between Albany and New York City along its Hudson River hinterland, see Patricia U. Bonomi, *A Factious People: Politics and Society in Colonial New York* (New York: Columbia University Press, 1971), p. 17; Thomas S. Wermuth, *Rip Van Winkle's Neighbors: The Transformation of Rural Society in the Hudson River Valley, 1720–1850* (Albany: State University of New York Press, 2001), pp. 12–13; Cynthia A. Kierner, *Traders and Gentlefolk: The Livingstons of New York, 1675–1790* (Ithaca: Cornell University Press, 1992), pp. 10–85; Robert Greenhalgh Albion, *The Rise of New York Port 1815–1860* (New York: C. Scribner's Sons, 1939), pp. 77–94; Clyde and Sally Griffen, *Natives and Newcomers: The Ordering of Opportunity in Mid-Nineteenth Century Poughkeepsie* (Cambridge: Harvard University Press, 978), p. 9.

15. A. J. Williams-Myers, *Long Hammering: Essays on the Forging of an African American Presence in the Hudson River Valley to the Early Twentieth Century* (Trenton: Africa Worlds Press, Inc., 1994), pp. 17–24; Berlin, *Many Thousands Gone,* pp. 56, 180–181; Sung Bok Kim, *Landlord and Tenant in Colonial New York: Manorial Society 1664–1775* (Chapel Hill: Institute of Early American History and Culture by the University of North Carolina Press, 1978), pp. 6–7, 8–43, 154; Wermuth, *Rip Van Winkle's Neighbors,* pp. 12–15; Kierner, *Traders and Gentlefolk,* pp. 65–66, 70–71, 89–91.

16. Shane White, " 'It Was a Proud Day': African Americans, Festivals, and Parades in the North, 1741–1834," *Journal of American History,* Vol. 81, No. 1 (June 1994), pp. 13–40.

17. Berlin, *Many Thousands Gone,* pp. 178–184, 188–193; Ira Berlin, "Time, Space, and the Evolution of African American Society" in Lawrence B. Goodheart, Richard D. Brown, and Stephen G. Rabe, eds., *Slavery in American Society,* 3rd edition (Lexington: D. C. Heath and Company, 1993), p. 44; C. Eric Lincoln and Lawrence Mamiya, *The Black Church in the African American Experience* (Chapel Hill: Duke University Press, 1990), pp. 56–57.

18. On this phenomenon, see Mark A. Noll, *A History of Christianity in the United States and Canada* (Grand Rapids: William B. Eerdmans Publishing Company, 1992), pp. 165–244; Carroll Smith-Rosenberg, *Religion and the Rise of the American City: The New York City Mission Movement, 1812–1870* (Ithaca: Cornell University Press, 1971); Whitney R. Cross, *The Burnt Over District: The Social and Intellectual History of Enthusiastic Religion in Western New York, 1800–1850* (Ithaca: Cornell University Press, 1950).

19. Edgar J. McManus, *A History of Negro Slavery in New York* (Syracuse: Syracuse University Press, 1966), pp. 174–179, 190–192; Berlin, *Many Thousands Gone,* pp. 237–238.

20. McManus, *A History of Negro Slavery,* pp. 174, 195.

21. See Gilbert Osofsky, *Harlem: The Making of a Ghetto,* 2nd edition (New York: Harper Torchbooks, 1971); David Levering Lewis, *When Harlem Was in Vogue* (New York: Oxford University Press, 1979); Nathan Irvin Huggins, *Harlem Renaissance* (New York: Oxford University Press, 1971); Jervis Anderson, *This Was Harlem: A Cultural Portrait 1900–1950* (New York: Farrar Strauss Giroux, 1981).

22. On black urban life outside of major cities, see Armstead, *"Lord, Please Don't Take Me in August,"* especially p. 3.

23. Kenneth T. Jackson, *Crabgrass Frontier: The Suburbanization of the United States* (New York: Oxford University Press, 1985), pp. 35–36, 84–85, 94–99, 166.

24. Joe William Trotter, *The Great Migration in Historical Perspective: New Dimensions of Race, Class, and Gender* (Bloomington: Indiana University Press, 1991), p. 6; Emmett J. Scott, *Negro Migration During the War* (1920 report, New York: Arno Press, 1969), pp. 106–134.

25. See Thomas Archdeacon, *Becoming American: An Ethnic History* (New York:

The Free Press, 1983), pp. 11–14, 19–20, 27, 34, 36, 45–46, 62, 71–73, 76, 78–79, 81, 83, 94; Edwin G. Burrows and Mike Wallace, *Gotham: A History of New York City to 1898* (New York: Oxford University Press, 1999), pp. 737–739.

26. Archdeacon, *Becoming American,* p. 212; Philip Kasinitz, *Caribbean New York: Black Immigrants and the Politics of Race* (Ithaca: Cornell University Press, 1992), pp. 54–59; Irma Watkins-Owens, *Blood Relations: Caribbean Immigrants and the Harlem Community, 1900–1930* (Bloomington: Indiana University Press, 1996), pp. 1–11.

27. [Sojourner Truth with Olive Gilbert], *Narrative of Sojourner Truth,* edited by Margaret Washington (New York: Vintage Books, 1993), pp. 30–31.

1

Graham Russell Hodges

The Emergence of a New Black Religious Identity in New York City and Eastern New Jersey, 1624–1807

The cosmologies that African captives brought to the Hudson Valley formed the core of their identities. These newly enslaved populations encountered alternative religious systems during the period of the legal trans-Atlantic slave trade that lasted in this country from the seventeenth century until 1807. By the end of this period, most overtly religious blacks in the region had assumed new religious identities as Christians. But this new identity formation must be understood as a synthesis resulting from two sets of oppositions: the challenge between white missionary advances and African attempts to preserve their own belief systems, and the confrontation between black enthusiasm for Christian baptism as a means to liberation from slavery and white slave owners' (especially Dutch Reformed) reluctance to proselytize because this prompted slave expectations of manumission. In reshaping the new religion they eventually embraced, black Christians in the Hudson Valley connected to those evangelicals, pietists, and rituals proven most friendly to African worship styles. Moreover, the black converts established independent black churches as a critique of segregationist practices in white denominations.

The Dutch West India Company was unsure about the legality of enslaving Christians permanently . . . and wanted all residents of the colony to accept Christ. Ostensibly, the Reformed Church was the sole permissible denomination in the colony. In the original terms of settlement in 1624, the Dutch West India Company announced that the Reformed Church should be the official

---

theology of the colony, though that dictum soon proved impossible to enforce. After the arrival of the Walloons, other European pietist denominations, including Lutherans, Swedish Reformed, Puritans, and others, settled in the colony. Many of them came from rural provinces of Holland or from other countries where popular attitudes maintained that Christianized slaves should be freed. The Angolans had probably converted to Roman Catholicism before their arrival in New Amsterdam. The Reformed faith did have a monopoly in one area: only the religious edifices of its church were allowed in New Netherland until the 1650s. Some dissidents quietly joined the Reformed congregation. To keep the peace and allow some observance of other creeds, the Reformed Church used a concept of the "hidden church" to allow other denominations to borrow time in the sanctuary. Because religion was the clearest avenue to freedom and civil equality, the first blacks in New Netherland sought membership in the state church.[1]

Because the Synod of Dort[2] permitted local ministers the right to refuse baptism and allowed clerics to own slaves and deny them Christian fellowship, slavery gained a de facto legality in New Amsterdam, thereby opening clerics to pressure from their parishioners to do little about the fate of Africans. . . . [T]he Dutch West India Company seeking to reconcile the Synod of Dort's mandates on pagan baptism with the allure of the slave trade, saw no contradiction in the purchase and sale of Christians. In contrast, pietist settlers, while eager to obtain slaves, remained anxious about converting their chattel and possibly losing them. . . . Dutch families arriving in New Amsterdam surely recognized that this conflict worked against their self-interest. In the future, settlers would solve this problem simply by refusing to let their slaves anywhere near a church pulpit.

Initially Dutch Reformed Church efforts to convert Africans in New Amsterdam depended heavily on the dominie, or minister, who was an employee of the Dutch West India Company. . . . As the company imported more blacks as lifetime slaves and sold them to private owners, Reformed clerics became leery about performing a rite that had powerful social and legal consequences. Also, although clerical reports suggest that blacks were eager to be baptized, the requirements included a solid understanding of the basic beliefs of the Reformed Church and patience with the solemn, unemotional sermons. The orthodoxy issued from the Synod of Dort ensured a strict hierarchical order in which blacks were far down the ranks. Blacks owned by patriarchal masters had the tough task of convincing the family head of the necessity of catechism and church membership. Together, these reasons were early signs that Christian denominations would make only partial headway in converting African Americans. Public anxiety over the black equation of baptism and freedom curbed the willingness of Dutch Reformed members to catechize their slaves. . . . As the Dutch curbed baptism of blacks to avoid the threat of emancipation,

Africans became unrecorded spectators in the Reformed churches. The Reformed Church discouraged lay preaching and approached theological disputes in a distinctly paternalist manner, diminishing any black contributions.[3] Blacks' participation in religious affairs became limited to annual public rituals. The liturgical year in New Netherland was richly celebratory and preserved traditional pietism in the church. In particular, the Dutch observed Pinkster, their version of Pentecost, as a sanctified revival of the early Christian church. Pinkster was already known to Africans. Even before arriving in New Netherland, Africans were exposed to Roman Catholic instruction from missionaries. Kongolese royalty became Catholic during the sixteenth century after conversion by Jesuits and Capuchin clergy, and so slaves exported from Luanda in the seventeenth century had been exposed to Christianity. Catholic missionaries in the Kongo regarded all aspects of the culture of the target country that were not directly contrary to the fundamental doctrine of the church as immaterial and left them unchanged. Thus blacks in New Amsterdam coming from Angola lead a syncretic rather than an assimilated understanding of Christianity.[4] This alchemy is visible in the anxieties European divines expressed over African use of the holiday. The Capuchin monk Denis De Carli baptized several Angolans on Pentecost Sunday, then watched with apprehension as "They fell a playing upon several instruments, a Dancing and Shouting So Loud that they might be heard half a league off."[5]

Pinkster was celebrated in New Amsterdam as early as 1628. In the New World, Pinkster celebrants met on Sunday and Pentecost Monday and kept Tuesday as a holiday, creating a long weekend holiday for slaves. Pinkster was a time of interracial celebration when African and Dutch music and dance intertwined and wine and ale flowed freely. Sundays were also free times for slaves. New Amsterdam was not as determined as New England to keep the Sabbath holy. Although the Dutch did attempt to cease all work, amusements, and drinking during worship, the city magistrates refused to publish Stuyvesant's decree that the entire 24 hours of the Sabbath be holy, declaring it to be too severe and contrary to the rights of the homeland. . . .[6]

The Sunday gatherings are direct evidence of the survival of African traditions. Though arriving from disparate parts of Africa and the Caribbean, enslaved blacks formed "nations" or cultural units fusing religious beliefs and customary behaviors.[7] These units were similar to those travelers found in Africa. Nathaniel Uring, visiting Luanda in 1701, observed young blacks carousing and dancing on Sundays. Uring noted that "the young men and women often meet together in small companies by moon-light and Sing and Dance most part of the night, which they choose for coolness, it being too hot during the day for those kind of diversions. This custom of dancing is kept up in all our American plantations. On Sundays when they have leave to visit their friends they get together in small companies in the streets." Similarly, blacks in

Barbados, the source for many New Jersey slaves in this period, reveled on Sundays and on special feast days, whether African or European.[8]

These events often occurred on European holy days. Among Africans there was no clear division between the sacred and the secular. As Jon Sensbach has observed, religion suffused and dominated every aspect of life. Accordingly, what Europeans saw as blasphemy of holy days was to Africans religious observance. Moreover, the European religious community in the region lacked consensus on Sabbath behavior. Presbyterians, an important denomination in East Jersey, did not keep the Sabbath. The Society of Friends regarded strict Sabbath-keeping as a relic of authoritarian New England. The Dutch often frolicked on Sundays and invoked order on the Sabbath only to corral their unruly servants.[9]

Black Sunday romps continued through the 1690s. The grand jury in Kings County complained on November 10, 1697, of "great concourse and Mobbing of Negroe Slaves from Yorke and other places to this Place on the Sabbath Day . . . to the horror of the majority of His Majesty's Loyal Subjects." The court accused John Norton, ferryman, of transporting slaves from "yorke on the Sabbath Day" and urged that he be fined for each and every slave. Frustrated by similar problems the following year, the same court urged that "no Negroes, male or female, shall presume to go out their Majesty's habitations from one town to another without a Ticket on the Sabbath Day, under penalty of a whipping." In 1702 Lord Governor Bellomont (Richard Coote) asked the Board of Trade for a law regulating slaves, which "is become so necessary through the great insolency that sort of people are grown to." By 1706 in New York black frolics grew so threatening that Bellomont's successor, Viscount Cornbury (Edward Hyde) issued a warrant to the justices in Kings County giving them authority to break up illegal assemblages of blacks and including "the extraordinary command that if the negroes could not be taken they might be fired upon and killed."[10]

Such turbulent behavior convinced English authorities that local slaves need greater instruction in servility. When whippings and executions failed to cow the slave populace, the English turned to religion. There was much to be done. Neglect by the Dutch Reformed Church and lack of interest by newer congregations in the region left Africans virtually unchurched in Christian mores. In 1730, David Humphreys, reviewing the efforts in New York of the Society for the Propagation of the Gospel in Foreign Parts (SPG), the missionary wing of the Church of England, reported that in the last decades of the seventeenth century, "the Negroes were much discouraged from embracing the Christian religion. . . . Their marriages were performed by mutual consent only, without the blessings of the Church; they were buried by those of their owne country or Complexion in the common field, without any Christian office; perhaps some ridiculous Heathen rites were performed at the Grave by some of their owne people. No notice was given of their being sick, that they might be visited, on the contrary, frequent Discourses were made in Conversation that they had no souls and perished as the Beasts."[11]

Humphreys's descriptions indicate that over a half-century after the arrival of the first nonindigenous settlers in the region, African religious practices were still prevalent among the colony's slaves and that little effort had been made to Christianize them. Newly arrived enslaved Africans had ether been exposed to Catholicism, which the English loathed, or lacked any Christian experience. Religion, which James Axtell has termed "the invasion within," was the most potent tool for acculturation. In English society, as in other Protestant nations, baptism was a foremost ritual in any person's life cycle. Although the ceremony of baptism was fraught with ambiguity and ideological debate, there was no disagreement about its fundamental importance as the foundation of Christianity. Blacks coming into contact with Christian nations shared this view and regarded catechism and baptism as powerful steps toward free membership into society.[12]

The Church of England made the strongest institutional effort to convert Africans in the New York region. In contrast to the flagging or timorous efforts in the West Indies and the southern colonies,[13] the educational missions of the SPG in New York and New Jersey at first were powerful attempts at acculturation. Anglican efforts in North America began in the 1680s, employing the rite of baptism as the doorway to salvation for Africans. Theologian Morgan Godwyn took pains to assure nervous colonials that baptism did not require emancipation. Godwyn was emphatic about bringing Christianity to slaves; failure to do so, he argued, invited a secular, licentious reading of the Bible and God's intentions. Secret instructions to royal governors contained orders to "facilitate and encourage the Conversion of Negroes and Indians to our Christian religion." The principal support for proselytizing blacks came from wealthy New Yorkers and Crown officials but from few other colonists. Puritans in particular had deep reservations about the lasting value of the baptism of pagans.[14]

That the Church of England was quite weak outside of New York City was evident early on. For example, when the Dutch briefly recaptured the city in 1674, magistrates instructed residents of surrounding towns to nominate a representative of the Reformed faith. All residents were ordered to worship according to the tenets of the Council of Dort. Extreme Labadist pietists attempted to ban celebration of Pinkster. Even after the English retook the colony in 1675, Dutch pietism gained strength in rural parts. After the Glorious Revolution of 1688, English clerics determined to stamp the Anglican faith on the colony but had little success. Charles II's policy of awarding large grants of land to his supporters and the ensuing desire to populate proprietary colonies like New York and New Jersey required appealing to diverse groups of immigrants. Crown mercantilist legislation inevitably came into conflict with the established church by encouraging an environment open to dissenters. Thwarted, Anglican missionaries took aim at Indians and Africans.[15]

In 1703, the SPG's plans bore fruit when Elias Neau opened the first Anglican school for New York's blacks. . . . Neau identified masters' fear that baptism mandated emancipation of slaves as the key problem for the school. He suggested that Parliament pass a law clarifying the issue, "according to the example of the French and Spanish who baptize all slaves without giving them temporal liberty."[16] Together with the Reverend William Vesey, the Trinity priest, Neau lobbied the New York Assembly to duplicate earlier laws in other colonies, which "confirmed the rights of masters over their slaves after baptism . . . for without that they will not suffer them to be instructed, for fear they should be baptized without their knowledge." Neau reported that masters threatened to sell slaves who asked to attend the school to Virginia and the West Indies.[17] In fact, Vesey did baptize enslaved blacks without their masters' knowledge. In 1706 and again in 1712, he acknowledged that "those who were baptized had it done to them without consent of their masters and there are . . . [some] who wish me ill and many negroes come to catechism unknown to their masters."[18]

Neau's first success came across the North (Hudson) River. In 1704, the New Jersey Assembly, led by Lewis Morris, proclaimed that "the baptizing of any Negro, Indian or Mulatto slave shall not be any reason or cause for setting them or any of them at liberty." Two years later the New York Assembly tacked onto general tax legislation a law that intended to end the "groundless opinion that hath spread itself throughout the colony" that baptism of slaves meant "that they would become free and ought to be set at liberty." Rather, the legislation declared that baptism "shall not be any cause or reason for the freeing them." Further, the law inscribed the lineage of slavery, providing that a child "shall follow the state and condition of the mother." An additional clause ordered that "no slave whatsoever in this colony shall at any time be admitted as a witness against any freeman" in any judicial matter.[19]

The laws showed the contradictions of Anglican liberalism. Intended to open the church to potential black adherents, they reduced blacks to the status of noncitizens, permitting the act of baptism to become a justification for racial bondage. . . . Despite Neau's efforts, the SPG worried that "the greatest part of the black people in New York remain unbaptized, thro' the indifference of their masters, notwithstanding the good laws that have been made . . . and the subsequent services of the Society." Neau turned to the governor for help. Responding to the schoolmaster's request for an endorsement in early 1712, Governor Robert Hunter issued a proclamation "to the effect that all slaves should be sent to Neau's school." On the eve of a slave conspiracy that rocked the colony, Trinity rector William Vesey refused to read the proclamation in church (although it was distributed widely), indicating sharp political disagreements toward black instruction, which could not have escaped notice among the enslaved population. On April 25, Neau reported that "Vessey refused to baptize a mulattress tho' she had a letter directing [him] to baptize her." The black woman was then baptized by the chaplain of the fort in his chapel. Baptism was a major issue in the revolt a few weeks later, after which the Reverend John Sharpe noted that "What is very observable the Persons whose Negroes have been found guilty are such as are declared opposers of Christianizing Negroes." Following the conspiracy, Elias Neau retreated to his rooms, canceled classes, and worried about possible involvement of his scholars: "(only one, Hendrick Hooglandt's slave, angry at his master's refusal to allow him baptism was involved)."[20] After the revolt was repressed, Neau reopened his school. Governor Robert Hunter and his wife endorsed Neau and his students with several visits. Without Hunter's patronage, it is unlikely that Neau's school would have survived.[21]

Neau's efforts to inculcate Christian religion in African slaves had mixed effects. His sincerity and willingness to allow Africans open admission surely gave the Church of England a better reputation among slaves than it deserved. It cannot be argued, however, even so early in the century, that his teachings reached all enslaved Africans locally or convinced them to submit docilely to their fates. In New York, he worked virtually alone. Though backed by the London bishopric and by the governor, he was opposed and disliked by other colonial clerics. His historical reputation is perhaps larger than his contemporary success. Jon Butler has contended that Anglican missions caused a holocaust of African religions in America.[22] Certainly, it is true that open worship was impossible because it threatened theological hegemony and undermined the authority of slave masters. It is possible, however, that local observers did not understand how blacks used Neau's classes for their own purpose. The eagerness of transient blacks to attend classes and grab reading material for their own purposes combined with the explicit threat of the weekly or holiday African celebrations and Neau's failure to erase them are perhaps the strongest, immediate contradictions of Butler's argument.

Other European faiths did not match Anglican efforts. The Dutch Reformed Church, easily the second strongest denomination in the region and in rural areas the most powerful, rejected its earlier efforts to proselytize among blacks. The church split at the close of the seventeenth century between urbanites willing to compromise with the official Church of England and pietists who resisted Anglicanism fiercely. Pietism was most influential in the Dutch counties of Bergen in East Jersey and Kings in New York. In Bergen County, a pietist personality emerged in the aftermath of the Liesler Rebellion, which shook New York in the early 1690s. During the brutal repression by English authorities, Dutch pietists fled to Bergen, which was already overwhelmingly Dutch. As Randall Balmer has suggested, the rural pietist personality emerged among people of peripheral social status, and its ecstatic religious expression derived from inner light conversion. Proof of conversion was necessary for membership in churches governed by parishioners who valued charisma over learning and illumination over doctrine. Sacraments were reserved to the faithful, though they were incidental to spirituality. Identity was local and dependent on an "inner elect" who had withdrawn from the outer world. These qualities helped Bergen slaveholders resist Anglican calls to catechize their slaves. Elias Neau recognized this problem, explaining: "I have not catechized [in New Jersey] because they are almost all Dutch there and for they that live in town are afraid that their slaves may demand their freedom after Baptism, the country people certainly believe there is some other design upon them, besides depriving them of their slaves." No law passed by English authorities would convince these Dutch to ignore customary beliefs that baptism mandated emancipation. It was better, they decided, to keep slaves out of church and share religious experiences with them only at festivals, especially the ecstatic moments of Pinkster. For blacks, this meant that they would not receive the religious instruction given by Neau (with its concomitant gift of literacy), but they would be able to maintain their own religious faiths and encounter the Dutch and Huguenots in the magical days of Pinkster.[23]

As the African population grew, political need for acculturation to Christianity increased. For Anglican purposes, the slave revolt of 1712 was a disaster. Elias Neau now had to work under a cloud of suspicion, with William Vesey and Anglican colleagues regarding his methods as dangerous. In the aftermath of the revolt, missionaries reported distrust of baptism for political reasons.[24]

Tensions over his mission to blacks ended with Neau's death in 1722. He had sustained the school despite social and bureaucratic opposition. For slaves, Neau was the epitome of godly governance. Although Neau did not question slavery and helped pass a law that protected the system, his school was a sympathetic world in which blacks could experience Christianity, learn the precious skills of reading and writing, and practice their beliefs openly and collectively.

In the decade after Neau's death, Anglicans gave little assistance to blacks.[25] Most missionaries felt little obligation toward slaves and believed Neau succeeded largely because of his proximity to urban slaves. In a typical letter, John Thomas of Hempstead reminded the society that Neau's "business is wholly with the slaves at New York City where they live contiguously and where they come to his house." Even after Neau's death, despite the reluctance of local missionaries to catechize blacks, the London offices of the SPG kept up a steady stream of instructions. In 1730 the bishop of London appealed to colonial clerics and slave owners to consider blacks "not barely as slaves and upon the same level with laboring beasts but as Men-Slaves and Women-Slaves, who have the same Frame and Faculties as yourselves and have Souls Capable of being made eternally happy, and Reason and Understanding to receive Instruction to it." Once again, imperial edicts conflicted with local perceptions and fears.[26]

Missionaries learned to accommodate local anxieties while fulfilling the orders of the faith. The Reverend Richard Charleton operated the Trinity Church school from 1733 until 1747. . . . Seventy black students attended Charleton's school, and 15 to 20 baptisms occurred annually. The skills required of candidates for baptism included literacy, memorization, and public theological explication. After Charleton's recovery from illness in mid-1744, he was assisted by Joseph Hildreth, who taught literacy through study of the Bible and psalm-singing. In 1747 Charleton, exhausted by his endeavors, transferred to Staten Island, where he served as cleric for St. Andrew's. He baptized blacks only occasionally in the years before his death in 1777.[27]

Blacks encountered various other European faiths. Members of the Society of Friends (Quakers), a denomination with heavy representation on Long Island and in mid-Jersey and influential in New York City, continued to use slaves on farms and in households. Although radical Friends such as John Hepburn and John Sandiford initiated a campaign to cleanse the church of slavery in this period, most Quakers kept their slaves. Indicative of this pattern is the fact that over half of the members of the Shrewsbury Meeting in Monmouth County bequeathed slaves to relatives before 1741. Quaker reforms were still in the future.[28]

Two European faiths were sufficiently open to black membership as to be considered interracial communities. The Lutheran Church, in particular, attracted rural blacks. Separated by language and culture from Anglican influences and strongly pietist in rural regions, Lutherans gave free blacks high-ranking positions in their churches. Arie Van Guinee came to New York City from Surinam as a free man in 1705 and, with his wife, joined the Lutheran congregation in New York City under the Reverend Justus Falckner. A few years later Van Guinee moved to the Raritan Valley in New Jersey, where he hosted the first recorded Lutheran service in the area in 1714. Van Guinee assisted in the baptisms of his niece and nephew. He and his family purchased sizable plots of land over the years, and he became a man of considerable means and influence in the church. In 1735 he married a second wife, Margareetje Peters, granddaughter of Solomon Peters, in Hackensack.[29] Lutheran liberality attracted other descendants of the original free blacks. Families whose children appear in church registers include the Matthys, Anthonys, Franciscos, and Peterses, whose ancestries can be traced to the first Angolans in the mid-seventeenth century. Other important Lutheran free black families included the Jacksons and Cromwells.[30]

The Moravian Church, whose American territory lay largely in Pennsylvania and North Carolina, permitted black conversion in East Jersey. Andrew, the communicant member of the Moravian church in Bethlehem, Pennsylvania, prepared a memoir telling of his capture from the Igbo nation in what is now southeastern Nigeria and sale to a merchant in New York City in 1741. After being resold to a Moravian merchant named Thomas Noble, Andrew learned to read the Bible and finally convinced Noble to allow him to be baptized. The ceremony was held in Bethlehem, where Andrew joined the communal congregation and its choir. He married a free black Moravian named Magdalena with whom he had three children. He died in 1779.[31]

The Dutch Reformed Church was far less liberal. Cultural divisions between the urbane Church of England and rural Dutch pietism widened. Dark suspicions that slave baptism inspired the revolt of 1712 darkened Dutch pietist attitudes toward English rule and Anglicanism.[32] In rural East Jersey, Theodore Frelinghuysen's evangelical movement emphasized spiritual rebirth, but older beliefs such as predestinarianism restrained Dutch confidence in blacks' spiritual potential. Suspicion of Anglican missionary efforts centered around customary beliefs about baptism and emancipation.[33]

The observance of Pinkster created a momentary equality and community among Africans and Dutch and was a safety valve for household tensions. More important, it served a greater purpose for Dutch and Africans. Ecstatic moments of the "Holy Wind" and speaking in tongues were a form of spiritual conversion which replaced church baptisms. Dutch slave owners could accept their slaves into the sanctity of the faith without apprehension about the effects of Anglican baptism on slaves' expectation of emancipation. Among slaves, moreover, Pinkster ceremonies sustained promises of sacred equality and nurtured their spiritual sensibility. Pinkster resembled the pietistic ceremonies at Elias Neau's school, differing from later Anglican education, which emphasized acculturation. Pinkster services did not require perfect English, literacy, or command of Scripture. Observed in nearly all the denominations in the mid-Atlantic, Pinkster or Whitsuntide became a social conversation among English, Dutch, German, and African cultures, a union possible only in New York and New Jersey.[34]

Blacks could also use Pinkster for their own purposes. A satire that appeared in the *New-York Weekly Journal* in 1737 noted use of African musical instruments during Pinkster. Africans from the Guinea Coast in particular were adept at drums and stringed instruments. Bangars, rattles, and fiddles were common at Pinkster festivals. Performance on the fiddle was very different from European methods, with a highly percussive style in which the musician plucked the bow energetically. Pinkster songs, with their emphasis on role reversal, complemented African songs and dances of derision. Finally, the use of several instruments at Pinkster created an orchestral style akin to the music of an African festival.[35]

The article noted that blacks were forming according to their "nations." Such nationhood did not allude to specific African ethnicity but to associations of blacks formed on shipboard or in the Americas. Most common in Latin America, nations were associations of people from similar African cultural areas who typically came together to bury the dead and conduct festivals. In a large celebration such as Pinkster, when the whole African American community might assemble, blacks divided up by these nations, which served otherwise as rudimentary self-help organizations and even as governments. . . .[36]

The cleavages between paternalist and patriarchal masters and their enslaved blacks [continued in the late eighteenth century and this] was no more apparent than in religion. The paternalist Church of England maintained its limited relationship with a few privileged slaves. The Reverend Samuel Auchmuty succeeded Charleton as instructor to the slaves at Trinity. He remained as catechist at Trinity until 1784, a term that brought further growth and stability to the school. Between 1747 and 1762 Auchmuty, though hampered by illness and the recalcitrance of slave masters, averaged about 50 baptisms each year. Auchmuty reported that his students "make no small proficiency in the Christian religion." He instructed his scholars by making them "repeat their catechism . . . also I endeavor to make them sensible of the true meaning of every question, which naturally opens and discovers to them the Christians scheme and the Duty and Obligation they are under to live as Christians." Auchmuty's students learned to read from books using symbols and pictures to give meaning to words. Pupils memorized maxims broken into syllables. One key proverb exhorted "ser-vants to be o-be-di-ent unto their Mas-ters. . . . Ser-vants o-bey in all things your master ac-cording to the Flesh." The messages may have preached docility, but the Anglican persuasion that all humankind was equal before God was a powerful antidote to the dismal slave condition. In short, the Anglican schools and their curricula became carefully constructed steps toward black initiation into white society. . . .[37]

For those few men in Anglican classes, church training could advance their status. Accepting the tenets of Christianity, these slaves prepared for leadership, usually as ministers in the black community during the Revolution and afterward. . . .

Politically, Anglican missionary efforts had important consequences. As the official church, its teachings stressed the prestige of royal and imperial bonds over local governance and the importance of sacred power over the temporal. Inadvertently, because of the better treatment received by the slaves of paternalist Anglicans and the occasional emancipation stemming from baptism, the church's behavior sustained the folk custom that admission to the church mandated freedom for slaves, an axiom still held by local blacks and pietist whites. Implicit in this tenet was the understanding that refusal of this rite placed slave masters in opposition to God and instilled among blacks a critique of slavery.[38]

As the Great Awakening disturbed religious orthodoxy in colonial America, the Dutch needed a stronger buttress against slaves' claims for equality. With very rare exceptions, Reformed churches still refused to baptize free or enslaved blacks. Members or not, blacks were constant, if rowdy, listeners at Sunday services. The Awakening's evangelical methods loosened the church's hierarchy and doubtless made black adherents question their lowly status.[39]

However Reformed members inculcated doctrine among slaves, salvation usually occurred outside of the church. This may be seen in the slave narrative of James Albert Ukawsaw Gronniosaw, who came to New York City as a slave from his home in Bournou, in the interior of the Gold Coast. After serving a Mr. Van Horne of New York City, Gronniosaw was sold to the Reverend Theodores Frelinghuysen of the Dutch Reformed Church, who instructed him in Christian prayer. . . . Gronniosaw found God while sitting under a tree one day: "A light inexpressible darted down from heaven and shone around me for the space of a minute." Rather than receiving God within the boundaries of a church and community, Gronniosaw got his revelation in the open air near a tree, a symbol of the presence of divinity in African culture. His private conversion enabled him to live as a slave in a white-dominated religion. At the same time, his inner light stemmed from an African conception of salvation.[40]

The attitudes of Dutch Reformed congregations toward slaves and chattel bondage created subtle effects. Their staunch opposition to slave baptism, church membership, and emancipation imparts the impression that the Dutch believed slaves had no souls. In the late colonial period, for example, the master of John Jea, a rural slave, informed him that Africans lacked souls.[41] At the same time, the intimacy and magical powers of the Pinkster experience performed within the home ensured compelling spiritual effects. The paradox of public refusal to convert slaves while sustaining sacred occasions at home generated a combination of European pietism and barely disguised Africanisms.

The Lutheran Church generally sustained its liberal inclusion of blacks. Lutherans held marriage ceremonies for free black families around Hackensack in Bergen County. Ceremonies included the rites of the marriage of Willem Smidt and Barbara Franssen of Hackensack and the marriage of Caspar Francis Van Sallee, the grandson of Anthony the Turk, and Johanna Cromwell, a free black, at Hackensack in 1746. By performing such rites without requiring deep personal investment, the Lutherans showed far greater liberality than any other denomination. The Lutherans also performed interracial marriages. On June 6, 1741, James Elsworth, an Englishman, and Mary Jorga, a "free Portuguese baptized negress who had received liberty of her mistress to marry," did so at the home of Nicolaus Emmings in Highland, New York. . . .[42]

By the mid-eighteenth century, other European denominations questioned the morality of slavery. Chief among them were the Society of Friends, who earlier had been unrepentant slave owners and traders.[43] In 1758 the Philadelphia Meeting voted to move against slavery and to visit member slave owners to convince them to manumit their slaves and end any involvement with the slave trade. John Woolman, the leading Quaker abolitionist, visited New Jersey Friends in 1761 to encourage them to free their slaves. Another leading Friend, Daniel Stanton, spoke out against slavery in large meetings in New Jersey and New York in the early 1760s. Such meetings were more open than regular services, and it is likely that slaves attended and heard the debate. Quakers worried greatly about abolitionists encouraging possible slave revolts. . . . East Jersey Quakers, influenced by the conservative New York Meeting, lagged behind Philadelphia Friends on the issue of slavery. Although Friends increasingly manumitted their slaves by will in Monmouth County, they usually required a term of years or cash payments as forms of quitrents. Even in the Revolutionary era, only after numerous visits did the Quakers finally excommunicate three Shrewsbury slave owners who refused to manumit their slaves. That they waited until their own deaths and even then required payments by the slave to their heirs shows that Quaker slave owners were determined not to lose money over conscience. Their policies anticipated the gradual emancipation laws of the late eighteenth century.[44]

The importance of the Quakers lies not in their congregation with blacks but in their equation of slavery and immorality. The question of Christians enslaving fellow believers had arisen before, but the Anglicans and Dutch Reformed dodged the issue. The Quakers met it head-on, determining to erase slavery from their faith. What is important for our concerns is that blacks listened with great interest to Quaker debates in public and, privately, during visits to recalcitrant Friends. During the Revolution these visits had severe consequences.[45]

If the Quakers were reluctant to view blacks as potential equals at prayer, the rising evangelical sects embraced Africans as brothers and sisters. Blacks attended the love feasts and mass rallies of the Great Awakening to hear messages of personal and bodily salvation. Outside of New York the Great Awakening animated greater Presbyterian efforts among blacks. The "sacramental season," which occurred in late fall, included fasting and lengthy family orations and prayers. Like Pinkster in the Dutch Reformed Church, the Presbyterian sacramental season was uncharacteristically egalitarian. Love feasts, open to all, instilled a temporary equality before God. At the same time Presbyterians held a cautious and hesitant attitude toward criticism of slavery in the colonial period.[46]

Methodism, unlike earlier European religions, did not require catechism before baptism, making it very attractive to the great masses of unlettered whites and blacks. The Wesleyan church, making its greatest impact in America in the prerevolutionary decade, was still a wing of the Church of England. Early leaders considered themselves Anglicans. They combined the liberal paternalism with the Pentecostalism inherent in pietist sects. Their difference from the latter was the absence of the patriarchalism that characterized the Dutch Reformed, Huguenot, and even Presbyterian Churches. Of primary interest to theologically marginalized groups like blacks were the Methodists' methods, which emphasized universal salvation, experiential religion, and sanctification. Church fathers promoted the faith in person. Benjamin Abbott, his mentor Francis Asbury, and George Wesley himself counseled American Methodists. Asbury preached in New York City in 1771 and itinerated on Long Island and in New Jersey in 1772. Of one gathering in New York Asbury characteristically wrote: "To see the poor Negroes so affected, to see their sable countenances in our solemn assemblies and to hear them sing with cheerful melody their dear Redeemer's Praise, affected me much and made me ready to say of a faith I perceive God is no respecter of Persons." Asbury also counseled slave owners about freeing their bondsmen. Methodism gained more than 5,000 converts in 1775. In New York, black women were among the first members of the Methodist Church. The beloved church sexton was Peter Williams Sr. Blacks flocked to Methodism in its formative years because it was openly antislavery, respected African spirituality, focused on immediate salvation, and sponsored a nascent black ministry.[47]

The black religious impulse was still masked by slavery. Unlike the South, where historians have found ample remains of African survivals, evidence of African religious traditions in the North has been scanty. Africans did adapt Christianity to their own uses within the structures of European religions; black leaders and audiences appear through the interstices of Protestant rituals. There are glimpses in the colonial period of the creation of a black ministry, which arose like a phoenix after the American Revolution. Runaway notices provide evidence of black preachers. Andrew Saxon, who fled from Jacobus Van Cortlandt of New York City, "professeth himself to be a Roman Catholic." He marked his shirt and coat with a cross. Simon, who escaped from James Leonard of Middlesex County, New Jersey, in 1740, was accused of having "Pretended to be a Doctor and very religious and says he is a Churchman." In 1775, Major Prevost of Bergen County advertised for Mark and Jenney. Mark was "a preacher, short, black, and well set and speaks slow; the woman is rather lusty, has a cast in one eye, bad teeth, smooth tongued and very artful." Other fugitive blacks passing through the region were described as "professors of religion," "preaches to his color," and "makes a great show of religion, on which he has much to say."[48]

Runaway notices offer fragments of black autobiographies, and those shreds are filtered through suspicious white eyes. By the 1750s, blacks recorded their own stories and conversions to Christianity, narratives that offer the contours of a developing African American Christianity. In their narratives, blacks who lived or passed through New York and East Jersey displayed a powerful cynicism about life, understandable in anyone kidnapped from a homeland in Africa and enslaved in America. Hope and conversion occurred in several ways. The luckiest received schooling, as in the case of James Albert Ukawsaw Gronniosaw, who was fortunate to live in the household of Theodore Frelinghuysen. More commonly, as in the instances of Katy Schenck of Monmouth County and John Jea of Brooklyn, religious instruction came only from deep personal conviction and effort. Helping their desires was a newfound absorption of radical views of human duty and destiny which characterized evangelical thought. A particularly radical idea, which appears in Jea's narrative, and the works of Boston King, Venture Smith, and John Marrant, was that Christian conversion was a vehicle for gaining freedom. Implicitly understood since the days of Dutch rule, this affirmation at once helped blacks endure slavery in the North and forced them to confront their masters and demand freedom.

Before that could happen, however, salvation was necessary. Most narrators recalled African life with the sadness of an exile. The reverence for African religion was replaced in virtually every colonial black narrative with a deep awe for the Christian ritual and the doctrine of reconciliation. Their religiosity, shown most cogently in Jupiter Hammond's poetry and in Jea's narrative, was overwhelming, quickly replacing godliness for loyalty to a master. The word of God appeared to each outside of a church, usually in a field or road, and inspired the narrator to ecstasy. The emotions expressed demonstrate that blacks felt that Christianity, if properly followed by true adherents, would lead to bodily freedom.[49]

[During the Revolutionary War] as in the colonial period, alliances between the British and blacks were built on religious foundations. Although the war seriously hampered religious observance, blacks and whites worshiped together. In 1776 as the American army fled New York City, a wounded British soldier observed returning Loyalists, particularly Anglicans, "mother and children, grandfather and grandchildren, etc. down to the black children of the slaves, hugging and kissing each other." Anglicans were generally loyal, particularly in New York and New Jersey, where support for the SPG and a bishopric was strong. While black and white Anglicans celebrated British control, a plot to destroy the city was afoot. Charles Inglis reported to his SPG directors in London in 1776, "Several rebels secreted themselves in the houses. . . . The weather being very dry and the Wind blowing fresh on Saturday, they set fire to the city in several places at one time, between 12 and 1 o'clock in the morning. The fire raged with the utmost fury and its destructive Progress consumed about one thousand houses, or a fourth part of the city."[50]

The fire destroyed Trinity Church and its charity school for blacks and forced Anglicans to borrow the Dutch Reformed Church for their services. The school for blacks reopened: "Mr. Hildreth opened his school, his scholars collected and. . . . The Number of Negroes is the same." Inglis reported to the SPG that "Mr. Bull regularly catechizes the Negroes on Sunday after the Evening Service, and the Reverend Mr. Walters, a worthy clergyman from Boston, generally gives them a Lecture or Sermon at the same time." Bull reported that many of the black refugees became communicants. By 1778 the rebuilt Trinity Church began to hold marriage ceremonies for freed slave couples. Another Anglican missionary, Abraham Beach, used flags of truce to travel from a refuge in New York City to New Brunswick, New Jersey, where he baptized six blacks each year.[51]

The fusion of Christian and black religion continued apace. One example was the free black leader Stephen Bleucke, who arrived in New York City in the late 1760s with his wife, Margaret, and became the head of the black Loyalists in the wartime city. Bleucke, described as an impressive, educated man, was the culmination of Anglican missionary efforts toward blacks. A member of the church and the leader of his people, Bleucke became very important in British postwar plans for black Loyalists. . . .[52]

In the years after the American Revolution, the reorganized Episcopal Church stayed in the vanguard of black conversion. Trinity Church in New York City became a center for black marriages. After conducting a few ceremonies during the Revolution, Trinity Church clerics Samuel Provoost and Benjamin Moore officiated at 30 to 40 marriages between blacks annually through 1806. Some of the ceremonies joined together free blacks and slaves given permission to marry by their masters.[53]

Despite the blessings of such rites, African Americans felt stymied in the Anglican faith. Although Episcopalians strongly believed that blacks were capable of true understanding of Christian faith, they were very reluctant to promote black leaders. For example, Peter Williams, Jr., trained by the Episcopalians in the 1790s, did not become a priest until 1826, despite his obvious erudition and high status among blacks. As part of their mission effort to retain black interest, Trinity and the uptown St. Paul's Parish of Bloomingdale opened Sunday schools for blacks with the purpose of "influencing many children who would otherwise be but profane violators of the sanctity of God's Holy Day." But desegregation of Episcopal Church ritual was not universal. Episcopalian parishes, including St. Mark's in the Bowery, St. Peter's Church in New Brunswick, New Jersey, St. George's, and Christ Church of Flushing, Long Island, baptized very few blacks in the years after the Revolution.

The Episcopalians did, however, create an institution for blacks with far-reaching implications. The African Free School, founded in 1789, was a direct descendant of the charity schools administered by Anglican missionaries in the colonial period. Within four years 160 students were enrolled; by the close of the century, about 140 students of both sexes stood for examinations. The African Free School was supported by city tax revenue. In the next few decades it became the foremost vehicle to success for aspiring blacks.[54]

Reform occurred, however gradually, even in the Dutch Reformed Church. Officially segregated since the 1660s, the church began accepting black communicants soon after the Revolution. The church constitution of 1792 resolved that "no difference exists between bond and free in the Church of Christ; slaves or blacks when admitted to the church possess the same privileges as other members; their infant children are entitled to baptism and ministers who deny them any Christian privilege are to be reprimanded." In the early postrevolutionary years, black members were usually servants or slaves of white worshipers. Several new communicants, however, were free blacks, with certificates of membership from Dutch Reformed parishes in outlying regions. The Dutch Reformed Church also performed marriages either among slaves, between slaves and free blacks, or among free people, and the Dutch Reformed cemetery accepted several black burials. Still, black membership in the Dutch Reformed Church, though far greater than in the colonial era, remained small compared with the number of African Americans owned by the Dutch. Colonial-era splits between rural pietists and urban paternalists affected this reform. The new liberalism was largely confined to the city.[55]

The experience of one slave demonstrates how contentious the issue of baptism remained between Dutch masters and their bondsmen. John Jea, an African who preached in New York and New Jersey in the 1700s, claimed that an angel taught him to read the Bible in Dutch and English. Following this miracle, Jea, who lacked permission from his master, persuaded a Presbyterian minister to baptize him. According to Jea, the laws of New York State required his Dutch Reformed master to emancipate him. His master, who had informed Jea that he did not need religious instruction because he lacked a soul, became enraged at this event though he eventually freed Jea. No such law existed, of course, but Jea's error demonstrates how contentious an issue slave baptism remained after the Revolution.[56]

Presbyterian churches in New York City and New Jersey welcomed several free blacks during the 1780s, while other Presbyterian churches waited until the second decade of the nineteenth century to admit blacks. In South Hempstead, Long Island, Christ's Presbyterian Church neither admitted nor married blacks until 1810. More active was the Old Tennant Church of Freehold, New Jersey, which accepted around five slaves and free blacks as members in the first decades after the Revolution. Significantly, however, the Old Tennant Church created a new plan for seating in 1790 and permitted no blacks on the main floor. Black Presbyterians' anger over "negro pews" kept African American membership low. Racist ministers also plagued the Presbyterians, especially in New Jersey, where the southern-oriented Princeton Theological Seminary produced most church leaders. Ashbel Green, one of the most respected members of the Presbyterian Synod, declared slavery "a gross violation of sacred rights" but argued that the "number of slaves, their ignorance and vicious habits, render immediate emancipation inconsistent alike with the safety and happiness of masters and slaves." The New York Synod also flinched at the idea of immediate emancipation. There, Presbyterians worried that newly freed blacks "may be in many respects more dangerous to the community" than slaves. The synod encouraged masters to provide "such good education as to prepare them for the better enjoyment of the future." If emancipation was gradual, freedom would best occur in Africa, an early sign of the colonization movement that would dominate church policy in the antebellum period.[57]

The Methodist Church, whose English founders were abolitionists, gained numerous black adherents in the last years of the colonial era and continued to accept blacks after the war. The Methodists combined American Revolutionary egalitarianism with their own evangelical "conscience" concerns, and, in 1782, passed a rule excluding slaveholders. The Methodist Church attracted charismatic black preachers, licensed and otherwise. The limitations of the Methodist Church, easily the most liberal toward blacks, are indicative of the difficulties Protestant sects had with a black membership. As Nathan O. Hatch has argued, the Methodist Church's position toward blacks was torn by the paradox of its egalitarianism on the one hand and its racism on the other. Increasing white discomfort with black membership meant less tolerance following the Revolution. In the 1790s, Methodists amended the constitutional ban against slaveholding to apply only when slavery was "contrary to the laws of the state." Methodist ministers and their flocks in the South and West welcomed masters but excluded their slaves. The Methodists limited the authority and status of black ministers.[58]

The limited leadership of the parent church notwithstanding, Methodism offered African Americans the greatest room for growth and religious self-expression. In 1795, the John Street Methodist Church in Manhattan had 155 black members enrolled in eight worship classes; only two of the classes included men, a total of 34. As in other denominations, female adherents were most numerous. Class number 31, led by a white preacher, Cornelius Warner, was filled with black men who soon would found the African Methodist Episcopal (AME) Zion Church. The roster included James Varick, Abraham Thompson, William Miller, William Hamilton, Francis Jacobs, Thomas Miller, George Moore, George White, Thomas Cook, David Bias, and Samuel Pointer, whose words and writings became significant instruments in the formation of the black community in New York City and beyond.[59]

The first indication of a separate black religious organization came in New York City in 1795 when a group of free blacks, calling themselves the African Society, petitioned the Common Council for assistance to purchase land in the seventh ward for a burial ground. The group's leaders complained that they were not allowed to incorporate as a religious body. They petitioned for assistance to "procure a place for the erection of a place of divine worship and the interment of the People of Colour." This last request hit a positive note with the council, which for seven years had been vexed by speculators' encroachments on the Old Negro Burial Ground behind the almshouse on Bowery Lane. Land investors had chipped away at the cemetery, in operation since the 1640s, and the city wanted closure of the problem. It granted £100 to the African Society to create a new church and graveyard. The same year, angered by continued white racism against the Haitian revolution and by the incessant irritation of "black pews," Peter Williams, Sr. led the black congregation out of the John Street Church to hold separate meetings. Six years later, this group of dissident black Methodists constructed the African Methodist Episcopal Zion Church on a lot at Church and Leonard Streets. The church obtained a charter from a bishop, James Varick.[60]

The creation of the African Methodist Episcopal Zion Church in 1796 led to other black congregations. The first of these in New York was the Abyssinian Baptist Church, formed by former members of the Gold Street First Baptist Church in 1807. The Reverend Thomas Paul, founder of the First African Baptist Church in Boston, mediated the split between white and black worshipers at Gold Street and became the first minister of Abyssinian Baptist when he led four men and twelve women plus three new members out of Gold Street to form the new church. In 1810 the congregation selected Josiah Bishop of Portsmouth, New Hampshire, as its minister.[61]

African American churches provided emotional support in the face of uncertainty and disappointment and enforced the norms and values of society. Black churches in the early nineteenth century engaged in gospels of moral improvement, charity, and benevolence. They offered peace, hope, and tranquillity through Christ. They used religion and the Scripture in black protest against slavery and racial caste and to emphasize the universal equality of humans.[62]

The careers of two black ministers in this era demonstrate the parameters of black religious zeal. George White, who arrived in New York City in the early 1790s, took part in a famous class for black leaders at the John Street Methodist Church and preached on Long Island and in Westchester County and rural New Jersey. His goal was to be licensed by the Methodist Church as an ordained minister. During this pilgrimage he suffered many disheartening rejections from the Methodist hierarchy, gaining his license only after a dozen years of trying. He remained, however, very faithful to the Methodist faith. In contrast, John Jea, a less educated but more charismatic preacher, itinerated throughout rural New Jersey in the 1790s, preaching to crowds of enslaved and free blacks. Jea preached a theology of rebirth by linking the story of Lazarus with the aspirations of an emerging free black congregation. Jea disdained denominational affiliation and eventually left the New York area for crusades that took him to South America, the Far East, England, Ireland, and France. His prophetic messages appealed to blacks and whites; his methods anticipated the

Pentecostal styles popular among black male and female preachers around New York from the 1830s on. Unlike White, Jea refused to be confined by the judgments of the Methodist hierarchy.[63]

Black churches were intrinsic parts of a developing black community. Concentration of blacks enabled the growth of black churches as did their imposed segregation in the lower classes. Independent black churches were part of an overall construction of benevolent societies, literary and political forums, and occupational structures. An important reason for independence was that the black ministry was engaged in the struggle to end slavery, a process that brought cooperation from few sympathetic whites. In contrast, blacks warmly embraced the radical views of man's destiny and duty which characterized evangelical Christian thought in this era. Unlike the South, however, where such theology also enabled blacks to endure slavery precisely because doctrine promised eventual deliverance without the demands of resistance, blacks in the North employed their beliefs as proof of equality and requisite liberty.[64]

Notes

1. For pietist settlers, see David Steven Cohen, *The Dutch-American Farm* (New York: New York University Press, 1992), pp. 16–18; Keith Sprunger, *Dutch Puritanism: A History of English and Scottish Churches of the Netherlands in the Sixteenth and Seventeenth Centuries* (Leiden: E. J. Brill, 1982, pp. 53, 111, 292–296, 364; Arnold J. F. Van Laer, ed., *Documents Relating to New Netherland in the Henry E. Huntington Library* (San Marino, California: Huntington Library and Art Gallery, 1924), p. 2; John Webb Pratt, *Religion, Politics, and Diversity: The Church-State Theme in New York History* (Ithaca, New York: Cornell University Press, 1967), pp. 3–24.

2. In 1618, at the Council of Dordrecht (Dort in English) in Holland, European Protestants gathered to hammer out a theology that would greatly affect the future of Dutch settlement and the texture of race relations in North America. This was the last general meeting of Reformed churches and included representatives from the Netherlands, England, Scotland, the German states, and Geneva. Decisions made at the Council of Dort strongly affected New Netherland.

3. For discussion of the conservatism of the Dutch Reformed Church in New Netherland, see George L. Smith, *Religion and Trade in New Netherland: Dutch Origins and American Development* (Ithaca, New York: Cornell University Press, 1973), pp. 79–82, 131–155.

4. For discussion of the syncretic nature of religion in Kongo, see Wyatt MacGaffey, *Religion and Society in Central Africa: The Bakongo of Lower Zaire* (Chicago: University of Chicago Press, 1986), pp. 200–208; John Thornton, "The Developments of an African Catholic Church in the Kingdom of the Kongo, 1491–1750," *Journal of*

African History Vol. 25 (1984), pp. 152–157. For conversions in Africa, see R. R. F. F. Michelangelo and Denis De Carli, "A Voyage to Congo in the Years 1666 and 1667" in John Churchill, *A Collection of Voyages and Travels Some Now First Published in English . . .* (London: Printed by Assignment from Messrs. Churchill for Henry Lintot and John Osburn, 1744), Vol. 1, pp. 491–503. On African Christianity before and during the process of enslavement, see Georges Balandier, *Daily Life in the Kingdom of the Kongo from the Sixteenth to the Eighteenth Century* (New York: Pantheon Books, 1968), p. 81; John Thornton, "On the Trail of Voodoo: African Christianity in Africa and the Americas," *Americas* Vol. 44 (1988), pp. 261–279.

5. Michelangelo and De Carli, "A Voyage to Congo," pp. 492–493. For Pinkster in Dutch culture, see Simon Schama, *The Embarrassment of Riches: An Interpretation of Dutch Culture in the Golden Age* (New York: Harper Collins, 1987), pp. 185–188.

6. I. N. P. Stokes, *Iconography of Manhattan Island* (New York: R. H. Dodd, 1915–28), Vol. 4, p. 130. For Pentecost in Africa, see Sorrento, "A Capuchin and Apostolick Missioner," in Churchill, *Collection of Voyages,* Vol. 1, p. 573. For Pinkster in New Netherland, see Donna Merwick, *Possessing Albany, 1630–1710: The Dutch and English Experiences* (New York: Cambridge University Press, 1990), pp. 74–76, and Cohen, *Dutch-American Farm,* pp. 160–163. For discussion of masters' obligations to let slaves have holidays, see Herbert S. Klein, "Anglicanism, Catholicism, and the Negro Slave" in Ann J. Lane, ed., *The Debate Over Slavery: Stanley Elkins and His Critics* (Urbana: University of Illinois Press, 1971), pp. 148–149, 151.

7. For nations, see John Thornton, "The African Background to American Colonization" in Stanley Engerman and Robert E. Gallman, eds., *The Cambridge Economic History of the United States,* Vol. 1: *The Colonial Era* (New York: Cambridge University Press, 1996), pp. 59–60.

8. Captain Nathaniel Uring, *A History of the Voyages and Travels of Captain Nathaniel Uring,* 2nd ed. (London: J. Peele, 1726), pp. 46–47. For dancing and drinking in the West Indies during this period, see Richard Ligon, *A True and Exact History of the Island of Barbadoes,* 2nd printing (London: P. Parker and T. Guy, 1673) and William Bosman, *A New and Accurate Description of the Coast of Guinea* (London: J. Knapton, 1705), pp. 189–191.

9. Winton versus Solberg, *Redeem the Time: The Puritan Sabbath in Early America* (Cambridge, Massachusetts: Harvard University Press, 1977), pp. 197–222; Jon F. Sensbach, *A Separate Canaan: The Making of an Afro Moravian World in North Carolina, 1763–1840* (Chapel Hill: University of North Carolina Press for the Institute of Early American History and Culture, 1998), p. 6.

10. Kings County Court and Road Records, New York Municipal Archives (NYMA), New York City, pp. 41, 46–47, 60, 74–76, 81–82; Miscellaneous Conveyances of Kings County, NYMA, Vol. 3, p. 70.

11. David Humphreys, *An Account of the Endeavors Used by the Society for the Propagation of the Gospel in Foreign Parts to Instruct the Negro Slaves of New York Together with Two of Bishop Gibson's Letters on That Subject. Being an Extract from*

Dr. Humphrey's Historical Account of the Society for the Propagation of the Gospel in Foreign Parts (London: n.p., 1730), pp. 238–239.

12. James Axtell, *The Invasion Within: The Contest of Culture in Colonial North America* (New York: Oxford University Press, 1985); David Cressy, *Birth, Marriage, and Death: Ritual, Religion, and the Life-Cycle in Tudor and Stuart England* (New York: Oxford University Press, 1997), pp. 98–100; Frank Klingberg, *Anglican Humanitarianism in Colonial New York* (Philadelphia: Church Historical Society, 1940), pp. 122–123.

13. On this point, see Margaret Washington, *"A Peculiar People": Slave Religion and Community-Culture Among the Gullahs* (New York: New York University Press, 1988), pp. 67–74, 96–97; David Brien Davis, *The Problem of Slavery in Western Culture* (Ithaca, New York: Cornell University Press, 1966), pp. 210–222.

14. Lords Commisioness of Trade and Plantation to Archbishop of Canterbury, 25 October 1700, Society for the Propagation of the Gospel (SPG) Papers, Rhodes Library, Oxford University, 13: 3–4; Extract from the Instructions to Earl Clarendon when Lord Cornbury & Governor of New York, 1 January 1702/3, SPG Letter Book B: 1 (Appendix); *Ec. Rec.,* Vol. 2, pp. 954, 1034. For Puritan reservations, see Cressy, *Birth, Marriage, and Death,* pp. 111–113.

15. For the Dutch, see Randall H. Balmer, *A Perfect Babel of Confusion: Dutch Religion and English Culture in the Middle Colonies* (New York: Oxford University Press, 1989), pp. 15, 25. For Whitsun, see David Cressy, *Bonfires and Bells: National Memory and the Protestant Calendar in Elizabethan and Stuart England* (Berkeley: University of California Press, 1989), pp. 6, 8. For the Anglicans and their frustrations, see Patricia Bonomi, *Under the Cope of Heaven: Religion, Society, and Politics in Colonial America* (New York: Oxford University Press, 1986), p. 31 and John Butler, *Awash in a Sea of Faith: Christianizing the American People* (Cambridge, Massachusetts: Harvard University Press, 1990), pp. 101–105.

16. Translation of Elias Neau to John Chamberlayne, New York, 3 October 1705, in Letter Book A2: 124–126, SPG Papers, Rhodes Library, Oxford University.

17. Neau to Secretary, 30 April 1708, Letter Book A2: 167, ibid. For examples of popular prejudices toward slave baptism at this time, see *A Journal of the Life of Thomas Story* (Newcastle-on-Tyne, U.K.: Isaac Thompson, 1747), pp. 176–177; John Cotton to Unknown Minister, 9 September 1699, Pierpont Morgan Library, New York City. Cotton may have been opposed for personal reasons. In 1711, he wrote the Reveren Rowland Cotton that "Negroes and other servants grow so intolerant that I am afraid what the issue will be." (John Cotton to Rowland Cotton, 27 October 1711, ibid.). For English cases, see Folarin Shyllon, *Black People in Britan, 1555–1833* (Oxford: Oxford University Press, 1977), pp. 17–19.

18. Klingberg, *Anglican Humanitarianism,* pp. 127, 130, 132.

19. Nicholas Trott, comp., *The Laws of the British Plantations in America: Relating to the Church and the Clergy, Religion and Learning* (London: B. Cowse, 1725), p. 257; *Colonial Laws of New York from the Year 1664 to the Revolution* (Albany: J. B. Lyon,

1894–96), Vol. 1, pp. 597–598; *Ec. Rec.*, 3: 1673; *Journal of the Legislative Council of the Colony of New York, 1691–1775* (Albany: Weed, Parsons, 1861), Vol. 1, pp. 243–245; Edgar J. McManus, *Black Bondage in the North* (Syracuse, New York: Syracuse University Press, 1973), pp. 101–102. Neau forwarded the laws to the SPG secretary, offering hope that it would "help the instruction of slaves." See Neau to Secretary, 22 July 1707, Letter Book A3: 80, SPG Papers, Rhodes Library, Oxford University.

20. Secretary to Neau, 24 May 1711, Lambeth Palace Papers, 14: 248; Neau to Secretary, 21 February 1712, Letter Book A7: 143–146, SPG Papers, Rhodes Library, Oxford University.

21. Neau to Secretary De La Matre, n.d. (1713), Letter Book A8: 42; Neau to Mr. Chamberlayne, 2 September 1713, Letter Book A8: 41, SPG Papers, Rhodes Library, Oxford University.

22. Butler, *Awash in a Sea of Faith*, pp. 129–163.

23. Graham Russell Hodges, *Slavery, Freedom, and Culture Among Early American Workers* (Armonk, New York: M. E. Sharpe, 1998), p. 37; Balmer, *Perfect Babel*, p. 101; Neau to Secretary, 5 August 1708, Letter Book A3: 128, SPG Papers, Rhodes Library, Oxford University.

24. Neau did not reveal Vesey's reaction for several years until a serious dispute arose between them. See Elias Neau to Mr. Taylor, 6 December 1715, Letter Book A 11: 293–294, SPC Papers, Rhodes Library, Oxford University. See also Neau to Secretary, 22 June 1721, Letter Book A 15:95; Neau to Secretary, 2 April 1722, Letter Book A 16: 196, and Neau to Secretary De La Matre, n.d. (1713), Letter Book A 8:42, ibid. In 1717 Vesey tried unsuccessfully to fire Neau. For memorials defending Neau see Letter Book A 13:44, 48 (1718) and Governor Robert Hunter and Nine Clergy on Behalf of Neau, 2 July 1718, Letter Book A 13:424, ibid. For Neau's own defense, see Neau to Secretary, 2 July 1718, Letter Book A 13:397, ibid.

25. See William Vesey to Secretary, 26 December 1726, Letter Book A 19:421–422; Rev. Thomas Colgan to Secretary, 23 January 1726/27, Letter Book A 19:430–431; Colgan to Secretary, July 1731, Letter Book A 23:330–336; Rev. Richard Charleton to Secretary, 5 June 1733, Letter Book A 24:462, ibid.

26. John Thomas to Secretary John Chamberlayne, Hempstead, 12 June 1709 in Letter Book A 5:9; see also Mr. Muirston to Secretary, 9 January 1707/08, Letter Book A 3:168, ibid; Humphreys, *Account*, pp. 27–30.

27. Rev. Richard Charleton to Society, 28 March 1743, Letter Book B 11:146; Charleton to Society, 30 September 1743, Letter Book B 11:147; Charleton to Society, 26 March 1745, Letter Book B 13:217, 219, SPG Papers, Rhodes Library, Oxford University. Charleton baptized nine blacks in 30 years in Staten Island. See William T. Davis et al., *The Church of St. Andrew, Richmond, Staten Island: Its History, Vital Records, and Gravestone Inscriptions* (Lancaster, Pennsylvania: Science Press Printing, 1925), pp. 128–129.

28. Graham Russell Hodges, *Slavery and Freedom in the Rural North: African Americans in Monmoth County, New Jersey, 1665–1865* (Madison, Wisconsin: Madison

House Books, 1997), pp. 70–72; Jean R. Soderlund, *Quakers and Slavery: A Divided Spirit* (Princeton: Princeton University Press, 1985), pp. 112–148.

29. For Arie Van Guinee and his family, see Graham Russell Hodges, "The Pastor and the Prostitute: Sexual Power Among African Americans and Germans in Colonial New York" in Martha Hodes, ed., *Sex, Love, Race: Essays on Crossing Boundaries* (New York: New York University Press, 1999).

30. Ken Stryker-Rodda, "Baptisms of the Lutheran Church of New York City," *New York Geneological and Biographical Record* (1966–72), pp. 97–102; "First Communions in the Lutheran Church of New York City, 1704–1769," *New York Geneological and Biographical Record* 104 (1973), pp. 28–52, 109–115, 181–186, 212–214. See also Hodges, "The Pastor and the Prostitute."

31. Daniel B. Thorpe, "Chattel with a Soul: The Autobiography of a Moravian Slave," *Pennsylvania Magazine of History and Biography,* Vol. 112 (1988), pp. 433–451. For a general history of black Moravians, see Sensbach, *Separate Canaan.* For the concept of interracial communities, see Jen F. Sensbach, "Interracial Sects: Religion, Race, and Gender among Early North Carolina Moravians" in Catherine Clinton and Michele Gillespie, eds., *The Devil's Lane: Sex and Race in the Early South* (New York: Oxford University Press, 1997).

32. Richard Pointer, *Protestant Pluralism and the New York Experience: A Study of Eighteenth Century Diversity* (Bloomington: Indiana University Press, 1988), pp. 72–99; Balmer, *Perfect Babel of Confusion,* pp. 72–99; Bonomi, *Under the Cope of Heaven,* pp. 73–74.

33. For religious divisions between governor and citizens in New York, see Joyce Goodfriend, "The Social Dimensions of Congregational Life in Colonial New York City," *William and Mary Quarterly* 3d ser., Vol. 46 (1989), p. 255. For Dutch pietism and isolation, see James Tanis, *Dutch Calvinistic Pietism in the Middle Colonies: A Study in the Life and Theology of Theodorus Jacobus Frelinghuysen* (The Hague: Martinus Nijhoff, 1968).

34. A. C. Bernard, "Die Pinksterfees in Die Kerlike Jaar," Ph.D. diss., University of Amsterdam, 1954, pp. 14–22, 24–25, 32, 40, 45–46, 48, 54, 57.

35. *New York Weekly Journal,* 7, 14, 18, 21 March 1737. See also Dom Rex versus Mary Holst, 4 November 1718, Court of General Quarter Sessions, *New York Weekly Journal,* 12 June 1738. For agreement on the concept of African "nations," see Ira Berlin, *Many Thousands Gone: The First Two Centuries of African American Slavery* (Cambridge, Massachusetts: Harvard University Press, 1998), pp. 189–190.

36. See John Thornton, *Africa and Africans in the Making of the Atlantic World, 1400–1680* (New York: Cambridge University Press, 1992), pp. 184–204; Richard Gray, *Black Christians and White Missionaries* (New Haven: Yale University Press, 1990), pp. 13–15.

37. Unfortunately, Auchmuty's book of baptisms burned in a fire, but his frequent reports to the SPG show constant attention to baptisms. See the various letters from Auchmuty to the society in Leeter Book B 19:67, B 20:56–57, B 2:1–5, 7, 58, SPG Papers, Rhodes Library, Oxford University. For means of instruction, see *The British*

Instructor or the First Book for Children Being a Plain and Easy Guide to the English Language (London: J. Andrew Oliver for Thomas Field, Bookseller, 1763), p. 3. In the text the author identified himself as a former missionary who wrote the book "to induce numbers of poor negroes to read."

38. For Titus, see Graham Russell Hodges and Alan Edward Brown, eds., *"Pretends to Be Free": Runaway Slave Advertisements from Colonial and Revolutionary New York and New Jersey* (New York: Garland, 1994), p. 60; for comments, see Hodges, *Slavery and Freedom,* pp. 70–71.

39. Adrian C. Leiby, *The United Churches of Hackensack and Schraalenburgh, New Jersey, 1686–1822* (River Edge, New Jersey: Bergen County Historical Society, 1976), p. 244; Abraham Messler, *Forty Years at Raritan: Eight Memorial Sermons with Notes for a History of the Reformed Dutch Churches in Somerset County, New Jersey* (New York: A. Lloyd, 1873).

40. James Albert Ukawsaw Gronniosaw, *A Narrative of the Most Remarkable Particulars in the Life of James Albert Ukawsaw Gronniosaw, an African Prince* (Bath, U.K.: Printed for W. Gye, 1770), pp. 27, 30–31, 33–40, 45–47; Robert Farris Thompson, *Flash of the Spirit: African and Afro-American Art and Philosophy* (New York: Random House, 1983), p. 6; Dominique Zahan, *The Religion, Spirituality, and Thought of Traditional Africa* (Chicago: University of Chicago Press, 1979), pp. 27–28. For a similar account, see Hodges, *Slavery and Freedom,* pp. 78–80.

41. Graham Russell Hodges, ed., *Black Itinerants of the Gospel: The Narratives of John Jea and George White* (Madison, Wisconsin: Madison House Books, 1993), p. 90.

42. See "Some Early Records of the Lutheran Church of New York," in *Year Book of the Holland Society of New York, 1902* (New York: Knickerbocker Press, 1902), pp. 8, 14–15, 17, 19, 20–22; "New York Lutheran Church Book, 1704–1723," *Year Book of the Holland Society of New York, 1903* (New York: Knickerbocker Press, 1903), pp. 6, 8, 15.

43. Soderlund, *Quakers and Slavery,* pp. 54–86.

44. For the Society of Friends in New Jersey, see Peter O. Wacker, *Land and People: A Cultural Geography of Preindustrial New Jersey, Origins and Settlement Patterns* (New Brunswick, New Jersey: Rutgers University Poress, 1975), pp. 178–183. For the conservatism of the New York Meeting, see Oblong (Pawling) Monthly Meeting, pp. 126, 141–145, Haviland Record Center, New York City; John R. Cox, *Quakerism in the City of New York, 1657–1930* (New York, Privately printed, 1930), pp. 57–62; Herbert Aptheker, "The Quakers and Negro Slavery," *Journal of Negro History* 25 (1940), p. 350; Soderlund, *Quakers and Slavery,* pp. 122–124; Vivienne L. Kruger "'Born to Run': The Slave Family in Early New York, 1626–1827," (Ph.D. diss., Columbia University, 1985), pp. 609–611.

45. See, for example, Hodges, *Slavery and Freedom,* pp. 91–93.

46. See Leigh Eric Schmidt, *Holy Fairs: Scottish Communions and American Revivals in the Early Modern Period* (Princeton: Princeton University Press, 1989), pp. 69–85, 196. For slavery, see Irving S. Kull, "Presbyterian Attitudes toward Slavery," *Church History,* Vol. 7 (1938), pp. 101–115.

47. Elmer T. Clark, ed., *The Journal and Letters of Francis Asbury* (London: Epworth Press, 1958), Vol. 1, pp. 9, 25, 43; Frederick E. Maser and Howard T. Maag, eds., *The Journal of Joseph Pilmore, Methodist Itinerant* (Philadelphia: Printed for the Historical Society of the Philadelphia Annual Conference of the United Methodist Church, 1969), pp. 74, 96, 131. See also Hodges, ed., *Black Itinerants,* pp. 10–44 and William J. Walls, *The African Methodist Episcopal Zion Church: Reality of the Black Church* (Charlotte, North Carolina: A.M.E. Zion Publishing House, 1974), pp. 40–41.

48. For Andrew Saxon, see *New-York Gazette,* I October, 1733; for Simon, see *Pennsylvania Gazette,* 11 September 1740; for Mark and Jenny, see *Rivington's New-York Gazeteer,* 8 June 1775. For other religious blacks, see Billy G. Smith and Richard Wojtowicz, eds., *Blacks Who Stole Themselves: Advertisements for Runaways in the Pennsylvania Gazette, 1728–1790* (Philadelphia: University of Pennsylvania Press, 1989), pp. 97, 110, 120, 124, 125, 152.

49. Hodges, ed., *Black Itinerants,* pp. 22, 114–117; Vincent Caretta, ed., *Unchained Voices: An Anthology of Black Authors in the English-Speaking World of the 18th Century* (Lexington: University of Kentucky Press, 1996); Timothy L. Smith, "Slavery and Theology: The Emergence of Black Christian Consciousness in Nineteenth-Century America," *Church History,* Vol. 41 (1972), pp. 497–512.

50. For a description of the fire, see Thomas Moffat Diary, Peter Force Collections, 8d, Reel 53, Item 106, Library of Congress and Ewald Gustav Schaukirk, *Occupations of New York City by the British* (New York: New York Times, 1969), pp. 253–255. For Anglican Loyalism, see David D. Holmes, "The Episcopal Church and the American Revolution," *Historical Magazine of the Protetant Episcopal Church,* Vol. 47 (1978), pp. 261–291.

51. See John Woolfe Lydecker, *The Life and Letters of Charles Inglis* (London: Published for the Church Historical Society, 1936), pp. 183–186, 193, 207; Sir Edward Midwinter, "The S.P.G. and the Church in the American Colonies," *Historical Magazine of the Protestant Episcopal Church,* Vol. 4 (1935), pp. 78–79, 81. See also Richard Pointer, "Religious Life in New York during the Revolutionary War," *New York History,* Vol. 66 (1985), esp. pp. 361–364. For marriages in Trinity Church, see Register of Marriages, Vol. 1, pp. 104–107, Trinity Church Archives. For Beach, see Walter H. Stowe, "The Reverend Abraham Beach, D. D.," *Historical Magazine of the Protestant Episcopal Church,* Vol. 3 (1934), pp. 81–86, 89–95. Only one other denomination performed rituals for blacks in the war-torn city. A Lutheran pastor baptized seven blacks recently arrived from the South and performed two marriages for blacks in New York City during the Revolution. See Stryker-Rodda, "Baptisms of the Lutheran Church of New York City," pp. 44, 157–158, 217, 219, 222–223. For Lutheran baptisms and marriages of blacks in New Jersey, see Amandus Johnson, ed., *The Journal and Biography of Nicholas Collin, 1746–1831* (Philadelphia: New Jersey Society of Pennsylvania, 1936), pp. 251, 258, 282.

52. Bleucke's career may be followed in Graham Russell Hodges, ed., *The Black Loyalist Directory: African Americans in Exile After the American Revolution* (New York: Garland, 1996), pp. xxiii–xxv, xxiv, 88.

53. Register of Marriages, Vol. 1, pp. 104, 107, 149–295, Trinity Church Archives.

54. White, *Somewhat More Independent,* p. 116.

55. For the constitution, see *Tricentenary Studies, 1928, of the Reformed Church in America: A Record of Beginnings* (New York: Reformed Church, 1928), p. 401; John Pershing Luidens, "The Americanization of the Dutch Reformed Church," Ph.D. dissertation, University of Oklahoma, 1969, pp. 331. See also "Records of the Dutch Reformed Church in the City of New York," *New York Genealogical and Biographical Record* 61: 277–279, 373–380, 62: 41–45; "Marriages from 1801–1866 in the Dutch Reformed Church, New York City," *New York Genealogical and Biographical Record,* 70: 35–40, 171–172, 277–279, 385–388, 71: 187, 300–301, 394–399; "Burials in the Dutch Church, New York," *New York Genealogical and Biographical Record,* 32, 73; "Church of Brooklyn" in *Year Book of the Holland Society of New York 1897,* 141; "Records of the Reformed Dutch Church of Harlem," *New York Genealogical and Biographical Record* (1986–1987), 117: 228–233, 118: 31–32; "Baptismal Records of Reformed Dutch Church of Cortland Town, Westchester County," *New York Genealogical and Biographical Record,* 75 (1945): 33.

56. Hodges, ed., *Black Itinerants,* pp. 22, 114–117.

57. For black Presbyterians, see "Records of the First and Second Presbyterian Churches in the City of New York," *New York Genealogical and Biographical Record* (1887–1889) 18: 170, 20: 177, 179, 181; Reverend John Robinson, *The Testimony and Practice of the Presbyterian Church in Relation to American Slavery* (Cincinnati: J. D. Thorpe, 1852), pp. 16, 27–29; "Christ's Presbyterian Church at South Hempstead, Long Island, Marriages," *New York Genealogical and Biographical Record* 53 (1922): 242–254; "Records of the Presbyterian Church, Newtown (Elmhurst) Queens County, Long Island, 1731–1793," *New York Genealogical and Biographical Record* 55 (1924): 291, 393–398; "Baptismal Records of Basking Ridge Presbyterian Church, Somerset County, 1795–1817," *Genealogical Magazine of New Jersey,* Vol. 7 (1931), pp. 23, 26–38; "Bound Brook, New Jersey, Presbyterian Church Records, 1805–1810," *Genealogical Magazine of New Jersey,* Vol. 37 (1962), p. 66; "Records of the First Presbyterian Church of Cranbury," *Genealogical Magazine of New Jersey,* Vol. 23 (1952), p. 60.

58. Nathan O. Hatch, *The Democratization of American Christianity* (New Haven: Yale University Press, 1989), pp. 106–108.

59. Walls, *African Methodist Episcopal Zion Church,* pp. 47–48.

60. For petition of the African Society, see *MCC, 1784–1831,* 2: 112, 151, 158 and Walls, *African Methodist Episcopal Zion Church,* p. 47. For problems over the Old Negro Burial Ground, see *MCC, 1784–1831,* 1: 554, 598, 610, 663, 709–710, 739, 769, 2: 22, 134, 218, 221, 252, 264, and John F. Miner, *A Tour around New York City and My Summer Acre, Being the Reminiscences of Mr. Felix Oldboy* (New York: Harper and Bros., 1893), p. 145.

61. Edward D. Smith, *Climbing Jacob's Ladder: The Rise of Black Churches in Eastern American Cities, 1740–1877* (Washington, D.C.: Smithsonian Institution Press, 1988), pp. 39–40.

62. Monroe Fordham, *Major Themes in Northern Black Religious Thought, 1800–1860* (Hicksville, N.Y.: Exposition Press, 1975), pp. 29–30.

63. Hodges, ed., *Black Itinerants.* For black ministers on Long Island, see Lynda R. Day, *Making a Way to Freedom: A History of African Americans on Long Island* (Interlaken, N.Y.: Empire State Books, 1997), p.113.

64. William B. Gravely, "The Dialectic of Double-Consciousness in Black Freedom Celebrations, 1808–1863," *Journal of Negro History,* Vol. 67 (1982), pp. 302–318; Timothy L. Smith, "Slavery and Theology: The Emergence of Black Christian Consciousness in Nineteenth-Century America," *Church History,* Vol. 41 (1972), pp. 497–498.

2

Aileen B. Agnew

"Living in a Material World"

African Americans and Economic Identity in Colonial Albany

Slave status did not necessarily preclude direct participation in the Hudson Valley's marketplace for African chattel. In the urban centers of the region, slaves not only procured goods for their owners, but frequently bought and sold on their own behalf as well, using their garden produce, wildlife, fish, lumber, and pigs for barter. The generation of such items itself was a subversion of the slave system that viewed blacks as passive, will-less dependents. Thus, even in their bondage, slaves secured an identity for themselves as independent, economic actors. Aileen Agnew demonstrates this phenomenon in her careful examination of the ledgers and account books of an eighteenth century merchant in colonial Albany who included slaves among her customers. Agnew further suggests that Albany's blacks fashioned a distinctive consumer identity for themselves that reflected not only the constraints of limited incomes but also African-derived values and social relations within the black community.

In October of 1754, Bat, a female slave belonging to Mr. Eldert Teymonsen, went to the store of Elizabeth Sanders and bought fine cloth, silk for sewing, and one dozen Breast Buttons. She paid for her purchases with dried apples, nuts, and corn. In doing so, Bat revealed herself to be both an active consumer and producer of goods, serving her own ends in both instances. African American slaves in colonial Albany, New York constructed economic and social identities for themselves by making the most of a limited access to Albany's busy commercial economy. As slaves, most of their waking hours did not belong to them, putting control of a work identity largely out of reach. Small openings to Albany's retail trade enabled bondspeople not only to develop economic identities as consumers, but also social identities built around appearance. Consumer purchases strengthened family identities through shared responsibilities for debts. A single transaction of a slave purchasing goods thus had multiple social implications.[1]

At mid-century, Albany marked a frontier between Anglo-Dutch New York and territories dominated by Native Americans and the French. The streets of Albany offered a panoramic view to the east of the Hudson River and the East Manor of Rennsselaerwyck. Perched on the banks above the river, the town and the fort that dominated it afforded excellent vistas of the river and its traffic, with boats of various sizes and shapes arriving regularly from the south, bringing goods from England via New York. Eighteen miles to the west sat Schenectady and the way west via the Mohawk River. Furs unloaded from bateaux in Schenectady arrived by wagon in Albany. To the north lay Canada, the source of frequent Native American traders. In the 1750s and 1760s, the thousands of New England and British soldiers sent to fight the Seven Years' War dramatically, though temporarily, swelled the local population and, as a consequence, the size of the city's trading public. Thus, Albany was both distribution center and market for goods arriving from several directions, and the city boasted a flourishing retail trade.

Attraction to consumer goods was not limited to the rich. Poorer residents and slaves also had an interest in the wide array of merchandise offered for sale by the numerous retailers of Albany. The slaves and few free blacks of Albany made their way along the streets and into selected stores even as wealthier members of the town did. Eighteenth-century observers noted the presence of these black Albanians. Kalm, for instance, noted that "the servants in the town are chiefly Negro." Slaves in Albany County did not act only as servants certainly; many also worked on farms or in more industrial settings.[2]

Africans and African Americans never formed more than a minority of the population of New York. Nevertheless, they were a fairly sizeable minority. In 1749, the population of the province of New York contained over 73,000 people. Of these, about 14.4% were black. The entire county of Albany had a population that was 13.9% black and concentrated in the city of Albany. Between the 1720s and the 1770s, the black population of Albany County grew from approximately 800 to over 3,700. By 1790, the city of Albany contained almost 600 African Americans, in a population of approximately 3,500.[3]

Slavery existed in the Dutch colony of New Netherland from the early days of settlement. Although important to the society and economy, slavery did not come to dominate the economy as it did in the southern colonies. Households with chattel tended to own one or two slaves. The New York Dutch of the Hudson Valley were certainly a slave-owning society, but not a slave society. That is, although slavery permeated the society, slave labor did not supply a major portion of the economy's labor demands, nor did slavery play an extensive role in the operation of commerce.[4]

Local economies provided access to the labor of slaves, even for those who did not own them. By hiring a slave owned by someone else, a person could have work done without any significant investment. Local farmers hired slaves to perform housework and farm work, among other tasks. In 1748, Hendrick Cuyler paid Evert Wendell for the work of Wendell's female servant Brit, "who scoured at his house 3 days at 2/ [2 shillings] pr day." Likewise in 1750 and 1751, Cuyler paid to have Brit clean his house for two days. In the back pages of his account book, Joseph Yates kept a list of the work that his bondsman, Sem, did for other people during the years 1758 and 1759. In 1759, for instance, Sem did farm work for Harmen Arent Vedder for 11 days, as recorded by Yates "min Neger In der bouw Gewerk 11 Dage, 2.4.0." Though such arrangements took place between whites, some slaves may have profited from these transactions.[5]

For most slaves, the work performed for their owners and as hired help did not provide much of an avenue for self-expression. But when work on their own time produced admittance to the world of consumer goods, that work became linked to their own identity as producers and consumers of goods. Participation in a commercial economy required some ability to pay. In the Albany area, African Americans used various work strategies to accumulate the means to pay for goods. These work strategies spoke to who they were as slaves, but principally to who they were as individuals.

New York's African Americans took advantage of resources they could control, as did slaves elsewhere. No blacks offered work of any kind as a payment, perhaps understanding that work time was not theirs to give away, or perhaps not wanting to spend *their* time doing any more of *that* work. Black women thus never sewed for credit, as white women did. They did not offer butter or dairy products in exchange for goods. The work of black women that potential slaveholders openly admired was not the work that black women used to buy goods. The qualifications cited in newspaper advertisements for the sale of female slaves related strictly to housework. When John Lindsay wrote from Oswego to William Johnson in 1750, he asked for a female slave to help his wife, to do his wife's work for her. He begged of Johnson, "I give you the trouble again to entreat you to buy me a Negro winch & send her as soon as possible, there is no woman here to assist or serve my wife & as she is on[e] of ye best am not able to see her undergo what she does at present . . . my wife is sickly and needs on[e] to attend her rather than to be obliged to serve herself and others."[6]

The skills of housewifery extended beyond sewing, cleaning, and the dairy, however. Through a combination of necessity and choice, bondswomen selected from an assortment of tasks to generate the assets needed to make purchases. Unfree blacks chose specific kinds of work to perform during their "free" time to produce acceptable items for exchange, thus exercising control over a part of their labor. The nature of payments made to Elizabeth Schuyler

Sanders for commodities purchased from her point to the choice of work that produced goods suitable to the retailer.

The gardening of Albany blacks played a major role in consumer exchange. Many of the credits to the accounts of Sanders's black customers took the form of garden produce. Anne Grant noted the presence of cottages in the pine barrens between Albany and Schenectady. "These cottages," she wrote, "were in summer occupied by some of the negroes who cultivated the grounds about them."[7] The resulting crops could have formed the basis of the purchasing power of Albany slaves. The harvest produced and traded reflected the influences of local geography and agricultural conditions. Black customers paid most often with Indian corn, then occasionally with dried apples, dried corn, beans, and potatoes. Women were more likely to pay with garden produce than men were, suggesting either that gardens were one of the few means of production that black women had access to, or that black women did more gardening than black men. That is not to say that black men did not garden, or at least use garden produce for trade. Tom, for instance paid Elizabeth Sanders with "6 begs Corren," while in Schenectady, a male slave paid a retailer, John Bradt, with corn and bunches of corn stalks.[8]

Locally grown goods that blacks did not use in exchange also have significance, illustrating the limits of African American involvement in the local economy. Just as African Americans in the American South and the Caribbean were generally prohibited from growing the staple crops of the region for exchange, New York blacks did not exchange wheat for goods. Nor did Sanders's black customers trade in beef, a commodity closely regulated by local selectmen. Pigs, however, were in evidence. One woman paid her bill to Elizabeth Sanders with a pig, and later with a hog.[9]

Men had only a few more options for payment than did women. One man paid in white pine. White pine was also used to pay off part of a woman's account, though she did have a husband who possibly was free, and therefore perhaps was the source of the white pine. In general however, it cannot be said that gender clearly defined one's payment choices. In the environment of frontier New York, most men had the skills to harvest white pine and saw the wood into boards. Whether black men had free access to white pine is questionable, but historian A. J. Williams-Myers writes that slaves regularly worked in sawmills and other places of industry. The white pine may have originated in that labor or some other exchange of work for pay. Both men and women exchanged small quantities of furs. Jack paid for a blanket with ten raccoon skins. A woman brought in musquash (muskrat) in payment. Catching muskrat or raccoon could be done without roaming very far afield. Fishing also provided payment, as when one woman paid with three strings of fish.[10]

On another occasion, Lane, a black woman and slave of Barent Sanders, the father of Robert, brought in 40 empty glass bottles for trade payment.

There is no evidence of how she accumulated these bottles. Most of her purchases of liquor from Sanders were for gallons of rum, too much for the common quart-size green bottles of the eighteenth century, which presumably the 40 bottles were. We cannot assume that a gallon of rum was delivered in a one-gallon container, however, so perhaps Lane brought them in to recycle for more purchases.

The array of work used in developing assets used for purchasing suggests the importance of the consumer marketplace to Albany's slaves. Blocked from paying with the means often used by whites, specifically sewing, wampum manufacture, and other forms of work, blacks drew on their own time and skills to afford imported grocery items and fashionable goods. In this way they positioned themselves as consumers, familiar with the mechanics of retail shopping.

The commercial economy of Albany provided slaves with an arena for self-expression in very precise ways, as they eschewed the purchase of necessities in favor of goods that represented their desires. In her memoirs of her childhood in eighteenth-century Albany, Anne Grant suggests what constituted necessities. While conceding the moral problematics of slavery as an institution, Grant went on to acknowledge how much a part of many white families Albany's slaves were. The owners, she said, were much attached to their slaves, always giving the young slave children to a member of the family when the slaves reached the age of three. In the eyes of Grant, keeping the young slaves in the family was a kindness to both slave parent and child. In her memory, the new young owner "to whom the slave was given immediately presented it with some piece of money and a pair of shoes."[11] Grant did not discuss the importance of the shoes or the money, but these items can be viewed both functionally and symbolically. Functionally, the shoes were shoes but symbolically, they served as a reminder of the responsibility of the owner to maintain his or her slave. Albany County Court minutes show occasional records of owners being chastised for failing to provide the necessities of life for a slave. On "being informed that a Negro Wench belonging to the Heirs of Hendrick Hallenbeck, dec'd is going about the streets naked and without any Sustenance whatever" the Court ordered the Heirs to "keep the said Wench & maintain her sufficiently for a servant."[12] Shoes apparently were part of what was expected from an owner. The account books regularly record the purchase of shoes by owners for their slaves. A shoemaker's accounts indicate the regular purchase of shoes for slave dependents. Owners also provided some clothing. John Butler's accounts contained a long list of items bought by "Capt Walter Butler for the Negroes," such as "a shift and pty cot shoss and stockns" (shift and petticoat, shoes and stockings) for Jen.[13] This does not mean that Albany blacks did not buy shoes or clothes. Quite the contrary, they often did. But their purchases did not represent life's barest necessities. Slaves elsewhere might have spent most of their spare money buying food and improving their diets, but African American shoppers in Albany selected goods that might be considered embellishments or luxuries. Albany's bondspeople did not buy retail for survival but to articulate identity.

Besides serving as a reward to the slave and demonstrating the benevolence of an owner, the gift of a coin implies a recognition that the slave had his or her own interest in possessing cash, an acknowledgment by the slaveholder that a slave might still like to buy goods or accumulate assets. Blacks commonly paid for goods in cash and received cash for certain kinds of work and produce.[14] John Sanders's own slaves paid him partly in cash for goods they purchased from him. In 63 entries for credit in Elizabeth Sanders's book, 37 represented payment in cash. Even though these black people were slaves, opportunities existed in their working lives for earning cash. Walter Butler paid a Negro for a burial. John Sanders paid another Negro for ginseng gathered. The control over cash earned in these extra jobs enabled African Americans in Albany to obtain some measure of small luxuries.[15]

Access to cash was especially important to slaves and other poor consumers, since long-term credit was not as available to them. Although Elizabeth Sanders sold goods to slaves, she did not give them the same kind of access to credit that she did for her white customers. The accounts of her black customers did not drag on unpaid for years. Many white and a few black accounts never were closed, but generally slaves paid off their debts quickly.

Black consumers shopped with only a few of the many retailers in the Albany area. In general, however, exchanges with blacks in retail settings represented uncommon entries in local merchants' records. Elizabeth Schuyler Sanders, a slaveholder herself, seems to have been a favorite resource for goods for some blacks. Other merchants did occasionally sell goods to slaves. In Schenectady, John Sanders, the brother-in-law of Elizabeth Sanders, sold items to his own slaves in the late 1760s, keeping their accounts at the back of his daybook. Another retailer, John Bradt, sold several items to "the Negro of My father London," in 1770. An unidentified Mohawk Valley trader also sold a few goods to area blacks in the late 1760s and early 1770s.[16] The 18 blacks who bought goods from Sanders over the ten years that she kept her accounts, were a select few of the perhaps 1,500 African Americans living in Albany County at mid-century.[17]

In Albany, the account book of Elizabeth Sanders shows slaves participating in the formal economy developed by white men. The records are those of the formal economy; the means of payment and the goods purchased all form part of the standard commercial system. The work revealed by the account is not the work demanded by slaveholders. This source reveals a piece of black economic life that depended on the intersection of black interests with formal white economic institutions.

The relationship of slaves and free blacks in Albany and Schenectady to formal markets is by no means clear. Albany had a meat market at least by the end of the eighteenth century, but it is unclear whether Schenectady had a market. In the years after the American Revolution, local governments regulated the meat markets strictly, specifically banning slaves from selling meat. Penalties included fines to the master and jail time for the slave caught breaking the rules. Peter Kalm noted in 1750 that a market in Albany met twice weekly and that the country people brought their goods there to sell. Participation by local African Americans could be expected, or even assumed, in this venue, but no good evidence has been found that describes an African American presence at weekly or seasonal markets.[18]

Subtle differences in the seasonal purchasing patterns of Albany African Americans suggest that regular fairs may have played a role in African American consumerism. Three small buying clusters appear for Sanders's African American customers, correlating loosely to the scheduling of fairs. Legislated for twice a year in the early part of the century, scant evidence exists for their regular incidence. The account book of William Kane mentions the cost to a customer for a cow "bought at the fear," in January but no other references occurred in the sources. These fairs originally were to be held during the third week of July in Albany and the third week of October in Crawlius (Crolius?) in Rensselaerwyck. A twice-yearly fair served as a great attraction for all local residents. The debit made to a customer in January by William Kane suggests that a fair was held, perhaps in October, but more likely closer to January.[19]

Small differences existed between the buying patterns of whites and blacks throughout the year. White women visited at a steady rate over ten months of the year, with the notable and not surprising exception of February and March when little shopping occurred. White men also made purchases throughout the year with a drop in January and February. Little existed in the way of a pattern for black men although they too did less buying in January, February, and March. Black women, on the other hand made many more purchases in July, December, and January than they did in other months. The clustering of purchases in July may relate to the summer fair scheduled for Albany, while the December and January purchases speak of the importance of the Christmas and New Year's season to the city's slaves.[20]

Historians have discussed the adoption by blacks of the Dutch Pentecost Festival, otherwise known as Pinkster. Pentecost falls seven Sundays after Easter, which places it from mid-May to early June. Purchases of fabric and rum by African Americans do not suggest any sort of buying binge in relation to Pinkster. As evidenced by the purchasing patterns, regular agricultural fairs may have been important to the local black population, in a way that Pinkster perhaps was not yet. Election Day, important to blacks in New England, perhaps did not have the same relevance to Albany-area African Americans. Albany's election day at the end of September did not coincide with active purchasing by blacks, but preceded the October purchases of slaves. Albany and Schenectady blacks may have developed holidays of regional importance to them, without necessarily following patterns established elsewhere.[21]

Sanders's black customers bought items very similar to those purchased by whites. Blacks bought a variety of fabrics, thread, hanks of silk, buttons, tea, rum, and a number of caps and hats. Less common purchases included handkerchiefs, buckles, stockings, shoes, a rug, a blanket, shot, and an iron trap. While black customers chose items from the same categories as Sanders's white customers, an analysis of purchasing patterns reveals differences not only between whites and blacks, but also between black men and women.

These differences extend beyond what was actually purchased to the ways that the various customers shopped. Eighteen black customers made 100 trips to Sanders's store while 87 white customers made 230 trips. For black customers that means an average of 5.6 trips per account holder, while white customers averaged just 2.6 trips per customer (or 5.9 versus 4.3 if you count as customers only those people who actually made purchases as opposed to all the names in the book). Those blacks who did shop with Sanders were more consistent customers than the whites, buying from her over a longer period of time. Perhaps the limited choice that unfree African Americans had in where they shopped ensured their loyalty to Sanders.

Four basic items of consumption—rum, tea, sugar, and fabric—illustrate the variation in purchasing patterns between Sanders's white and black customers. The reasons for these differing patterns of consumption cannot be put down solely to cultural dissimilarities between the groups. For example, blacks may have bought rum from Sanders because they had nowhere else to buy it. Whites on the other hand, especially white men, likely had access to several nearby dram shops and taverns. Loudoun's List of 1756 contains the names of nine or so such establishments, as well as a large number of retailers from whom rum could be purchased. More than one of Sanders's white customers appeared on the list as purveyors of liquor.

Among the black customers, however, we also see a gendered division in the choices made by the purchasers. Of the 19 purchases of tea, black women made 15. Two of these women also bought teakettles for themselves. Tea, which drew many white customers into Sanders's shop, and in England supported an entire complex of stores, held much less allure for Albany's blacks. For those who bought rum, 32 of 38 purchasers were women. We cannot assume that female slaves necessarily drank more than men, but we can perhaps surmise that black women had an even more restricted set of places to buy rum than did black men. Women used at least some of the rum in celebrations. Sanders noted that one purchase of rum was for "when yr son Marryd." Women also bought sugar more often than men did, perhaps because they did more cooking than men, or perhaps the sugar was used with the rum. While the numbers of people borrowing cash were quite small, it is perhaps important that here we see black men borrowing cash more often than women.[22]

The consumer merchandise most often purchased by Sanders's black customers was fabric. For Albany blacks, the purchase of fabric meant new clothing. Given that bondspeople could be bought or sold without warning, and that few slaves had their own homes, the investment of slave assets in clothing makes good sense. Clothes were portable wealth, as well as the means to imaginative self-expression. Clothing not only disclosed community standing, but also made known riches or poverty. We can discuss the status and identity of some slaves in Albany using our understanding of the meaning of dress to interpret their purchases. This interpretation draws from the following assumptions: first, that clothing was important in establishing identity and expressing status. Second, that a slave buying from Elizabeth Sanders very likely had good standing in the slave, and perhaps the white, world.

Dress actually formed identity. Historian Shane White has discussed the importance of dress to New York City blacks in identity formation during the late eighteenth century. Albany blacks, especially those of higher status, were no less interested in their dress.[23] When in the late eighteenth century, Pomp stole money and ran away to New York City from Albany, his purchase of a "bright red, cloth coat cut in the prevailing fashion, and adorned with gilt buttons," allowed him to "parade" down Broadway. He went out of his way to create a new, swaggering identity for himself. Likewise, when the King of Pinkster dressed in festive clothes, he transformed himself from an ordinary slave into the chief of a rowdy, popular celebration.[24]

Sanders's black patrons were among the more highly ranked in Albany's black and white social hierarchy. Prominent slaves in the North derived some measure of their status within the black community by their association with their socially important white owners. The servant of a politically important white man, for instance, could be recognized in both the black and white communities as an individual of higher stature than an ordinary slave.[25] The town of Albany and its surroundings certainly contained enough African Americans to support a stratified community in keeping with both the local white society and the cultural influences of an African heritage. The eighteen slaves that purchased goods from Elizabeth Sanders drew on their personal acquaintanceships with Sanders when they shopped for new consumer goods in that formalized setting of exchange. Their connection to families recognized as socially important to Sanders gave these blacks a privileged access to consumer goods. Nor were Sanders's customers confined to slaves resident in Albany proper. A few traveled some distance from where they lived; Bat and Susan both came from Niskayuna while others crossed the Hudson River. Many of those listed belonged to members of Elizabeth Sanders's extended family, such as "Father Peter Schuylers Negroman Mink," or "Uncle Jacob Glens Negro Piet." Other blacks were identified as belonging to prominent members of the community such as "Patroons Negrowench Deen."

The four slaves who bought goods most regularly from Elizabeth Sanders belonged to very prominent families, specifically the Van Rensselaers, the Schuylers, and the Sanderses. Barent Sanders's bondspeople, Cate and Lane, by Peter Schuyler's bondsman, Mink and by Killiaen Van Rensselaer's servant, Tom, slaves of comparative privilege and status, spent their money on clothing and imported grocery items. Lane bought "flower" in 1755 and one half of a cheese in 1757, but these were the only food items listed in the accounts of these four consumers.

Lane visited Sanders's house consistently over the course of ten years, averaging about 2.5 visits a year. Mink and his wife, Sarah, between them made 15 stops over the same ten years. Cate went to Elizabeth Sanders's 21 times in ten years, but nine of those calls came in one year, 1755. From 1759 through 1761, Cate never made a purchase from Sanders. Mink and Lane each apparently went for a year at a time without making the journey to the Sanders's house, at least for the purpose of purchasing goods. The purchases by blacks declined somewhat during the years of the Seven Years' War, perhaps reflecting the turmoil in the city during those years.

Much of what Lane, Cate, Mink, and Tom bought consisted of articles of dress or recreation. Tom, for instance, bought the materials for a complete, or nearly complete, suit of clothes not once but twice. These purchases however, occurred seven years apart. In October of 1756, Tom bought cloth, shalloon (for lining), buckram (to reinforce the coat), silk, thread, mohair, and 2 1/2 dozen buttons. After a lapse of six years, Tom bought tea and borrowed cash, returning later for rum. In June of 1763, he bought stockings, a large amount of fustian fabric, shalloon, buckram, linen, thread, two dozen buttons, and one shilling cash. The high cost of material perhaps tempered the interest of Albany blacks in clothes. Tom might have preferred not to wait seven years for new clothes of his choosing, but likely had no choice.

Clothing and appearance mattered as much to African American men in identity formation as it did to African American women. Black customers of both sexes made more purchases of clothing and dress items per person from Sanders than did white customers. The availability of other places to shop could have determined this proportion. However, we should also consider the possibility that faced with a widening array of consumer choices, Sanders's black customers still chose to spend their time and money on clothing rather than on other goods. Black men made more purchases of fabric per customer than black women while white men made substantially fewer purchases than white women. This is startling only because we assume that women are more interested in clothing and fabrics than men. It is also entirely possible that men bought fabric for women who had no opportunity of their own for purchasing such material.

The clothing worn by these black servants showed attention to both the type of the fabric and the details of dress. Cate's position may have been especially high among local blacks. She was one of very few blacks who witnessed the baptism of a child in the Dutch Church of Albany, standing up at the baptism of the small daughter of a male slave. Cate's age is uncertain, but she was married herself and had her own account. She and Mink's wife, Sarah, each purchased large quantities of black crepe and black bombazine, which may have had associations with mourning even in the eighteenth century, but certainly conveyed dignity. A nineteenth-century article on early Albany claimed that prior to the Revolution, adult Albany women commonly wore black and that colors only became popular after the war. Indeed, the white women who bought fabric from Sanders bought black fabric with much greater frequency than any other color. By wearing black, Cate positioned herself as a person of dignity and authority. In a further statement of her position Cate may have worn a cap, kerchief, or decorative apron of lawn. She was one of only three black women who bought a small quantity of this expensive linen.[26]

Lane, her co-worker at Barent Sanders's, chose a very different wardrobe for herself. In the 1750s, Lane had a son of marriageable age and therefore she was not very young. Lane, or her husband John Burn, cared enough about appearance to pay a tailor for his work. Elizabeth Sanders twice paid Jellis Winne (a local tailor) five shillings cash for Lane, once specifically for "making the Coat." Since Lane bought green ratteen on two occasions perhaps she liked the way she looked in green, and perhaps clothing in this fabric enabled her to distinguish herself from Cate's more sober character. The materials she chose, green and later red, ratteen, certainly differed considerably from Cate's black crepe.[27]

To a much greater extent than the white customers, Albany blacks bought plain fabrics. Most of the fabric bought by black customers was not described as decorated, or even colored. Overall, 65% of fabric purchases by blacks were of plain fabric, while just over 45% of the purchases by white customers were. In general, fabrics with patterns or colors cost more than plain fabrics, and some patterns or colors cost more than others. New striped or colored fabric constituted a real luxury.[28]

Dress accentuates authority and social position. When Mink bought black cloth, shalloon for lining, and two dozen buttons, he purchased the materials for an impressive suit. Likewise, when London bought a pair of "Pomps" and silver buckles, he certainly planned to make a social statement, perhaps especially to other blacks, but these status symbols surely also spoke to whites.[29] These African Americans adopted the symbols of the local white society to reinforce their own position. The "John London Negro" aged 40 and born in "Jemaica" who appeared on the militia lists for Richard Rea's Albany County unit in 1761,was one of a handful of men of color listed on the rolls. This may not have been the same London, but his choice of dress likely advanced the position he made for himself, straddling both the black and white worlds.[30]

The dress of blacks during the colonial and early Federal period has been noted for its retention of African characteristics. The articles of clothing worn by blacks in the North were the same as those worn by whites, but "the overall effect was distinctive," as blacks pieced together outfits that defied the dress conventions of white northerners. Small differences in the cut of a suit or the placing of buttons could have spoken volumes to the wearer. Adapting common items in an uncommon way formed the heart of black style in Federal period New York, and it almost certainly did during the colonial period as well. Black consumers, even consumers privileged to buy new material, could not depend on the richness of the fabric alone to make the same kind of statement that well-dressed whites made.[31]

One clothing choice often discussed in relation to African and African American consumers is that of headgear. Purchases at Sanders's show a number of black purchases of hats and handkerchiefs, more proportionally than for white customers. When Tom bought a "Bever hat," or Brit bought a "4 Ells hat Band Crape and 1 Castor hat," they each certainly intended to make a fashion statement. White women bought quite a lot of lawn and cambric, fine linens, in small quantities, perhaps for caps. Black women rarely made similar purchases. The small white cap commonly associated with colonial dress perhaps was not chosen by black consumers, who preferred instead to wear a felt hat or to use a new silk handkerchief.[32]

Historians and other observers of the spending habits of slaves have sometimes suggested that slaves squandered their money on frivolities, when they might have been better served by saving that money to buy their freedom. Historian Edgar McManus judged that some slaves "wasted whatever came into their possession on frivolous luxuries" such as fine clothing. He considered that this unhealthy interest in fancy clothing drew slaves into the commission of petty crimes while forcing owners to pay slaves bribes in the form of clothing, liquor, or cash in order to obtain work.[33] Slaves, however, may have viewed things from a different perspective, using whatever means afforded to individualize their wardrobes.

Elizabeth Sanders's accounts document one of the ways that African Americans worked to bind themselves more closely as family members by using economic links to reinforce a family identity. Black families functioned as economic units even though the members may not have lived as a nuclear family. Typically, in the North, marriages between black men and women did not include co-residence. Northern blacks maintained marriages and parent–

child relationships despite the fact that the parties involved often did not live together. The owner of a slave runaway from New York City in 1773 did not know whether Jack would have gone to his mother in Rocky Hill, New Jersey, or to his wife at Anthony Ten Eyck's in Albany. Both relationships exerted a strong pull, and Jack was both a husband and a son. The small numbers of slaves owned by individual whites meant that blacks only rarely lived in nuclear families and faced serious difficulties in maintaining family ties between households, especially when faced with great distances. In Albany County, and other frontier areas, men outnumbered women. This was true for both blacks and whites, although the difference was even more striking among blacks. In addition, across the whole colony, Africans and African Americans had fewer children per adults than the whites did. Family ties could be maintained but only with effort.[34] We may not be able to speak of black households as little economies the way we speak of white households, but we can certainly see that in important ways, Albany African American family members connected to each other through a family economy, if not a household economy.

Elizabeth Sanders took care to note exactly who paid what or bought what, leaving behind a useful, albeit scanty, record of the familial relationships between some Albany blacks. Cate, for instance, had a husband named Jan who both borrowed money on Cate's account and made payments to it. Mink's wife Sarah made several purchases while Mink's father borrowed cash, putting it on Mink's account. Lane's husband, John Burn, actually had a last name suggesting that he was a free black. The accounts of Tom, owned by Killian Van Rensselaer, contained no references to other family members. Elizabeth Sanders's own slave Tom, however, had a partner with whom he jointly owned a horse. Black family relationships depended in part on the extension of economic ties beyond the bounds of a single household. If white families derived their power from the accumulation of wealth in the hands of the father or parents, black families created strength from the distribution of whatever assets they had. Some comparable support between white family members also appears in the records, such as David Springer "accepting to pay for acco[un]t of your Sister Abigail" or Nenne Brown taking responsibility for the debts of her sister Wyntjie Bath but in a more formally recorded way. Both blacks and whites used economic means to express their family connections, but not identically.

In Elizabeth Sanders's accounting of black marriages, the husband does not always emerge as the dominant figure. The key to which partner had more economic substance rested on their acquaintance with the merchant or retailer. Elizabeth Sanders did not label Cate's account with the name of her husband, Jan, in part because she likely knew Cate better and saw her more frequently. Cate was ultimately responsible for the purchases made against her account, even as Mink was responsible for the purchases made on his account by his wife, Sarah. Sarah likewise felt responsible for their joint purchases. She brought in cash payments on more than one occasion.

One difference between these accounts and the accounts of white couples is that even when Sanders listed accounts in the names of white women, their husbands did not use the accounts for purchases. White women made payments on their husbands' accounts and made purchases debited from their husbands' accounts but white men did not similarly make purchases under their wives' names. On the one occasion when a white man made a payment on his wife's debt, her name appears over the debt while his is written over the credit. The entries of whites contain evidence of the separate interests of husband and wife. The economic concerns of black family members entwined in partnerships not seen in white marriages.

These economic ties in black families extended beyond husbands and wives to other generations. Lane, for instance, provided two gallons of rum when her son got married. The gift of rum by a mother on the day of her son's wedding suggests Lane's celebration of her son's happiness, declared through a simple purchase. Mink and his father had a more complex economic relationship. On more than one occasion, Mink's father borrowed cash against Mink's account. Mink's father, however, also paid off part of Mink's account in pine boards which Sanders noted "must be Deducted out fathers Boards of 1755." In 1757, Mink paid off £1.16.0, "By Debiting yr father for the Ballance Due to him in Book A." These accounts show a family balancing their purchases precariously by moving resources around between family members as needed. The ledgers also suggest that the balance of power in black families may not have relied as heavily on the centralized and overt authority of the husband as white families did.

In no way do the records of a few transactions tell the entire story of family finances but they do tell part of the story. Black families in Albany acted in economic unity to take advantage of the white formal economy. The effect was to strengthen the family itself, while giving family members the resources to be individuals. Slaves used goods grown or made to purchase various consumer goods, and in the process test the limits of slavery. As profoundly, however, they used these exchanges to maintain their families and fortify their identities as family members.

Notes

1. The Account Book of Mrs. Robert Sanders, Albany, New York, 1753–1764, Sanders Family Papers, New York Historical Society (Hereafter ESS Accounts).

2. Peter Kalm, *Peter Kalm's Travels in North America,* ed. by Adolph Benson (New York: Dover Publications, 1987), p. 346.

3. Robert versus Wells, *Population of the British Colonies Before 1776: A Survey of*

the Census Data (Princeton, N.J.: Princeton University Press, 1975), pp. 112, 122, 119, 116.

4. Philip D. Morgan, "British Encounters with Africans and African Americans," in Bernard Bailyn and Philip D. Morgan, eds., *Strangers Within the Realm: Cultural Margins of the First British Empire* (Chapel Hill: University of North Carolina Press, 1991), pp. 157–219, 163; Joyce Goodfriend, "Burghers and Blacks: The Evolution of A Slave Society in New Amsterdam," *New York History* 59(1978): 125–144, argues that by 1664, New Amsterdam was a slave society. However, Morgan's more recent definition and the structure of the Albany area economy suggest that this was not the case in the eighteenth century; for a discussion of slave labor in the Hudson Valley, see A. J. Williams-Myers, "Hands That Picked No Cotton: An Exploratory Examination of African Slave Labor in the Colonial Economy of the Hudson River Valley to 1800," *Afro-Americans in New York Life and History,* 11(1987):25–51.

5. Evert Wendell Account Book, Albany, 1708–1758, New York Historical Society; Joseph Yates Account Book, 1749–1769 (in Dutch), W.T. Hanson Collection, New York State Library.

6. James Sullivan et al., eds., *The Papers of Sir William Johnson,* 14 vols. (Albany, 1921–1965), 3:321–322, 348; 4:95–96.

7. Anne Grant, *Memoirs of an American Lady with Sketches of Manners and Scenes in America as They Existed Previous to the Revolution* (Freeport, N.Y.: Books for Libraries Press, rep. 1972, orig. 1901), I: 78.

8. Account of Mr. Killiaen Van Rensselaer's Negro Tom," October 1755, ESS Accounts; Account of London, Sept. 27, 1770, John Bradt Account Book, Schenectady, 1762–, NYSL.

9. Albany Common Council Minutes, sale of meat regulated 1792 and 1795, on microfilm 88–02947, #66, 95, Albany Hall of Records, Albany, N.Y. The Common Council regulated both the behavior of slaves and the sale of meat during the 1750s and 1760s as well; Account of Fathers Negerin Cate, 10/28/1754 and 11/3/1754, ESS Accounts.

10. Williams-Myers, "Hands That Picked No Cotton," 38; Accounts of Fathers Negerin Cate, 11/3/1754 (white pine, some bad); Mr. Jacob LaGrange Negro Jack, 12/8/1755 (raccoon); Madam Elizabeth Van Renslaer Negerin Brit, 12/31/55 (muskrat); Madam Negrowench Briel, 7/24/1759 (fish).

11. Grant, *Memoirs of an American Lady,* I: 80, 81.

12. Albany County Court Minutes, October 5, 1768, on micro-film, Albany Hall of Records.

13. Unidentified Account Book of a Shoemaker, 1733–1774 (in Dutch), Jacob Lansing Family Papers, NYSL; John Butler Account Book, Butlersbury, 1759–1744, W. T. Hanson Collection, NYSL.

14. Payment in cash became more common for all consumers in the Hudson-Mohawk region during the 1750s and 1760s, owners as well as slaves. See Aileen B. Agnew, "Silent Partners: The Economic Life of Women on the Frontier of Colonial New York," (unpub. Ph.D. dissertation, University of New Hampshire, 1998) ch. 3.

15. Walter Butler Account Book, 1733–1743, W. T. Hanson Collection, NYSL. John Sanders and Jacob Glen Account Book, Schenectady, 1752–1765 and 1765–1771, N-YHS; Account Book of an Unidentified Indian Trader of the Mohawk Valley, 1762–1776, found in the papers of Jelles Fonda, N-YHS.

16. Sanders-Glen Account Book; John Bradt Account Book, Schenectady, 1762–1780, NYSL; Account Book of an Unidentified Indian Trader of the Mohawk Valley, 1762–1776, found in the papers of Jelles Fonda, N-YHS; Historian Elizabeth A. Perkins notes that several slaves bought goods from a merchant in late eighteenth-century Kentucky. "The Consumer Frontier: Household Consumption in Early Kentucky," *Journal of American History* 54(1991): 486–510.

17. Wells states that in 1749, 13.9% of Albany County's resident population of 10,636 was black, suggesting that approximately 1,500 blacks lived in Albany County. *Population of the British Colonies,* p. 112.

18. Kalm, *Peter Kalm's Travels,* 342; A watercolor of the Albany Market in 1805, completed by Albany artist James Eights in 1850, depicts an African American woman in the foreground, perhaps an unconscious statement of the prominence of local blacks in the market. See Albany Institute of History and Art, 200 Years of Collecting, ed. by Tammis K. Croft and Mary Alice Mackay (New York: Hudson Hills Press 199X), pp. 58–59.

19. A fair is a periodical gathering, defined as to time and place by statute or custom. Markets generally were (are) open more regularly; "An Act for Settling Fairs and Markets," *Acts of the Assembly Passed in the Province of New York From 1619 to 1718* (London, 1719), 13, American Colonial Records, Micro-film Reel 1, Dimond Library, UNH; William Kane Day Book, 1764–1792, Jan. 4, 1771, Albany, NYSL.

20. According to a nineteenth-century author, New Year's Day was an important visiting day and day of celebration, while Christmas Day largely passed unnoticed. "A Glimpse of an Old Dutch Town," *Harper's New Monthly Magazine,* No. CCCLX, 62 (1881): 523–539.

21. For Pinkster, see, for example, A. J. Williams-Myers, "Pinkster Carnival: Africanisms in the Hudson River Valley," *Afro-Americans in New York Life and History* 9 (1985): 7–17; Graham Russell Hodges, *Slavery and Freedom in the Rural North: African Americans in Monmouth County, New Jersey, 1665–1865* (Madison, Wisc.: Madison House, 1997) 56–58; Shane White, "'It Was a Proud Day': African Americans, Festivals, and Parades in the North, 1741–1834," *JAH* 81(1994): 13–50; Sterling Stuckey, "African Spirituality and Cultural Practice in Colonial New York, 1700–1770," in Carla Gardina Pestana and Sharon versus Salinger, eds., *Inequality in Early America* (Hanover, N.H.: University Press of New England, 1999), pp. 160–181.

22. Account of Fathers Negrowench Lane, 6/20/57, ESS Accounts.

23. Shane White, *Somewhat More Independent: The End of Slavery in New York City, 1770–1810* (Athens, Georgia: University of Georgia Press, 1991) pp. 196–197; Lydia Jean Wares, "Dress of the African American Woman in Slavery and Freedom: 1500–1935," (unpub. Ph.D. dissertation, Purdue University, 1981), 134; Linda

Baumgarten, "Plains, Plaids, and Cotton: Woolens for Slave Clothing," *Ars Textrina* 15(1991): 203–222, 203.

24. "Character and Eccentricities of the Slave Pomp," *Collections on the History of Albany,* 4 vol., Joel Munsell, ed. (Albany: Joel Munsell, 1865) 2:382–383; Stuckey, "African Spirituality and Cultural Practice," 171.

25. William D. Pierson, *Black Yankees: The Development of an Afro-American Subculture in Eighteenth-Century New England* (Amherst: University of Massachusetts Press, 1988), p. 130.

26. "Character and Eccentricities of the Slave Pomp," *Collections on the History of Albany,* 2: 383; *Records of the Reformed Dutch Church of Albany, New York* (Baltimore: Genealogical Publishing Co., 1978).

27. Ratteen was a "thick, twilled, woolen cloth, usually friezed or with a curled nap"; Crape (crepe), in the eighteenth century was "a sort of thin worsted stuff," and later a "transparent gauze-like fabric, chiefly of black silk and used for mourning dress." All definitions taken from the *Oxford Universal Dictionary* prepared by William Little et al. (Oxford, Clarendon Press, 1955). In Elizabeth Sanders' accounts, the ratteen was relatively expensive, at 9 to 12 shillings per ell (39 inches), while crepe sold for just over 2 shillings an ell.

28. Linda Baumgarten, "'Clothes for the People': Slave Clothing in Early Virginia," *Journal of Early Southern Decorative Arts* 12(1988): 26–70, 50–52.

29. ESS Accounts; Account of Fathers London, John Bradt Accounts; Some of the possible explanations for the high numbers of buttons on slave sites include the use of buttons in medicine bundles or for magical purposes, for musical instruments, or buttons may have been discarded as slaves collected fabric for quilts. Patricia A. Samford, "The Archaeology of African American Slavery and Material Culture," *WMQ* 3rd Ser. 53(1996): 87–114, 109, 111. Baumgarten thinks the buttons may have been used as beads, "Slave Clothing," 59.

30. Florence Christoph, *Upstate New York in the 1760s: Tax Lists and Selected Militia Rolls of Old Albany County, 1760–1768* (Camden, Maine: Picton Press, 1992), p. 243.

31. Quotation from White, *Somewhat More Independent,* 196; Piersen, *Black Yankees,* p. 101.

32. Baumgarten,"Clothes for the People," 59, discusses the use of handkerchiefs as headgear by slaves.

33. Edgar J. McManus, *A History of Negro Slavery in New York* (Syracuse: Syracuse University Press, 1966), pp. 63, 61, 64.

34. Piersen, *Black Yankees,* 94; Graham Russell Hodges notes the particular challenges faced by northern blacks on small farms in *Slavery and Freedom in the Rural North,* pp. 16–19; Graham Russell Hodges and Alan Edward Brown, eds., *"Pretends to Be Free": Runaway Slave Advertisements from Colonial and Revolutionary New York and New Jersey* (New York: Garland Publishing, Inc., 1994), p. 166.

3

Michael E. Groth

Laboring for Freedom in Dutchess County

Between Dutchess County slaves and masters, a dialectic existed. Masters exerted absolute legal power over black chattel. Yet owners' economic calculations regarding the most profitable use of slaves, conscience pangs over their exploitation of those held in bondage, and/or their desires for a tractable labor force all served as wedges whereby slaves negotiated greater freedoms for themselves. Utilizing this leverage, slaves hired themselves out and cultivated garden plots to acquire monies to purchase their freedom and the freedom of loved ones. They requested their own sale to locations near family and loved ones. If owners proved uncooperative, slaves reciprocated in their job performance—reporting fake illnesses, slowing their work pace, damaging tools—or by running away (quitting). Thus slaves established identities for themselves as independent economic actors despite their economic debasement. While similar patterns of behavior occurred in other slaveholding sections of the country, slave efforts to secure their freedom by these means intensified once state gradual abolition laws were in place after 1799. Slaves, in other words, often leveraged their identities as economic agents through increasingly aggressive activity towards freedom.

During the past decade historians of American slavery have charted exciting new directions in the study of early African American history and culture. Moving beyond merely demonstrating the existence of a vibrant black community in bondage, scholars have embarked upon the more difficult task of defining and interpreting the very nature of that community. Historians have enlivened scholarly debate by redirecting attention to the question of work and the exceedingly complex and ever-changing relationship between master and slave. The struggle for power lay at the heart of the master–slave relationship. Slavery was ultimately the constant and daily negotiation between slave and master, requiring both accommodation and resistance. The slave occupied a clearly inferior position in such dealings, but the master's authority was never absolute, nor were slaves completely powerless in their dealings with their owners. In the incessant negotiation and "give-and-take" between master and slave, slaves exercised a significant degree of economic power. Recent scholarship has demonstrated the existence of a vibrant and autonomous slave economy in the Americas. Work and economic activity, broadly defined, permeated every aspect of slaves' social and cultural lives. Selling the fruits of their own labor, slaves acted as producers, sellers, and decision-makers. By engaging in their own economic activity, slaves acted as independent agents who carved out what Larry Hudson has described as a "social space" between themselves and their owners that allowed slaves to fashion personal and communal autonomy.[1]

The experience of African Americans in New York's Hudson River Valley demonstrates that slaves wielded economic power in the incessant negotiation that took place between slaveowner and slave on a daily basis. By the end of the eighteenth and beginning of the nineteenth centuries, slaves in Dutchess County were exploiting their position in the regional economy to exact concessions from their masters. African Americans in the Mid-Hudson Valley not only relied on their economic value to their owners but also capitalized on the nature of slavery and patterns of slaveholding in rural New York. Slaves struggled with their owners about the types and amount of work they actually performed on a day-to-day basis and exerted some voice in determining whom they would serve and even the terms of their own labor. In the wake of the Revolution and the bitter struggle over slavery in New York after the war, slaves grew increasingly assertive and insistent in their demands, ultimately exploiting their own labor to negotiate their own freedom.

As elsewhere in the Americas, Europeans brought Africans and African Americans to the Mid-Hudson Valley to meet the pressing demand for labor. European settlement of the region and Dutchess County in particular originally proceeded slowly. For decades, the Hudson Valley and the colony as a whole remained unattractive to prospective immigrants. Preoccupied with the fur trade, the Dutch had limited interest in cultivating the Hudson Valley during the seventeenth century. From the English conquest of the colony in 1664 to the middle of the eighteenth century, the proximity of the hostile French, the military threat posed by powerful Indian nations, the physical challenge of clearing forests, ethnic conflict, the lack of representative government, and rampant political corruption combined to restrain settlement of the province. The system of land tenure in the Hudson Valley allegedly served to impede immigration as well. Beginning in the latter part of the seventeenth century, colonial governors granted large tracts of land throughout the region as a means of dispensing political patronage. Political patrons and land speculators held title to hundreds of thousands of acres by the early eighteenth century.[2] In Dutchess alone, fewer than one dozen landlords held title to virtually every acre in the county.[3] In theory, the landlords of such vast tracts assumed responsibility for enticing migration to their estates and stimulating economic development. The granting of such large patents to a privileged elite, however, arguably precluded the establishment of freeholds in many areas and retarded population growth for at least the first decades of the eighteenth century. An allegedly oppressive leasehold system, moreover, discouraged the long-held ambitions of aspirant yeoman who preferred settlement in Pennsylvania and the Chesapeake, which boasted greater economic opportunities. Although some scholars have refuted the argument that New York's system of land tenure retarded population growth and economic development, it is clear that European settlement of Dutchess County proceeded exceptionally slowly. Early census figures reflect the county's anemic growth. It is unclear whether any European resided in the county when it was organized in 1683, and its subsequent growth was so slow that colonial authorities provisionally attached the county to neighboring Ulster until 1713. As late as 1731, the county ranked dead last in population of the colony's ten counties, numbering a mere 1,724 (non-Indian) persons.[4]

Profound economic changes beginning in the second quarter of the eighteenth century, however, brought about a dramatic reversal in Dutchess County's fortunes. A long-term recession in the fur trade beginning in the latter part of the seventeenth century encouraged the colonial government and entrepreneurs to diversify their economic activities.[5] With a rapidly expanding intercolonial market for foodstuffs and other agricultural commodities, producers looked longingly at the exceptionally fertile soils of the Mid-Hudson Valley and Dutchess County in particular. The county's terrain was less rocky than the western bank of the Hudson. A temperate climate and adequate rainfall enhanced the fertility of the soil, and gently rolling hills provided drainage and irrigation. The many creeks and streams that traversed the county provided water power for a variety of manufacturing enterprises, while the Hudson River provided ideal access to distant markets. A rapidly growing population mirrored the county's economic expansion. After decades of halting growth, Dutchess was the fastest growing region in the colony during the middle of the eighteenth century. While the population of colonial New York less than doubled between 1731 and 1756, Dutchess's population increased more than seven times, jumping from 1,724 persons to 14,157. During the half-century between 1723 and 1771, the county's population increased an astounding twenty times, from fewer than 1,100 people to more than 22,000. Dutchess jumped from last in county population to second within a mere 25 years, a rank it held for the rest of the century.[6]

The county's fantastic growth during the middle of the eighteenth century, however, only exacerbated the demand for workers in the rapidly expanding economy. While a chronic shortage of labor afflicted virtually every employer in the Americas during the colonial period, the need for laborers was especially acute in the Hudson Valley, where immigration proceeded only slowly. Although reduced by the mid-1700s, the threats posed by different native populations and the French remained, and the break-up of large estates into smaller freeholds proceeded only slowly during the decades preceding the Revolution. Although landlords offered a variety of incentives to entice tenants to their holdings and even sold portions of their estates to smaller farmers, neither European immigrants nor the steady flow of land-hungry New Englanders to the region met the growing demand for labor. In many cases, immigrants left as quickly as they arrived, as employers had difficulty keeping them. Hector St. John de Crevecoeur, the French commentator on eighteenth-century American life who himself became a landholder and slaveowner in nearby Orange County, bemoaned:

> As to labour and labourers,—what a difference! When we hire any of these [white] people we rather pray and entreat them. You must give them what they ask: three shillings per day in common wages and five or six shillings in harvest. They must be at your table and feed . . . on the best you have.[7]

Nor was bound European labor a viable option for many New Yorkers. The rising costs of indentured servants, legal restrictions, and other limitations associated with indentured servitude restrained the employment of white servants in New York throughout the colonial era.[8]

Impediments to European immigration and the costs and unreliability of European laborers forced producers in the Mid-Hudson Valley to turn to Africans and African Americans, who provided New Yorkers a comparatively cheaper and more convenient labor source. As opportunities for slave ownership grew with the expansion of the transatlantic and domestic slave trade over the course of the eighteenth century, the black population of the colony increased dramatically. The number of Africans and African Americans in New York doubled between 1723 and 1756 and tripled during the six decades between 1731 and 1790, jumping from 7,231 to 25,983 persons, making the province the largest slave society north of the Chesapeake. The even more remarkable increase in Dutchess County itself points to the particular importance of slavery to the Mid-Hudson Valley. During the three decades between 1723 and 1756, the number of blacks in the county increased twenty-fold, skyrocketing from 43 to 859. The number of Africans and African Americans increased almost three times between 1756 and 1790, again exceeding the rise for the colony and state as a whole. By 1790, Dutchess was home to 2,300 people of color, 1,856 of whom were slaves. The institution of slavery was firmly entrenched in the society and economy of eighteenth-century New York and the Hudson Valley in particular, where more than half of the colony's slave population lived and worked.[9]

Slaveowners in Dutchess County valued not only the specific skills of their slaves but also their adaptability to the myriad labor demands of the regional economy. Northern agriculture was more diversified than southern. Grains like barley, maize, oats, rye, and especially wheat were the mainstay of the eighteenth-century economy of the Hudson Valley, but farmers increasingly diversified their activities over time. Horticulturists cultivated flax, hay, and hemp, while vegetables such as cabbages, onions, peas, potatoes, pumpkins, and turnips supplemented farmers' incomes as well as their diets. Virtually all farmers tended orchards that produced fruits such as cherries, plums, peaches, melons, pumpkins, and most importantly, apples. The rhythm of work changed with the changing seasons. When not engaged in planting and harvesting, slaves busied themselves felling trees, clearing fields, raising livestock, constructing barns, repairing fences, fixing tools, and carting produce to market.[10] The phrase "understands all kinds of farm work" appeared regularly in advertisements for male slaves during the late eighteenth and early nineteenth centuries. Colonial farmers and their slaves were "jacks of all trades" who labored as their own blacksmiths, butchers, cobblers, coopers, distillers, carpenters, joyners, masons, rope makers, sawyers, tanners, tailors, and weavers. Abel Noble boasted that his 27-year-old slave was "a handy fellow at many sorts of business."[11] Zachaeus Newcomb's slave Pomp, while familiar with cobbling, was purportedly "handy and ingenious about anything else."[12] Such versatile slaves were also highly skilled. Charles Clinton's slave Bob was one exceptionally intelligent craftsman. Clinton described the literate slave a "mechanical genius" who, in addition to being knowledgeable of all kinds of farm work, could "do the business of the carpenter on a farm, turn, make shoes, & c." and "work in the mortar in a doctor's shop."[13]

The versatility of male slaves extended beyond the farm to include rural manufacturing and commerce. Mill operators in the Mid-Hudson Valley employed slave labor, and slaves also labored in local forges. Merchants utilized Africans and African Americans in their warehouses, while black teamsters and boatmen transported goods along local highways and waterways. Well acquainted with farm work, one 20-year-old offered for sale in 1802 was also "used to the boating business," while another farm laborer came well recommended as "an excellent teamster."[14] In addition to engaging in agricultural labor, rural manufacturing, and commerce, male slaves also worked in masters' households. Boys typically labored as house servants, while men in more genteel families served as coachmen, gardeners, porters, and waiters. Slaveowners particularly valued young men capable of work on both the farm and in the home. One young man offered for sale in 1782 labored not only on the farm, but also served as both a "genteel waiter" and "good teemsman [sic]."[15] Similarly, another young man of 17 offered for sale in 1806 was a talented farmer, horseman, and waiter.[16]

Slave women and girls labored predominately as domestics, whose responsibilities around the home were likewise numerous and wide-ranging. While the phrase "understands all kinds of farm work" typically appeared in ads for male slaves, advertisements for women regularly noted that the women were knowledgeable of "all kinds of house work." Responsibilities within the household were many. Individual skills noted in advertisements for women during the late eighteenth and early nineteenth centuries included baking, clearing starch, cooking, dairying, ironing, knitting, making butter, milking, needleworking, scrubbing, sewing, spinning, and washing. Responsibilities of slave women, however, extended beyond the domain of the household. As they valued the versatility of their male slaves, slaveowners prized the adaptability of female slaves to different working environments. James Latta described his 28-year-old slave as "exceeding [sic] handy."[17] An "excellent cook, washer, and ironer" advertised for sale in 1802 allegedly understood "all kinds of work," while another woman was purportedly qualified for "any kind of business."[18] In 1796 Henry Livingston offered for sale a woman familiar with "plain cooking, washing, ironing, and baking" and suggested that the slave was "well calculated for a tavern."[19] Other sellers specified that their female slaves were suitable for either the town or country. One slaveowner considered his female slave—a woman who could be well recommended for her "sobriety and honesty"—"a most compleat [sic] house wench" capable "of all kinds of country work."[20] Women were not absent from the fields, particularly during harvest and other busy times. One 24-year-old woman offered for sale by Thomas Palmer in 1783 was not only familiar with "kitchen work" but also "capable of working in hay or harvest, as a common Negro man."[21] Henry Livingston likewise noted in 1795 that the woman he offered for sale was "accustomed to work in haying and harvesting."[22]

Usually laboring alongside their owners in the fields or within the home, Dutchess County slaves became intimately acquainted with their owners. Patterns of slave ownership in the region reinforced such intimacy. Almost three-quarters of Dutchess County slaveowners at the beginning of the final decade of the eighteenth century held fewer than four slaves. The average slaveholding in the county in 1790 was 2.8 slaves, while two of every five slaveowners held only a single slave. Only 14 slaveholders in the entire county—a mere 2% of all slaveowners—owned ten or more slaves.[23] Often residing in attics, basements, cellars, garrets, or kitchens of their masters and mistresses, Hudson Valley slaves were integral, if clearly subordinate, members of their owners' households. Such spatial intimacy had a devastating impact on black family life, depriving black men, women, and children of privacy. Proximity also invited cruel emotional, physical, and sexual abuse. However, if the familial nature of slavery bred cruelty and nurtured fear and distrust, it also fostered bonds of genuine affection between slaves and their owners. Slaves became companions, trusted friends, confidants, and even lovers. Whites and blacks in Dutchess County worked together, ate and drank together, sang and danced together, worshiped together, and slept together.

Slaves in the Hudson River Valley exploited the intimacy of their relationships with their masters and mistresses and their importance to the regional economy to make demands on their owners. Slaves undoubtedly exerted some say in the tasks to be performed and lobbied their masters for extra provisions, time off, and opportunities to visit loved ones.[24] Among the different concessions slaves forced from their masters was some voice in determining where and for whom they were to labor. According to his master's 1771 last will and testament, William Doughty's slave Sampson could not be sold against his will.[25] Harry, a slave belonging to John Hageman, likewise enjoyed the right to remain on the family homestead as long as he desired.[26] In other instances, valuable and assertive slaves refused to relocate with their masters when their owners left the area. A versatile 20-year-old man belonging to Henry Livingston adept at farming, the care of horses, and domestic service compelled Livingston to sell him to a local buyer when the man objected to moving to New York City.[27] A 21-year-old woman belonging to Thomas Tillotson similarly induced her owner to sell her in 1803 when she simply refused to relocate with her master's family to Albany.[28]

Efforts to maintain or improve their positions could involve requesting as well as rejecting a sale. An October 1795 advertisement in the *Poughkeepsie Journal* for the sale or exchange of a young slave couple and their two-year-old child noted that the family was being sold at their own request.[29] Although bequeathed to his deceased master's heirs, Philip Cinceboe's slave Prince enjoyed the right to initiate a sale if he so desired.[30] Some slaves even enjoyed the right to choose their owners. Upon her master's death, Benjamin Roe's slave Nann had full "liberty to chuse herself a master to live with," and Abraham Kip of Rhinebeck stipulated in his last will and testament that his slaves were to be free to be hired by "honest persons," "as they shall think best."[31]

While slaves who opposed their relocation may have done so to maintain a privileged and advantageous position, the ardent desire to preserve families often lay behind slaves' efforts either to oppose or instigate sales. In the case of Thomas Tillotson's female slave, it was the young woman's refusal to be apart from her husband that forced Tillotson's hand. The advertisement appearing in the *Political Barometer* noted that the woman's free black husband could be well recommended for a position in the buyer's family.[32] It was apparently another young woman's desire to be with her husband in Poughkeepsie that compelled another slaveowner to offer the woman's sale in 1812.[33] In a few instances, entire families were kept intact. One seller in August 1799 offered for sale a young man of 22, his wife of 19, and their young child of four months.[34] Seven months later, a slaveholder advertising another young family indicated that he would consider selling the husband, wife, and one-year-old boy separately only if they were sold in the same neighborhood.[35] While human compassion and the owners' moral sensibilities obviously informed a slaveholder's willingness to grant such concessions, it is equally likely that such agreements were the result of lobbying by slaves themselves. The frequent sale of women with their infant children was undoubtedly attributable in many cases to the entreaties, pleas, and even threats brought to bear by the mothers themselves. In 1803 John Pottenburgh explicitly stated that his 25-year-old female slave was to be sold with her 18-month-old child.[36]

The leverage slaves wielded vis-à-vis their owners should not be overestimated. Although some slaves successfully negotiated concessions from their owners, others were sold or bequeathed to heirs without a second thought. When advertising an 18-year-old woman in 1798, Abraham Teller stated plainly that the woman came "with or without a male child of about 1 year old, as may best suit the purchaser."[37] Even when acceding to slaves' demands, moreover, slaveowners typically placed limitations on slaves' freedom of action. Masters in their wills, for example, sharply restricted slaves' choice of new owners by confining that selection to their heirs.[38] In other instances, the executors of a slaveowner's estate retained the authority to veto any prospective sale. Samuel Field's slaves enjoyed protection from sale to anyone outside of the family and the right to choose their own masters when they came of age, but Field restricted their choice to "such as my executors shall think well of for masters."[39] Masters' and executors' insistence that slaves command sufficient remuneration also curtailed choices for new owners. Benjamin Roe stipulated that his slave Nanna was to be sold "for such price as my executors shall agree upon."[40] John Montross' slave enjoyed the right to select a new owner only if he would "give a reasonable sum."[41] Any right to negotiate or reject a sale usually required some accommodation on the part of the slave. An uncompromisingly rebellious and recalcitrant slave did not earn the master's good will. Peter Jay, Abraham Kip, and Catherine Reade maintained that it was only in recognition of loyal and obedient service that they granted their slaves some say in determining their new masters upon their owner's deaths.[42]

Although slaveholders restricted slaves' choice of new masters, demanded fair compensation, and insisted on the involvement of their executors, the fact that such masters and mistresses allowed such concessions at all is suggestive of the influence slaves could exercise. The seasonal nature of the regional economy and the prevalence of slave hiring during the late eighteenth and early nineteenth centuries enhanced the bargaining position of those held in bondage. Hiring slaves out for days, weeks, or months or selling them for longer terms proved quite lucrative for slaveholders in the Hudson Valley. By allowing slaveowners to adjust their labor needs to the changing seasons and shifting economic fortunes, the practice provided masters with income and relieved them of the costs of maintenance. Slave hiring had broader implications as well. The notably cheaper cost of hiring versus buying a slave put slave labor—particularly skilled labor—within reach of smaller farmers, artisans, and others with more modest means.[43] The hiring out of slaves became even more attractive after the passage of a gradual abolition law in 1799. Although the statute provided for an exceptionally conservative scheme of emancipation that affected only children of slave women born after July 4, 1799 and required them to serve their mother's masters until adulthood, the law significantly undermined the position of masters when negotiating with their slaves. With the eventual demise of the institution assured, slaveholders assumed an even greater risk that their increasingly impatient slaves, emboldened by the law, would abscond or otherwise become more restive. Indeed, advertisements for slaves for hire or for sale for terms ranging anywhere from a few to a dozen or more years were common in the local press during the first decades of the nineteenth century.[44]

The number of masters individual slaves served during their lifetimes reveals the frequency by which slaves were sold or hired out in the Mid-Hudson Valley. The experience of Thomas Lee was typical. Born a slave in the Westervelt family in Poughkeepsie, Thomas Lee was ultimately sold to Henry Diemond for a term of six years and then to Caspar Ganse of Fishkill for four.[45] Other slaves were even more well-traveled. Phillis Anthony spent the most productive years of her life serving no fewer than seven different masters, including Thomas Langdon, Joseph Wood, Robert Williams, Gilbert Livingston, Cadwallader Colden, and Ebenezer Babock before finally procuring her freedom from her last master, Kurt DuBois of Clinton.[46] Born a slave in New Jersey, Rachel Pride served no fewer than eight different masters.[47] Another woman, Diana Jackson, noted simply that she was "sold from one Person to another" during her life in bondage.[48]

The hiring of slaves had contradictory implications. By relieving owners of costs of maintenance and providing them with supplemental income, and by making slave ownership accessible to the middling sort, the practice of slave hiring and selling slaves for terms could ultimately strengthen the institution of slavery. Hiring and frequent sale, however, had unintended consequences. While proving lucrative for buyers and sellers of slaves, frequent sale also provided slaves with economic and psychological weapons of resistance. Hiring allowed slaves to improve their situations and carve out a degree of personal autonomy. Versatile and skilled slaves sold for specified terms or hired out by their owners, for example, could often determine the conditions of their own employment. A young man offered for sale in August 1799 for a term of 12 years advertised as an "excellent house servant" and farmer knowledgeable of the care of horses enjoyed the right to stipulate the terms of his own sale.[49]

The impact of such autonomy was far-reaching. Refining existing skills and learning new ones, slaves working for others grew increasingly self-confident. Earnings provided purchasing power and allowed slaves to supplement their diets and procure additional clothing, household items, and gifts for family members. Additionally, hiring and frequent sale meant that many slaves were well-traveled, giving them a broader knowledge of the wider world. The case of Hagar Davis is illustrative. Born in Fairfield, Connecticut, circa 1750, Hagar Davis was first sold at the age of seven to Abraham Barlow, who ultimately sold her to Abraham Duryee of Fishkill. Relocating to Poughkeepsie after her purchase by Abraham Losee, Hagar moved yet again to Nine Partners to live with her subsequent owner, Hans Coonly. Her purchase by Richard Everett brought her back to Poughkeepsie, but Everett himself subsequently sold Davis to yet another buyer.[50] Movement from place to place brought slaves like Davis into contact with new people—black as well as white—expanding their knowledge of the larger world and their place in it. In sum, hiring and frequent sale increased slaves' sense of self-worth and eroded slaves' material and psychological dependence on their owners. Its effect, moreover, was cyclical. Working for others and themselves in different settings, increasingly self-confident slaves grew more assertive in their dealings with their masters and mistresses, demanding yet greater concessions from their owners.[51]

Such freedom of action constituted virtual emancipation for some slaves. When Rachel Pride received a full year's leave from her master to attend to her ill daughter across the river, it is likely that Rachel moved and acted as a free woman of colour during that time.[52] Rachel's experience was not necessarily unique. Given permission to work for himself, Peter Livingston's slave John Francis lived ostensibly as a free man during the beginning of the nineteenth century.[53] Samantha Lewis was a young woman who was a slave in name only during the final months of her bondage. Although her deceased master's will stipulated that she was to be manumitted at the age of 22, Samantha Lewis effectively earned her freedom before that time. Lewis left Fishkill to relocate to Poughkeepsie on October 1, 1814, some time before her 22nd birthday, when her new master agreed that he no longer required her services.[54]

Slaves who worked for themselves labored to make virtual freedom real by purchasing their freedom outright. Thomas Atkins, hired out by his master's widow, ultimately earned the 50 pounds required to purchase himself, paid in installments to the estate's executors.[55] A woman named Betty similarly "undertook to pay her freedom" from James Emott of Poughkeepsie in 1807.[56] Nevertheless, while self-purchase provided an avenue to freedom, it was an exceptionally arduous and time-consuming process. Costs were sizeable and undoubtedly prohibitive for some. Slaveowners insisted on adequate compensation for their loss and frequently acceded to plans for self-purchase only if they or their estates were fairly compensated.[57] Slaves like Thomas Atkins and

James Vandeburgh's slave Ompador who earned wages by working for themselves could pay for their freedom in installments.[58] A series of smaller payments, however, only delayed emancipation, and many slaves with limited means found even smaller installments difficult to meet. According to the agreement she reached with Robert Livingston, Caty Stevenson was to receive her freedom after a period of six years, at which time Stevenson was to pay Livingston $30. After hiring herself out for four years, however, Stevenson had managed to earn merely five dollars toward her purchase price.[59] Those without opportunities to earn wages could pay for their emancipation only with their own labor. Robert Newkirk negotiated an agreement with his master, Abraham Flagler of Clinton, in 1804 that granted Newkirk his freedom after a specified term of service.[60] As Tom Williams, Prince, and William Wright discovered, however, self-purchase agreements whereby slaves worked for their freedom could be oppressive. Tom Williams labored for two and one-half years before earning his emancipation.[61] Williams, however, was relatively fortunate. Prince did not receive his freedom until February 1810, after he had served Doctor John Masten of Rhinebeck for a full seven years.[62] Under the contract he concluded with his master, William Wright was to receive his freedom only after five and one half years of "honest" and "faithful" service. Wright's failure to conduct himself appropriately would postpone his emancipation for an additional year.[63]

The formidable obstacles to self-purchase meant that economic assistance from relatives and friends was often indispensable. Absalom Titus, "a man of colour supposed to be free" contracted to purchase his brother-in-law Jacob Tabor in Pawling shortly after the passage of the 1799 gradual abolition act.[64] Husbands in particular endeavored to purchase their wives and children. After his own manumission by Ezra Thompson of Stanford in 1800, Robert Churchill bought his wife's freedom from her owner, Captain Reed of the Oblong.[65] Permete Bloom endeavored to purchase his wife's freedom within one year of his own manumission.[66] Working together, couples and families at times could overcome seemingly insurmountable odds. Jane Hallem was only 17 years of age in 1801 when her master allowed her to work for herself in consideration of a promise made by Moses Hallem, a black man, to pay $100 at a future date. Amazingly, the couple met that price and married shortly after Jane's manumission.[67]

Even with the assistance of kin and the opportunities to work for themselves, however, self-purchase remained a very uncertain and even dangerous proposition. Any contract required the willingness of the slaveowner to enter into it, which was itself shaped by a host of economic, familial, and moral considerations. Moreover, in the eyes of the law, slaves could not contract, and self-purchase agreements made between slaves and their owners had no legal standing. Slaveowners could—and did—alter and even abrogate such agreements. In such instances, slaves like Anthony Murphy had no legal recourse. Although he had originally contracted to buy his wife's freedom for $10, for unknown reasons Murphy ended up paying twice that figure.[68] Even an agreement made in good faith by both parties was threatened with dissolution. A slaveowner could die before manumitting a slave, and desperate financial circumstances could force an owner to sell his slave property before the slave had purchased his freedom. In either case, the slave had no legal claim to any payments the slave had already made toward self-purchase.[69]

Although slaveowners could abrogate self-purchase agreements with their slaves, it was not in their long-term interest to do so. Entering into contracts with their slaves whereby slaves bought their own freedom either in cash installments or by their own labor guaranteed slaveowners a reliable source of labor, encouraged the good behavior of their bondmen and women, and provided compensation for the loss of the slave. As Ira Berlin has noted, manumission through self-purchase provided slaveholders with opportunities to satisfy both their consciences and their pocketbooks.[70] It would be a serious error, however, to presume that such agreements between slaveowners and their slaves were simple business transactions or, even more misleading, were indicative of masters' moral qualms over the institution. Dutchess County slaveowners actively resisted the antislavery impulse of the late eighteenth and early nineteenth centuries. For two decades, slaveholders in the Hudson Valley and their downstate allies successfully thwarted legislative efforts to eliminate slavery. Even after the adoption of New York's gradual abolition statute in 1799, slaveholders in Dutchess retained their slaves as long as possible. The number of manumissions increased only slowly during the end of the eighteenth and the beginning of the nineteenth centuries, and masters typically postponed manumission for several years or otherwise made it conditional upon obedience, dutiful service, or a slave's ability to indemnify the slaveowner or his estate.[71] In light of their opposition to emancipation, then, it is clear that self-purchase agreements between masters and slaves were made largely at the instigation of slaves themselves. The case of Rachel Pride—who approached Moses Downing to negotiate her own sale for two years of service and $50—was not necessarily atypical.[72]

An obdurate slaveowner who refused to accede to the entreaties and demands of his or her slaves risked retaliation. Slowing the pace of labor, feigning illness, performing shoddy work, stealing property, and sabotaging tools were just some of the many economic weapons slaves wielded on a daily basis to resist their enslavement. Running away constituted another effective weapon, and Dutchess County slaveowners became increasingly vulnerable to flight during the Revolution and after the adoption of gradual abolition at the very end of the eighteenth century. Although Dutchess County did not see a major battle during the War for Independence, the Mid-Hudson Valley occupied a pivotal strategic position during the conflict. The proximity of British forces in New York City, the presence of a large American encampment in Fishkill, social unrest and partisan activity in the countryside, and economic dislocation allowed slaves to challenge their owners and abscond. Newspapers published advertisements for as many as 60 slaves from the Hudson Valley region between 1777 and 1783, and that figure almost certainly underestimates the actual number of fugitives.[73] Slaves continued to take to the road after the termination of hostilities. Between 1785 and 1827, when slavery technically ended in New York State, more than 200 slaves from the Mid-Hudson region fled their owners. The adoption of the gradual abolition law in 1799 was an important turning point. Although the number of fugitives appearing in the local press dipped slightly during the decade and a half after the Revolution (46 runaways, or 3.1 per year), 108 fugitives appeared in Dutchess County newspapers between 1799 and 1817, or an average of six annually.[74]

Oftentimes literate, multilingual, and skilled, fugitives tended to be particularly intelligent and resourceful. Some deliberately took advantage of the prevalence of slave hiring and the autonomy it afforded. Ananias Cooper's fugitive slave Tom carried a counterfeit pass to look for a master, and Pomp, a literate and particularly "ingenious" slave who spoke good English, allegedly forged his own pass as well.[75] Lewis Barton speculated that his runaway slave Tom carried with him a document the fugitive had secured from a free black named Caesar the preceding spring "when he went into nine months service."[76]

Not surprisingly, slaveowners perceived such actions in insidious terms. Masters not infrequently described their runaways as cunning and deceitful. Hezekiah Collins considered his 25-year-old fugitive slave Nero a "smooth-tongued fellow."[77] Margaret Poyer of Fishkill described her fugitive slave Caesar as a man capable of writing a "very good hand" who had run away previously using an alias.[78] Slaveowners were probably especially sensitive to the duplicity of women and girls who also challenged gender conventions when defying their masters. Cornelius Haight was obviously unsettled by the flight of his slave Prim in 1780. The 23-year-old woman had evidently planned her escape well in advance, secreting all of her clothing to an unknown location before her flight. Haight predicted that Prim would go to the hiding place to change her appearance and warned readers of the *New York Journal and General Advertiser* and *New York Packet* to be "particularly careful to secure her, so that she does not give them the slip, as she is very sly and artful, . . . and if they trust her [she] will certainly deceive them."[79]

Crafty slaves who were openly defiant bred fear in the hearts of their owners. Advertisers for runaways occasionally noted the recalcitrance and intractability of their fugitives, describing them as having a "sour look," "surly countenance," a "sulky temper," a "down look," or an "ungovernable temper."[80] Dealing with cantankerous and uncooperative slaves undoubtedly wore on many slaveowners and took their psychological toll. Any success in duping or defying their owners, moreover, only bred self-confidence on the part of slaves. Aaron Black was a "remarkably strong" and "tolerably well formed" man who had escaped arrest for an unspecified felony. According to the advertisement for his capture, Black had "a habit of boasting and threatening in an extravagant manner, and of giving himself ludicrous airs of quality and importance." The author of the advertisement, Edward Thompson, speculated that a slave who so defied conventions of servile behavior had to be slightly insane.[81] Insane or not, however, defiant slaves could be particularly dangerous, as Ebenezer Hulsted of Nine Partners discovered. Hulsted's 35-year-old slave Rachel—"as cunning and subtle a creature as any of the kind"—stole clothing and other articles when she absconded in late May 1781. After absenting herself for a week, Rachel surreptitiously returned and torched Hulsted's home before fleeing to the British.[82]

By running away, fugitives undermined the master's authority and rendered slaveholding more onerous and costly to their owners. Some slaveowners responded by imposing harsh punishments or by simply selling their troublesome property. In advertising for the recapture of the fugitive Simon in 1818, John Drake indicated that he intended to sell the remaining time of the 16-year-old after Simon had fled "for the fifth time within a few months."[83] Henry Charlick likewise indicated his intent to sell his fugitive Ephraim on his capture.[84] In other instances, however, slaveowners reached some accommodation with their slaves to avoid flight in the future. Although his slave Adonijah had absconded from him in 1795, Daniel Lewis of Stanford provided for the slave's eventual emancipation when Lewis drafted his last will and testament in 1798. Lewis stipulated that Adonijah, who was approximately 19 years of age when Lewis made his will, was to receive his freedom on his 30th birthday if he behaved properly. According to Lewis, Adonijah could not be "guilty of any crime such as Stealing, running away, or some other criminal misdemeanor." What is revealing in this case is less Lewis's attempt to enforce Adonijah's good behavior than the fact that Lewis made any provision for the slave's manumission at all.[85]

Slaves pressured their masters into not only negotiating agreements but also adhering to them. If a slaveowner could unilaterally abrogate a contract for freedom or some other agreement between master and slave, the slave could break the contract by running away. The relationship between Gilbert Livingston and his slave Sam and that between Israel Vail of Clinton and his slave James provide insight into the complexity of the master–slave relationship and the different perspectives slaves and their masters had of the agreements they reached. Livingston placed an ad in the *Political Barometer* in July 1804 for his 19-year-old slave who had "ungratefully" left his employ. Livingston considered Sam's "dereliction of service" to be particularly "base," since Sam had allegedly solicited Livingston to purchase him for $225 "on an express contract to work out his freedom."[86] A similar struggle for power between James and his master Israel Vail lasted for years. Like the contract concluded between Livingston and Sam, James's original purchase agreement stipulated that the slave was to receive his freedom after serving Vail for a specified term of years. James, however, ran away before the end of the term, absconding from Vail on the night of July 30, 1803. Either authorities apprehended James or the fugitive returned voluntarily. For unknown reasons, the terms of the original purchase agreement remained in force. James, however, fled again in September 1805. If James had no qualms about violating the agreement he had concluded with Vail, his owner was indignant at James's breach of faith a second time. In a postscript to the advertisement for James's apprehension, Vail fumed, "As the aforesaid Negro man was purchased at his own request, this dereliction of service must be considered by every person as notoriously base." Vail entreated "printers throughout the United States" to place the advertisement in their newspapers.[87] In the eyes of Israel Vail and Gilbert Livingston, contracts for freedom were beneficent gifts awarded for loyal service, and the terms of such agreements were binding on slaves as well as masters. For slaves like Sam and James, however, such contracts were only a means to an end—their ultimate freedom—to be discarded whenever a better opportunity for freedom arose.

If slaves never really achieved the upper hand in their dealings with their owners, their bargaining position clearly improved over time. The restiveness of slaves during and immediately after the Revolution revealed the vulnerability of slaveowners, while the adoption of gradual abolition in 1799 placed masters in the position of having to accede to at least some of their slave's demands or risk retaliation or flight. Guaranteeing labor for a set period of time and securing some form of compensation for the eventual loss of the slave was preferable to losing the slave altogether. The effect of such concessions, moreover, was cyclical. The success of some in securing concessions from their owners and in negotiating freedom contracts encouraged others in bondage and also increased the likelihood of their success.[88]

The agitation of young women, for example, demonstrates the increasing restiveness of slaves during the first decades of the nineteenth century. A perilous undertaking, running away typically was not a realistic option for most women. Fugitives in the Mid-Hudson Valley, as elsewhere in the Americas, were disproportionately young (and usually single) men, who accounted for more than eight in ten fugitives during the half-century between the Revolution and the end of slavery in New York State in 1827. The increase in both the number and proportion of female runaways during the decades after the Revolution, however, is striking. Accounting for merely nine of 106 fugitives between 1777 and 1799, female runaways were particularly rare during the late eighteenth century. Both the number and proportion of female fugitives, however, increased in the wake of the 1799 statute. Advertisements for 18 women appeared in the local press during the decade and one-half after 1799, comprising 17% of all runaways. Young women grew yet bolder after the passage of an 1817 law that stipulated the formal end of New York slavery ten years later. Women accounted for fully one-third of the 45 fugitives appearing in the local press between 1818 and 1827. The descriptions of two 16-year-olds bound to service under the terms of the 1799 law provide some insight into the personalities and temperament of such women. Jerome Scofield's 16-year-old runaway allegedly had a "disposition much averse to fidelity and truth," and Matsey, another young woman of 16 who wore a "sour look," was allegedly so sly that she was "artful enough to deceive Satan himself."[89]

Growing assertiveness of African Americans in the decades after the Revolution and increasing economic leverage vis-à-vis their owners clearly hastened emancipation in Dutchess County and the Hudson River Valley. Ironically, the position of African Americans in the regional economy would deteriorate during the three decades preceding the Civil War, as the unavailability and cost of land and increasing competition for employment from native-born residents and European immigrants constrained the ability of free blacks to fashion economic autonomy. Any interpretation of the African American experience in the Hudson Valley during the Revolutionary and Early National eras, however, must account for the economic power slaves exercised in the region. Slaves in Dutchess County, exploiting the value of their own labor and the intimate nature of slavery in the regional economy, were independent actors who played central roles in the demise of slavery in New York.

Notes

1. See, for example, Ira Berlin, *Many Thousands Gone: The First Two Centuries of Slavery in North America* (Cambridge: Belknap/Harvard University Press, 1998); Ira Berlin and Philip Morgan, eds., *Cultivation and Culture: Labor and the Shaping of Slave Life in the Americas* (Charlottesville: University Press of Virginia, 1993); Ira Berlin and Philip Morgan, eds., *The Slaves' Economy: Independent Production by Slaves in the Americas* (London: Frank Cass, 1991); Larry Hudson, *To Have and to Hold: Slave Work and Family Life in Antebellum South Carolina* (Athens: University of Georgia Press, 1997); Larry Hudson, ed., *Working Toward Freedom: Slave Society and Domestic Economy in the American South* (Rochester: University of Rochester Press, 1994).

2. See for example, Thomas Wermuth, *Rip Van Winkle's Neighbors: The Transformation of Rural Society in the Hudson River Valley, 1720–1850* (Albany: State University of New York Press, 2001).

3. James H. Smith, *History of Dutchess County, New York* (Syracuse: D. Mason & Co., 1882), pp. 47–55.

4. Evarts B. Greene and Virginia D. Harrington, *American Population before the Federal Census of 1790* (New York: Columbia University Press, 1932), pp. 95–97. Evidence of the first settlement in the county is inconclusive, but Nicholas Emigh is generally credited as being the county's first permanent white resident, arriving some time in the 1680s. James Smith, *History of Dutchess County,* pp. 56–57. For an exploration of colonial development and the debate over land and labor in New York, see Patricia Bonomi, *A Factious People: Politics and Society in Colonial New York* (New York: Columbia University Press, 1971), pp. 179–228; David M. Ellis, et al., *A History of New York State* (Ithaca: Cornell University Press, 1967), pp. 71–77; Michael Kammen, *Colonial New York: A History* (New York: Oxford University Press, 1975), pp. 5, 37–38, 112, 176–180, 295–296; Sung Bok Kim, *Landlord and Tenant in Colonial New York: Manorial Society, 1664–1775* (Chapel Hill: University of North Carolina Press, 1978), pp. 3–43, 130–131, 235–238. Henry Noble MacCracken, *Old Dutchess Forever!: The Story of an American County* (New York: Hastings House, 1956), pp. 113–114; A. J. Williams-Myers, "Hands That Picked No Cotton: An Exploratory Examination of African Slave Labor in the Colonial Economy of the Hudson River Valley to 1800," *Afro-Americans in New York Life and History* 11 (July 1987), pp. 28–33.

5. On the growth of New York's economy during the middle part of the eighteenth century, see Kammen, *Colonial New York,* pp. 161–172; and Samuel McKee, Jr., "The Economic Pattern of Colonial New York," in Alexander C. Flick, ed., *History of the State of New York,* vol. II (New York: Columbia University Press, 1933), pp. 249–268.

6. Greene and Harrington, *American Population,* pp. 96–104.

7. Hector St. John de Crevecoeur, *Sketches of Eighteenth-Century America,* Henri L. Bourdin, Ralph H. Gabriel, and Stanley T. Williams, eds. (New Haven: Yale University, 1925), pp. 82–83.

8. A. Leon Higginbotham, Jr., *In the Matter of Color: Race and the American Legal Process: The Colonial Period* (New York: Oxford University Press, 1978), pp. 115–116; Samuel McKee, "A Century of Labor," in Flick, *History of the State of New York,* pp. 305–307; McKee, *Labor in Colonial New York, 1664–1776* (Port Washington: Ira J. Friedman, Inc., 1963; originally published 1935), pp. 93–94.

9. Greene and Harrington, *American Population,* pp. 96–104. Thomas Davis explores the demography of New York's eighteenth-century slave population in "New York's Black Line: A Note on the Growing Slave Population," *Afro-Americans in New York Life and History,* 2 (January 1978), pp. 41–59. See also Edgar McManus, *A History of Negro Slavery in New York* (Syracuse: Syracuse University Press, 1966), pp. 24–25, 42–46.

10. Horticulture in colonial New York is discussed in McKee, "A Century of Labor," pp. 291–298.

11. *New York Packet,* July 31, 1777.

12. *New York Journal and General Advertiser,* September 4, 1780; *New York Packet,* September 7, 1780.

13. *New York Packet,* July 17, 1783. On slave labor in New York and the North, see

Graham Hodges, *Root and Branch: African Americans in New York and East Jersey, 1613–1863* (Chapel Hill: University of North Carolina Press, 1999), pp. 43, 82–83, 107–111; Hodges, *Slavery and Freedom in the Rural North: African Americans in Monmouth County, New Jersey, 1665–1865* (Madison: Madison House, 1997), pp. 44–47; James Oliver Horton and Lois E. Horton, *In Hope of Liberty: Culture, Community, and Protest Among Northern Free Blacks, 1700–1860* (New York: Oxford University Press, 1997), pp. 14–15; William P. McDermott, "Slaves and Slaveowners in Dutchess County" *Afro-Americans in New York Life and History* 19 (January 1995), 20–25, 31–32; McManus, *Slavery in New York,* pp. 47–48; Richard S. Moss, *Slavery on Long Island: A Study in Local Institutional and Early African American Community Life* (New York: Garland, 1993), pp. 74–79; William D. Piersen, *Black Yankees: The Development of an Afro-American Subculture in Eighteenth-Century New England* (Amherst: University of Massachusetts Press, 1988), pp. 42–43; Shane White, *Somewhat More Independent: The End of Slavery in New York City, 1770–1810* (Athens: University of Georgia Press, 1991), pp. 10–13, 21–22, 94; Williams-Myers, "Hands That Picked No Cotton," pp. 36–43; Donald Wright, *African Americans in the Colonial Era: From African Origins Through the American Revolution* (Arlington Heights: Harlan Davidson, 1990), pp. 71, 106–107.

14. *Poughkeepsie Journal,* May 11, 1802; *Political Barometer,* January 27, 1808. For similar examples, see *New York Packet,* January 24, 1782, and March 20, 1783; *Poughkeepsie Journal,* January 15, 1794. For slaves in rural manufacture in Dutchess County, see William P. McDermott, *Clinton, Dutchess County, New York: A History of a Town* (Clinton Corners: Clinton Historical Society, 1987), pp. 58, 60, 63–64; McDermott, "Slaves and Slaveowners," pp. 20–22; Frank Hasbrouck, ed., *The History of Dutchess County, New York* (Poughkeepsie: S. A. Matthieu, 1909), p. 347; Roberta Singer, "The Livingstons as Slave Owners: The 'Peculiar Institution' on Livingston Manor and Clermont," in Richard T. Wiles, ed., *The Livingston Legacy: Three Centuries of American History* (Annandale-on-Hudson: Bard College, 1987), pp. 72–75.

15. *New York Packet,* January 24, 1782.

16. *Poughkeepsie Journal,* February 11, 1806. A young man of approximately 15 or 16 years of age who had labored as a house servant for several years also purportedly understood farming and the care of horses. *Poughkeepsie Journal,* March 6, 1804. For similar examples, see *Poughkeepsie Journal,* August 17, 1802; November 30, 1802; June 13, 1810; and April 15, 1818.

17. *New York Packet,* June 27, 1779.

18. *Poughkeepsie Journal,* April 13, 1802; May 26, 1791.

19. *Poughkeepsie Journal,* December 21, 1796.

20. *New York Packet,* August 14, 1783. For similar examples, see *New York Packet,* May 3, 1781; July 18, 1782; January 9, 1783; *Poughkeepsie Journal,* May 26, 1791; February 6, 1793; July 2, 1799; February 18, 1800; April 13, 1802; June 7, 1803; May 8, 1804; June 10, 1807; January 8, 1812; and *Political Barometer,* December 21, 1808.

21. *New York Packet,* August 14, 1783.

22. *Poughkeepsie Journal,* October 7, 1795.

23. Statistics compiled from *Heads of Families at the First Census of the United States Taken in the Year 1790: New York* (Baltimore: Genealogical Publishing Company, 1976); "Population Schedules of the First Census of the United States, 1790," Microcopy 637, Roll 6, New York, vol. 2 (Washington, D.C., 1965). Figures for Dutchess are comparable to those of the six downstate counties of New York. See Vivienne L. Kruger, "Born to Run: The Slave Family in Early New York, 1626 to 1827" (Ph.D. dissertation, Columbia University, 1985), p. 139; Moss, *Slavery on Long Island,* pp. 70–73; White, *Somewhat More Independent,* pp. 14–18, 88–89.

24. On the bargaining power of slaves in New York and elsewhere in the North, see McManus, *Slavery in New York,* pp. 61–62; Gary B. Nash and Jean R. Soderlund, *Freedom by Degrees: Emancipation in Pennsylvania and Its Aftermath* (New York: Oxford University Press, 1991), pp. 139–140; Piersen, *Black Yankees,* pp. 29–31; White, *Somewhat More Independent,* pp. 49, 106–111, 152.

25. "Abstracts of Wills," *Collections of the New York Historical Society,* vol. VII (New York: The Society, 1898), pp. 458–459. Eighteenth-century wills are on file in the New York State Archives in Albany and recorded in *Collections of the New York Historical Society* for the Years 1892–1908, vols. I–XVII (New York: The Society, 1893–1909).

26. "Will Book D," Dutchess County Surrogate's Court, Poughkeepsie, New York, p. 192.

27. *Poughkeepsie Journal,* November 30, 1802.

28. *Political Barometer,* November 22, 1803.

29. *Poughkeepsie Journal,* October 7, 1795.

30. "Abstracts of Wills" (1900), pp. 219–220.

31. "Will Book A," p. 211; "Abstracts of Wills," (1896), pp. 99–100.

32. *Political Barometer,* November 22, 1803.

33. *Poughkeepsie Journal,* January 8, 1812.

34. *Poughkeepsie Journal,* August 6, 1799.

35. *Poughkeepsie Journal,* March 25, 1800.

36. *Poughkeepsie Journal,* November 8, 1803. For similar examples, see *New York Journal and General Advertiser,* April 19, 1779; March 27, 1780; June 19, 1780; November 12, 1781; *New York Packet,* July 8, 1779; August 19, 1779; August 31, 1780; September 7, 1780; January 31, 1782; May 2, 1782; November 14, 1782; August 14, 1783; *Poughkeepsie Journal,* October 13, 1785; February 18, 1795; December 21, 1796; March 8, 1797; April 19, 1797; May 30, 1797; March 13, 1798; April 3, 1798; August 6, 1799; August 12, 1800; January 5, 1802; June 7, 1803; November 8, 1803; May 8, 1804; July 31, 1804; May 21, 1805; February 4, 1806; May 10, 1809; November 15, 1809; October 14, 1812; October 13, 1813; August 31, 1814; and *Republican Herald,* January 8, 1817.

37. *Poughkeepsie Journal,* March 27, 1798. For similar examples, see *Poughkeepsie Journal,* March 1, 1792; August 14, 1798; and February 18, 1800.

38. See "Will Book H," pp. 290–291, "Abstracts of Wills," (1900) pp. 262–263; (1903) pp. 227–228; (1904) pp. 111–112.

39. "Will Book A," p. 48.

40. "Will Book A," p. 211.

41. "Abstracts of Wills," (1898), p. 429.

42. "Abstracts of Wills," (1900), pp. 262–263; (1896), pp. 99–100; "Will Book H," pp. 290–291.

43. T. Stephen Whitman, *The Price of Freedom: Slavery and Manumission in Baltimore and Early National Maryland* (Lexington: University Press of Kentucky, 1997), pp. 13–17, 24–25, 110–111. See also Joyce Goodfriend, *Before the Melting Pot: Society and Culture in Colonial New York City, 1664–1730* (Princeton: Princeton University Press, 1992), pp. 118–119; Hodges, *Root and Branch,* pp. 41–42, 83; McKee, *Labor in Colonial New York,* pp. 129–130; McManus, *Slavery in New York,* pp. 47–52; Nash and Soderlund, *Freedom by Degrees,* pp. 85–86. McManus argues that hiring was more prevalent in New York than in any other colony and state.

44. White, *Somewhat More Independent,* pp. 149–152. See also Whitman, *Price of Freedom,* pp. 56–62, 73–78.

45. "Record of the Overseers of the Poor, Town of Poughkeepsie, 1807–1815," Adriance Memorial Library, Poughkeepsie, New York, p. 324.

46. "Overseers of the Poor," pp. 130, 322.

47. "Overseers of the Poor," pp. 233–234, 327–329.

48. "Overseers of the Poor," p. 396.

49. *Poughkeepsie Journal,* August 13, 1799.

50. "Overseers of the Poor," pp. 150–151.

51. On the significance of hiring, see Hodges, *Root and Branch,* pp. 106–110; McManus, *Slavery in New York,* pp. 145–153; Moss, *Slavery on Long Island,* pp. 74–80; Whitman, *Price of Freedom,* chapter 3, especially pp. 62–63, 75–78, 89–90.

52. "Overseers of the Poor," pp. 233–234.

53. "Overseers of the Poor," p. 192.

54. "Overseers of the Poor," p. 389.

55. "Overseers of the Poor," pp. 207–208.

56. "Overseers of the Poor," p. 49.

57. "Will Book B," pp. 562–564, "Will Book F," pp. 225–227.

58. "Overseers of the Poor," pp. 207–208; "Town of Beekman Record Book, 1772–1827," Dutchess County Archives, Poughkeepsie, New York, p. 405.

59. "Overseers of the Poor," p. 124.

60. "Overseers of the Poor," p. 256.

61. "Town of Beekman Record Book," p. 414.

62. "Rhinebeck Town Records, 1748–1863," Rhinebeck Historical Society, Rhinebeck, New York, February 21, 1810.

63. "Smith Thompson File," Franklin Delano Roosevelt Library, Hyde Park, New York.

64. "Overseers of the Poor," pp. 3, 43.

65. "Overseers of the Poor," pp. 164–165, 192.

66. "Overseers of the Poor," p. 184.

67. "Overseers of the Poor," p. 162.

68. "Overseers of the Poor," p. 399.

69. Whitman provides an outstanding detailed analysis of manumission and self-purchase in Whitman, *Price of Freedom,* chapters 4–5, pp. 93–139. See also Herbert Aptheker, "Buying Freedom," in Aptheker, *To Be Free: Studies in American Negro History* (New York: International Publishers, 1969; originally published 1948), pp. 31–32; Mary Beth Corrigan, "'It's a Family Affair': Buying Freedom in the District of Columbia, 1850–1860," in Hudson, *Working Toward Freedom,* pp. 163–192; Hodges, *Root and Branch,* pp. 172–175; Hodges, *Slavery and Freedom in the Rural North,* pp. 128–129, 137; Kruger, "Born to Run," pp. 763–767; Sumner Eliot Matison, "Manumission by Purchase," *Journal of Negro History* 33 (April 1948), 146–167; McManus, *Slavery in New York,* pp. 145–155; Moss, *Slavery on Long Island,* pp. 50–51, 59–60.

70. Ira Berlin, "The Revolution in Black Life," in Alfred F. Young, ed., *The American Revolution: Explorations in the History of American Radicalism* (DeKalb: Northern Illinois University Press, 1976), p. 358; Matison, "Manumission by Purchase," pp. 161–162; Whitman, *Price of Freedom,* pp. 87–88, 98–108.

71. Michael Groth, "Slaveholders and Manumission in Dutchess County, New York," *New York History* 78 (1) (January 1997), 33–50.

72. "Overseers of the Poor," pp. 233–234, 327–329.

73. Michael Groth, "Forging Freedom in the Mid-Hudson Valley: The End of Slavery and the Formation of a Free African American Community in Dutchess County, NY, 1770–1850" (Ph.D. dissertation, Binghamton University, 1994), pp. 84–86.

74. See Michael Groth, "The African American Struggle Against Slavery in the Mid-Hudson Valley, 1785–1827," *Hudson Valley Regional Review* (March 1994) 11 (1), 63–79. Editors of the *New York Journal and General Advertiser* and *New York Packet* resumed publication of their respective sheets in the Mid-Hudson Valley after evacuating New York City in 1776.

75. *New York Journal and General Advertiser,* May 1, 1780; September 4, 1780.

76. *New York Packet,* June 28, 1781.

77. *New York Packet,* October 30, 1777.

78. *New York Packet,* November 27, 1777.

79. *New York Journal and General Advertiser,* June 5, 1780; *New York Packet,* June 8, 1780.

80. *Poughkeepsie Journal,* July 15, 1800; October 16, 1816; November 20, 1797; *Republican Herald,* September 22, 1813; May 3, 1815.

81. *Poughkeepsie Journal,* August 11, 1824.

82. *New York Packet,* June 7, 1781.

83. *Poughkeepsie Journal,* August 19, 1818.

84. *Poughkeepsie Journal,* October 21, 1818.

85. *Poughkeepsie Journal,* September 9, 1795; "Will Book B," pp. 120–121. Zachaeus Newcomb of Poughkeepsie similarly instructed the manumission of his slave Pomp in his 1790 will. Newcomb had advertised a runaway by the same name ten years earlier. *New York Journal and General Advertiser,* September 4, 1780; "Will Book A," p. 260.

86. *Political Barometer,* July 10, 1804.

87. *Poughkeepsie Journal,* August 2, 1803; October 8, 1805.

88. Matison, "Manumission by Purchase," p. 167; Berlin, "Revolution in Black Life," pp. 365–368.

89. *Dutchess Observer,* March 6, 1822; *Poughkeepsie Journal,* July 15, 1800. See also *Dutchess Observer,* July 14, 1824.

4

Myra B. Young Armstead

A Geography of Slavery and Freedom in Antebellum Ulster County and New York City

Isabella Van Wagenen and Her Family

When Isabella Van Wagenen lived in the Hudson Valley, she resided mainly in Ulster County as a slave domestic and farm worker and in New York City as a free woman who labored at housework. After leaving New York City, she gained fame as Sojourner Truth—abolitionist, feminist, and preacher-orator. How does one account for such a personal transformation? By focusing on Truth's earlier incarnation—the lesser known, local historical figure, Isabella Van Wagenen—I explore the ways in which her later identity shift may have been predicated on the meanings she attached to the varied physical environments she confronted in the region. I map her physical movements in religious space, residential space, work space, and judicial space to suggest that her decision to shed her old identity for a new one as an itinerant preacher resulted from the lessons she learned about her life chances in those locations.

Both slavery and freedom, while often considered in metaphysical and philosophical terms alone, historically have also had a material dimension for Africans in the New World. In the past, these terms have found their meaning in objects. Thus, for example, chains were associated with slavery, while books with freedom. But slavery and freedom have also acquired significance because of their association with the built environment and with natural landscapes. African captives about to be sold as slaves huddled together in West African coastal forts and crossed the Atlantic while squeezed onto the floors of ship galleys while free people had access to marketplaces, legislative halls, and courtrooms. Black chattel were mostly confined to farms and plantations while cities were often a refuge for the free and would-be-free. Thus it makes sense to talk about a geography of slavery and a geography of freedom. Blacks in the Hudson Valley experienced these ostensibly opposing geographies from 1613 when the black Atlantic Creole, Jan Rodrigues, left a Dutch vessel to remain on Manhattan Island until July 4, 1827, when slavery in New York State was made illegal. A study of Isabella Van Wagenen and her family as residents of Ulster County and New York City provides an illuminating example of these phenomena.

Prior to 1843, that towering, thunder-voiced, itinerant preacher called Sojourner Truth did not exist as such. These are the relevant details of her period of bondage: She was born a slave some time around 1797, the daughter of Mau-Mau Bett and James or Bomefree—both of whom were slaves in the household of the low Dutch-descended farmer, Colonel Johannes Hardenburgh. Her parents named her Isabella. The household lived in Hurley in Ulster County, New York. When Johannes died, Isabella, her younger brother, Peter, and their parents were passed on to Charles Hardenburgh, Johannes's son; Isabella was just a baby at the time. Upon Charles's death and the settlement of his financially pressed estate in 1808, John Nealy, a Massachusetts Yankee-merchant new to the area, purchased Isabella (along with a sheep) at a local auction. Peter was sold away separately while Isabella's parents, by then too elderly to fetch a good price, were granted their freedom. Mr. and Mrs. Nealy spoke only English, while John could understand some low Dutch. Isabella, who only spoke low Dutch, was forced to learn English the hard way in the Nealy household. John Nealy was an impatient, physically abusive master to Isabella, and Mrs. Nealy was a demanding, verbally abusive mistress. Through the intervention of Bomefree, however, Isabella was purchased after roughly a year from the Nealys by Martin Schryver, a tavernkeeper in Kingston. In 1810, when Isabella was about 13, John J. Dumont of New Paltz successfully offered $300 for her. Isabella remained with the Dumonts for 16 years, married one of their slaves, Tom, and bore five children—Dinah, Peter, Hannah, Elizabeth, and Sophia. In 1826, Isabella fled the Dumont household with her infant, Sophia, and found shelter with a nearby family, Isaac and Maria Van Wagenen.[1]

These are the relevant details of Isabella's period of freedom: When on Independence Day of 1827 all slaves in New York State were emancipated by law, Isabella, now known as Isabella Van Wagenen, elected to stay with the Van Wagenens as a paid house servant. However, she learned later that year of the plight of her son, Peter. He had been illegally moved out of New York State and was held a slave in Alabama by the relatives of Solomon Gedney, an Ulster County doctor to whom he had been sold earlier. Isabella promptly removed herself to Kingston, New York—the county seat—where she filed a complaint with the Grand Jury and won her son's return to the state and to her custody in 1828. During the next year, Isabella worked and visited relatives in Ulster County from Newburgh to Kingston. Upon the advice of a fellow-Methodist schoolteacher, she moved with Peter to New York City in 1829. For the next 14 years, she performed various domestic duties in the households of several wealthy, white New York evangelical reformers. During this period, from 1832 to 1834, she participated in a utopian religious community called The Kingdom of Matthias. Peter, who experienced several brushes with the law, was finally convinced to go to sea in 1835 and remained in touch with his mother by letter until 1839. Four years later, Isabella opted to leave New York City and the Hudson Valley entirely for points east. This decision was accompanied by an equally momentous one: Isabella Van Wagenen chose at this point to discard her name and become Sojourner Truth.[2]

Isabella's 30 years of bondage and 16 years of emancipation were marked by physical movement within a multi-layered physical environment. While a resident of Ulster County and New York City, she either was relocated or relocated herself from countryside to town, town to town, house to house, workplace to workplace, outdoors to indoors, downstairs to upstairs, room to room, and corner to corner. Each of these spaces held particular meaning(s) for Isabella and her family over time as social relations were produced and reproduced within them. Over the span of their lives, it was within specific material locations that Isabella and her kin learned the meaning of their status as slaves in relation to free whites and how this varied by age, gender, and class. Similarly, it was within defined physical spaces and places that Isabella and her relations discovered the meaning of freedom and how this, too, varied by age and gender for black people in the Hudson Valley. Dolores Hayden has asserted, ". . . [I]t is place's very same assault on all ways of knowing (sight, sound, smell, touch, and taste) that makes it powerful as a source of memory, as a weave where one strand ties in another."[3] Thus it is from the assorted places—both natural and human-made—in which Isabella Van Wagenen and her family circulated that their history in the Hudson Valley may partially be constructed.

Religion, home, work, and the law derived their significance from the spaces in which blacks encountered them. Isabella's religion preceded her formal conversion to Methodism and, in its primal stages, was associated with outdoor spaces. Her mother was either the daughter of an African-born slave or "of all-black African ancestry." Mau-Mau Bett taught Belle to say the Lord's Prayer, to obey her master in all things, and never to lie or steal. Gathering her children at day's end under a starry, nighttime canopy, Bett delivered her catechism: "My children, there is a God, who hears and sees you . . . He lives in the sky . . . and when you are beaten, or cruelly treated, or fall into any trouble, you must ask help of him, and he will always hear and help you."[4] When on these occasions, Mau-Mau Bett sorrowfully remembered the eight or more of her children who had been sold to owners beyond her knowing, she would peer mournfully upward at the sky and explain to Peter and Isabella, "Those are the same stars, and that is the same moon, that look down upon your brothers and sisters, and which they see as they look up to them, though they are ever so far away from us, and each other."[5] Erlene Stetson and Linda David have suggested, rather vaguely, that Bett's outdoor, nocturnal prayers under the stars and moon "issued from deeply-rooted African Traditional or Islamic religion."[6]

From this instruction, Isabella concluded that God was a benefactor, remote, but accessible through audible, deliberate invocation which could best be accomplished in the wild—out of earshot of owners and, perhaps, because such spaces were in closer proximity to the sky. Consequently, while living within the Dumont household, Isabella carefully and secretly surveyed the surrounding countryside to determine the location of her altar. Having discovered an island in the middle of a stream whose babbling noises concealed the sound of her petitions, she began building. There, she wove willow branches into a wall high enough to hide her body while she spoke with God. Historian Nell Painter concludes that such a prayer site was "much like the shrines of black southerners" and, rather generally, that Isabella "worshiped God as though she were in a West African river cult."[7] Streams, trees, sky, stars, moon—these were the pastoral elements in which a young Isabella connected to God while a slave. These external, bucolic surroundings were an antidote to her forced legal confinement and comforted her with intimations of an unrealized freedom.

And it was out-of-doors that Isabella received two critical, divine messages in her flight from slavery. In the first message, she was encouraged to run. John Dumont, impressed with her industry, had promised Isabella and Tom manumission on July 4, 1826—a year earlier than the date stipulated by New York State law—and that he would fix the couple in a cabin of their own. At the appointed emancipation date, however, Dumont reneged. Isabella had cut her right hand badly in the intervening time and this accident had decreased her productivity. Dumont claimed that Isabella owed him more work. Finally, after 16 years of near fanatically dutiful service, the 30-year-old Isabella reached her limit. She decided that after the fall harvest and "the wool was spun," she would leave the Dumonts and take along Sophia, her infant youngest child.[8]

In the predawn hours of an autumn day in 1826 Isabella made her escape and, after walking six to seven miles without detection, she reached the top of a hill just as the sun arose brightly in the sky. According to the narrator of her first memoir, "She thought it never was so light before, indeed, she thought it much too light." In this physical setting, fugitive Isabella asked God, "Where, and to whom, shall I go?" Receiving instructions "soon" thereafter, she quickly make her way to an elderly, white acquaintance, Levi Rowe, whose wife directed her to the abode of Mr. and Mrs. Van Wagenen. In this way, the God of the sky had helped her escape slavery.[9]

In the second message, Isabella received a fierce rebuke from this God of nature that prevented her voluntary return to bondage. The Van Wagenens, who were anti-slavery, had paid Dumont $25 to satisfy his claims against Isabella and Sophia. Isabella had been well treated in the Van Wagenen household, but despite the family's kindness, she had found its routines too cheerless, monotonous, and placid.[10] As Pinkster season approached in the spring of 1827, Isabella longed for the gaiety of this festival in which "black people crowned a king, drummed, paraded, danced, sang, drank, and staged elaborate ceremonies in which those who had been born in Africa instructed the American-born."[11] Moreover, Isabella perhaps recalled an earlier Pinkster celebration in which she may have met another slave, Robert, her first and perhaps only true love and by whom she may have borne her first child. As the 1827 festivities approached, Isabella yearned to participate in the annual Hudson Valley holiday. One day she had an intimation that her old master, Dumont, would come calling for her and informed Maria Van Wagenen of this. When later that very day Dumont did appear, Isabella prepared to depart with him and leave the Van Wagenens permanently. But as she approached the Dumont carriage, a supernatural intervention blocked her look backward to Egypt and was reported as follows by Isabella's narrator:

> God revealed himself to her, with all the suddenness of a flash of lightning, showing her, 'in the twinkling of an eye, that he was *all* over'—that he pervaded the universe—'and that there was no place where God was not.' She became instantly conscious of her great sin in forgetting her almighty Friend and 'ever-present help in time of trouble.' All her unfilled promises arose before her, like a vexed sea whose waves run mountains high; and her soul, which seemed but one mass of lies, shrunk back aghast from the 'awful look' of Him whom she had formerly talked to, as if he had been a being like herself; and she would now have fain hid herself in the bowels of the earth, to have escaped his dread presence.[12]

In a few trance-like seconds known only to Isabella, apparently her God had furiously prevented her return to Dumont, had in fact obstructed her return to slavery. Outside, in broad daylight and on the Van Wagenen walkway, God revealed a burning wrath toward Isabella's "sin"—her misguided nostalgia for activity linked to her former bondage. Apparently, God's indignation was persuasive. Immediately, Isabella did a mental and physical about-face. She walked back to the Van Wagenen house—her refuge, her place of safety and freedom—and found that the "burning sun" and turmoil of God's anger which she had just felt were now replaced by a friendly presence, a vision of light beaming "with the beauty of holiness, and radiant with love." She inquired more deeply of this God, "Who are you?" "Jesus," the answer came. She later told her biographer that suddenly, at that instant, she knew that Jesus had always loved her, that he was intimately acquainted with her, and readily accessible to her in ways she had not previously known.[13] Of significance here, however, is that this mysterious, divine presence confirmed the safe, predictable democracy of the Van Wagenen homestead.

The deeper revelation Isabella received at this time had, in fact, a physical dimension. Since this God of love, approval, and liberation was now everywhere, she need not look for him only in the open ranges of the out-of-doors. Any space, any location, any spot could and should be a place of freedom. This incident is generally recorded as Isabella's moment of explicit Christian conversion. Noteworthy here is that the evangelical religion she embraced was one of liberation, one of personal empowerment, one that condemned slavery, and one that linked these ideals to physical spaces.

Emancipation and religious conversion, in other words, converged in Isabella's case and in this process, a shift occurred in her symbolic orientation towards space. An omnipresent God was now accessible in every space—outdoors and indoors. Following the logic of evangelicalism, every space should then be accessible to everyone. Thus, from this episode forward, Isabella would increasingly find herself drawn to the company of nineteenth century integrationists who objected to the partitioning of space on racial grounds. At this stage of her life, however, this objection was entirely personal; it was not expressed in explicit political protest. Rather, it simply led her, on an individual level, whenever possible to exact compliance with an egalitarian notion of physical interaction between free people, black and white. For instance, when she happened upon her first Methodist meeting in Ulster County, rather than sit in the customary "Negro pew" of the church, Isabella stood outside and observed through an open window. Despite her hunger for Methodist instruction, she resigned her membership in New York City's John Street Church to join an all-black church, Zion Church, rather than endure the former's racial segregation of space for at John Street, blacks attended separate class meetings.[14]

Hearth, home, or residence were also places full of multiple meanings for Isabella and other Hudson Valley blacks as they were shifted from owner to owner or from slave to free status. On the one hand, home for a slave always meant relatively meager accommodations in marginal spaces within the master's domain. But what form these accommodations took and the connotations they held depended on the means and will of the master. While held by Johannes Hardenburgh who was a large landholder, Isabella, her brother, and parents were cottagers on their owner's estate. They lived together, apart from their master, in a small house on hilly acreage lent to them by Johannes, and farmed "tobacco, corn, and flax" in exchange for a set number of days of labor. This relatively privileged residential space disappeared for Isabella and her nuclear family after Johannes's demise, however. Charles Hardenburgh housed the group in a space more common to Hudson Valley slaves—his cellar. It was dark and cold there at all times. The floor was earthen. Slaves ate their meals there and slept on straw-covered wood pallets arranged atop the dirt floor. On wet days, the boards sloshed in mud. It was in such a home that Mau-Mau Bett expired—palsied, rheumatoid, choking, "helpless and senseless on the earth." Such institutionalized spatial arrangements amounted to living pictures by which owners reinforced the depressed, subordinate status of bound blacks. The space beneath the feet of whites was black space. It is no wonder that some years later when Isabella was offered lodging by sympathetic Quakers during her legal battles for her son, Peter, she marvelled at the "nice, high, clean, white, *beautiful* bed" proffered by her hosts and required some coaxing in order not to sleep in her usual space, the floor.[15]

Spatial mobility, generally regarded as a great boon of freedom for blacks, could become a curse for the elderly, however. Isabella's parents experienced this reality. Only because they had outlived their economic usefulness did the Hardenburgh family manumit Mau-Mau Bett and Bomefree at Charles's death. At first they were permitted to remain in their familiar home—the humid, dark cellar—by the new occupants of the former Hardenburgh residence. Mau-Mau Bett cared for her aged and crippled husband, probably by doing domestic work when she could and when it was available. But after Mau-Mau Bett died, the now blind Bomefree became too much of a burden to the renters with whom he resided. "I am *so old,* and *so helpless,*" he cried to Isabella during one of the infrequent visits with him permitted her by the Nealys. "What *is* to become of me? I can't do any thing more—my children are all gone, and here I am left helpless and alone." Isabella had no solution to offer. Eventually, the Hardenburghs showed some pity on Bomefree and offered to share responsibility for him.[16] What this in fact meant was that Bomefree was doomed to homelessness—perpetual spatial liminality until his death. Whenever one of the Hardenburghs tired of him, they pushed Bomefree off onto another of their relations. His situation is described in a passage from Isabella's *Narrative:*

> If, when he made a removal, the place where he was going was not too far off, he took up his line of march, staff in hand, and asked for no assistance. If it was twelve or twenty miles, they gave him a ride. While he was living in this way, Isabella was twice permitted to visit him . . . but when she reached the place where she hoped to find him, he had just left for a place some twenty miles distant, and she never saw him more. The last time she *did* see him, she found him seated on a rock, by the roadside, alone, and far from any house. He was then migrating from the house of one [Hardenburgh] to that of another, several miles distant . . . [H]e was blind . . . and his gait was more a creep than a walk.[17]

This state of affairs was relieved only briefly when Bomefree was taken into his last abode—"a rude cabin, in a lone wood, far from any neighbors"—which had been granted Caesar, Mau-Mau Bett's brother, and his wife—themselves old and infirm and, for this reason, also recently emancipated by the Hardenburghs. As part of a story with a cruel refrain, when Caesar and his wife died, another elderly woman and an emancipated slave named Soan, too old and weak to do regular work, made sick visits to Bomefree from time to time before his demise. Similarly, after emancipation, Isabella's husband, Thomas, a man some years older than she and unable to care for himself especially after her departure from the Dumont household, "died in the poorhouse." Thus, an erstwhile landscape of freedom was transformed for the aged into what Michael Dear and Jennifer Woloch would call "a landscape of despair" by the cruel trickery of pecunious slaveholders.[18]

Work sites similarly reinforced the status of Hudson Valley blacks as slave or free, but the extent to which they did so varied according to gender. In this particular region, the economic utility of female slaves owed not so much to their fecundity, but to their skills in traditional domestic duties—cooking, laundering, sewing, cleaning, nursing the young and ill, gardening, dairying—and planting and harvesting on area farms. Emancipation did not alter this range of work options for Hudson Valley black women.[19] The locations in which their labor was performed—whether interior or exterior—were privately held and defined the normative environment of antebellum women (black and white).[20] Thus female work space was tightly circumscribed space. Moreover, for black women, even emancipated black wage-earning women, it was socially devalued space.

Isabella was well acquainted with the kitchens, yards, and fields of the Hudson Valley in which were performed female work rhythms in slavery and in freedom. Within the households she knew as a slave—those of the Nealys and Dumonts—Isabella cooked, cleaned, spun, and harvested. Later, as an emancipated wage earner, household domestic work sustained her in Kingston and New York City. As a member of the perfectionist cult, The Kingdom of Matthias, she served as a kitchen maid and nurse to the sick, and helped bring in the hay.[21]

Isabella was also familiar with the disdain with which those who labored in female work spaces were often regarded and handled. The Nealy barn where she milked the cows each morning was where she received her first severe beating. The Nealy kitchen was the scene of verbal castigation for inevitable miscommunications as the then Dutch-speaking Isabella collected pot hooks when ordered to bring frying pans by her English-speaking mistress. The Dumont kitchen was the site of endless scrutiny under that mistress's watchful eye, ever on guard against "half-performed" work.[22]

Furthermore, Isabella understood the class dynamic informing the difference between culinary space occupied by wage-earning female domestics—black and white—and bourgeois white housewives: The former was linked to social denigration while the latter to social respectability. Isabella's perceptiveness on this point was revealed in the manner in which she conveyed her disapproval of one of the events that transpired during her period in The Kingdom. A white servant girl had been joined to a middle-class businessman in the group's wife-swapping practices, but Isabella felt that this woman "was only fit to be in the kitchen with her."[23]

For a woman to abandon traditional female work space in the private realm and to venture into the public marketplace was to draw certain moral suspicion and/or reproach. Thus, antebellum female slaves and black and white poor women, who out of necessity plied public sidewalks as peddlers selling wares, washerwomen bearing their clients' laundry, or sewing-trade workers on their way to and from mills, risked popular association with their less reputable sisters—the original streetwalkers.[24]

In two instances, Isabella's work required her entry into public space. The first met with disapprobation from a contemporary, her biographer, and perhaps from a later reconstructed Isabella herself. As the slave of the innkeeper Schryver, Isabella circulated broadly outside the confines of traditional female work space. Her antebellum narrator recorded the following about her movements at this time: "Here she lived 'a wild, out-of-door kind of life'; she carried fish, hoed corn, and searched the woods for roots and herbs to be used in beer-making. When she was sent 'to the Strand [a commercial area in the Rondout section of Kingston] for a gallon of molasses or liquor,' she would 'browse around.'" Of note here is the negative commentary assigned Isabella's public circulation as a worker by her narrator, Olive Gilbert, herself apparently a paragon of antebellum female virtue. With characteristic bourgeois restraint, Gilbert remarked that Isabella's life during this stretch was "wholly unimproved" and that "morally, she retrograded, as [the] example [of the Schryvers] taught her to curse."[25] By this account then, female labors performed in public, heterosocial spaces led to corruption.

The only exception to this "rule" condemning female, out-of-doors, public work was, of course, labor that amounted to social housekeeping, for instance the performance of the traditional female activities of uplift and nurture within the public sphere on a volunteer, unpaid basis. Women could "work" as benefactors in the public realm by raising money for the poor, crusading against prostitution, advocating for temperance, lobbying for abolition, and the like. The social acceptability of this variance was itself incipient in the early 1830s, but Isabella took early advantage of it in her efforts as a Methodist public exhorter. Before joining Matthias's Kingdom, she was known among New York City evangelicals for "preach[ing] and pray[ing] loud and long."[26] Among white Methodists and later friends, she was highly respected for her effectiveness as a preacher. They reported that she was "the means of converting some by her zeal" and that "the influence of her speaking was miraculous."[27] But because Isabella at this time specifically wanted to reach New York City *blacks* with her preaching and felt rejected by this audience (she felt they preferred "great preachers, . . . not ignorant ones like herself"), she initially regarded this public ministry a failure.[28] The point to be underscored here, however, is that she had begun to discover and explore a public work space for herself that met with at least some measure of approval and success.

Whereas exterior work space was scarcely available to Hudson Valley black women, it abounded for their male counterparts. For black men like Isabella's son, Peter, public space offered many work options. They might labor in the Hudson Valley from Albany to New York City on docks as longshoreman; on canals and railroads as builders; in retail outfits as restaurateurs and barbers; on streets as hawkers, pavers, ditch diggers, construction workers, carters, and chauffeurs; and in fields as farmhands. When compared to the work sites of white men, black men tended to labor outside where the availability of a day's wages depended on favorable weather conditions. White men enjoyed the more predictable and better sheltered environments of office, shop, and factories.[29]

The choices made for and by Isabella's Peter illustrate that, of the public work spaces available to black men, one of the most compelling was the sea. Historians have long observed the heavy representation of black sailors in antebellum maritime industries characterizing especially the nation's port cities. Blacks, in fact, held 18% of all American seaman's jobs in 1803. For free blacks in the North, a stint as a sailor was often viewed as a stepping-stone to middle-class status since black mariners sailing on voyages originating above the Mason-Dixon Line received equal and sometimes more pay than whites. This fact prompted "the 'best' black families in the North [to send] their sons to sea."[30] It was only logical then that when Isabella first moved from Ulster County to New York City with Peter in tow, her plan was to enroll her son in a navigation school. With the financial aid of a white friend, she was able to do this.[31]

Besides the promise of economic independence associated with the sea as a work place, the ocean proved attractive to some black men as the location for their labors because of its association with a free-wheeling, unrestricted lifestyle. Work on seafaring vessels, especially deep sea ships like whalers, was especially dangerous and violent. For antebellum free black men, the sea could be a site for recapture, re-enslavement, and kidnapping. But experience at sea also enhanced a sailor's sense of worldliness and masculine bravado—qualities denied land-bound, free, black men even as such qualities were valued in their white counterparts during this period. As W. Jeffrey Bolster has explained, seafaring . . . throughout the nineteenth century . . . affirmed blacks' capacity for . . . transcendence of the ordinary." It is not entirely surprising therefore that despite truancy and initial abandonment of his mother's maritime plan for him, the restless Peter eventually elected to set sea from Nantucket upon a whaling vessel.[32]

The geography of race prohibited blacks equal access to yet another space, courts of law, especially during slavery. In New York a dual legal system existed until the early nineteenth century. First, black testimony against a white person was not permitted and, from 1708 to 1788, special slave courts existed for slaves accused of capital crimes; three justices of the peace and five freeholders heard such cases. After 1788, slaves facing charges for crimes punishable by death were granted jury trials. Finally in 1813, jury trials were permitted for all slaves facing criminal charges and statutes preventing black testimony against whites were nullified.[33]

The geography of freedom thus extended equal access to judicial space to blacks by law. But in the pre-Civil War years in New York State, the extent to which this new geography held real meaning was a matter to be tested. It is extraordinary that Isabella Van Wagenen was willing to participate in such an experiment. She was at least triply hampered. As a woman of the era, she had no political rights. She could not vote, and social conventions conspired against her entry into any public arena. Moreover, she was an uneducated, poor woman who was not supposed to understand the law or be able to pay for its practitioners. Finally, she was a black woman subject to the general racial biases which barred African Americans even from jury service in the antebellum North.

Isabella successfully exploited her access to judicial space as a free woman of color on two occasions. The first time, she won Peter's return from illegal enslavement.[34] The radical novelty of this recently emancipated black woman's physical presence in previously forbidden space is perhaps best conveyed in her *Narrative:*

> By a little inquiry, she found which was the building she sought, went into the door, and taking the first man she saw of imposing appearance for the *grand* jury, she commenced her complaint. But he very civilly informed her there was no grand jury there; she must go up stairs. When she had with some difficulty ascended the flight through the crowd that filled them, she again turned to the *"grandest"* looking man she could select, telling him she had come to enter a complaint to the grand jury. For his own amusement, he inquired what her complaint was; but when he saw it was a serious matter, he said to her, "This is no place to enter a complaint—go in there," pointing in a particular direction. She then went in, where she found the Grand Jurors indeed sitting, and again commenced to relate her injuries.[35]

The court building, its portal door, its lobby stairs, its jury chambers all loomed before Isabella quite literally as unknown territory. Yet she understood that freedom entitled her to occupy these spaces as a litigant. Despite sexist, classist, and racist prejudices and conventions, she therefore exercised her legal right by stepping into this new terrain.

In a second instance, Isabella brought suit in a libel case following the demise of The Kingdom of Matthias. The cult's leader, Robert Matthews, was on trial for the murder of one of The Kingdom's adherents, and two disillusioned followers now claimed that Isabella was an accomplice in the alleged crime. Upon the advice of Matthews's lawyer, Isabella agreed to sue her accusers for slander as a way of clearing her name so that she might become a more credible witness for her former spiritual mentor. Although Isabella won this case, she never appeared in the court as a witness in her own defense—an opportunity she desperately wanted. As "the public" insisted by convention on the testimony of whites, Isabella's white employer testified in court on her behalf that her accusers had privately admitted that they had lied in implicating her.[36]

Four years after the sensational Matthias case, when Isabella Van Wagenen decided to become a new person, her identity shift had much to do with the early national and antebellum geography lessons she had learned as a slave and free black woman. Her religious experiences had taught her that God was ubiquitous, in every place and must be shared abroad, everywhere. Her residential experiences had taught her that no physical home was secure for those who owned no real estate. Her work experiences underscored that only pulpits and lecterns, established and makeshift, offered a measure of equal treatment. And her legal experiences confirmed that courtrooms were capricious spaces—sometimes receiving black voices, sometimes not, and sometimes only permitting blacks to be spoken for.

The ostensible opposition of slavery and freedom had not always meant respectively opposite encounters with the physical environment for Isabella Van Wagenen. Having passed from slave to free, she did not yet own, either literally or figuratively, the spaces in which she moved. She was now a free black woman in New York State. But, as a live-in domestic in the Hudson Valley, her workplace options were sequestered, limited, and not especially remunerative. Nor could she claim possession of any place in which she resided. Judicial spaces were now open to her, but these required mediation on her behalf by men. Religious space, in contrast, held the most promise since its ideal and practice combined in her experience to confirm that it could provide an accessible, rewarding, and public arena of expression. To live permanently in this arena—in this liberated space—was an attractive possibility.

Summarizing these lessons, according to her *Narrative,* Isabella concluded two things. On the one hand, persistence in her current location was foolish since "every thing she had undertaken in the city of New York had finally proved a failure."[37] On the other hand, embracing transience as a sojourner was likely to minimize any future disappointments and cognitive dissonance. Transient space, itinerant space—untrammeled and unfettered by permanent, stationary obstacles—constituted an ideal geography of freedom for this poor, black woman seeking self-validation and self-advancement in an uncooperative age. She would no longer be blocked for she would always be on-the-move. She would, in fact, sojourn. Committing herself to public preaching on this ever-shifting ground, she might speak The Truth as she perceived it without question or interruption. During the Matthias trial, Isabella Van Wagenen had told her lawyer, "I have the truth, and I know it."[38] Prevented from speaking this truth by law and custom, Sojourner Truth could now do so on a new and endless road.

Notes

1. [Sojourner Truth with Olive Gilbert], *Narrative of Sojourner Truth,* edited by Margaret Washington (New York: Vintage Books, 1993), pp. 3–30; Gilbert Vale, *Fanaticism: Its Source and Influence, Illustrated by the Simple Narrative of Isabella* (New York: G. Vale, 1835), Part I, p. 2; Carleton Mabee with Susan Mabee, *Sojourner Truth: Slave, Prophet, Legend.* (New York: New York University Press, 1993), p. xiii.

2. *Narrative,* pp. 30–82; Mabee, *Sojourner Truth,* pp. 26–76.

3. Dolores Hayden, *The Power of Place: Urban Landscapes as Public History* (Cambridge, Massachusetts: The MIT Press, 1995), p. 18.

4. *Narrative,* p. 7; Mabee, *Sojourner Truth,* pp. 1–3.

5. *Narrative,* p. 7.

6. Erlene Stetson and Linda David, *Glorifying in Tribulation: The Lifework of Sojourner Truth* (East Lansing, Michigan: Michigan State University Press, 1994), pp. 32–33.

7. Nell Painter, *Sojourner Truth: A Life, A Symbol* (New York: W. W. Norton and Company, 1996), p. 25; *Narrative,* pp. 44–45.

8. *Narrative,* pp. 20–21, 26–27; Mabee, *Sojourner Truth,* pp. 12–13; Painter, *Sojourner Truth,* pp. 20–25; Stetson and David, *Glorifying in Tribulation,* pp. 41–42.

9. *Narrative,* p. 28; Painter, *Sojourner Truth,* p. 25; Stetson and David, *Glorifying in Tribulation,* pp. 43–44.

10. *Narrative,* pp. 29–30, 48; Stetson and David, *Glorifying in Tribulation,* p. 10.

11. *Narrative,* p. 48; Mabee, *Sojourner Truth,* p. 21; Painter, *Sojourner Truth,* p. 28. On Pinkster, see Stetson and David, *Glorifying in Tribulation,* p. 10, Shane White, "Pinkster: Afro-Dutch Syncretization in New York City and the Hudson Valley," *Journal of American Folklore,* Vol. 102 (January/March 1989), pp. 68–75; Albert James Williams-Myers, *Long Hammering: Essays on the Forging of an African American Presence in the Hudson River Valley to the Early Twentieth Century* (Trenton, New Jersey: Africa World Press, 1994), pp. 85–95.

12. *Narrative,* p. 49. Regarding Robert, see *Narrative,* pp. 22–23; Mabee, *Sojourner Truth,* pp. 6–7.

13. *Narrative,* pp. 49–51; Mabee, *Sojourner Truth,* pp. 21–22; Painter, *Sojourner Truth,* pp. 22, 27–30; Stetson and David, *Glorifying in Tribulation,* pp. 48–50.

14. *Narrative,* p. 62; Mabee, *Sojourner Truth,* pp. 22, 25; Painter, *Sojourner Truth,* p. 39; Stetson and David, *Glorifying in Tribulation,* pp. 65, 48–51. On antebellum black efforts for full citizenship rights in New York State, see Williams-Myers, *Long Hammering,* pp. 115–125. For treatments of racialized space, see David Delaney, *Race, Place, and the Law 1836–1948* (Austin, Texas: University of Texas Press, 1998), pp. 30–32, 39–41, 45–49 and Richard Thompson Ford, "The Boundaries of Race: Political Geography in Legal Analysis" in Kimberle Crenshaw, Neil Gotanda, Gary Peller, and Kendall Thomas, eds., *Critical Race Theory: The Key Writings that Formed the Movement* (New York: The New Press, 1995), pp. 449–464.

15. *Narrative,* pp. 1–5, 9–10, 33; Mabee, *Sojourner Truth,* pp. 2, 17; Painter, *Sojourner Truth,* p. 13. For a confirmation of early nineteenth-century black residential consignment to cellars elsewhere in the Hudson Valley, *viz.,* New York City, see Shane White, *Somewhat More Independent: The End of Slavery in New York City, 1770–1810* (Athens, Georgia: The University of Georgia Press, 1991), p. 178. For verification that antebellum free blacks often lived in cellars generally throughout the North, see Leon Litwack, *North of Slavery: The Negro in the Free States, 1790–1860* (Chicago: The University of Chicago Press, 1961), pp. 168–169.

16. *Narrative,* pp. 8–11; Mabee, *Sojourner Truth,* p. 3. On the unmarketability of older slaves, see Edgar J. McManus, *A History of Negro Slavery in New York* (Syracuse, New York: Syracuse University Press, 1966), p. 44.

17. *Narrative,* p. 11.

18. *Narrative,* pp. 13–14, 54. See Michael J. Dear and Jennifer R. Woloch, *Landscapes of Despair: From Deinstitutionalization to Homelessness* (Princeton: Princeton University Press, 1987).

19. Litwack, *North of Slavery,* p. 155; Graham Russell Hodges, *Root and Branch: African Americans in New York and East Jersey 1613–1863* (Chapel Hill: University of North Carolina Press, 1999), pp. 41, 108, 154, 159, 201–202, 232, 270.

20. Ira Berlin, *Many Thousands Gone: The First Two Centuries of Slavery in North America* (Cambridge, Massachusetts: The Belknap Press of Harvard University Press, 1998), p. 185; Don Mitchell, *Cultural Geography: A Critical Introduction* (Oxford: Blackwell Publishers, Ltd., 2000), pp. 204–205.

21. *Narrative,* pp. 14–15, 17, 20–21, 29, 40, 68–69, 75; Vale, *Fanaticism,* Part I, pp. 54, 60, 67; Painter, *Sojourner Truth,* pp. 55–56; Paul E. Johnson and Sean Wilenz, *The Kingdom of Matthias: The Story of Sex and Salvation in 19th Century America* (New York: Oxford University Press, 1994), pp. 105, 117–118, 120, 127–128, 139; Williams-Myers, *Long Hammering,* p. 25; Berlin, *Many Thousands Gone,* pp. 182, 246.

22. *Narrative,* pp. 14–15; Mabee, *Sojourner Truth,* pp. 4, 8; Painter, *Sojourner Truth,* pp. 13–15.

23. Vale, *Fanaticism,* Part II, pp. 17, 20; Mabee, *Sojourner Truth,* pp. 34–35;

Painter, *Sojourner Truth,* pp. 53, 57; Johnson and Wilenz, *The Kingdom of Matthias,* p. 127; Litwack, *North of Slavery,* p. 158.

24. Christine Stansell, *City of Women: Sex and Class in New York 1789–1860* (Urbana, Illinois: University of Illinois Press, 1987), pp. 3–30; Alice Kessler-Harris, *Out to Work: A History of Wage-Earning Women in the United States* (New York: Oxford University Press, 1982), pp. 50–53. For a critique of the cult of domesticity and its inability to account for the realities of antebellum black women in the United States, see Jean Fagan Yellin, *Women and Sisters: The Antislavery Feminists in American Culture* (New Haven: Yale University Press, 1989), pp. 78–87.

25. *Narrative,* pp. 16–17; Mabee, *Sojourner Truth,* p. 4; Painter, *Sojourner Truth,* p. 14. On Olive Gilbert and the perspectives held by her white, female contemporaries, see *Narrative,* pp. xxxi–xxxii; Stetson and Gilbert, *Glorifying in Tribulation,* pp. 13–14; Painter, *Sojourner Truth,* pp. 103–104; Yellin, *Women and Sisters,* p. 25.

26. Mabee, *Sojourner Truth,* p. 25; Stetson and David, *Glorifying in Tribulation,* p. 66.

27. Mabee, *Sojourner Truth,* pp. 24–25; Painter, *Sojourner Truth,* pp. 43–44; Stetson and David, *Glorifying in Tribulation,* p. 66.

28. Mabee, *Sojourner Truth,* p. 27; Painter, *Sojourner Truth,* pp. 69–73.

29. Litwack, *North of Slavery,* pp. 4, 154–155; E. Anthony Rotundo, *American Manhood: Transformations in Masculinity from the Revolution to the Modern Era* (New York: Basic Books, 1993), pp. 167–221.

30. W. Jeffrey Bolster, *Black Jacks: African American Seamen in the Age of Sail* (Cambridge, Massachusetts: Harvard University Press, 1997), pp. 6, 160–161; Berlin, *Many Thousands Gone,* p. 246; Litwack, *North of Slavery,* pp. 154–155.

31. *Narrative,* p. 57; Painter, *Sojourner Truth,* pp. 36–37, 66; Stetson and David, *Glorifying in Tribulation,* p. 78.

32. Bolster, *Black Jacks,* pp. 5, 30–31, 91, 93, 117–118, 180–182; *Narrative,* pp. 56–57; Mabee, *Sojourner Truth,* p. 43; Painter, *Sojourner Truth,* pp. 66–68; Stetson and David, *Glorifying in Tribulation,* p. 78.

33. McManus, *Negro Slavery in New York,* pp. 91–93, 166–167, 178. A liberalized code giving slaves jury trials in cases involving possible death penalities and eliminating special slave courts was enacted in New York State in 1788, according to McManus, *Negro Slavery in New York,* pp. 166–167.

34. Mabee, *Sojourner Truth,* pp. 16–21; Painter, *Sojourner Truth,* pp. 32–34; Litwack, *North of Slavery,* p. 94.

35. *Narrative,* pp. 33–34.

36. Vale, *Fanaticism, passim* but especially Part II; *Narrative,* pp. 75–76; Mabee, *Sojourner Truth,* pp. 35–40; Painter, *Sojourner Truth,* p. 58; Johnson and Wilentz, *The Kingdom of Matthias,* pp. 141–168.

37. *Narrative,* p. 78; Mabee, *Sojourner Truth,* p. 43.

38. Vale, *Fanaticism,* Part II, p. 116; Mabee, p. 37; Nell Irvin Painter, "Representing Truth: Sojourner Truth's Knowing and Becoming Known," *Journal of American History,* Vol. 81, No. 2 (September 1994), p. 463.

5

Edythe Ann Quinn

The Kinship System in *The Hills,* An African American Community in Westchester, New York, in the Mid-Nineteenth Century

Throughout the nineteenth century, scattered and isolated enclaves of blacks lived in the rural sections of the Hudson Valley. Small minorities within their townships, villages, and counties, these populations nonetheless exhibited a distinct community consciousness. In her study of one such black cluster, The Hills community of Westchester County, Edythe Ann Quinn demonstrates the importance of stable kinship ties—nuclear, extended, and fictive—in the construction of African American community identity. She further illustrates how this identity was strengthened through involvement with such institutions as racially separate church, school, and mutual aid societies. In these ways, otherwise remote collections of blacks maintained a sense of connection to each other, to the larger African American world, and to mainstream American society. Ironically, however, it was these broader connections, in fact, which led to the demise of The Hills community in the decades following the Civil War.

> *Give my love to all and kiss them all for me, especially to Mother Weeks. Give my love to the old man Weeks, Mother Tierce, the old man Tierce, and all enquiring friends; and find out where Solomon is, the name of the place, and how he is. [sic]* Sergeant Simeon Anderson Tierce of the 14th Regiment, Rhode Island Colored Heavy Artillery, United States Colored Troops, stationed at Fort Saint Leron, Camp Kenyon, Department of the Gulf of New Orleans, LA, to his wife, Sarah Jane Tierce, residing in the African American community, *The Hills,* Harrison, Westchester County, NY, March 11, 1864.[1]

The above passage from Simeon Anderson Tierce's letter holds both valuable clues and aggravating mysteries in the search to determine the kinship system operating in *The Hills,* the African American community located on the rugged lands crossing the town borders of Harrison, White Plains, and North Castle in Westchester County, New York (see tables 5.1 and 5.2).

At the heart of this chapter is an analysis of the kin relationships between members of *The Hills* community in the 1860s, with supporting evidence from the 1830s through the 1860s, its most significant period in terms of population and community-institution building. In establishing the concepts embodied in the kinship patterns, I have looked to Herbert G. Gutman's classic study, *The Black Family in Slavery and Freedom, 1750–1925,* recognizing that, although his work is based on the southern experience, it is also relevant to enslavement and freedom in the North. *The Hills* family data will support Gutman's thesis of the survival of the African American family through slavery and freedom. Graham Russell Hodges's comprehensive history, *Root & Branch: African Americans in New York and East Jersey, 1613–1863,* provides the broad context in which to place *The Hills* community. For a comparison with other free black communities of the period, I have used anthropologist Joan H. Geismar's study, *The Archaeology of Social Disintegration in Skunk Hollow: A Nineteenth-Century Rural Black Community.* Skunk Hollow in the Palisades on the New York–New Jersey border shared some common

Table 5.1 *African American Populations in Major Westchester Towns, 1860*

Town	*Total Population*	*African American Residents*	*Percent of African Americans*
Harrison[a]	1,413	213	15
Scarsdale Village	548	50	9
New Rochelle	3,519	212	6
North Castle[b]	2,487	97	3.93
Rye, including Portchester	4,447	142	3.19
White Plains	1,846	48	2.6
Bedford	3,639	90	2.47
Greenburgh	8,929	133	1.5
Yonkers	11,848	170	1.43
Cortland, including Peekskill	10,074	140	1.4

Source: U.S. Department of the Interior, Bureau of the Census, *Eighth Census of the United States, 1860: Population Statistics* (Washington, D.C.: Government Printing Office, 1864).

[a] Of the 213 African American residents, 115 resided in the Harrison section of *The Hills*. There was also a small neighborhood of blacks in downtown Harrison, and others were scattered throughout the town, for example, living on farms and in homes as laborers or domestic workers.

[b] Of the 97 African American residents, 69 resided in the North Castle section of *The Hills*.

Table 5.2 *Characteristics of African American Population of The Hills, 1860*

Total Population	191
Adult Men	52
Adult Women	55
Children up to/including 16 years	84
Households[a]	44
Nuclear Family Households	30
Extended Family Households	12
Nuclear and Extended Family Households	42
Nuclear and Extended Family Households Headed by an Adult Man	39

Source: Eighth Census of the United States, 1860.

[a] Of the 44 households in The Hills, 27 were in Harrison, 15 were in North Castle, and 2 were in White Plains.

characteristics with *The Hills,* the larger and older of the two communities. Besides enlisting the research of other historians, such as A. J. Williams-Myers, I returned to my own research, *The Hills in the Mid-Nineteenth Century: The History of a Rural Afro-American Community in Westchester County, New York,* published by the Westchester County Historical Society in 1988. For this broader study of *The Hills,* I drew from a variety of materials: The U.S. Federal Census, the New York State Census, *The Weekly Anglo African* newspaper for the years 1859–1865, from church and school records, Harrison town records, and from the compiled military service and pension records of *The Hills* men who served in the Civil War, in particular from the five letters written by Sergeant Simeon Anderson Tierce of the 14th Regiment, Rhode Island Colored Heavy Artillery.[2]

While questions remain unanswered, my research reveals that the African American family in *The Hills* was the dominant, stable social unit for that community and the majority of families were headed by an adult man. Many of the families were related and were descendants of blacks enslaved by local whites. Also, the system of kinship in *The Hills* cannot readily be separated from the concept and reality of community. In the fluid and fragile environment of the first half of the nineteenth century, African Americans rarely had the luxury of limiting kinship to the nuclear family or even to the extended family. Endangered by rampant racism locally and nationally, made specific in the anti-abolition riot in New York City in 1834, the Fugitive Slave Act of 1850, the Dred Scott Decision of 1857, and the Draft Riots of 1863, and severely constrained by social, economic, and political inequalities, the family unit needed the buffer of community, church, and mutual aid associations to survive. For the individuals residing in this settlement, *The Hills* was community, and in a more intimate sense, extended family. *The Hills* provided protection in its isolated location on rugged terrain; stability in its familial structure, its gender balance, land ownership patterns; and cultural continuity in its own church, school, and burial grounds. However, the residents were not immune to the outside threats that impinged on their welfare, especially on their economic viability. The community formed an extended kinship system, whether expressed in honorific titles of Mother or Uncle bestowed on fictive kin, in the camaraderie of neighbors during military service in the United States Colored Troops (U.S.C.T.), or simply in references to being "school boys together" in the district's Common School for Colored Children. The now well worn African proverb, "It takes a village to raise a child," gains new life in its application to *The Hills*.

In the late 1700s, *The Hills* community began as a settlement for blacks freed by their masters, especially by members of the Society of Friends, the Quakers in the Purchase [Harrison] Meeting, and slowly coalesced as a community as other freed blacks joined them, in a pattern of chain migration and family reunification that culminated in the mid-nineteenth century. The majority of residents settled along Stony Hill Road, on the Lake Street, Harrison side of *The Hills*. From the 1830s through the 1860s, the community and its families exhibited strength and viability through the church, school, mutual aid society, and contacts with other African Americans in other communities, such as nearby Rye, and in cities, especially New York City and New Haven, Connecticut. Through these connections, *The Hills* residents came into contact with black abolitionist ministers, the black press, and African American recruitment efforts for the United States Colored Troops.

The Civil War ushered in the demise of *The Hills* community. During the Civil War, at least 34 men associated with *The Hills* served in the U.S.C.T. and amassed a significant record of promotions and military engagements. Five men became noncommissioned officers: four received promotions to the rank of corporal and one to sergeant. Their service took a toll on the community: four Hills men died in service, one in battle and three from illness; four men were wounded and several others suffered disabling illnesses. In the post-war years, the deaths and disabilities weakened the economic strength of the community, as widows, aged parents, and disabled veterans tried to survive on reduced incomes. Other men gathered up their families and moved out of *The Hills,* for example, to Providence, Rhode Island, Brooklyn, or nearby White Plains.

As the late nineteenth century passed into the twentieth, the community's decline reached its conclusion. In the 1920s, the Bronx Parkway Commission established a green belt, The Bronx River Parkway Reservation, a series of parks along the length of the Bronx River Parkway. In 1924 and 1925, the Commission received authorization to acquire land encompassing *The Hills* for

Silver Lake Park, part of the Westchester County Park System. Thus, the ruins of *The Hills* community, especially foundations along Stony Hill Road, were preserved and the land reverted to the rugged, forested environment which the first freed blacks settled.[3] In 1983, Stony Hill Road in the Harrison section of *The Hills* was declared a Westchester County Tri-centennial Historic Site. In April 1999, Stony Hill Cemetery, the burial ground for *The Hills* received New York State Historic Site recognition. In August 1999, Stony Hill Cemetery was entered into the National Register of Historic Places.

The history of *The Hills* follows the late eighteenth and early-nineteenth-century time line of gradual emancipation in New York State and incorporates religious and ethnic influences of the time. The manumission of enslaved African Americans and their subsequent resettlement in a region were often linked to the ethnic and religious character of the white population itself, that is, British or Dutch. In areas of heavy Dutch settlement, such as Kings and Queens counties in New York and Bergen County in New Jersey, the slave owners were inclined to continue enslavement until state statutes forced their compliance. In contrast, according to Hodges, "large numbers of free blacks lived in those areas where Quakers, Anglicans, and Presbyterians were a significant proportion of the population," evincing a greater propensity towards abolition.[4] This religious composition mirrored that of late eighteenth century Westchester County. However, Methodists may well be added to this list, as Westchester County was the circuit of Methodist Bishop Francis Asbury who preached openly that "people should not be in bondage, nor should men hold other men in bondage."[5] In 1784, the Methodist-Episcopal Conference had insisted upon "full and entire emancipation of every slave in the possession of the members of the Church." North Castle town histories record Asbury as preaching to whites and blacks in that town in June 13, 1787. This period of Methodist-Episcopal Church activities coincides with the years in which the Quakers freed their enslaved blacks.[6]

The standard explanation for the origins of *The Hills* was the account included in the section on Harrison in J. Thomas Scharf's 1886 *History of Westchester County, New York* and reprinted in Alvah P. French's *History of Westchester County of New York,* published in 1925:

> When the Quakers of Purchase liberated their slaves, they settled them upon their rough lands in the northwestern portion of the town of Harrison, and thus the negro community, still existing northeast of the village of White Plains, was begun.[7]

Indeed, in 1767, at its Quarterly Meeting, the Purchase Society of Friends in Harrison acknowledged the moral incompatibility of Friends owning slaves:

> If it is not consistent with Christianity to buy and sell our fellow men for slaves, during their lives and their posterity after them, then wherefore is it consistent with Christian spirit to keep those in slavery that we already have in our possession, by purchase, gift or other ways.[8]

The issue of slavery was prominent in the Society's business until the 1780s, when all blacks enslaved by Purchase Meeting Friends had been freed and resettled. The Purchase Minutes of 1784 record that "proper settlements had been made between the Friends who had set their negroes free and the negroes so set free."[9] However, the details of settlement are not clear. It is not known whether the land was granted outright to the freed blacks, or whether the freed men and women were tenants on their former masters' lands, with the options of purchasing these rough lands when they had acquired the funds. An 1837 indenture suggests that "settled" did not mean that former masters uniformly granted freeholds to the freed blacks. In this indenture Jeremiah Mitchell, a long time member of *The Hills* community, was identified as "Coloured Man" [sic] purchased four and a half acres "in a place commonly [called] the "Hills," a "lot of land . . . occupied" by Mitchell and purchased from Thomas H. and Elizabeth Burling of New Rochelle, a family name associated with the Society of Friends. The deed describes the land's borders, naming those who own or occupy the surrounding acreage, including several black men, for example, "[The land] is bounded and described as follows *viz:* . . . land of David Halstead possessed [*sic*] by Charles Halsted (so called)."[10] This indenture and others from that period for parcels of land in this area call into doubt the generous overtones of the pious history of *The Hills,* for instance, "When the Quakers of Purchase liberated their slaves, they settled them upon their rough lands. . . ."[11] "Settled" did not necessarily mean the land was given to these blacks, but over time they acquired the means to purchase their parcels outright, parcels on which they had been living and farming since the late 1700s. This indenture and other records of the time illustrate the problems in concretely defining the settlement process of *The Hills* until well into the 1830s. By the 1830s, however, *The Hills* community was well established.

Religious conviction and church mandate account for only some of the manumissions. Other area residents acted under state laws of gradual emancipation in 1799, 1817, and 1827, manumitting their enslaved workers. Although Quaker surnames are found among *Hills* residents, many of the African Americans in *The Hills* bear Anglo surnames belonging to the non-Quaker residents.

This settlement pattern was common to several towns in Westchester, Rockland, Ulster, and Dutchess counties in New York and in border counties in New Jersey, with the historical accounts repeating a similar description of "rough lands," for example: "When the slaves of Bedford [in Westchester County] were set free they were given rough land on the southern side of Aspetong Hill, where quite a colony became established."[12]

In *Long Hammering: Essays on the Forging of an African American Presence in the Hudson River Valley to the Early Twentieth Century,* A. J. Williams-Myers noted the African American concentrations on marginal land "on the peripheries of some towns in the region." Besides *The Hills,* he mentioned Sparkill near Nyack in Rockland County; Skunk Hollow in Bergen County, New Jersey, in the Palisades, "just south of the New York–New Jersey state line"; the settlements in the Ramapo Mountains of New York and New Jersey; Eagles's Nest in the mountains west of Hurley in Ulster County; and Freemanville (Poughquag) in Dutchess County, "pejoratively referred to as "Nigger Hill," but . . . now known as Depot Hill."[13] To these I would add the small settlement of freed blacks in the Saxon Woods area (known as Saxton Forest in the eighteenth century) on the Scarsdale—White Plains border in Westchester County. While these marginal lands reflected the marginality of free blacks, these rugged sites, surely not fertile, flat farmlands, afforded protection from land speculation, marauding white mobs, and perhaps decreased acculturation and allowed revival of African traditions manifest in material culture and architecture. With *The Hills* as my example, I believe that the isolation of the black communities fostered rather than hampered the formation and maintenance of the family unit, often a subsistence farm unit.

I chose the period of the 1840s through the 1860s to analyze the family and community structures of *The Hills* as documentation was possible, reducing the need for supposition. I focused on 1860 as the defining year for close analysis because it was the last census before Simeon Anderson Tierce's letters, and his references may more readily reflect the census manuscript. Also, this census enumeration closely follows the outline of the residences in *The Hills* as they appear on the highly detailed 1867 F. W. Bears *Atlas of Westchester County* (see tables 5.1 and 5.2.). As helpful as the census record and maps may be for the later decades of the 1800s, they reflect the community past its prime, after it had suffered the cataclysmic effect of the men's military service in Civil War. However, as devastating as that experience was to the community in the long term, the community's family structure was made more visible through the testimonies in the Civil War veterans' and widows' pension records.

Before discussing particular family relations, the statistical evidence from the census material will demonstrate the overall importance of *The Hills* as an African American community in Westchester County and the stability of its family structure, an essential ingredient of the overall community's stability. The 1855 population for Westchester County totaled 80,687, with whites numbering 78,750 and blacks (including mulattos) numbering 1,928. (In 1860, Westchester County's population had risen to 99,497.)[14] Harrison was the Westchester County town with the largest percentage of African Americans in the population, according to the 1860 census. Of the 1,413 people in Harrison, 213 were black; that is, 15% of Harrison's population was black. Of the 213 blacks, 115 of them resided in the Harrison section of *The Hills* (see Table 5.1). There was also a small neighborhood of blacks in Harrison village and others were scattered throughout the town, for example, living on farms and in homes as laborers or domestic servants.[15]

As in the days of slavery, in Westchester County in 1860, African Americans were generally scattered throughout the towns and villages, living in small clusters surrounded by white neighbors. Rarely did more than four or five black families live in close proximity. *The Hills* population of 191 black people in 44 households represented the largest settlement of African Americans in Westchester County. The settlement spanned three towns, with 27 households in Harrison, 15 in North Castle, and two in White Plains. As such, *The Hills* may have been the largest, rural concentration in the Lower Hudson River Valley. Thus, findings and conclusions drawn from the archival and statistical record for *The Hills* are important in understanding the status of family and community for rural African Americans in this region of New York.

To our immediate interest is the centrality of the family itself to the stability of the community and by extension the stable community's role as an extended family. Herbert Gutman identified the core or nuclear family and the enlarged kinship group as central to both the enslaved and the post-Civil War African American communities. He refuted such sociological theorists and historians as E. Franklin Frazier, Kenneth M. Stampp, Stanley M. Elkins, and Daniel Patrick Moynihan who claimed that enslavement had destroyed the African American family and that the distorted family units that resulted were generally headed by a woman. *The Hills* evidence further substantiates Gutman's findings of family stability with male heads-of-households, in this case, for a northern, rural black community. In both Gutman's mammoth work and in this small case study, evidence demonstrates that stability and responsibility from family and kinship system extended to community. According to Gutman, "Kin obligation among Afro-Americans survived enslavement and enlarged social obligation emerged out of kin obligation."[16]

In Table 5.2, the recognized patterns of strong family stability become evident, not only in the number of male adult-headed households, but also in the ratio of adult men and women, 52 and 55 respectively, and the strong presence of children, that is, 84 children. However, the main focus is on the nuclear family unit and its head. The nuclear family is defined as a husband and wife, two parents and their children, or a single parent with one or more children. When the nuclear family expands, taking in kin, it is called an "extended household." The 12 extended households sheltered grandchildren, nieces and nephews, and elderly relatives. Of the combined total of nuclear and extended households, 42 in number, 39 were headed by an adult man.[17] In reviewing the

African American populations in other Westchester towns, the predominant pattern was the nuclear or extended household, headed by an adult man. This pattern was also very evident in the African American settlement, Skunk Hollow, in Bergen County, New Jersey, a smaller, rural, free black community that shares many characteristics with *The Hills*.[18]

Important Families and Interactions among Them

These numbers from the census records are significant, but they do not reveal relationships outside of the immediate household, that is, between households, which constitute the dynamics of the kinship system. Archival documents, such as wills and deeds, church and school lists, and nineteenth century maps provide additional historical records of the families in *The Hills*. One might suggest that the first place to look for kinship patterns is through shared surnames in these documents. Although surnames can be important in identifying family relationships, at best, they offer clues, but not firm data concerning familial interactions. The surnames of blacks may indicate individual and family origins among white slaveholders. However, there are few guarantees that these lines of descent are direct, or that blacks with a common surname are related. African Americans exerted their own agency in choosing a surname. At best, black surnames shared with white families seemingly confirm what we already know from tax and census manuscripts and wills and the town and county histories. Most of the residents of *The Hills* (and the other Lower Hudson River Valley communities) were formerly enslaved persons or descendants of enslaved persons of local families.

Another hindrance to the use of surnames for conclusive evidence regarding family patterns exists. While surnames can be family markers, in the eighteenth and early nineteenth centuries, free blacks were rarely identified through surnames in legal documents and church registers. Enslaved blacks were identified through their owner's name, which might not be the name they assumed after manumission. An example of this gap in the historical record is demonstrated in the baptismal, marriage, and burial records of Christ's Church of the Town of Rye. The church served the parish of Rye, which was founded in 1695, and originally comprised the towns of Rye (including White Plains and Harrison), Mamaroneck and Bedford, and later included Scarsdale and North Castle, all towns from which *Hills* residents may have originated. Therefore, the extant church records of baptisms, marriages, and burials performed for blacks could be important indicators of kinship. Unfortunately, through the first decade of the 1800s, surnames are inconsistently designated for free blacks, and enslaved blacks are identified by their owner's name. For example, on April 15, 1792, the rector, Reverend David Foote, baptized Mary, a black infant, "belonging to David Haight." In June 1792, he baptized Abraham, an enslaved black "[b]elonging to Capt. Purdy." Free blacks who came for baptism are recorded, but surnames are not always given. On June 10, 1805, the record indicated the baptisms of "Harry & Alce [*sic*] his wife (black people of Mamaronac [*sic*]) and four sons, *viz:* Harry & Abraham; the other names forgotten." Likewise, on September 20, 1807, the church recorded the baptism of "Lanis, son of Simon & Susan, black people; age 13 months." On September 20, 1807, the rector recorded the baptism of "John, son of Easter, black woman; born May 17, 1807."[19]

Nor are the marriage records any better for reliable identification through surnames. Among the marriages recorded, Lett and Tone were married on April 26, 1791, no surnames given. On September 16, 1804, a marriage was performed and recorded for "Prince to Dinah, black people of this place." [Rye] We know these two couples were free blacks, as enslaved blacks were identified by their owners. For example, among the marriages performed in 1805, on July 15, Cuff and Phillis, identified as "black people belonging to David Brown of the Purchase, were married. Another marriage performed for enslaved persons was listed on July 28, 1805, "Jack, belonging to Philoman Halsted, Jun[ior], to Nanny, belonging to N. Penfield." Significantly, this marriage crossed the barriers of ownership by two different masters and the couple's choice of a surname after emancipation is not guaranteed to be either Halsted or Penfield, as will be discussed later. As late as 1828, black couples were still being registered without surnames; for example, on February 9, 1828, the marriage is recorded for "Peter to Hannah (a black couple)."[20] Rather than clarifying identifications, these records simply provide a sense of the diversity of situations of bound and free black people, and the willingness of this particular church to perform their baptism, marriage, and burial services. In the 1830s, for baptisms and marriages and burials, surnames are consistently used in the church records; still there remain limits to their usefulness in identifying family heritage.

In his chapter, "Somebody Knew My Name," in *The Black Family in Slavery and Freedom,* Herbert G. Gutman discussed the processes through which blacks acquired surnames. He referred to the proceedings of the First Lake Mohonk Conference on the Negro Questions, held in Ulster County, New York, in June 1890. At that conference, C. C. Gaines, a Hudson River Valley college president, recalled that slave surnames sometimes revealed a "mark peculiar to the person or incident to his history." For example, sold slaves "often were known by the surname of an original master who might then be dead." Gaines commented: "You will find many negroes to-day who do not retain the surname of their last owner, but are known by that of a remote ancestor who years ago came out of another estate. [Ex-slaves] chose such names as they pleased, and many of them observed such reasonable rules as to ancestry as naturally applied."[21] Gutman's research showed that "ex-slaves put aside a final owner's surname and replaced it with either the surname of an earlier owner or the surname of a parent's or a grandparent's owner. . . . Sale, or separation for other reasons, from a slave family of origin encouraged slaves to retain different surnames from their new owners."[22]

The system of enslavement in Westchester County and throughout the North carried the same reality of sale and separation from one's enslaved family as it did in the South. Although the surnames of *The Hills* residents are often those of local whites, it is difficult to ascertain whether these were the names of the last owners or the original owners of the individuals or their ancestors. One cannot assume that families with the same surname are related.

While the research on slave naming practices has emphasized surnames, I suggest that given or Christian names or middle names carry weight as well in shaping an identity separate from enslavement, yet carrying one's ancestry. For example, the first generations of enslaved blacks were burdened with fanciful names, classic names, or abbreviated names as their owners deemed fit. (Occasionally, enslaved blacks carried African names, for example, Cuffee or Cuff, a Kongo name.) Wills, runaway slave advertisements, church documents, and the 1790 census record such names as Caesar, Mose, Pompey, Jupiter, Herculus, Tobe, Dick, Prime, and Lew for men; and Bell, Sibb, Gine/Gin, and Dinah for women. Using *The Hills* residents as examples, I contend that, with emancipation, blacks chose given names for themselves and their children that more closely resembled Anglo-Saxon, Christian names. However, they may have also chosen first or middle names to reflect family ties.

The William Tierce family serves as a case study of how first and middle names reflected family history. Tierce is not a surname common to Westchester County. William and Deborah Jane Tierce may have given their first son, Simeon Anderson Tierce, his middle name to trace his lineage on his mother's side to black residents of *The Hills* in 1820, who previously may have been enslaved by the white Andersons, a Harrison-based family with enslaved blacks. In his will, dated January 26, 1796, William Anderson deeded land and an enslaved black man named Dick to his son, Jeremiah. To his wife, Elizabeth, "as long she remained [his] widow," he bequeathed "a negro girl called Gin." In an addendum, he explained that he had "sold the said Negro Girl Gin & in lieu thereof I give my wife the Negro boy Crinee." Crinee was to be set free at age 26.[23]

In the 1820 Federal Census for *The Hills* section of Harrison, under "Free Negro Heads of Households," Richard Anderson is listed as a "free coloured person. [sic]" His household totaled six "free coloured persons [sic]" as follows: one man in the 26–45 age category, presumably Richard; one man in the 14–26 age category; two men under 14 years; and two women, one in the 26–45 age category, and one in the 14–26 age category.[24] Richard Anderson is possibly the enslaved black named "Dick" mentioned in William Anderson's 1796 will, an example of a black man changing his name after enslavement and claiming the surname of his former master. Also, we do not know how the members of the household are related, whether this is a nuclear family with Richard and the woman in the age 26–45 category as the parents of the four younger blacks, or whether they are related at all. In these early years of gradual emancipation and settlement, the other five free blacks may simply be sharing the household of William Anderson, before moving on or forming separate households. In the 1830 Federal Census, there is no Anderson household listed for *The Hills,* and several heads of households present in *The Hills* in 1830 are missing from census records during the more stable decades of *The Hills* community.[25]

Indeed, signs of a transient population in the early decades of *The Hills* suggest a problem in forming or reforming families and building a community resulting from New York State's laws of gradual emancipation. Rather than outright emancipation of all enslaved people, permitting the immediate reuniting of families and the settlement of free, united kin and kith, the 1799 and 1817 Acts drew out the process, probably frustrating efforts at uniting families and forming communities. The 1799 law granted freedom to enslaved children born after 1799, but bound them to serve in the household of their mother's owner for a designated period. Men acquired their freedom at age 28; women at age 25. Although the 1817 law specified that every enslaved black person born before 1799 was to be free as of July 4, 1827, it did not achieve universal freedom. The 1817 statute stipulated, "Children born after that date could continue in indenture as servants until they were of age." Finally, the 1841 law established total emancipation and extinguished "all privileges of slave owners, and all ownership in slaves within the state."[26]

Further clues to the Tierce family origins are found in examining the Jeremiah Mitchell family. Like the Tierce family, the Jeremiah Mitchell family illustrates how kinship history may be traced through first and middle names. As mentioned previously, in 1837, Jeremiah Mitchell purchased four and a half acres of land "in a place commonly [called] the "Hills," from Thomas H. and Elizabeth Burling of New Rochelle, land that been conveyed in 1804 to Thomas H. Burling's father (then deceased), also named Thomas. Perhaps Jeremiah was the free black in the residence of Thomas Burling of Harrison, noted in the 1800 Federal Census. In the 1810 Federal Census for Harrison, a free black by the name of "Jerry Mitchell" appears.[27]

In 1815, Jeremiah Mitchell had land dealings with Hagar Anderson of Harrison, a woman whose race is not indicated on the indenture, as it normally was for a black person; however, Hagar is often an African American name. In the documents I have examined, the Anderson family did not include a female member named Hagar. However, she could have been the woman, between the ages of 26 and 45, living in the African American household of Richard Anderson, as enumerated in the 1820 Census.[28] In the 1850 federal census, Jeremiah Mitchell, a "laborer," age 69, is listed as married to Hester, age 55.[29] This listing suggests several possibilities. In this instance, is Hester a variation of Hagar, a means to continue the female name? If so, had Jeremiah Mitchell married into the Anderson family, perhaps to the woman between the ages of 14 and 26? Silas does not appear in the household, but two women, Hannah Valentine, age 10, and Hester A. Hatfield, age 4, are listed. Both Valentine and Hatfield are *Hills* family names and these two young women may be grandchildren. In particular, Hester A. Hatfield's first name and middle initial are again suggestive of family lineage. Further evidence linking the Mitchell and Tierce families is found in an 1851 land transaction. In that year, Jeremiah and Hester Mitchell sold property in *The Hills* to William Tierce, who was already occupying the land. As noted on the deed, this one-acre parcel was part of the land conveyed by Thomas and Elizabeth Burling to Mitchell in March 1837.[30]

In the 1860 census, 45 years after Jeremiah Mitchell's transaction with Hagar Anderson, Silas A. Mitchell, Jeremiah's son, age 21, was living in lower Harrison, adjacent to Rye, where, as a minister, he was associated with other *Hills* and Rye blacks in two religious organizations. The census lists him as having two children, Hager Ann and George B., living with him. In choosing Hager/Hagar for his daughter's name, Silas may have been using a name to commemorate his family history. Possibly, he was using his grandmother's name. Perhaps the middle initial B in the name of his son, George B. Mitchell, stands for Burling, the Quaker family with whom his father had strong ties.[31]

Silas A. Mitchell, who is prominently mentioned in Simeon's correspondence, ministered to the religious needs of *The Hills* community and had established links to the black abolitionist press and ministry in New York City and New Haven, Connecticut. Given realty transactions between William Tierce and Jeremiah Mitchell, their being neighbors in *The Hills,* and Simeon's fondness and respect for Silas, I believe the young men were cousins.

Furthermore, Simeon Tierce's first name is the same as "old man Weeks," to whom he sent fond regards in his letters. He referred to Simon/Simeon Weeks's wife Lena as "Mother Weeks." Simeon/Simon and Lena Weeks resided near the Tierce families in *The Hills*. In the 1870 census, after Lena's death, Simeon/Simon, age 69, lived in a separate household on William Tierce's dwelling site. Whether they were blood or fictive kin, the coincidence of a shared first name is suggestive. (Weeks was the surname for a slaveholding family in North Castle, that is, in 1755, Able Weeks is documented as having one enslaved man named Lewis.) Thus, I believe in examining kith and kin relations one should take into account given Christian names as well as surnames.[32]

To complicate matters further, a free black's chosen surname may not have been readily accepted by the white community and its legal system. The following example again involves Jeremiah Mitchell. The 1837 land indenture for

Jeremiah Mitchell is extremely important for several reasons; as previously stated it raises questions about land ownership patterns and establishes ties between Mitchell and the Burling family. In this indenture Mitchell is identified as a "Coloured Man" [*sic*]. However, in naming the African American men who owned or occupied the surrounding acreage, a question of legality was raised concerning their surnames. For example, "[The land] is bounded and described as follows *viz:* . . . land of David Halstead possessed [*sic*] by Charles Halsted (so called) . . . by the land of Michael Brown (so called) . . . by the land of Ichabod Lewis (so called)." Halsted/Halstead, Brown, Lewis were all surnames of white slaveholding families in the surrounding towns. Whites' acceptance of the blacks' claim to these same surnames may have come grudgingly and slowly.[33] Interestingly, in this deed, Mitchell's name is not challenged, as he may have been better established in the larger community.

If *The Hills* community and its families could only be reconstructed through the legal documents, such as deeds and wills, and census manuscripts, the record would be severely limited. White enumerators, operating with the racial biases of their times, collected the information in census manuscripts, and the African American population was seriously undercounted and devalued, for example, concerning its occupations and literacy rate. In two editions of the New York City newspaper, *The Weekly Anglo African,* the editors warn their readers of the errors and incompleteness of the census enumeration.[34] Fortunately, for *The Hills* community and its families, we have the five letters from Sergeant Simeon Anderson Tierce and the pension records for many of the U.S.C.T. veterans and their widows, with depositions describing relationships and community activities. Simeon Anderson Tierce grew up in *The Hills*. In 1856, he married Sarah Jane Berrian, a widow with a young daughter, Sarah Ann, who was called Sissy. In 1863, Simeon enlisted in the 14th Regiment, Rhode Island Colored Heavy Artillery, was promoted to Sergeant, and served with the occupation forces near New Orleans. He died of typhoid on July 8, 1864. His widow Sarah Jane applied for a pension for herself and Sissy, claiming Simeon had treated her daughter as his own. She sent five of his letters to the Pension Review Board in Washington, D.C., to substantiate her claim, and in that way these letters were preserved, providing us with much of the information and clues for reconstructing this community.

By coupling the letters with census data and information in the veterans' depositions, the following excerpts from his letters shed light on the depth and extent of family relations and friendships and on the dominance of certain families in *The Hills*.[35] In his letters, Simeon sent Sarah Jane regards from his neighbors who served beside him in the regiment. For example, "Jacob, Uncle Alfred [Seymore] and all of the rest of the boys from this way send you an abundance of love." He also wrote of his *Hills* comrades who regularly visited him when he was ailing and alone in his tent.

Throughout the history of *The Hills,* several large families dominated its kinship system, including the Seymore family of the North Castle section. Alfred Seymore was the patriarch of the family in 1860, when the census listed his age as 50 and his occupation as a gardener. He volunteered along with his sons, James Shipman and John Wesley, and his nephew William Henry Seymore, all enlisting in the 14th Regiment. William Henry Seymore's parents, Jane Halstead Seymore and Harvey Seymore, lived in *The Hills;* his mother's stepfather's surname was Gaul, probably David Gaul, an early and long-time resident to the community.[36]

Another family, entrenched in The Hills, was the Barker family and their descendants still retain property in *The Hills,* adjacent to county park land. At least three of the Barker men, Benjamin, David, and Elisha, served in the 14th Rhode Island Regiment with Simeon and men of the Seymore family. Benjamin Barker, kinsman to Simeon Tierce, addressed a proclamation within Simeon's letter, assuring Sarah Jane of his loyal care of her husband and his close affection for her: "I, Benjamin Barker, intend to be Simeon's nurse and will do all I can to restore his health and all I ask in return is your prayers and the pleasure of sitting beside you on the sofa that I ask you to get home."[37] Simeon and Sarah Jane were obviously close friends, if not relations, of Benjamin Barker. Benjamin's wife Elizabeth was the widow of Charles Berrian of Harrison, who died in the 1850s. Sarah Jane Tierce had also been married to a Berrian, possibly a brother of Charles.[38] One gets a sense of peer relations here, and the willingness to introduce suitable newcomers into the community, in this case as a suitor to Benjamin's sister, Mary Barker: "There is a young man coming home with me when I come—I don't know when that will be—by the name of Mr. Johnson. Tell Mary to have her cap set for him when I come home as he is the handsomest man on the ground."[39] Simeon hoped Mary would write to him, as he reminded Sarah Jane, "Tell Mary [Barker] not to forget to write me a letter."[40] His relationship with Mary Barker seemed to have indeed been close, as Simeon asks for her picture to be included along with his wife's and stepdaughter's: "I want you to have your daguerreotype and Mary's and Sis all in one case if you can and send it by the next letter; and if you don't put them in one case, have them taken separate as I should like to have to look at, being that I cannot see your face."[41] Mary Barker must have objected on the grounds that she was not pretty enough to have her picture taken, a message Mary sent in her letter to Simeon or one that Sarah Jane conveyed in her next letter to Simeon, who responded: "I want you to please not forget your likeness and tell Mary [Barker] that she need not be afraid of her likeness frightening me, according to her statement."[42]

All was not always peaceful in *The Hills,* in its gender relations. Although the reference is not entirely clear and open to interpretation, one gathers that Simeon was accused of impregnating another *Hills* woman, a situation that infuriated Sarah Jane when it became known. Another Hills resident informed him of this either directly or perhaps in a letter to a Hills comrade in his regiment. Simeon responded, "It made my heart ache when I hear that you cursed and swore." He continued in the next paragraph, "Tell Old Adeline that she had no business to name that child before I came home for I never put in for it, and the next one she names after me I want to be there."[43] Old Adeline may be the *Hills* midwife and the custom may have persisted that a midwife asks for the father's name when an unwed mother is in labor, recording the name the mother gives as the child's father.[44] Simeon had a substantial reputation in *The Hills* community, was now the top-ranking enlisted man from the community, and a good prospect for a father figure. Simeon denied this paternity and his expression of a desire to be there might have forced the mother to be honest or confront him. Whether he was innocent or guilty, he was undaunted in his expressions of love for Sarah Jane in this letter, as he was in the others.

In the veteran and widow pension records, the history of the Brown family in *The Hills* is fleshed out from its appearance in the census records and early deeds. "Micha Brown" was mentioned in an 1815 real estate indenture; this is probably the "Michael" listed as a "free negro" and head of a household in *The Hills* area in the 1800 Harrison census. "Michael Brown (so called)" appeared in Jeremiah Mitchell's 1837 land indenture. The Brown surname is common to whites and blacks in several Westchester towns, such as Rye, in connection with slavery. In 1838, the School District Report listed Michael Brown as having two children in the local school, which was then still integrated. Thomas Lea Brown, who served in the 29th Infantry Regiment, Connecticut Colored Volunteers from *The Hills,* is probably Michael's son. He signed an affidavit for Solomon Tierce's widow's pension application, in which he described his relationship with his friend and neighbor, Solomon G. Tierce, Simeon's brother. He stated, "We were school boys together." Thomas and Chloe Carrier Brown raised three children in *The Hills,* Cyrus Everet Brown, Thomas Tierce Brown, and Ernest Ulisses [sic] Brown, born 1863, 1871, and 1874, respectively. Given the date of Thomas's birth, 1871, his middle name, Tierce, might honor Simeon's death in the Civil War, or Brown's neighbor, William Tierce, Simeon's father, or his school boy friend, Solomon Tierce.[45]

These are a sampling of the connections between members of *The Hills* community, demonstrating both family relationships and friendships, and supporting the view that the community itself was an expanded family. In a study of rural black families of the 1880s, Crandall A. Shifflett concluded that the "solidarity of strong black kinship networks" relieved the burden of poverty.[46] I believe this conclusion may be applied to northern black families as well. The circumstances described here have not included an economic analysis. *The Hills's* economy was based on land ownership, subsistence farming with small market crops, and diverse occupations, more complex than simply "laborer." However, it was still vulnerable to the restraints on black opportunity in the trades, on outside market forces, and internal circumstances, for example, illness and death. Thus, while poverty might not describe *The Hills,* certainly the "solidarity of strong black kinship networks" provided some protection and sustained the community as a whole.

Tracing Community through Church Ties

The Hills relationships were intertwined with school and church ties and ties to blacks in other communities, for example, in the village of Rye. This Rye connection can especially be seen in church relations. Although church history in *The Hills* includes several affiliations within the community and outside the community as well, the starting place is the community. In the nineteenth century African American community in slavery and freedom, the church was the central institution. In fact, it was so intimately linked with all the goals and movements of the African American people throughout the period that church and community were practically one and the same. The black leader and scholar Martin R. Delaney wrote to Frederick Douglass in 1849, "the Church is the Alpha and Omega of all things."[47]

Before archival records officially document the establishment of a church in *The Hills,* personal testimony provides a sense of early religious practice among the families. Jane Halstead Seymore explained that at the time of her marriage, circa 1837, "We did not have a regular church building then, and had services around among each other's houses. Later, at the time of her son's birth and baptism, circa 1839, she recalled, "We [had] a new minister every year. . . . "[48]

On May 1, 1844, five black men, all residents of the North Castle section of *The Hills,* acting as trustees of the Methodist Episcopal Zion Church of Colored People of the Town of Harrison, signed a mortgage with Charles A. Purdy, a white resident of Harrison. Previously, Frederick and Deborah Stephens, white residents of North Castle, had deeded approximately one quarter of an acre to the community for use as a church or meeting house lot. The money borrowed in this mortgage may have been used to finance the building of a church on the property. Mount Hope A.M.E. Zion Church of White Plains, the congregation that traces itself directly to the church in *The Hills,* reported that additional land was purchased for the church in the 1850s and the trustees at that time included Henry Seamore [Seymore] and William Henry Baker [Barker].[49]

The church building also served as a school, as explained in the 1886 *History of Westchester County:*

> A small frame building was erected in the northwestern part of the town of Harrison, just over the line of North Castle, which was used by the colored people as a schoolhouse and chapel.[50]

The school began in 1843 when the school district trustees authorized a "colored school district" for *The Hills* children. The circumstances surrounding this "colored school" are complex and open to different interpretations. Was the segregated school imposed from the outside, after the black children had previously been attending a neighborhood school? Or, inspired by the call for community control by the era's Negro Conventions, did the black parents take advantage of a 1841 state law permitting segregated schooling? Historian Carleton Mabee acknowledged that black parents sometimes petitioned for segregated public schools, hoping to improve their children's education or provide a more encouraging classroom experience, free from ridicule. Whichever the cause, *The Hills* school, operating in the church building, educated Simeon Tierce and other *Hills* children. Given the high level of literacy in Simeon's letters and the documentation of books used at the school, the education was substantial. The church and school further enhanced the sense of community in *The Hills*.[51]

In his correspondence, Simeon Anderson Tierce referred to his position as "church assistant secretary" in *The Hills* church.[52] He also mentioned the preaching of Silas Mitchell. In his letter of February 22, 1864, he wrote, "We have a minister out here by the name of George Mitchell but no Silas Mitchell." In his last letter of the series, he commented further on "Brother George Mitchell, the minister. [He's] not the man that Silas Mitchell is but he is the chaplain of the battalion.[53]

One of the most prominent figures in the history of *The Hills's* religious observance is the Reverend Silas A. Mitchell, mentioned earlier. Silas, probably the son of Jeremiah Mitchell and raised in *The Hills,* was living in lower Harrison, near Rye, in 1860. He was the preacher at the Second Colored American Congregational Methodist Church in Rye Neck, a section of Rye, the town adjacent to lower Harrison.[54] Both in Rye Neck and in New York City, Reverend Silas Mitchell associated with the Reverend Levin Tilmon (1807–1863), a black abolitionist minister and pastor of the First Colored American Congregational Church of New York City. Tilmon was also the president of the First Colored American Congregational Grove Company of New York City, which operated a grove in "Barry's Woods" in Rye Neck. At the 1854 organizing meetings for the Rye Neck church and the grove company, members of *The Hills* community participated, including Jeremiah Mitchell, who served as one of the directors of the grove association.[55]

The grove was a parcel of land set up for summer gatherings, similar to camp meetings but usually of shorter duration, that is, one-day events. In *The History of the Negro Church,* Carter G. Woodson describes camp meetings as "social as well as religious" and explains that they "sometimes partook of a festive nature."[56] The grove in Rye Neck attracted blacks from the surrounding area and New York City, who traveled there on the New Haven Railroad. In June 1860, Tilmon advertised the attractions of the Congregational Grove in the *Weekly Anglo-African:* "It is easy of access, beautifully located, and well adapted for excursion, grove and camp meetings. The improvements consist of wood shanties, a well of never-failing water, a small dwelling house, etc. [sic]."[57] He further wrote, "This grove deserves the patronage of the colored people of the city and county of New York, who are accustomed to celebrate the First of August and hold picnics [sic], Sabbath-school excursions, and camp and grove meetings, and is every way adapted for the same."[58] In Simeon Anderson Tierce's letter to his wife Sarah Jane, of February 15, 1864, he mentions a revival meeting at his army post, Camp Kenyon, near New Orleans. His description suggests the importance of grove meetings to the Hills residents: "[W]e had a class meeting here yesterday morning, Sunday, the 14th, by John Thomas, Jacob Smith and myself and we had a glorious time. Brother Jacob got all off, worse than he was once at Rye Neck and it made me think of home."[59]

John Thomas and Jacob Smith were comrades from *The Hills*. Along with Simeon's participation, Jacob Smith's attendance at Rye Neck further links *The Hills* with religious activities in the larger African American community. Thus, *The Hills* families were served by their own church and school, sometimes receiving the services of Reverend Silas Mitchell, probably the son of one of their early settlers. Members of the community, for example, Simeon Anderson Tierce, Jeremiah Mitchell, and Jacob Smith, were also affiliated with religious associations in nearby communities that had ties to New York City and its black abolitionist movement. In 1864, Reverend Silas Mitchell moved to New Haven, CT, where he served as pastor of that city's A.M.E. Zion Church and an agent for *The Weekly Anglo-African,* a New York City newspaper and an aggressive voice in the black press. Any reference to blacks in New Haven, a center of black activism in religion, education, and abolition, must include mention of Reverend Amos G. Beman, the peripatetic Congregational minister who was always headquartered in New Haven, no matter where else his work took him.[60] Through this network, I believe *The Hills* community was associated with the forces at work in the black abolition movement, dispelling the sense of a socially isolated community.

The establishment of the church and its burial ground and the school in *The Hills* further confirms my thesis that *The Hills* was a stable community. The close web of relationships and support that existed between family members and friends, augmented by their interactions in the church and school and larger black community, confirms my view that the community was the extended family in *The Hills.*

The Civil War and the Postwar Decline of *The Hills*

In one of the most stirring passages in his long letters, Sergeant Simeon Anderson Tierce captured the fulfillment of the yearnings of African Americans through the long dark night of slavery.

> God is about to do the work that has been prayed years and years before we thought about praying, for God has seen and answered prayer. He is about to pluck out root and branch in the south and I see in some of the states he has been to work already. In the City of New Orleans, . . . I saw that God had been to work there and had moved the old slaveholders out and colored people were keeping stores themselves and I saw that they were men and women capable to doing it.[61]

The sustained prayers of the African Americans in *The Hills* community had been answered when the Union took up arms against the Confederacy and when Lincoln issued the Emancipation Proclamation. *The Hills* blacks answered the call for volunteers to serve in the United States Colored Troops, sending at least 34 men associated with their community to fight. In April 1863, one man enlisted in the 54th Regiment, Massachusetts Colored Infantry. In September 863, 13 black men from *Hills* families enlisted in the 14th Regiment, Rhode Island Colored Heavy Artillery. In December 1863, 16 men, associated with *The Hills,* enlisted in the 29th Regiment, Connecticut Colored Infantry. Then, in 1864, four *Hills* men enlisted in the 10th Regiment, New York Colored Infantry. Five men became noncommissioned officers: four received promotions to the rank of corporal and one to sergeant. Four men were wounded, one was killed in battle, and three others died from illness while in service. Many of the others were hospitalized for illness at some time during their enlistment and several were discharged for disabilities.[62]

Many of the men returned to *The Hills* in weakened conditions from illness and injuries, incapable of returning to the labor they had performed before the war. This reduced ability to labor on their own land or earn a living in turn reduced the economic security of the community. Some veterans and their families, anxious for more opportunity than *The Hills* offered, left the community for nearby White Plains, for other towns in Westchester, for the Boroughs of New York City, for Providence, and for Connecticut, especially New Haven. Thus, in the postwar years, one observes the slow and steady decline of the community, especially in its core families. Although several families stayed on and newcomers occasionally joined the community, the steady decline continued. The old houses were without electricity and modern plumbing, and people moved away for better housing or to be closer to job opportunities in urban centers.[63]

In the early 1920s, the Westchester County Park Commission commenced a major program of land acquisition for public parks along the Bronx River Parkway. The Commission purchased land from property owners, both blacks and whites, in the vicinity of *The Hills* in order to establish Silver Lake County. The acquisition of much of *The Hills* as county park land assured its preservation in the rugged state in which the original free African Americans came to it and made it their home.[64]

Census records nonetheless confirm the residual tenaciousness of the historic *Hills* family ties for at least one old-timer even into the early twentieth century. Sarah Jane Watson was located in the 1925 New York State Census manuscript. There I found a listing for Sarah Watson, age 74. Sarah Watson was the daughter of Sarah Jane Tierce, stepdaughter of Simeon Anderson Tierce, referred to as "Sissy" in his Civil War letters. Over those long years, some 62 years, in fact, Sarah Ann held on to her property, to her home. Simeon's words to Sarah Jane, back in 1864, had been heeded: "I want you to have that place fixed so that if me or you should die, it will always be a good home for Sis as long as she lives."[65] For Simeon, his descendants, and others like them, *The Hills* had been a "good home," and Sarah's home stood as a visible reminder of its place in the once vital families that constituted its African American community.

Notes

1. The National Archives and Service Administration, *[Widow's] Pension Files, 1861–1934,* "Case of Sarah Jane [Tierce] Depeau, No. 257.715," Letter: Simeon Anderson Tierce to Sarah Jane Tierce, 11 March 1864 (hereafter cited as SAT to SJT, 11 March 1864, *Widow's Pension File*).

2. Herbert G. Gutman, *The Black Family in Slavery and Freedom: 1705–1925* (New York: Vintage Books, 1976); Graham Russell Hodges, *Root & Branch: African Americans in New York & East Jersey, 1613–1863* (Chapel Hill: University of North Carolina Press, 1999); Joan H. Geismar, *The Archaeology of Social Disintegration in Skunk Hollow: A Nineteenth-Century Rural Black Community* (New York: Academic Press, 1982); A. J. Williams-Myers, *Long Hammering: Essays on the Forging of an African American Presence in the Hudson River Valley to the Early Twentieth Century* (Trenton, New Jersey: Africa World Press, 1994); Edythe Quinn Caro, *"The Hills" in the Mid-Nineteenth Century: The History of a Rural Afro-American Community in Westchester County. New York* (Valhalla, New York: Westchester County Historical Society, 1988).

3. Jay Downer and James Owen, Chapter LIV. "Public Parks in Westchester County," in Alvah P. French, ed., *History of Westchester County, New York,* Vol. II, p. 983.

4. Hodges, *Root & Branch,* 164–165.

5. Sweet, William Warren, *Methodism in American History* (New York: Abingdon-Cokesbury Press, 1933), pp. 230–233.

6. Richard Lander, "Methodism at North Castle," *North Castle History* Vol. 14 (1987) 7–14.

7. J. Thomas Scharf, ed., *History of Westchester County, New York* (Philadelphia: L. E. Preston & Co., 1886), Vol. II, 717; Alvah P. French, ed., *History of Westchester County, New York* (New York: Lewis Historical Publishing Co., Inc., 1925), Vol. I, 42.

Also, Ernest Freeland Griffen, ed., *Westchester County and Its People, A Record,* p. 131.

8. Griffen, *Westchester County and Its People, A Record,* p. 131. Also, Society of Friends, "Minutes of the Purchase Quarterly Meetings" (1746–1777) and "Minutes of the Purchase Monthly Meetings" (1777–1812), Purchase, New York, located in the archives of the Society of Friends Yearly Meeting. John H. Light, "The Purchase Quakers and The Black Settlement of Stony Hill" (Purchase, New York: State University of New York at Purchase, 1986, unpublished senior thesis; Mary Ellen Singsen, "The Quaker Way in Old Westchester," *The Westchester Historian,* Vol. 58, No. 1 (Winter, 1982), pp. 8–22.

9. Griffen, *Westchester County and Its People,* 131. Society of Friends, "Minutes of the Purchase Quarterly Meetings" (1777–1812).

10. *Record of Deeds,* "Thomas H. Burling of New Rochelle to Jeremiah Mitchell of Harrison," 1 March 1837.

11. Scharf, *History of Westchester County, New York,* Vol. II, 717; French, ed., *History of Westchester County, New York,* Vol. I, p. 42. Also, Griffen, ed., *Westchester County and Its People, A Record,* p. 131.

12. Alvah P. French, ed., *History of Westchester County, New York* (New York: Lewis Historical Publishing Co., Inc., 1925), Vol. II, p. 622.

13. A. J. Williams-Myers, Long Hammering, pp. 119, 166. *Eighth Census of the United States.*

14. R. French, ed., *Gazetteer of the State of New York* (Syracuse, New York: R. Pearsall Smith, 1860), 150. U.S; *Eighth Census of the United States.* Department of the Interior, Bureau of the Census, *Eighth Census of the United States.*

15. *Eighth Census of the United States.*

16. Gutman, *The Black Family in Slavery and Freedom,* p. 229. Gutman's monumental work in its entirety, and especially xvii–xxi and Chapter 10, pp. 432–460, refutes such historians as E. Franklin Frazier, *The Negro Family in the United States* (1939), Kenneth M. Stampp, *The Peculiar Institution* (1956), Stanley M. Elkins, *Slavery: A Problem in American Institutional and Intellectual Life* (1959), and sociologists Nathan Glazer and Daniel P. Moynihan, *Beyond the Melting Pot: The Negroes, Puerto Ricans, Jews, Italians, and Irish of New York* (1963), and Daniel P. Moynihan, *The Negro Family in America: The Case for National Action* (1965). With convincing evidence, Gutman argued that neither enslavement nor migration to the North destroyed the black family.

17. *Eighth Census of the United States*. Gutman, *The Black Family in Slavery and Freedom,* pp. 443–444.

18. Geismar, *The Archaeology of Social Disintegration in Skunk Hollow: A Nineteenth-Century Rural Black Community,* pp. 53–56.

19. Thomas T. Sherman, *Christ's Church at the Town of Rye in the County of Westchester and State of New York: Transcription of Vital Records, 1790–1880,* pp. 4, 5, 10, 146. In possession of Rye [NY] Historical Society. Interestingly, concerning Easter, the mother of John born May 17, 1807, in the 1755 census of slaves in Westchester County, in the borough of Westchester, an enslaved woman by the name of Easter was listed in the household of Nathaniel Underhill. No age was given for Easter, a somewhat distinctive name among the enslaved women in the county. Perhaps the woman recorded in 1807 is her daughter. Underhill is a name associated with *The Hills*. "Census of Slaves in Westchester County. 1755," *Papers Relating to Westchester County,* p. 511.

20. Sherman, Christ's Church, Transcription of Vital Records, 1790–1880, pp. 148, 149, 257, 282.

21. Gutman, *The Black Family in Slavery and Freedom,* p. 231.

22. Gutman, *The Black Family in Slavery and Freedom,* pp. 248, 251.

23. "A list of all the Slaves taken within my Limets [sic] In the year 1755 . . . in West Chester County," in "Census of Slaves in Westchester County. 1755," *Papers Relating to Westchester County,* p. 512. "Last Will and Testimony of William Anderson, 26 January 1796," Charles Dawson History Center, Harrison, New York. In Rye, New York, the Westchester County town adjacent to Harrison, the prominent citizen, Jacob Pierce was the master of Rose who received her freedom when Jacob and his wife Mary died. I have long wondered if the Tierce surname was changed from Pierce. Did the Pierce family insist that their name not be used by blacks, or did William Tierce prefer to alter the name for his own use? In several instances, surnames of prominent white, slaveholding families are not used by blacks, perhaps by the insistence of the whites. For example, although members of the Haviland family of Westchester County owned slaves, I have found no blacks by that surname. "Inventory of Jacob Pierce Estate, *Record of Deeds, Westchester County,* Vol. B, 183, Westchester County Archives, Elmsford, New York and Rye [NY] Historical Society.

24. U.S. Department of the Interior, Bureau of the Census, *Fourth Census of the United States, 1820* (Washington, D.C.: Gales and Seaton, 1821).

25. U.S. Department of the Interior, Bureau of the Census, Fifth Census, or, Enumeration of the Inhabitants of the United States, 1830 (Washington, D.C.: Duff Green, 1832); Carter G. Woodson, Free Negro Heads of Families in the United States in 1830, Together with a Brief Treatment of the Free Negro, Washington, D.C.: The Association for the Study of Negro Life and History, 1925, p. 110.

26. Carl Nordstrom, "The New York Slave Code," *Afro-Americans in New York Life and History,* 4: 1 (January 1980), 19–20.

27. *Record of Deeds,* "Thomas H. Burling of New Rochelle to Jeremiah Mitchell of Harrison," 1 March 1837; U.S. Department of the Interior, Bureau of the Census.

Second Census of the United States, 1800 (Washington, D.C.: Printed by order of the House of Representatives, 1801); U.S. Department of the Interior, Bureau of the Census, *Third Census of the United States, 1810* (Washington, D.C., 1811).

28. *US Census, 1820, Harrison, 467.* New York, Westchester County, *Record of Deeds,* "Hagar Anderson to Jeremiah Mitchell," 19 April 1815, Liber of Deeds, No. 37, 286.

29. *US Census, 1850, New York, Westchester County, Harrison.*

30. New York, Westchester County, *Record of Deeds,* "Jeremiah and Hester Mitchell to William Tierce," 12 February 1851, Liber of Deeds, No. 159, 32.

31. *US Census, 1860, Harrison, NY.*

32. SAT to SJT, 11 March 1864, Widow's Pension File; *Eighth Census of the United States, 1860; Ninth Census of the United States, 1870;* "North Castle, A list of ye Nagros [*sic*] . . . for the year 1755," Papers Relating to Westchester County, 512.

33. New York, Westchester County, *Record of Deeds,* "Thomas H. Burling of New Rochelle to Jeremiah Mitchell of Harrison," 1 March 1837, Liber of Deeds. The parcel had been conveyed in 1804 to Thomas Burling, who in 1837 is noted as "deceased"; presumably Thomas H. Burling of New Rochelle is his son.

34. *The Weekly Anglo-African,* "Taking the Census," Vol. I, No. 47, 9 June 1860, "Statistical," Vol. II, No. 30 (Whole No. 82), 9 February 1861.

35. National Archives and Service Administration, *[Widow's] Pension Files, 1861–1934,* "Case of Sarah Jane [Tierce] Depeau, No. 257.715.

36. SAT to SJT, 15 February 1864 and 11 March 1864, *Widow's Pension File. US Census, 1860,* New York: North Castle, p. 59, No. 427/457. National Archives and Service Administration, *Service Record,* "Case of Alfred Seymore." National Archives and Service Administration, *Pension Files, 1861–1934,* "Case of Jane Seymour, mother, No. 258.672."

37. SAT to SJT, 22 February 1864, *Widow's Pension File.*

38. National Archives and Service Administration, *[Widow's] Pension Files, 1861–1934,* "Case of Elizabeth Barker, No. 290.660."

39. SAT to SJT, 24 November 1863, *Widow's Pension File.*

40. Ibid.

41. Ibid.

42. SAT to SJT, 22 February 1864, *Widow's Pension File.*

43. SAT to SJT, undated, circa Spring 1864, *Widow's Pension File.*

44. In Colonial New England, a practice existed that may still have been practiced by midwives in the mid-nineteenth century. As explained by Laurel Thatcher Ulrich, a midwife asked "unwed mothers to name the father of their child during delivery." See Laurel Thatcher Ulrich, *A Midwife's Tale: The Life of Martha Ballard, Based on Her Diary, 1785–1812.* (New York: Random House, 1990), p. 149.

45. *Record of Deeds,* "Hagar Anderson to Jeremiah Mitchell," 19 April 1815, Liber of Deeds, No. 37, p. 286; *Second Census of the United States;* "Thomas H. Burling of New Rochelle to Jeremiah Mitchell of Harrison," 1 March 1837, Liber of Deeds.

"School Report, 1839, District Number One" (Harrison and North Castle, New York), in possession of the Town Historian, North Castle, New York. National Archives and Service Administration, *Pension Files, 1861–1934,* "Case of Thomas L. Brown, #860,882." Also, *[Widow's] Pension Claim,* "Case of Chloe Brown, No. 731.391." National Archives and Service Administration, *[Widow's] Pension Files, 1861–1934,* "Case of Carolina A. Tierce, No. 352.335." Questionnaire, 17 March 1896.

46. Crandall A. Shifflett, "The Household Composition of Rural Black Families: Louisa County, Virginia, 1880," *Journal of Interdisciplinary History,* VI (Autumn 1975), 235–260, quoted in Gutman, *The Black Family in Slavery and Freedom,* p. 448n.

47. Benjamin Quarles, *Black Abolitionists* (New York: Oxford University Press, 1969), pp. 68–69.

48. "Deposition A, 5,7," *Pension Files, 1861–1934,* "Case of Jane Seymour, mother, No 258.672."

49. New York, Westchester County, *Record of Mortgages,* "Indenture: Trustees of Methodist Episcopal Zon's Church to Charles A. Purdy," 5 December 1844, Liber of Mortgages, No. 88, pp. 183–185. Mildred Mitchell and Mae Malone, *Mt. Hope A.M.E. Zion Church: History and Memoriam* (White Plains, New York: n.d., circa late 1970s) no pagination.

50. Scharf, ed., *History of Westchester County, New York,* Vol. II, p. 73.

51. Letter: "S Young, New York Superintendent of Common Schools to Commissioners of Common Schools of the Towns of Harrison, North Castle and White Plains," 09 March 1843, in the possession of Town Historian, North Castle, New York, "Common School Amendment," Chap. 260: 15, *Statutes (1841).* Howard Holman Bell, *A Survey of the Negro Convention Movement, 1830–1861* (New York: Arno Press and the New York Times, 1969). Carleton Mabee, *Black Education in New York State, From Colonial to Modern Times* (Syracuse: Syracuse University Press, 1979), pp. 72, 73, 76. "School Report, 1846, District Number Six" (Harrison, North Castle, and White Plains, New York), in possession of Town Historian, North Castle, New York.

52. SAT to SJT, 24 November 1863, *Widow's Pension File.*

53. SAT to SJT, 22 February 1864, and undated, circa Spring 1864, *Widow's Pension File.*

54. *Record of Religious Societies, Vol. B.,* "Certificate of Incoporation of The Second Colored American Congregational Methodist Church," pp. 184–185.

55. *Record of Religious Societies, Vol. B.,* Certificates of Incorporation: "Zion Mission Church of Rye-Neck Village" and "The First Colored American Congregation Grove Company, Rye Neck, Westchester Co.," pp. 264–265, 189–190. For details of Reverend Levin Tilmon's early life, see Levin Tilmon, *A Brief Miscellaneous Narrative of the More Early Part of the Life of L. Tilmon, Pastor of a Colored Methodist Congregational Church in the City of New York,* electronic edition, University of North Carolina at Chapel Hill Libraries, *Documenting the American South,* 1999 (*http://metalab.unc.edu/docsouth/tilmon/tilmon.html*).

56. Carter G. Woodson, *The History of the Negro Church,* 3rd ed., Washington,

D.C.: The Associated Publishers (Publishing Agency of the Association for the Study of Negro Life and History), 1921, p. 125.

57. *The Weekly Anglo-African,* Vol. I, No. 45, 26 May 1860.

58. *The Weekly Anglo-African,* Vol. I, No. 50, 30 June 1860.

59. SAT to SJT, 15 February 1864, *Widow's Pension File*.

60. Caro, *The Hills in the Mid-Nineteenth Century,* 52. Also see Robert Austin Warner, *New Haven Negroes, A Social History*. (New Haven, Connecticut: Yale University Press, 1940; reprint ed., New York: Arno Press, 1969).

61. SAT to SJT, 15 February 1864, *Widow's Pension File*.

62. Edythe Ann Quinn, "*The Hills* in the Mid-Nineteenth Century: The History of a Rural Afro-American Community in Westchester County, New York," *Afro-Americans in New York Life and History*. 14:2 (July 1990), 45.

63. Ibid., pp. 46, 47.

64. Ibid., p. 47. Downer and Owen, "Public Parks in Westchester County," 983.

65. Quinn, "The Hills," p. 47. *New York State Census, 1925,* Westchester County, Harrison, 6, #14. (A-0026), Westchester County Archives, Office of the County Clerk, Elmsford, New York. SAT to SJT, 11 March 1864, *Widow's Pension File*.

6

Joan H. Geismar

The Rise and Fall of Skunk Hollow

Critical cultural institutions and social leaders can engender and nurture black identity. Without such facilitators and symbols, black identity is threatened and may even disappear. In such circumstances, those who would continue to identify as black may be required to relocate to new areas offering this type of cultural representation and race cultivation. The following selection provides some understanding of this aspect of black identity as it operated historically in the lower, western reaches of the Hudson Valley—Bergen County, New Jersey. In this excerpt from her larger monograph on the subject, historical and archeological methodologies are employed by historical archaeologist, Joan Geismar, to link the emergence and demise of Skunk Hollow, a nineteenth-century, rural black settlement in the northeastern corner of the county, to the appearance and departure of a key, local figure. In so doing, it makes the argument for the necessity of salient, individual leadership and institutional development as anchors grounding a black-identifying community. While this chapter mainly focuses on historical documentation, archaeological data were an integral part of the study.

Skunk Hollow began as a black settlement in 1806, peaked in population around 1880, and then entered a period of slow disintegration until 1905, when it was virtually abandoned. The fortunes of Skunk Hollow compare with those of Hilltown, the fictional name for the New England village that served as a model for sociologist George Homans in his study of community social disintegration. In both places, internal cohesion was marked by a discernible social

Adapted from *The Archeology of Social Disintegration in Skunk Hollow: A Nineteenth-Century Rural Black Community* by Joan H. Geismar. See original volume for full bibliography.

class structure headed by community leaders and the central role of a local church or churches as a catalyst for the high level of community social interactions. In both Skunk Hollow and Hilltown, a decline of internal cohesion was fostered by many factors. Among them was an exposure to a wider regional and national network, the far-reaching effects of industrialization, and the disappearance of "ranked individuals" as community leaders standing "at the center of the web of communications." Of all these factors, the last two weighed heaviest in Skunk Hollow's demise.[1]

Skunk Hollow, also known as "the Mountain," was located atop the Palisades in the extreme northeastern corner of New Jersey. At its inception in 1806, the community was situated in Harrington Township, a division of Bergen County created by royal charter in 1775.[2] Prior to this in the eighteenth century, earliest settlement of the area was predominantly by those of Dutch origin.[3] With the building of railroads and roads in the last half of the nineteenth century, communication increasingly improved within this rural township and between it and other areas, including New York City.[4] Geographically, Skunk Hollow was only four miles north of Closter, the largest village in the township, and less than one mile south of the Village of Rockland, or Palisades, in Rockland County, New York. In the early 1870s, the building of a new road provided a link between these rural villages and Skunk Hollow, yet the relative isolation of the community appears to persist until its demise in the beginning of the twentieth century. Through an act of legislature signed April 8, 1903, the section of Harrington Township that included Skunk Hollow became the Borough of Alpine, the area's present political designation.[5]

Using all available sources—deeds, census manuscripts, tax records, relevant information from a diary, and oral histories—and with full cognizance of the limitations imposed, it is possible to construct a profile of Skunk Hollow and its inhabitants. The ensuing history of the community is based primarily on information about household heads, household numbers, land transactions recorded in deeds, and any relevant miscellaneous information recovered in research.

Early Black Settlement

The first known deed to a black settler in Skunk Hollow was granted to Jack Earnest, a freed slave. On January 1, 1806, paying $87.50 for a "lot and parcel of land lying situate and being in the township of Harrington in the County of Bergen and in the state of New Jersey," Earnest purchased five acres and 30 square rods of land.[6] According to township tax records, by 1822, Earnest's holding had increased to 11 acres, although no deed or deeds for this additional land have been located; this same tax record indicates that at this time, out of approximately 22 black householders and as one of two who owned land, Earnest was the largest land-owning free black in the township.[7] On November 19, 1841, at about the age of 71, Jack Earnest died of burns believed incurred from a live ash falling upon him while he slept before his fire. In his diary, Nicholas Gesner, a local white resident and Jack's former owner, sadly reminisces about Jack, his origins, and his successful manipulation to gain freedom.

Earnest was not buried in the community although there are at least two burial grounds at Skunk Hollow.[8] His gravestone is documented in a cemetery near Norwood, a town to the west of Skunk Hollow.[9] This might have been the private burial ground of a white family, although it is more likely it was a cemetery reserved for black burials.[10]

At his death Jack Earnest had no family. Yet the 1840 federal census, taken just a few months before he died, indicates several people in Jack's household: 4 boys under 10, 1 man 10–23, 1 man 36–54, 1 man 55–100 (obviously Jack), 1 girl under 10, 1 woman 10–23, and 2 women 24–35.[11] From a mortgage granted the day he bought his property, we know that Jack had a wife, Susan, but Gesner's failure to mention her in his diary, and the dispensation of Earnest's property after his death, suggest that she might have predeceased her husband. Unfortunately, no names other than heads of households are given on censuses prior to 1850, but it is possible—indeed likely—that the unidentified members of Earnest's 1840 household included William Thompson and his family; Thompson was the man to whom Earnest, reputedly from his deathbed, sold his land.[12]

The William Thompson who purchased Jack Earnest's land was or became an African Methodist Episcopal preacher.* On the 1850 census, his occupation like that of all Skunk Hollow men was that of "laborer"; after the community church was built on land he deeded to the "trustees of the Methodist Episcopal Church of Coulored [*sic*] people of the Township of Harrington" in 1856, Thompson became its minister.[13] In the 1860 census, Thompson's occupation is listed as "Methodist Preacher," a position he appears to have maintained for the remainder of his life, which was spent as a resident of Skunk Hollow.[14] Apparently, Thompson died in August 1886.[15]

Although Thompson's origins are unknown, it is likely he was born free, perhaps in New York State.[16] Tradition has it that he was an itinerant preacher who fell in love with a young slave girl, bought her, and married.[17] This girl is "Aunt" Betty, or Betsy (Elizabeth), Thompson who reputedly lived to be 102 years old, and died in 1907.

---

*A William Thompson first appears as a single man on the tax record of 1822 (HTR 1822: 17), but he would be too old to be the William Thompson documented at Skunk Hollow. It is possible that this elder man was a relative, perhaps even the father, of the William Thompson documented in the community, but this is merely speculation.

A month before Jack Earnest's land was purchased by William Thompson, Jim Oliver, a former slave like Earnest, also acquired property in Skunk Hollow.[18] Oliver is listed on the 1813 and 1822 tax records, but his residence at Skunk Hollow is an enigma; tracing his occupation illustrates one of the more frustrating Skunk Hollow family reconstructions, yet Oliver is better documented than many of the community's inhabitants. Although he is found on the 1830 census, the James Oliver listed on the 1840 census is too young to be the same James Oliver and too old to be one of Oliver's sons, James Oliver, Jr.[19] Also, there are two James Olivers on the 1844 tax record, but no James Oliver appears on the 1850 tax record or on the 1850 census.[20] Oliver is again listed on the 1854 tax record, and he died in 1855 according to an inventory to this effect.[21] It is possible that Oliver moved from the township some time after 1844 when he last appears in a tax record, but this is highly unlikely.[22] Although it would explain why he is not found on the 1850 census, it does not explain why he is missing from that of 1840, or why he reappears in 1854.

There are two known entries in Gesner's diary concerning Jim Oliver. The first, dated November 12, 1841, mentions legal issues being circumvented so that Oliver, considered a slave, could legally own the mountain land that he had bought the month before; Jim's master, Johannes Blauvelt, gave a certificate promising that at Blauvelt's death Oliver would be freed.[23] The fact that Oliver's acreage is not listed in the 1844 tax record may indicate that his former master was still living and that Oliver might not yet have had the legal right to own this land. The second entry, from January 8, 1842, notes Gesner's payment to Jim Oliver's wife for work done by Jim.[24]

When Oliver died, his goods were inventoried with one-third of their value going to his widow, Cady Oliver, and two-thirds being equally divided among his five children, Joseph Oliver, William Oliver, James Oliver, Jr., Jane Sisco, and Susan Sisco, wife of Pompey Sisco.[25] Although no will has been located requiring this provision, his land appears to have been similarly distributed.[26]

Three other families are part of the early history of the community. Benjamin Charlton, a contemporary of Earnest and Oliver in the settlement, was also a freed slave evidently born in Bergen County; he is the sole Skunk Hollow resident for whom a manumission paper was located.[27] Although this paper, made in the name of Resolvert Auryansen of Harrington Township, refers only to "my negro slave named Ben," its recorded association with two land deeds strongly suggests it refers to Benjamin Charlton.

The first deed to Charlton, dated March 14, 1833, the manumission paper, dated March 9, 1833, and the second deed from March 24, 1835, in this order, were entered in the County Clerk's Office on March 25, 1835.[28] The property is not specifically located, but for approximately 20 years, Charlton and his family were part of the Skunk Hollow community.

By Skunk Hollow standards, Charlton owned a great deal of land (by deed 18.75 acres), yet by 1850 he is no longer recorded as a head of household.[29] In 1859, he sold more than 15 acres in the Skunk Hollow area to Elisha Ruckman,[30] a wealthy Harrington Township landowner and speculator.[31] The date of Benjamin Charlton's death, March 16, 1860, is recorded on a gravestone found in the cemetery where Jack Earnest is buried. In this same cemetery are the graves of Charlton's daughter, Phoebe, who died at 18 in 1852, and a young son, James, who died in 1832 when he was five years old.[32]

Two other early Skunk Hollow residents were John Cartwright and John Whitehead. Cartwright is mentioned in Gesner's 1841 account of Jack Earnest's death. Both are on the census from 1840 through 1860, both are in the 1844, 1850, and 1854 tax records, and both listed New Jersey as their state of birth on the 1850 census and Virginia in 1860. While deeds for Whitehead's land—a considerable holding of at least 12 acres—are recorded and his dwelling can be located, no deeds for Cartwright have been found nor has his property been definitively identified.[33]

By 1840 Cartwright was the head of a household in Skunk Hollow and continued to be so for at least 20 years. Tax records indicate Cartwright was a householder in 1844 and 1850 and a landowner by 1854, possessing two acres.[34] From Gesner's diary, we know that he lived approximately one-quarter of a mile from Jack Earnest, whose dwelling has been located from deeds and an unpublished map.[35] Deeds citing Cartwright's property as a boundary indicate that his land was just south of John Whitehead's property, but this is not where Whitehead built his house and resided.[36] It is not known whether these two acres were where Cartwright lived. It is possible that when Jack Earnest sought help in 1841 (for his burns), Cartwright's dwelling was not on the land he later purchased, and it is also possible that he continued to live in the house he occupied in 1841, perhaps one he rented, and not on the land he acquired after 1850. In 1856, he was a trustee of the community church, and his death might have occurred between 1860 and 1870.[37] It appears that none of his children became heads of households at Skunk Hollow.

There are several deeds in John Whitehead's name, and he lived in Skunk Hollow at the same time as Cartwright.[38] His dwelling has been identified, and his male and female children remained at Skunk Hollow as wives and as heads of households. Geographically, the eastern extension of Turkey Ridge where Whitehead lived after 1858 was somewhat removed from the core of Skunk Hollow. This land was separated from other Skunk Hollow houses by more than a quarter mile of swampy, uninhabitable land.

Based on census manuscripts, by 1850 Whitehead possessed wealth almost equal to that of the minister, William Thompson, who was the most well-off resident of Skunk Hollow by 1860.[39] Widowed between 1850 and 1860, Whitehead died some time between 1865 and 1870.[40] There is an 1865 land transaction made in his name, but he does not appear on the 1870 census or any subsequent census manuscript.

Finally, among the pioneer Skunk Hollow settlers there is a Joe Johnson clustered with Jack Earnest, Jim Oliver, and the elder William Thompson on the 1822 list of Harrington Township tax rateables. On this record, Joe Johnson and Jack Earnest were the only blacks in the township documented as landowners.*

The Community's Apex

Deeds recorded in 1857 indicate that each of James Oliver's children received approximately one acre of land. These deeds also reveal that one son, James Oliver, Jr., living at the time in Goshen, New York, sold his one-acre share to his brother, Joseph Oliver, for $80.00.[41] The others all kept the land they inherited, and Joseph Oliver, Jane Sisco, and Susan Sisco, who are found in the 1854 tax schedule and on the 1855 state census, resided in the cluster of households comprising Skunk Hollow. Earlier, in 1844 and again in 1850, a William Oliver, perhaps James Oliver's eldest son, is found in the cluster, but this is the only concrete record for him. The acre that he inherited in 1856 included a small family burial ground and perhaps was not intended or needed for habitation.[42]

Joseph Oliver, probably Jim and Cady Oliver's second son, and his wife Flora lived at Skunk Hollow at least from 1840 to 1885. Since they are not recorded on the 1870 census, a break in their residency is suggested, but this is contradicted to a degree by the recording of Joseph Oliver's name on an 1867 road proposal; they could, in fact, be among the most enduring of Skunk Hollow's residents.[43] Certainly Joseph was one of the more active land transactors, with located deeds recording four purchases and two sales.[44] Theirs was also one of Skunk Hollow's more prolific unions, producing at least 11 children. Both husband and wife appear to have been born in New Jersey around 1812, but whether they were originally slave or free is unknown. At least three children and four grandchildren became heads of households in the community, and the last resident of Skunk Hollow was their direct male descendant.

By 1870, a James Oliver (Jr.), probably Jim and Cady's youngest child who had returned from Goshen, was living in Skunk Hollow, apparently on land purchased from his brother, Joseph. From the deed, we know this land was part of a 9.25-acre parcel Joseph bought in 1856 from Abraham Post, a white resident of Rockland County.[45] The deed from Post reserves the sole right to

* Like William Thompson, this Joe Johnson's age conflicts with that of the Joseph Johnson who lived at Skunk Hollow until 1885. Joe Johnson might have been a relative of the younger man, perhaps his father, and the absence of a deed to Joseph Johnson may indicate that he inherited the land.

cut the wood on the land for four years; after this restriction was lifted in December 1860, Joseph sold a little more than 3.5 acres to his brother.[46] Although James Oliver, Jr., is not listed on a census until 1870, the deed suggests that he was a resident of Skunk Hollow for almost a decade prior to appearing on any known local record, and it appears that he continued to live at Skunk Hollow for at least 20 years.

The second generation of Skunk Hollow Olivers also includes Jane Oliver Sisco, whose husband, John, is found on the 1840 census and in the 1844 and 1850 tax records; the Siscos buried a 14-day-old infant in 1846, a fact documented by the only headstone to survive in the aforementioned family burial ground.[47] By 1854, John had either died or deserted since Jane Sisco is listed as a taxpayer in 1854 and as a household head on the 1855 census.[48] Although this is the only census on which she appears, Jane is believed to have resided at Skunk Hollow until at least 1867 when she, too, is mentioned in the road proposal and was paid 10 cents in compensation as was everyone along the road's proposed route.[49] The proposal's description of the location of her dwelling suggests that at this time she may have occupied her father's house. There is no information concerning her whereabouts after 1867.

The remaining Oliver legatee, Susan Oliver Sisco, lived at Skunk Hollow with her family and husband, Pompey, until his death. Pompey Sisco appears for the last time as a head of household on the 1860 census.[50] His land, and the 10-cent compensation are also noted in the 1867 road proposal, so it appears that he was still living in Skunk Hollow at this time.[51] What Pompey Sisco's origins or status at birth were remain a mystery, as do those of John Sisco. It is not known if these two men were related; since John Sisco is not documented on a census after 1840, it is not even known if they were born in the same state. However, Siscos are believed by some to be the single largest and oldest black family in Rockland.[52] The name is also documented in Harrington Township census manuscripts, but here the names Oliver and Thompson are each almost twice as common as Sisco. "Pompey" is known to have been a slave name; based on census records, Pompey Sisco came from Bergen County, New Jersey, and was perhaps a freed slave.[53]

Although Susan Sisco and her family are not found on the 1870 census, they do appear in 1880, with Susan listed as a widow.[54] She is not on the state census of 1885, but four of her children are documented in the household of her brother, Joseph Oliver.[55] When quite elderly, Susan is again listed as a head of household, with her son Samuel, his family, and an older woman—perhaps a relative of Samuel's wife—living with her.[56] Several of his children were living in Skunk Hollow by 1870, and in 1872, his son, Samuel, bought the five-acre parcel of land on which his father's house and outbuildings were located for $1.00.[57] This purchase was made from four of his siblings, one married to a Sisco and three married to Olivers; the latter three all resided in Skunk Hollow.

Samuel married a woman from outside the community, and after his death some time in 1880, his property was sold to a Marie Lawrence for back taxes.[58] Mrs. Lawrence might have been a member of a prominent New York family who began to acquire land in the area after the Civil War.[59]

Another enduring community resident was the aforementioned Joseph Johnson. Although he settled in Skunk Hollow after Jack Earnest and Jim Oliver, Johnson's connection with Skunk Hollow as a householder may antedate concrete documentation. While no deeds are recorded in his name, Johnson is first noted in the 1844 tax record and then again on the 1850 census. His absence from the 1860 census suggests a break in occupation, yet he appears to have lived in Skunk Hollow through 1885.[60] He paid taxes on a house and lot in 1844 and 1850 and by 1854, he owned four Skunk Hollow acres.[61] The records specify that the Joseph Johnson documented at Skunk Hollow was born in New Jersey in about 1817. He and his wife Rebecca lived in Skunk Hollow with at least seven children, but reconstruction of his occupation is speculative. For example, no Joseph Johnson is found on the 1850 census, but there is a Joseph Jackson, and his wife, Rebecca, their children, and a Nancy Jackson, aged 73, in his household.[62]

In the 1840 census, a Nancy Johnson, apparently a widow, and her family are documented near Jack Earnest and others in Skunk Hollow.[63] This could conceivably be the Nancy Jackson who is 73 years old on the 1850 census. Confirming this is difficult, however, since neither a Johnson nor a Jackson are on the 1860 census; but by 1870, Joseph and Rebecca Johnson, whose ages coincide with those of Joseph and Rebecca Jackson, reappear.

Johnson was widowed by 1880, and his daughter, Susan, aged 37, and her children were living with him in Skunk Hollow. Thirty years earlier Susan Jackson, aged 6, was the eldest child of Joseph and Rebecca Jackson. By 1885, the last year he appears on the census, Johnson was over 60 and was living with a youth, perhaps his grandson.[64]

Disintegration

Except for intermittent occupation of the area slightly northwest of the core of Skunk Hollow by two Oliver-Sisco-Whitehead families, the Skunk Hollow community was fundamentally defunct by 1905.[65] After 1880, the descendants of the original free black settlers gradually began to move to towns and villages in Bergen and Rockland Counties, although some went further afield.[66]

After her husband's death in 1886, William Thompson's widow Betsy left Skunk Hollow and lived with her married son and his family in the nearby town of Alpine.[67] It appears that none of the sons born to William and Betsy ever became householders in Skunk Hollow, and, after 1885, no Thompson is recorded living in the community.

Susan Sisco died between 1895 and 1900, and Samuel and his family, who at some point had been living in Palisades, New York, lived in her Skunk Hollow house for at least a year but moved again in 1906 when the house burned.[68] Sisco family lore tells of the house being burned by a woman, Alice Gulliver, supposedly angered at being put out by Samuel.[69] The 1905 Alpine tax record documents Samuel as the last direct male descendant of Susan and Pompey Sisco living in the core area of Skunk Hollow.

A deed indicates that by 1893 James Oliver, Jr., was a resident of the nearby town of Cresskill, New Jersey, and he finally sold his Skunk Hollow property in 1898.[70] The 1900 census confirms this break with the community noting that he was then renting a farm that evidently was not in Skunk Hollow.[71]

The last Whitehead documented as a full-time resident of Skunk Hollow is Sarah Jane Whitehead Oliver, John's daughter married to Nick Oliver, son of Joseph and Flora; she and Nick were childless. Sarah Jane Oliver died some time between 1905 and 1907, and her husband sold at least part of their land to Sisco-Whitehead-Oliver descendants who lived in the area intermittently into the 1920s.[72] Since Nick Oliver's transaction does not appear in the tax records until 1911, it is possible that he continued living in Skunk Hollow after his property was sold.[73]

Benjamin Charlton's only surviving child, Thomas, married Susan Thompson, daughter of William and Betsy; although Thomas and Susan Charlton lived in Harrington Township, they do not appear to have been part of the Skunk Hollow community. Their granddaughter, Charlotte Charlton See, great granddaughter of William and Betsy Thompson and Benjamin and Susan Charlton, died in August 1979 at the age of 97; at her death, she was living with a son and residing in Nyack, New York.[74]

As is the case with William Thompson, it appears that none of Joseph Johnson's children became heads of households in the community, and in 1918, his estate, or part of it, was sold to the Borough of Alpine for back taxes.[75]

By 1905 only three Skunk Hollow households remained, all of them headed by Olivers: one was headed by Nick Oliver, a son of Joseph and Flora, and two were headed by their grandchildren, Albert Oliver and Margaret Ann Oliver Palmer.[76] Some time between 1908 and 1911, either Nick or Albert Oliver, both of them descended in a direct line from James and Cady Oliver, became the last official resident of Skunk Hollow.[77]

Explaining Skunk Hollow's Demise

Based solely on historical data, the reason for this abandonment remains a question. Considering the rapid changes that occurred during the nineteenth century, Skunk Hollow's history is relatively stable. Records document an insular community composed of family units primarily headed by men, with descent in the community coming predominantly from one family, the Olivers. Its isolation from outside events is suggested by the lack of evidence for any Skunk Hollow man performing military service in any war in which a black could serve prior to the twentieth century. While the men whose histories are recorded at Skunk Hollow were too young to fight in the Revolutionary War, none is known to have participated in the Civil War.

New transportation connections and regional economic transformations do not explain Skunk Hollow's decline and disappearance. In fact, the community's population peak coincides with many potentially fragmenting external factors, such as the building of roads and railroads and the increasing accessibility of the area.[78] After 1860, deeds and township census manuscripts document an influx into the Skunk Hollow area, if not into the community, of both the foreign born and wealthy white families from New York City.[79] The former were workers in growing industries such as brick-yards and the building trades, the latter commuters from New York City.[80]

While the population rise in the township was more than likely a consequence of deruralization, the population increase at Skunk Hollow, beginning between 1855 and 1860, and its documented decline before 1885 appear to coincide with two major events within the community itself: the building of the Skunk Hollow church some time between 1856 and 1860, and the death of its minister, William Thompson, probably in 1886. Although a Methodist Episcopal Church was established in the village of Closter as early as 1841, the Skunk Hollow church appears to have been the first of this denomination in Harrington Township solely for blacks.[81] It is conceivable that it was the first church of its kind in all of Bergen County.

Evidently, just prior to or after Thompson's death, the church foundered. Some time around 1880, members of the Skunk Hollow community might have attended other churches in the area.[82] Local history tells of the founding of a new church at Sparkhill, New York, in 1897, and many descendants of Skunk Hollow's early settlers are now among its longstanding members.[83]

With the number of households dropping from 13 in 1880 with 75 individuals, to 6 in 1885 with 28 individuals, migration of many Skunk Hollow families is documented. However, data from Nyack, New York, a town approximately six miles north of Skunk Hollow, illustrate that the drop in the community's population did not represent a general decline in black populations in the area; here, between 1860 to 1910, the number of blacks steadily, if slowly, increased. In addition to population decline, the household composition at Skunk Hollow, which at first documented an increasing number of children, exhibited a decline after 1885 that suggests the abandonment of the community by its young families, so that by the end of the nineteenth century, Skunk Hollow was no longer a vital entity.

Skunk Hollow was an enclave of free blacks while slavery persisted, and it remained so for 15 years after slavery's abolishment, a fact reflected in the population peak documented in 1880. This peak occurred, however, without the influx of blacks that other neighboring areas experienced when growing industries imported blacks.[84] This might have been a reflection of the strength of familial and spiritual ties within the community at this time.

Economic and social conditions, both within and outside the community, were unquestionably factors in the community's growth and ultimate demise. The fact, however, that the period of greatest population growth and community development was the time in which the church also functioned cannot be ignored. Although the cause–effect relationship is purely speculative when based solely on sparse records, the correlation requires investigation.

From 1918 to 1952, well after abandonment of the community, properties in the area were actively bought and sold but apparently not inhabited, and by the 1930s, the land constituting the core of Skunk Hollow was purchased by the Rockefellers and donated to Palisades Interstate Park.[85] This resulted in the preservation of many, but not all, Skunk Hollow cellar holes, foundations, and boundary walls. These undisturbed ruins, and fragmentary archaeological material, provide information crucial to understanding the decline of this cluster of nineteenth-century blacks for whom there is such a paucity of written records.

For approximately 75 years, members of the Skunk Hollow community maintained an economic independence and a relative affluence when compared with other local free blacks. In addition to documentation, ceramic analysis also suggests the comparatively elevated status of Skunk Hollow's residents. Analysis based on ceramic forms indicates that, while poor, Skunk Hollow's blacks were more prosperous than blacks, both slave and free, at two other nineteenth-century African American sites, the Black Lucy's Garden site in Massachusetts and the Cannon's Point Plantation site in Georgia. Archeological documentation indicates that some time after 1880 this favorable condition declined.

Evidence for economic and social ranking within the group is also recorded. Written historical data establish that by 1860, the Reverend William Thompson, the minister of the community church and the only Skunk Hollow man not a day laborer prior to 1870, exhibited the highest economic standing in the community. While cause and effect can only be suggested, a rise in population can be chronologically correlated with Thompson's rise in status and the building of the community church. But except for sparse unemployment statistics from 1871 until 1903, when the community became part of the borough of Alpine, no economic data relevant to a population decline have been located. It is for this period of the analysis that archaeological data are invaluable.

Using a controlled systematic collection of artifacts located on the surface in and around the site's 21 structural ruins, archaeological data were recovered that proved pertinent to analyzing the rise and decline of the community. These data provide information pertaining to feature identification, chronology, and status differentiation.

Feature identification, a prerequisite to understanding the community organization through archaeology, was based on field observation and a statistical comparison of differences in artifacts from the site's features. This analysis determined that the single-family compound, composed of one dwelling and auxiliary outbuildings, was the basis of community organization, an organization documented historically. It also indicated that a large, anomalous building, although more characteristic of a dwelling than an outbuilding, could not be classified as either. From archaeological evidence, this building appeared to be a public structure, an interpretation substantiated by deed information and a sketch map identifying it as the community church.

The data all suggest that, indeed, the disintegration of Skunk Hollow can be chronologically tied to the loss of its most highly ranked individual, the Reverend William Thompson. And further, Thompson's position as the minister of the community church indicates a correlation between economic status and social standing. And finally, in the period marking the loss of this individual of relatively high status, perhaps the result of his death or inactivity, a decrease in general status differentiation within the community is also suggested. This is a circumstance considered by sociologist George Homans to be an indication of social disintegration. Apparently, Thompson's crucial leadership role as pastor was permanently vacated upon his death. Without Thompson or his successor, the defining and sole community institution for Skunk Hollow faltered. Only at this point did the other possible disintegrative influences result in gradual desertion of the settlement.

This is not to imply that the demise of the Skunk Hollow community—its population decline occurring within a five-year period, but its total abandonment delayed for more than another 20 years—was solely the result of the loss of status of a ranked individual. Undoubtedly, a combination of internal and external factors caused this disintegration. Yet this must be considered: Although slavery was unquestionably a factor in the community's inception and early growth, its abolition does not appear chronologically tied to the community's florescence or demise.

While the community's population peak was reached in 1870, four years after slavery was legally abolished in New Jersey, evidence for a sharp rise in population is found prior to this in 1860. And, theoretically, slavery's restrictions were removed 15 years before the community's documented population decline. Further, although railroads in the mid-nineteenth century and road building after 1867 potentially linked Skunk Hollow to a larger sphere, the isolation and tenacity of the community persisted. Whatever the external factors involved and whatever the cause and effect, the years of the community's population peak and those of its decline can be tied most closely to the fortunes of the Reverend William Thompson. It seems that the institution of slavery, which may have originally served as a unifying force for Skunk Hollow's free blacks, was replaced by the bond of a powerful individual and his church.

Notes

1. George C. Homans, *The Human Group* (New York: Harcourt, Brace and World, 1950), pp. 334–368.
2. John P. Snyder, *The Story of New Jersey's Civil Boundaries 1606–1968. Bulletin 67.* (Trenton, New Jersey: Bureau of Geology and Topography, 1969), p. 79.
3. John Allison, "Vanished Folk of the River," *The Bergen Record,* Vol. 1 (March 1937), p. 5; W. Woodford Clayton and William Nelson, *History of Bergen and Passaic Counties, New Jersey* (Philadelphia: Everet & Peck, 1882), p. 210.
4. Clayton and Nelson, *History of Bergen and Passaic Counties,* p. 210.
5. *New Jersey Laws* (NJL), 1903, Chapter 163.
6. *Bergen County Liber* (BCL) Y, pp. 86–88.
7. *Harrington Township Tax Rateables* (HTR) p. 17.
8. *BCL 1857* A5, pp. 569, 680; *BCL 1865,* p. 403.
9. George Budke, Tombstone Inscriptions, Bergen County, New Jersey, 1916–1918, Budke Collection, Vol. 42:58, New York Public Library Manuscript Room, BCDCHA Archives, 1918, p. 48.
10. New Jersey Historical Society (NJHS) Proceedings 1916, p. 56; Budke, Tombstone Inscriptions, 1918, p. 48.
11. *Federal Census, Harrington Township (FCHT) 1840,* p. 5.
12. *Bergen County Mortgage Book (BCMB) C, 1806,* p. 356; *BCL J10 1841,* pp. 178–180.
13. *BCL B5 1856,* pp. 144–147.
14. *FCHT 1860,* p. 122.
15. Cornelia F. Bedell, *Now and Then and Long Ago in Rockland County* (New City: The Rockland County Historical Society, 1941), p. 186.
16. *FCHT 1850,* p. 285.
17. Sisco Frances Pierson, "Black History, Rockland County," *We, Too,* Vol. 2 (1976), pp. 2–3, Staten Island Institute of Arts & Sciences, Staten Island, New York.
18. *BCL 14 1841,* p. 409.
19. *FCHT 1830,* p. 40.
20. *HTR,* pp. 33–34.
21. *Bergen County Record of Inventories (BCRI) 1855,* pp. 51–52.
22. *HTR 1844,* p. 33.
23. Nicholas Gesner, Diaries 1830–1850, Palisades Free Library, Palisades, New York.

24. Gesner, Diaries, p. 8.
25. *Bergen County Orphan's Court Records (BCOCR)* Book G48, 1855, pp. 48–49.
26. *BCL A5 1856,* pp. 556–578.
27. *BCL A,* p. 226; *BCL N3* 1833, p. 249; *FCHT 1850,* p. 28.
28. *BCL N3,* pp. 246–250.
29. *FCHT 1850,* p. 287.
30. *BCL H5,* pp. 503–504.
31. Clayton and Nelson, *History of Bergen and Passaic Counties,* p. 217.
32. Budke, Tombstone Inscriptions 1918, p. 48.
33. *BCL L5 1848,* p. 582; *BCL L5 1858,* p. 584.
34. *HTR,* pp. 21, 34, 39.
35. John H. Serviss, Sketch Map, Northeastern Corner of Bergen County, New Jersey and Southeastern Rockland County, New York (charted between 1867 and 1884, Palisades Free Library, Palisades, New York, n.d.).
36. For examples of deeds citing Cartwright's property as a boundary, see *BCL 680 1858,* pp. 403, 405.
37. *BCL B5 1856,* p. 144.
38. *BCL L5 1848,* p. 582; *BCL L5 1858,* p. 584.
39. *FCHT 1850,* p. 285; *FCHT 1860,* p. 121.
40. *FCHT 1850,* p. 285; *FCHT 1860,* p. 121; *BCL E6 1865,* pp. 395–397.
41. *BCL A5 1856,* p. 566.
42. *BCL A5 1856,* pp. 568–570.
43. *Bergen County Book of Roads (BCBR) H,* p. 155.
44. *BCL A5 1856,* pp. 567, 568; *BCL N5,* pp. 50, 51, 53; *BCL E10* 1878, p. 447.
45. *BCL N5 1860,* p. 53.
46. *BCL N5,* p. 51.
47. *FCHT 1840,* p. 5; *HTR 1844,* p. 34; *HTR 1850,* p. 39.
48. *HTR 1854,* p. 21; *State Census, Harrington Township (SCHT) 1855,* p. 196.
49. *BCBR H,* p. 155.
50. *FCHT 1860,* p. 122.
51. *BCBR H,* p. 155.
52. Carl A. Nordstrom, Phoenician Tales, Nyack Public Library, Nyack, New York as cited in Isabel Savell, "Harry L. Sisco," *South of the Mountains,* Vol. 20, No. 2, pp. 3–7.
53. Donald Sinclair, Personal Communication, 1977, Rutgers Special Collection, Rutgers University; *FCHT 1850,* p. 285; *FCHT 1860,* p. 122.
54. *FCHT 1880,* p. 34.
55. *SCHT 1855,* p. 73.
56. *SCHT 1895,* p. 3.
57. *BCL 08,* p. 650.
58. *FCHT 1880,* p. 31; *BCL 630 1880,* p. 31.
59. Richard Peck, "Bashful Sneden's Landing: Rich in Past and Present," *New York*

Times, 4 December 1977, Section 8, pp. 1, 8; *BCL T10 1880,* pp. 630–631; *BCL A11 1880,* p. 662–663.

60. *SCHT 1885,* p. 73.

61. *HTR 1844,* p. 34; *HTR 1850,* p. 21; *HTR 1854,* p. 21.

62. *FCHT 1840,* p. 285.

63. *FCHT 1840,* p. 5.

64. *SCHT 1885,* p. 73.

65. *Alpine Town Rateable (ATR) 1907–1923;* Sisco Personal Communication; Charles Lundstrom, Interview, 1969, Palisades Free Library, Palisades, New York.

66. Francis Sisco Pierson, Personal Communication 1977–81, Piermont, New York.

67. *State Census Harrington Township (SCHT) 1895,* p. 45; *SCHT 1900 District 19.*

68. *ATR 1907,* p. 25.

69. Pierson, Personal Communication, 1977.

70. *BCL 467,* p. 75.

71. *FCHT 1900,* p. 10A.

72. *BCL 680 1907,* pp. 409, 412.

73. *ATR 1911,* p. 23.

74. Charlotte Charlton See, Personal Communication, 1979 Nyack, New York; Pierson, Personal Communication, 1979.

75. *ATR 1918,* p. 34.

76. *State Census, Alpine (SCA) 1905,* p. 2.

77. *ATR 1909,* p. 22; *ATR 1911,* p. 23.

78. John Scott, "The Slote, Piermont, and Erie Railroad," *South of the Mountain,* Vol. 20, No. 3 (1976), pp. 5–21.

79. *FCHT 1870,* p. 39; *BCL B7 1868,* p. 315; *BCL Z7 1871,* p. 380.

80. FCHT 1870, p. 39.

81. Clayton and Nelson, *History of Bergen and Passaic Counties,* p. 216.

82. Pierson, "Black History, Rockland County," p. 3.

83. Pierson, Personal Communication, 1979.

84. Nordstrom, Phoenician Tales, p.195.

85. BCL 2706 1946, p. 389ff; Charles Quadri, Personal Communications, 1977–81, Palisades Interstate Park Commission, Alpine, New Jersey.

7

Irma Watkins-Owens

Stepladder to Community

The range of black political identities expanded in Harlem during the 1920s. Often the appearance of the New Negro—a militant race advocate—is attributed to the frustrations of disillusioned black veterans returning from a European war they had fought for democracy only to face virulent race hostility on the homefront (see, for example, Cedric J. Robinson, Black Movements in America [New York: Routledge, 1997]). Yet historian Gloria Watkins-Owens offers an alternative explanation for the development. International labor displacements launched twentieth-century immigration from the British West Indies to the Hudson Valley during World War I. The marginal status of activists among the newcomers prevented their ready access to established African American political venues. These arrivals instead invented a new platform, literally, from which to air their views—the street corner stepladder. The street corner orator and rabble-rouser subsequently acquired an established position as a source of radical, alternative race-advancement strategies, usually nationalist- or socialist-tinged.

From World War I through the 1930s, the unclaimed terrain of the Harlem street corner became the testing ground for a range of political ideologies and a forum for intellectual inquiry and debate. The open-air arena claimed other adherents as well—barefoot prophets, musicians, healers, and traders—competing for the souls and pocketbooks of the urban masses. Space does not permit the treatment of all of these groups here, but on any day of the week, including Sunday, homebound Harlemites emerging from the subway at 135th Street and Lenox Avenue would most likely encounter congested sidewalks

---

and the well-toned voice of the street orator, often of African Caribbean descent, positioned atop a stepladder and surrounded by crowds of listeners.

Farther west on Seventh Avenue, between 137th and 138th Streets, other stepladder speakers (or "soap boxers") often espousing competing ideas, drew street audiences, too.[1] The meetings attracted larger and larger street crowds by the mid-1920s, and Harlem police often arrested speakers on charges of "obstructing traffic." "This street talk was virile and unconventional . . . unchained, free even daring," wrote an unidentified reporter from the African American *New York News* in 1926.[2]

The early radicals, the group who came together around 1917, those who invented the Harlem street corner speaking tradition were self-educated, mostly Caribbean immigrants. The mentor among them, Hubert Harrison, and a slightly younger Richard B. Moore, Frank Crosswaith, W. A. Domingo, Grace Campbell, Elizabeth Hendrickson, Marcus Garvey, and native migrants A. Philip Randolph and Chandler Owen and others articulated the urban generation's most urgent discontents and aspirations.[3] The street corner became the most viable location for an alternative politics and the place where new social movements gained a hearing and recruited supporters. Here a speaker did not have to be concerned with losing favor with political bosses or offending sources of influence.

After 1930, the street corner meetings retained their vitality and became an even more popular forum for airing public grievances. But in this decade a new breed of speaker was emerging. Claude McKay noted that "these soapboxers were rough men of the people whom educated Harlemites considered amusing or dangerous, according to the speaker's choice of subject."[4] One woman speaker, Louisiana native Audley Moore, recalled in an interview that "none of the churches would let us in with our kind of talk. . . ."[5]

Indeed the street corner provided an alternative to Sunday service, where unconstrained attacks upon black established leaders, landlords, and business people, not to mention the deity of Jesus Christ, were not likely topics of discussion. On the street corner, individuals, even those unknown to the community, who had a superior facility with the spoken word, wit, and a worthy topic could earn the respect of tough-minded Harlem working folk. "It is here where the West Indian shines," noted a Works Progress Administration researcher.[6]

Influential activist women, among them Audley Moore (Queen Mother Moore) and Bonita Williams, of African Caribbean descent, were to make their mark here as well. But even in this initially most untraversed of political spaces, women had fewer opportunities to articulate their own viewpoints, though women's issues, such as birth control, were among the topics raised. Socialist Helen Holman became well known in Harlem for her street corner speeches in favor of woman suffrage before the 1917 New York law was enacted. In the broader realm of activist politics, women were often the liaisons between leftist organizations, speakers, and bedrock community institutions.[7] They were also financial backers of important social movements growing out of the street corner tradition.

Why did such a politics emerge? In what ways did Harlem's immigrant radicals diversify and shape the direction of racial politics in New York City? And what has been the legacy of the ferment they helped create?

The restricted political space and the narrow political objectives of Tammany-controlled machine politics account in part for the appearance of a growing radical voice among the new black, urban generation as it had been among white, particularly Jewish, immigrants. In addition the proliferation of new ideas, particularly after World War I and the questioning of old values, including religious-based assumptions, influenced the young immigrant intellectuals. The appeal of socialism had been compelling enough for 94,000 Americans who voted for Eugene Debs on the socialist presidential ticket in 1900. The Bolshevik Revolution's overthrow of an undeserving elite; the rising discontent of Third World colonial peoples of color; and the growing sense of an internationalism evident in contacts between dispersed Africans from the colonial dependencies as well as American blacks were factors making a less provincial politics imaginable. The Harlem orators sometimes collaborated and shared platforms with Jewish Socialists or Communists from stepladders on Wall Street, Hanson Place (across from the Long Island Railroad) in Brooklyn. Stepladder forums sprang up also in Chicago and other major urban black centers across the North. But Harlem street corners nurtured the most active marketplace of ideas.[8]

Although some radical organizations made it possible for speakers to earn a partial income from their open-air lectures, the audiences who heckled and challenged some speakers helped mold, promote, and sustain the tradition. Ultimately the stepladder tradition was shaped not by organizations, but by the personality, skill, and ability of the speakers. Street audiences were drawn to the oratory of the individual speakers rather than to the organizations they represented, although the Universal Negro Improvement Association (UNIA) during its heyday is a possible exception to this. To the same unknown New York *News* reporter, indoor talks were "platitudinous, artificial, and lack[ed] courage." Moreover, "a fellow who is burdened with the weight of a church, a school, a lyceum or some other institution is afraid to say some of the things which [Hubert] Harrison said boldly on this street corner [137th and Seventh Avenue]. The indoor talks are generally limited, muzzled, tongue tied."[9]

The open-air meetings were not just political forums; they became the university of the streets, Harlem's first adult education centers. Speaker Audley Moore claimed, "That's where I got my Ph.D., on the street corner." Listeners could get an education in "everything from the French Revolution, the history of slavery, to the rise of the working class."[10] The New York *News* reporter made this rare observation about a summer 1926 Hubert Harrison street meeting:

> The Age of Pericles and Socrates in ancient Athens had nothing on the present age of Harlem in New York. Coming out of the "movies" between 137th Street and 138th Street on Seventh Avenue, we saw one of the biggest street corner audiences that we have ever met in this block, which is famous for street corner lectures, and the subject was "Evolution." This was not a selected audience but the "run of the street," and their faces were fixed on a black man who stood on a ladder platform, with his back to the avenue and the passing buses and his face to the audience who blocked the spacious sidewalk. . . . And what was he talking about? . . . The theory of evolution, and its illustration in different lines of material and biological development—the Darwinian science of the evolution of life, and the Marxian philosophy of the evolution of capitalism—and a possible development from capitalism to a state of communism.[11]

The reporter claimed he had "never seen a more attentive audience on a subject of this magnitude," as double-decker buses, autos, and clanging fire engines passed by. The listeners' serious absorption was broken only when Harrison "bore down on the fixed, immovable and unprogressive science of the pulpit." At these times there seemed to be "smiles and bits of merriment." Contemporaries believed that it was such meetings that inspired the New Negro movement of the Harlem Renaissance, though later scholars rarely make this connection. Immigrant street speaker Frank Crosswaith recalled in 1926 that "Negro Harlem had never before witnessed such inspiring spectacles as those intensely active nights when . . . thousands of darkskinned individuals of both sexes and all ages [stood] motionless for four and five hours drinking the message of the 'New Negro.'"[12]

Not all Harlem residents thought the street speakers were inspiring, however. For "the best people of the community"—some in the black middle-class and the pulpit—Harlem business people, and the police, the street meetings were a source of constant irritation. In 1916 the editors of the *Harlem Magazine,* which represented the interests of those who tried to stem the tide of the black "invasion," termed the intersection at 135th and Lenox, where "self-appointed orators" held forth nightly, "bug house corner."[13]

But if credit is given to one individual for establishing the open-air forums both as political and educational institutions in New York City as well as in Harlem, it would be Hubert Harrison, a brilliant scholar and biting social critic. A man of stocky build, dark complexion, and booming voice, he was known around New York as the "Black Socrates."[14] Even before World War I,

Harrison, a Socialist, was speaking with other Socialists in Madison Square Park, 96th Street off Broadway, and other locations. As a young immigrant Richard B. Moore was particularly impressed, as was Florida native A. Philip Randolph, both of whom later became two of Harlem's most magnetic street speakers. But before newer Harlem residents got to know Harrison's biting rhetoric, he had already earned his bricks and bats from mainstream native-born African American leaders.

Soon after he graduated with honors from De Witt Clinton High School, Harrison ran into trouble with the New York arm of Booker T. Washington's Tuskegee Machine. While holding a much-coveted colored job as a postal clerk, he sought direct involvement in the African American race struggle. As a speaker for St. Benedict The Moor Lyceum in San Juan Hill and a contributor to the New York *Sun* and New York *Call,* Harrison came to considerable public notice. In his New York *Sun* articles, he made his position against the accommodation views of Booker T. Washington quite clear. As the Tuskegee sage's emissary in New York, African American Republican Charles W. Anderson kept close tabs on Washington's critics. In a September 1911 note to Washington he wrote:

> Do you remember Hubert Harrison? He is the man who wrote two nasty articles against you in the New York "Sun." He is a clerk in the Post Office. The Postmaster is my personal friend, as you probably know. Harrison has had charges preferred against him and I think he is liable to be dismissed from the service. If not dismissed, he will get service punishment. Can you see the hand? I think you can. Please destroy this that it may not fall under another eye—unless it is Emmett's [Emmett J. Scott, Washington's personal secretary]. I will attend to Harrison. If he escapes me, he is a dandy.[15]

By the end of October, Harrison had lost his job. "I'm sure you will regret to learn that Mr. Hubert Harrison has been dismissed from his position as clerk in the New York Post Office," Anderson wrote Washington on the thirtieth.[16] Harrison never again worked in a similar job and made his living from his lectures and the sale of his books. He struggled to make a livelihood for his large family until his death from an attack of appendicitis in 1927.

Shortly after his dismissal from his post office job, Socialist party leaders in New York approached Harrison, who had been a member of the party since 1969, with the proposal that he be "made a paid speaker and organizer for Local New York for special work in negro districts."[17] Although the Socialists' poor record on civil rights was known to Harrison, he had arrived at his own independent political position, and their offer provided remuneration for the work he was already doing. Between 1911 and 1915 he actively tried to recruit African Americans into the party.

Feeling the young Harrison no longer a threat to Washington after dismissal from the post office job, Charles Anderson gleefully observed, "He is now stomping for the Socialist Party. . . ."[18] In the pre-war years, Harrison was one of the party's leading speakers, taking his soap box to the very site of capitalist power on the corner of Wall and Broad Streets, between the Stock Exchange and the office of J. P. Morgan. Here the young Henry Miller, noted novelist/essayist, said he received an education at the "foot of Harrison's soapbox."[19] Harrison provided a rationalization for his ideas in a 1912 essay, "The Black Man's Burden," which appeared in the *International Socialist Review* and later in his 1917 publication *The Negro and the Nation.* He located racial injustice within the structure of the capitalist system. Blacks were "the most ruthlessly exploited class in America . . . hanging on the ragged edge of the impending class conflict." He believed socialism was the means by which the working classes could be empowered.

Harrison was an early proponent of workers' struggles, and he was involved with Industrial Workers of the World (IWW) leaders Elizabeth ("Rebel Girl") Gurly Flynn, William ("Big Bill") Haywood, and Morris Hillquit in their leadership of the 1913 New Jersey silk-mill strike. It was Harrison who brought the Socialist movement to Harlem and encouraged the careers of the up-and-coming native-born and immigrant radicals. He helped establish the Harlem School of Social Science and the Modern School.[20]

But the Socialist party was not Harrison's main source of inspiration. During and after his Socialist party period, he maintained ties with a small group of native African American and African Caribbean scholars and bibliophiles, among them the Puerto Rican Arthur Schomburg and African American journalist John E. Bruce, who had in 1911 formed the Negro Society for Historical Research. This group of self-trained historians devoted themselves to reconstructing the history of people of African descent, mainly through their far-ranging collection of books and materials on Africa and the African diaspora. Their private libraries and bookshops became the reference tools of street speakers. For instance, the Rev. Charles Martin, a native of St. Kitts, maintained a library on the second floor of his brownstone on 134th Street and made it available to lay historians. Schomburg maintained an extensive library in his home on Kosciusko Street in Brooklyn. Family members reported that "there were bookshelves all over the house, even in the bathroom." He was also a supporter of Marcus Garvey and loaned him books from his collection and translated letters and documents for him.[21]

Harlem book dealers, like the street speakers, became freelance educators in history, philosophy, religion, and politics. Book dealer George Young was a Pullman porter who, according to Richard B. Moore, owned the first African American bookshop in Harlem at 135 West 135 Street. "In Young's Book Exchange, known then as *The Mecca of Literature Pertaining to Colored People,* there was . . . an astonishing array of material [about Africa] and her dispersed descendants." Moore began collecting himself in 1918, "having been led into the field by Hubert Harrison."[22] In the 1940s Moore opened his own bookshop, the Frederick Douglass Book Center, on 125th Street.

Harrison's and other speakers' involvement with research societies devoted to Pan-African topics was a crucial distinction between themselves and others who also spoke from street corners. In addition, the Caribbean scholars led by Schomburg provided an important international perspective to the study of the black experience. Schomburg's biographer notes that "to Schomburg the United States was merely a part, albeit an important one, of the wider American nexus, and he regarded himself as an historian of that greater southern land mass which also was America." Harrison, Moore, and others reflected this same perspective in their lectures.

By 1915 Harrison had severed ties with the Socialist party over disagreements with party leaders about the party's lack of a position on African American civil rights. He objected to the view that the grievances of the black masses were no different than those of white workers. Refusing in "this crisis of the world's history to put either socialism or the Socialist Party above the call of [his] race," Harrison moved his stepladder permanently to Harlem, where black grievances as well as his trademark liberal arts lectures became the focus of his street discourse.[23]

After years on street corners in Union Square, Wall Street, and in Harlem, the New York City Board of Education hired Harrison to give a series of lectures in 1923. But according to several contemporaries, Harrison had never been recognized by the "Negro leaders" and had never been mentioned in W. E. B. Du Bois's *Crisis*.[24] In a WPA biography of Harrison, Jamaican journalist and popular historian J. A. Rogers wrote that Harrison's "plainspokenness brought him many enemies among the leading Negroes, one of whom was Dr. Du Bois. . . ." Claude McKay recalled that Harrison had a "personal resentment against the NAACP and nicknamed it the 'National Association for the Advancement of Certain People.'"[25] Harrison apparently was never admitted nor sought admission to the inner circles of African American leadership. When he was hired as a lecturer by the Board of Education, William Pickens wrote an article for the *Amsterdam News* in recognition of the first black to be hired for such a position. Concerned that Harrison be elevated from the "obscurity" of the street corner, Pickens added that Harrison "ought to be a lecturer in some great American University," perhaps Columbia. In response Harrison dashed off a note to Pickens, thanking him for his "goodwill." "I can only hope that the other 'big Negroes' who have known for years what you have but recently discovered may not jump all over you."[26]

His ability to mingle with the masses was a quality his supporters admired in him. Few barriers appear to have existed between Harrison and his native

African American audiences. Upon his death in 1927, African American newspapers memorialized his unique contributions. In the view of the Boston *Chronicle,* a Caribbean-owned newspaper, he did Harlem a great service that was not fully appreciated. "He belonged to none of the uplift organizations because he refused to be fettered by any policy but his own, which was to dig out the truth and proclaim it on the highway without fear."[27] Journalist Hodge Kimon noted in the *Negro* World, "No trace of the Brahmin spirit was to be found in Harrison. He lived with and amongst his people; not on the fringe of their social life. He taught the masses and he drew much of his inspiration from them."[28] Nor did Harrison underestimate his audiences, the *Pittsburgh Courier* editorialized:

> To those who have little faith in the ability of the common man and woman on the street to appreciate "deep" subjects . . . it was a revelation to see Hubert Harrison, mounted on his street corner ladder and surrounded by a crowd of several hundred Negroes, discussing philosophy, psychology, economics, literature, astronomy or the drama.[29]

The New York Times added that on his stepladder platform throughout the city Harrison influenced "countless thousands" of whites as well.

Although after 1917 Harrison carried on his stepladder discourse primarily as a freelance lecturer, others who saw an opportunity in the open-air forums were increasingly affiliated with organizations, which often absented a street speaker from his or her audience. These were as divergent as the Socialist party, the Communist party, and Marcus Garvey's UNIA. Between 1916 and 1930, individuals and organizations of national prominence emerged from an initial grounding in street corner politics.

Florida native A. Philip Randolph, who later became head of the Brotherhood of Sleeping Car Porters and Maids, the first African American national labor union, began his public career at the corner of 135th and Lenox Avenue in 1916. When Randolph, the son of an African Methodist Episcopal (AME) preacher, arrived in the city in 1911, he sought out opportunities for intellectual exchange among young people and found that, with the exception of the Epworth League of the Salem Methodist Church, most churches "allowed no secular interests to intrude upon their study of the Bible."[30]

After giving up on an acting career, Randolph discovered that with an academic diploma he could attend City College for free.[31] During this period he developed a friendship with Ohio native Chandler Owen, who was a political science student at Columbia University and whose iconoclastic views he admired. He withdrew from the Epworth League and formed his own political study group with Owen, while honing his speaking and debating skills at City College. During the fall of 1916 the pair, largely due to Randolph's gifts as a speaker, became "the most notorious street corner radicals in Harlem exceeding even Harrison in the boldness of their assaults on political and racial conditions in the country." Although Harrison had left the Socialist party, he praised Randolph and Owen as "two brilliant young leaders."[32] They set up their stepladder on weekday nights and "if other soapboxers wanted to hold on to their audience, they had to be careful not to hold their meeting too close to where Randolph was preaching."[33]

But Randolph's sporadic employment could hardly have sustained his political activities without the active support of his wife, Lucille Green Randolph, a successful businesswoman and protégé of black hair-products millionaire Madame C. J. Walker. "Chandler and I had no job and no plan for the next meal. But I had a good wife. She carried us," Randolph later acknowledged.[34] Jervis Anderson, Randolph's biographer, notes that Lucille Randolph's financial backing was crucial in the launching of the two soapboxers' monthly magazine, the *Messenger,* in the fall of 1917.[35]

Having proved themselves on the streets, the *Messenger* editors also helped launch the 21st Assembly Branch of the Socialist party. The Harlem Socialist Club was composed of a group of outspoken, largely immigrant young men and one woman, Jamaican Grace P. Campbell. The men included street speakers Barbadian Richard B. Moore, Jamaican W. A. Domingo, and Virgin Islander Frank Crosswaith. After starting the *Messenger,* Randolph and Owen apparently were not among the regular speakers. In 1917–1918, according to Richard B. Moore, aside from himself the list of Socialists included the following: W. A. Domingo, Otto Huiswoud, Rudolph Smith, Frank Poree, Anna Jones, Elizabeth Hendrickson, Frank Crosswaith, Herman Whaley, John Patterson, Victor C. Gasper, Thomas Potter, and [John] Ramsay.[36] Others, including Ethelred Brown, were added to the list after 1920.

This group also formed a study seminar known as the Peoples Educational Forum, which met every Sunday afternoon at Lafayette Hall on 131st Street and Seventh Avenue. The meetings' format included a lecture and a discussion afterwards, which also perhaps served as a warm-up for street oratory. Moore characterized these meetings as "intellectual battlegrounds" where a speaker would have to be prepared "to battle for his ideas."[37] Joyce Moore Turner points out that by 1921 the Socialists were rotating their stepladders from nine different sites, several of them in Harlem:

> On the same evening Moore, Ethelred Brown, and H. Leadett would be speaking at Lenox Avenue and 128th Street, while Domingo, John Patterson, and Frank Poree were holding forth at Lenox Avenue and 133rd Street.[38]

A favorite assembly spot of course was 135th Street and Lenox because of the expansiveness of the sidewalk and the avenue. Turner and Turner continue:

> Once the stepladder was hauled from a fellow socialist tailor or cigar shop on 135th Street, the comrades assembled for a street meeting put a standing question to one another: "Well, what shall it be tonight? Shall it be propagate straight socialism or shall we talk Negro-ology?" They were prepared to discuss the meaning and significance of socialism or to deal with the problems and suffering of the Afro-American people and the potential solutions to those problems. Since the Socialist Party had not been able to come to grips with the "Negro Question," there remained two separate topics rather than an integrated approach.[39]

The younger group of Caribbean immigrants may have been drawn to the Socialists by the early example of Hubert Harrison. The party's educational programs, including the Rand School of Social Science, also attracted young people. But their own consciousness of class contradictions and the exploitation of colonial systems combined with the brunt of American racism would have appealed to these young intellectuals. Joyce Moore Turner notes that in relationship to the Socialist party, "the Harlem group . . . had little connection with headquarters and developed their study group and educational forum according to their own ideas."

Clearly it was their independence of thought and the aggressive, daring style of the speakers, rooted in the black oral tradition, which appealed to Harlem audiences.[40] The Socialist party itself failed to address key complaints of the black masses, including racism within Socialist-led unions. A major disadvantage was the absence of a mass-based, black-controlled community organization where grievances and aspirations could be addressed.

Hubert Harrison, now advocating "race first" and black self-determination but not rejecting Socialist theory, was the first of the soapboxers to attempt such an organization. In 1917, in the wake of the antiblack East Saint Louis Riots, he issued a call for a mass meeting to protest lynching and disfranchisement. Over 2,000 Harlem residents attended the meeting held at the Bethel AME Church on June 12. "It was made clear that the 'New Negro Movement' represented a breaking away of the Negro masses from the grip of the old-time leaders none of whom was represented at the meeting." A number of "new" leaders were present, however, including Marcus Garvey, who spoke on behalf of his Jamaica-based UNIA and gave his endorsement to the movement. A new organization, the Liberty League, was formed with Harrison as its president and editor of the new publication the *Voice*.[41] Though his street corner speeches are lost to posterity, the *Voice* and Harrison's book *When Africa Awakes,* largely a collection of his articles, remain sources of his ideas.

In his lectures Harrison confronted directly one of the key class grievances of the Harlem masses: the promotion of light-skinned African Americans over those of darker skin in public and private life. He openly condemned the practice, particularly as a criterion for selecting leaders. "So long as we ourselves acquiesce in the selection of leaders on the ground of their unlikeness to our racial type, just so long we will be met by the invincible argument that white blood is necessary to make a Negro worthwhile."[42] Statements like this could be interpreted as an assault on African America's "Talented Tenth" and "representative Negroes," over half of whom were light complexioned. His continued criticism of African American leaders on other grounds, including an article in the *Voice* entitled "The Descent of Du Bois," could hardly have induced the *Crisis* editor to have reviewed his work in the NAACP's monthly journal.

But stepladder speakers such as Harrison continued to focus their discourse on issues of immediate concern to the community. Among these were questions of the use of violence or self-defense, high rents and high prices, and police brutality. The increase in violence against African Americans, much of which occurred in centers of recent African American migration, was a grievance which found its effective response in Harlem street and mass meetings. A series of race riots between 1917 and 1921 and scores of street clashes between migrating blacks and mostly working-class whites not only challenged any expectation of a nonracial urban proletariat, but helped to usher in a new era of black militancy. While established leaders cautioned restraint and trust in the judicial system, Harrison was now joined by other young immigrant street speakers who urged blacks simply to defend themselves and their property.

One incident took place on May 30, 1917, when a crowd estimated at 200 tried to free a black man arrested in Harlem.[43] Just four days earlier, blacks in San Juan Hill had battled white residents and police after officers had shot into the store of a well-liked black immigrant grocer, wounding him and a small child.[44] Following this episode Harlemites were enraged when a white police officer struck the Rev. Dr. George Sims, pastor of Union Baptist Church, with a nightstick during an unrelated street disturbance. Sims had previously led a citizens protest of the San Juan Hill shootings.[45] Still another incident occurred on July 4, two days after the bloodiest day of the East Saint Louis Massacre. Police ordered 25 members of the all-black 15th Regiment to move from a street corner. When police arrested one of the soldiers who questioned the validity of the order and refused to move, black residents and other soldiers attempted to rescue the prisoner. At the height of the disturbance, 2,000 people had gathered, according to *The New York Times,* most of them fighting with knives, clubs swinging, and bricks flying in the air.[46]

The day after the 15th Regiment incident, Harrison called a meeting at the Metropolitan Baptist Church. *The New York Times* printed its report of the meeting directly beneath its story of the soldiers' riot to demonstrate the connection. According to *The Times,* Harrison told an audience of 1,000 cheering Harlemites: "We intend to fight, if fight we must. . . . This thing in East St. Louis touches us too nearly. We must demand justice and make our voices heard."[47]

The 1917 East Saint Louis race riot, or "massacre" as Harlem soapboxers preferred, the bloodiest of the century up to that time, touched off an intensity of community feeling in Harlem and around the United States. Reports that white mobs had driven thousands of blacks from their homes and had shot, burned, and hanged scores of others shocked Harlemites. On the surface, both established and emerging black spokesmen in Harlem were as one in their outrage and calls for a community response decrying such savagery. A coalition of leaders, including Hubert Harrison, W. E. B. Du Bois, black ministers, the NAACP, and the Urban League, organized the silent protest parade and marched down Fifth Avenue to midtown Manhattan on July 28, 1917. However, the masses of New York blacks in skirmish after skirmish before and after the July 28 march demonstrated that they were in no frame of mind for silence and were inclined to test the effectiveness of any coalition of black leaders. Self-defense became one of the major issues separating urbanized African Americans from the counsel of old-line leaders.

Fred R. Moore had a revealing exchange with Harrison over the issue of violence after the East Saint Louis riot. He wrote in the New York *Herald Tribune:* "The representative Negro does not approve of radical socialistic outbursts such as calling upon Negroes to defend themselves against whites." In the *Age* he advised, "No man, or woman, either, for that matter, is a friend to the race, who publicly advises a resort to violence to redress wrongs and injustices to which members of the race are subjected in various sections of the country at the present time." To this Harrison wrote a stinging reply: "Now, although the *Voice* seeks no quarrel with the *Age* we are forced to dissent from this cringing, obsequious view which it champions. And we do this on the ground that cringing has gone out of date, that the *Age*'s view does not represent any influential or important section of Negro opinion."[48] Spurred on by Harlem's expanding boundaries and the restless post-World War, mass-based community, a series of new organizations and publications emerged, sharing connections to the stepladder tradition.

Harlem's 21st assembly district Socialists Club provided a third-party alternative to the Democratic or Republican platforms, and Harlem's leading black politicians found themselves in direct competition with the growing presence of irreverent, young Socialists. The presence of the black Socialist party candidates was particularly irksome to those who hoped to elect the first black candidates from the 21st and the 19th assembly districts. A reader wrote the *Crusader* to complain about the magazine's support of black Socialist candidate Rev. George Frazier Miller, who ran unsuccessfully for Congress in 1918. In the opinion of the writer, a Republican, Miller's and others' candidacy on the "defeatist Socialist party" ticket served only to split the black vote and ensure the election of a Tammany Democrat. "Does this not conclusively show that you think more of your Socialism than you do of race representation, more of party than of race rights?"[49] In view of the party's lack of a position on civil rights, the reader's point could not be set aside easily. Harlem voters ultimately chose the Democratic party by 1930, but in the meantime, from 1917 and throughout the 1920s, Harlem street audiences helped shape political alternatives.

In these years the race's "representative Negroes" faced new challenges, if not a lapse in influence. One highly publicized incident occurred the year before, in October 1917, when Theodore Roosevelt came to the Palace Casino to speak on behalf of mayoral aspirant John P. Mitchell, a Fusion candidate. Rev. Adam Clayton Powell, Sr. chaired the meeting, and other distinguished Harlem "Old Guard Negroes" were on the platform. By prearrangement, the supporters of the Socialist mayoral candidate, Morris Hillquit, strategically placed throughout the audience, hissed and heckled, nearly disrupting the meeting altogether. Characterizing the hecklers as "soapbox orators" who made themselves "obnoxious," the *Age* fumed about the incident in its next issue: "Even Roosevelt was insulted by these ruffians. . . . They insulted everybody, even the prominent ministers who spoke." But Socialist street orator Frank Crosswaith had a different recollection of the incident: "Roosevelt's speech was literally drowned out in a turbulent sea of cat-calls and hoots. The 'New Negro' was out of control and could not be defeated."[50] Actually the Socialist candidate lost the election, but the party gained significant recognition in Harlem, polling nearly a quarter of its votes according to an undisputed *Messenger* estimate.[51]

Black Socialists attracted considerable support from Harlem street audiences as well as in the polling places. Numbers of new black women voters may have been impressed with Grace Campbell, who ran for State Assembly from the 19th district in 1920 and received a quarter of the ballots cast. A native of Jamaica, Campbell was known for her pioneer social-service work among young black women. She worked as a parole officer for the city of New York from 1921 to 1924 and set up the Empire Friendly Shelter, a home for unwed mothers and a forerunner of the Katy Ferguson Home in Harlem. According to Richard B. Moore, Campbell used much of her own salary to start the shelter.[52] She may not have been a regular stepladder speaker, but she was a well-known public speaker, and her activities were carefully watched by federal agents. An FBI informant reported that in a 1920 campaign speech, she "made a few remarks on the need of women waking up to the fact that they are being driven to prostitution and other evils by the low scale of wages. She promised to work hard among the women, not only of her race but all of the women."[53] Despite the paucity of information available to researchers about her life and activities, Campbell obviously helped influence the direction of Harlem radicalism. In 1923 an FBI informant's report described her as a "prime mover of the African Blood Brotherhood" (ABB) in Harlem.[54]

The ABB was formed in 1919 by Nevis native Cyril Briggs, who had immigrated to the United States in 1905. Among the founding members were Harlem stepladder speakers and African Caribbeans Grace Campbell, Richard B. Moore, W. A. Domingo, and Arthur Reid. Briggs himself was not a public speaker, due to a speech impediment.[55] He worked as a journalist for the *Amsterdam News* from 1912 until 1918, when he was forced to resign after refusing to have his editorial columns censored. With the financial backing of several Harlem businesspeople, Briggs launched the monthly magazine *The Crusader* in August of 1918. The *Crusader* and Randolph and Owen's *Messenger* were important repositories for stepladder speakers' ideas.

The ABB was a secret fraternal order whose aim was armed self-defense, the struggle for equal rights, and self-determination. It was one of the first Harlem-based organizations to affiliate with the new American Communist Party. Briggs and most of the ABB charter members, including Moore and Campbell, became Communists. Membership in the ABB remained relatively small nationwide, though chapters were set up in major urban centers. Campbell's involvement and apparent leadership rule in this predominantly male self-defense organization need further investigation. ABB recruits included native-born World War I veterans as well as workers in the building trades—plumbers, electricians, and bricklayers. The federal government charged that in the Tulsa riot of June 1921, when white mobs attacked the black community, the local chapter of the ABB played a leading role in the armed resistance of black neighborhoods.[56]

Just after the Tulsa riot, ABB speakers in Harlem passed out fliers inviting "every Negro tired of lynching and peonage, jim crowism, and disfranchisement to come out and hear our plan of action to remove these injustices which we suffer with others. You have nothing to lose but your chains. You have your liberation to achieve." "Our aim," W. A. Domingo said from a stepladder platform, "is to allow those who attack us to choose the weapons. If it be guns, we will reply with guns."[57] This very practical notion about self-defense was simply a reflection of what African Americans had demonstrated in Tulsa and elsewhere between 1917 and 1921.

If these years witnessed the most militant performances on Harlem streets, by 1921 very clear ideological differences had taken shape. Communists, Socialists, Nationalists, freelancers, and educators provided street audiences with an eclectic menu, usually at agreed-upon street corner locations. Disputed spaces occasionally resulted in street fights, though just as often the ideological battles took place in newspapers, magazines, and journals. By 1922 disputes reflected ethnic antagonisms as well as ideological differences.

One of the speakers who became involved in such disputes was W. A. Domingo, who arrived in New York in 1912 from Boston, where he had spent the last two years. In Harlem, Domingo resumed his political activities and journalistic interests which he had begun while still in Jamaica. He landed a job as a post office clerk and organized the Jamaica Benevolent Association in 1917. Between 1912 and 1916 Domingo met and formed a close political association with Randolph, Owen, Moore, Campbell, and other Socialists. Later he joined the Socialist Speakers Bureau and took part in the Peoples Educational Forum. Unlike most of the other Caribbean Socialists, Domingo did not join the Communist party. At some point in the early 1920s he left his post office job and started a business as a successful importer of Caribbean foods, mostly fresh vegetables and fruits. Of all the Harlem radicals, Domingo was probably the most financially secure. The stereotypical description of a Harlem radical as "an over-educated West Indian without a job" never applied to him.

While he still had his post office job, Domingo came to work for Marcus Garvey as the first editor of the *Negro World,* which Domingo used in part to spread Socialist ideas. The two parted in 1919 over Domingo's editorials, which were not in keeping with the program of the UNIA. Domingo also claimed he refused to write editorials and make street corner speeches in support of Garvey's Black Star Line.[58] When Garvey arrived in New York in 1916, he sought out Domingo, whom he had known in Jamaica. Apparently Domingo helped Garvey make contacts for his fledgling organization and perhaps helped to set up some initial speaking engagements. Garvey eventually became one of Harlem's most popular street corner speakers before the organization moved to Liberty Hall, but his first speaking date was a disaster. According to an account written by Domingo, Garvey arranged a lecture at St. Mark's Church Hall in May 1916.

> Shaking like an aspen leaf and with a tremor in his voice he started to deliver his oration. He hadn't gone very far when the audience began to vent its disgust by whistling and hooting. . . . He looked around in affright and pulling a manuscript from his pocket began to read. The more he read the great[er] was the din created by the audience.

Despite the sympathy of several supporters Garvey apparently could not continue and in his nervousness lost his balance and "fell off the stage and lay prostrate on the floor."[59] But Garvey—perhaps ill on this occasion—apparently recovered quickly. A. Philip Randolph, who claimed to have presented Garvey to his first public forum on 135th and Lenox Avenue in 1916, gave a conflicting account of the speaker's abilities. "Garvey got up on the platform and you could hear him from 135th to 125th Street. He had a tremendous voice."[60] James Weldon Johnson reported that Hubert Harrison's 1917 meeting was "Harlem's first real sight of Garvey, and his first real chance at Harlem. The man spoke and his magnetic personality, torrential eloquence, and intuitive knowledge of crowd psychology were all brought into play. He swept the audience along with him."[61] By 1919 the UNIA leader had established himself as one of the most exciting street corner speakers in the community. His emphasis on economic nationalism and race pride appealed to listeners. Furthermore, Garvey appeared to have a concrete program in the Black Star Line and the Negro Factories Corporation. The UNIA's community connections with local churches and with the fraternal orders, plus the pageantry and regalia of its activities, attracted broad-based audiences to Garvey's stepladder. John E. Bruce, a Garvey supporter, claimed "his street corner audiences were larger than those of the Socialist orators on the other corners a few blocks away, and they stayed longer."[62] Bruce became involved in the movement after hearing Garvey speak from a street corner.

By 1920, criticizing Garvey from the street corner must have required tact and possibly police protection. Garvey supporters threatened at least two preachers from the relative safety of their pulpits. Toward the end of August 1920, the *Age* reported an incident in which the nationally known Baptist minister Rev. Charles S. Morris of Norfolk, Virginia, had to be escorted to his lodgings by police when he spoke against Garvey during a revival meeting at the Abyssinian Church tent, located on the future site of the new 138th Street structure. The Abyssinian meeting coincided with the UNIA convention being held at Liberty Hall just next door. According to the *Age,* the demonstration against Morris became "so violent and the threats so earnest" that he had to be taken to his stopping place on 134th Street by an alternate route. However, Morris's host, Abyssinian pastor Powell, Sr., refused to exit by this route. Instead, he walked through the crowd, ignoring the insults.[63]

Garvey's loyalists may have been devoted to the image of an early militant UNIA leader who, like other stepladder speakers, demanded equal rights in America. But by 1921 he retreated politically, making some alliances which were interpreted as reactionary by many both in and outside the stepladder community. His highly publicized meeting with the Grand Wizard of the KKK in the summer of 1922 set off an explosion of criticism from a variety of fronts. All of the 1917 radicals—including the Caribbean Socialists and Communists—who had earlier been associated in one way or another with the organization in Harlem denounced Garvey as a "demagogue" or charlatan. But native black critics also labeled him as a "foreigner" and his followers as "ignorant West Indian Negroes."[64] A series of vituperative public exchanges between native and foreign-born radicals ensued. . . .

Harlem's nationalists, many of them Garveyites, created their own stepladder discourse. After Garvey's incarceration in 1925 and subsequent deportation in 1927, nationalist street speakers emerged as community leaders in their own right. Their Harlem-based street meetings focused much of their rhetoric on local issues. Jamaican St. William Wellington Grant, head of Harlem's local Tiger Division, claimed Lenox Avenue between 133rd and 135th Streets as UNIA territory. The Garveyites often appeared in paramilitary dress, carrying parade muskets and sabers and advocating a militaristic approach to black nationalism. A number of violent confrontations with Communists, the Harlem police, and even the rival Garvey Club occurred during their open-air meetings.[65]

Meanwhile, the stepladder meetings were increasingly connected with larger organizational movements. The labor organization was one of the most important outgrowths of the street meetings. Barbadian Moore and Virgin Islander Crosswaith were two of the better-known speakers who became worker advocates. Moore was also active in the Communist party's International Labor Defense and the Negro Labor Congress, but Crosswaith strictly avoided any Communist affiliation. As the activist head of the Harlem Tenants League, Moore was instrumental in using strikes to halt huge rental increases and to improve housing conditions in the 1920s. The strikes were aimed at both white and black landlords whose names he cited on the stepladder. Moore's Harlem Tenants League met each Monday evening at the 135th Street branch of the public library until library officials, unnerved by the militant tone of the meetings, refused to allow any further gatherings. Undaunted, members moved to another location, vowing to "make the rent gouging landlords squirm." The League targeted St. Philips Corporation and black millionaire Watt Terry in their campaign against Harlem slumlords.[66] Moore was a skillful orator, and audiences often came to street corners just to hear him. When fellow Communist Harry Haywood first heard Moore speak at an indoor meeting, "he brought the house down with an impassioned speech. . . . I had never heard such oratory."[67]

Frank R. Crosswaith was also one of the most polished orators in any setting. He traveled widely and became the most recognized stepladder speaker outside of Harlem. "In Chicago, in Saint Louis, in Denver, and in San Francisco his great booming voice is known even as it is on the corner of Seventh Avenue and 137th Street."[68] Born in Frederiksted, St. Croix, Danish West Indies, in 1892, he came to New York City as a teenager, enlisted as a sailor in the U.S. Navy, and later worked as a porter and as a garment worker. He aspired to go to law school, but involvements in the labor and Socialist movements in Harlem cost him his job and his plans. In 1917 he took to the street corners. Always smartly attired—boutonniere in his coat lapel, white scarf about his neck, clothes faultlessly pressed—he was known as "a Negro Debs."[69] According to the *Amsterdam News,* during the campaign season Crosswaith, who frequently ran for political office on the Socialist ticket, nightly drew the largest outdoor crowds.[70]

In Harlem Crosswaith organized the elevator operators, elevator constructors, mechanics, barbers, laundry workers, and motion picture operators. Politically, Crosswaith distinguished himself from some stepladder speakers by his willingness to work with mainstream labor and black establishment groups. He was a general organizer of the International Ladies Garment Workers Union and was instrumental, with the NAACP and Urban League, in increasing black women's numbers in that union, particularly after 1929. In 1925 he organized the Negro Labor Committee in order to get more black workers into predominantly white labor unions.

But while Crosswaith was willing to make alliances with black establishment organizations, he readily excoriated black as well as white landlords who exploited residents. In support of tenant organizing he wrote that "certainly it is utterly absurd to claim because Negro landlords are securing exorbitant rents from Negro tenants and are growing wealthy that fact should be the yardstick by which the race's progress should be measured. . . . Social and economic progress never comes through a parasitical class as such."[71]

One of the lasting labor outcomes of the street corner brigade was the formation of the Brotherhood of Sleeping Car Porters and Maids. Pullman porters approached A. Philip Randolph, who helped launch the organization on August 25, 1925. Virgin Islander and porter Ashley Totten talked to Randolph about leading the new union because Randolph was not a porter and subject to dismissal by the Pullman Company. Pullman porters also knew Randolph by reputation as a street corner speaker and editor of the *Messenger.* Porters were among the most reliable agents for the magazine. There is a suggestion also that Totten approached Randolph to head the national union because he was an American-born black whose right to leadership would not easily be challenged by anyone biased against the leadership of foreign blacks.[72] Moreover, the labor union, comprised of many native blacks and immigrants living in New York and elsewhere on the East Coast, was a good example of intragroup cooperation and was hailed by all sectors of the community. Crosswaith later claimed that in the union's "fierce but fascinating fight, the question of birthplace plays no part in one man's estimate of the other."[73]

But street speakers were perceived as a growing threat to some in the community. By the mid-1920s arrests, and therefore threats to street orators' First Amendment rights, increased. In September of 1926 police arrested Richard B. Moore on charges of "speaking without a permit" and disturbing the peace. In addition to his work with the Harlem Tenants League, Moore also headed a group which had been distributing handbills in Harlem calling upon residents to fight police "terrorism." On the evening of Moore's arrest, a crowd of 2,000 gathered to hear the stepladder veteran and his comrades speak in front of the Lafayette Theater in support of striking motion picture operators. When Moore refused to stop talking upon police orders, officers drove an automobile into the crowd. No one was reported injured, but Moore and his companions stood their ground and were taken to jail and fined $10 each.[74]

Supporters viewed Moore's arrest as not only a violation of free speech, but part of the general atmosphere of police suppression of the community. A meeting of 500 gathered at Liberty Hall in protest. The *Amsterdam News* reported that before the Moore incident, a group of Harlem citizens met at Abyssinian Baptist Church to draft a letter to the mayor requesting that street speakers be barred in Harlem. This action was believed to have been motivated by an attempt to prevent speakers from criticizing political candidates in the coming election. Hubert Harrison charged Harlem politicians with using their office to protect "crooks and criminals" while failing to protect law-abiding residents.[75] Socialist A. Philip Randolph, who had parted with Moore over the issue of Communism, nonetheless editorialized in the *Messenger* that "things are coming to a pretty pass in Harlem when a man or woman is hustled off to jail on some trumped charge of disorderly conduct or blocking traffic."[76] Communist community leader and school teacher Williana J. Burroughs, who, with Grace Campbell and others, formed a committee in support of the street meetings, sent out letters urging residents to preserve the gatherings at all costs, describing them as "the chief agency for spreading the leaven of improvement."[77]

The story of Harlem's female activists, immigrant and native, awaits a fuller investigation, but there are indications that they, like women in other African American movements, were key organizers behind the more public performances of male colleagues. But they also participated in predominantly or exclusively female groups. Williana J. Burroughs, Hendrickson, and Campbell were involved in a network of Harlem community organizations. Hendrickson's work with the American West Indian Ladies Aid Society and the Virgin Islands Catholic Relief Organization has already been mentioned. Although Campbell, Audley Moore, and others became active in the Communist party during the late 1920s and early 1930s, their concerns appear to have been rooted in the practical needs of the community. This approach, rather than a commitment to party dogma, brought Grace Campbell into conflict with male leadership in the 1930s. According to a Claude McKay account, Campbell favored the establishment of cooperative stores run by working-class Harlemites as a solution to unemployment and to establish community control of commercial development. When introducing the proposal to a Harlem audience, "Miss Campbell made a simple, earnest speech and the audience was moved. But when she had finished speaking, Comrade leader James W. Ford took the floor and declared that real Communists could not support their own comrade's scheme because it was not Communist enough!"[78]

Audley Moore, seldom modest about her own considerable abilities, asserted that although "I was little people, I was enthusiastic about my freedom and I could organize. That was the reason the Communists found it hard to deal with me, because I was such a great organizer. I was the best organizer they ever had."[79] Moore, whose politics shifted from the Garvey Movement to the

Republican party and then to the Communists, claimed she inducted a reluctant Adam Clayton Powell, Jr. into the activism. As an initiator of the Harlem jobs campaign, Moore sought a committee of "respected Harlem leaders" to negotiate with Harlem's business community. "I went to [Powell] and asked him would he head my job campaign. He said, 'Oh, I'm too busy.' 'Oh, Reverend Powell, you don't have to do a thing, just say, "yes." I'll organize the committee, if you say you'll head it.'" Moore claimed she got Rev. William Lloyd Imes to co-chair the committee and Arnold Johnson [probably John H. Johnson] to serve as secretary. Powell made Moore captain of the picket line. Once initiated, Moore claimed, "You never saw anybody develop so quickly in the struggle as Adam Powell did."[80] Moore also claimed she inaugurated the Association of Colored Women's Clubs, an organization of middle-class women, of which she was a member, into labor consciousness. "Under communist influence" she got them to establish a labor committee, "a thing they'd never thought of before."[81]

The speakers who took to the streets after the mid-1920s were perhaps less polished than the 1917 radicals. These speakers "knew their audiences like a rent party piano player knew his dancers," wrote Harlem writer Wallace Thurman.[82] The passage of time saw an increase in African American leaders' complaints about the influence of stepladder speakers. This objection to "soapboxers" grew throughout the 1920s, when street meetings often became violent and individuals McKay characterized as "rough men of the street" took up the tradition. In 1928 one Amsterdam *News* reader wanted such speakers, whom he characterized as "enemies of the race," removed from the streets:

> Can you use the influence of your newspaper to drive from the sidewalks of Harlem the crop of ignorant stepladder orators that has infested it? As one stops to listen, one hears the most ridiculous misstatements of facts of history and government, of science and geography, of art and literature imaginable. Yet these impostors are able to attract audiences. If the audience, as well as the would-be leaders and orators, would avail of the evening high schools in and near Harlem, they would easily secure truthful information.[83]

Crosswaith identified the critics of stepladder radicals as the "best people of the community"—politicians, preachers, and landlords. "As the radicals relentlessly pressed forward, the old and contented crowd became desperate. Frantically they raised the false alarm of 'foreigners.'"[84]

But the popularity of the tradition carried over into the 1930s, and while federal and local authorities continued to keep an eye on their gatherings, during the depression Evangeline Pollard claimed that stepladder speakers were "the nearest thing to leadership the Harlem community seems to have."[85] As leaders they continued to function most effectively outside traditional forums. The new breed included the flamboyant, turbaned, emerald-robed organizer of the Jobs for Negroes Campaign American-born Sufi Abdul Hamid. Jamaican Arthur Reid and southern migrant Ira Kemp were partners and organizers of the grass roots Harlem Labor Union. Kemp and his mentor Reid made quite a pair on Harlem streets. Reid, master of inflammatory invective, had an "unfailing talent for arousing Negroes to action." A native of Macon, Georgia, Ira Kemp was "a redoubtable soapbox orator who inveighed against landlords and high rents, the sale of rotten meats in Harlem, police brutality, and the prevalence of prostitution in certain sections of the community, and many other evils in the Negro district." While meetings flourished on 135th Street and Lenox and 137th and Seventh in the 1930s, open-air gatherings were increasingly staged in front of white-owned businesses targeted as discriminatory in employment or otherwise a "menace" to the community. In addition an entirely new thrust in stepladder oratory revolved around the Italian occupation of Ethiopia in 1936.[86]

We have seen that stepladder speaking linked the immigrant speakers to the native-black community, who could accept or reject their discourse on the spot. But speakers' connections to Harlem's Caribbean community are important to note as well. Immigrant speakers' affiliations provide information about the kind of often ethnically based social environments that sustained them. For instance, Socialist meetings were held at Caribbean immigrant Martin Luther Campbell's Tailor Shop, and the first meeting place of the African Blood Brotherhood was at the brownstone lodge building owned by the American West Indian Benevolent Association at 149 West 136th Street. Ethelred Brown had also held the first meetings of his Harlem Community church in the rooms of the 136th Street association. In 1917 Jamaican W. A. Domingo was a founder of the Jamaican Benevolent Association, which had its own headquarters. Several Virgin Island associations, including Hendrickson's American West Indian Ladies Aid Society were part of the social network in which activists operated. In addition, correspondence files of other Caribbean benevolent associations show a connection between their officers, particularly female officers, and progressive community causes supported by stepladder speakers. There was also a clear connection between stepladder speakers, Harlem Caribbean organizations, and the anticolonial movements which expanded in the Caribbean after 1930.

In Harlem stepladder speakers' legacy lay in a number of key areas. They introduced an alternative politics, whether in more structured movements like those of the Socialists, Communists, or nationalist UNIA or simply by giving voice to the basic concerns of the community. Speakers like Hubert Harrison challenged Eurocentric history and provided ordinary Harlemites with the first information they had ever heard about the African past. Street speakers most effectively introduced protest tactics, the boycott, demonstration, and the protest rally tactics taken up by twentieth-century African American social movements. The concept of protracted agitation—"bughousing" the power structure and "respectable Negroes"—helped alter strategies of conventional politicians and perhaps made them more responsive to community concerns. By the 1940s the methods of the street speakers were being utilized by candidates for electoral office, who harangued crowds from 125th Street and Seventh Avenue. Perhaps the tactics employed by Harlem's first congressman, Adam Clayton Powell, Jr., best illustrate the "leavening" of traditional politics. WPA researcher Sadie Hall wrote that Powell "moved the soapbox into the church" or, more accurately, moved the church into the street.[87] In 1938 Powell started a column in the *Amsterdam News* entitled "Soapbox," thus helping to legitimize the "tell it like it is" approach for those Harlemites who may earlier have dismissed the practice as a tool of the rabble-rouser. Stepladder speakers influenced growing numbers of community activists. By the mid-1920s Tyrell Wilson saw that he could do little for his race through the Seventh-day Adventist Church structure and, disillusioned by his unsuccessful search for a decent job, joined the Socialist brigade in Harlem. He recalled being greatly impressed by Socialist A. Philip Randolph and Communist Richard B. Moore. By 1929 Wilson was a "full-fledged activist for the poor generally and the blacks particularly."[88]

Historians have rarely treated the street corner in black communities as an institutionalized location for the proliferation of political ideas, although sociologists and anthropologists have focused on it as a particularly vital locality for a study of grass roots urban culture. Indeed the oral nature of the often unrecorded street meeting and the transient and unidentified audiences make it difficult to document or define the street corner meeting as a historical institution. But by 1930 Harlem street corners became the sites of regular meetings with identifiable speakers and locations. Moreover, sidewalk locations became the sites of two merging traditions carried by black immigrants and southern migrants whose most effective organizing technique was their direct contact with their audiences. This kind of organizing did not require a pulpit, newspaper, or meeting hall, though all of these forums came to be tools of the most successful street speakers. Only inclement weather or the Harlem police stood between the speaker and his or her audience.[89] Caribbean speakers gained an acceptance from native-born audiences and the audiences shaped their politics as well. But in the shaping of the stepladder tradition, birthplace was not an irrelevant issue; critics stereotyped many speakers as "foreign rabble-rousers." And particularly during Marcus Garvey's most controversial Harlem period, even the radicals themselves failed to rise above ethnic divisions.

Notes

1. Jervis Anderson, *A. Philip Randolph: A Biographical Portrait* (New York: Harvest, 1972), p. 77.

2. *New York News,* 1926. Clipping, Gumby Collection, Columbia University, n.d.

3. Richard B. Moore, "Afro-Americans and Radical Politics," in Joyce Moore Turner and Burghardt Turner, *Richard B. Moore: Caribbean Militants in Harlem* (Bloomington: Indiana University Press, 1988), p. 217.

4. Claude McKay, *Harlem: Negro Metropolis* (New York: E. P. Dutton & Company, Inc., 1940), p. 192.

5. Audley Moore, interview conducted by the Black Women's Oral History Project, Schlesinger Library, Radcliffe College, p. 23.

6. Harry Robinson, "West Indians in New York," (WPA Research Paper, SCRBC).

7. A list of Harlem's female radicals remains incomplete, as does biographical information about women whose names recur in the literature. More information about the following women's activities may help us understand distinctions between female and male activism in this period: Helen Holman, Layle Lane, Hermie Huiswood, Williana Burroughs, Anna Brown, Claudia Jones, Elizabeth Hendrickson, Grace Campbell, Maude White, Marie Houston, Bonita Williams, Louise Thompson, Audley Moore, and others. See Mark Naison, *Communists in Harlem during the Depression* (Urbana: University of Illinois Press, 1983); Philip S. Foner, *American Socialism and Black Americans: from the Age of Jackson to World War II* (Westport, Connecticut: Greenwood Press, 1977); Angela Davis, *Women, Race and Class* (New York: Random House, 1981).

8. "In Chicago the street university centered around Washington Park and State Street. Here Noble Drew Ali recruited many of the ten-thousand member Peace Movement of Ethiopia followers. Scores of Garveyites, Communists, Socialists, and black labor organizers could be found haranguing crowds along Southside Chicago Streets." Gary Hunter, "Don't Buy from Where You Can't Work: The Jobs for Negroes Campaign of the 1930s" (Ph.D. diss., University of Michigan, 1977), p. 35.

9. *New York News,* August 28, 1926.

10. A. Philip Randolph, quoted in Anderson, *A. Philip Randolph,* p. 77.

11. *New York News,* August 28, 1926.

12. Frank Crosswaith, "The Newer Negro," *Vanguard Press,* July 1928, Clipping in Vertical File, Schomburg Collection; "New Negro" was a term the World War I generation applied to themselves, a generation attempting to make a clean and permanent break with past censorship of free expression and the councils of accommodation. See Alain Locke, *The New Negro* (1925. Reprint, New York: Atheneum, 1060), pp. 7-8.

13. *Harlem Magazine,* December 1916, quoted in Anderson, p. 77.

14. Claude McKay, *A Long Way from Home,* (New York: Lee Furman, 1937), p. 41; *New York News,* August 28, 1926.

15. Charles W. Anderson to Booker T. Washington, September 10, 1911, in Booker T. Washington Papers, Box 52, Library of Congress.

16. Charles W. Anderson to Washington, October 30, 1911, in Ibid.

17. Foner, *American Socialism and Black Americans,* p. 206. Foner quotes from Samuel M. Romansky to Julius Gerber, New York, October 12, 1911, in Local New York Socialist Party Papers, Tamiment Institute, Bobst Library, New York University.

18. Anderson to Booker T. Washington, in Washington Papers.

19. Quoted by Wilfred Samuels, "Hubert Harrison and the 'New Negro Manhood Movement,'" *Afro-Americans in New York Life and History* (January 1981), p. 34. According to J. A. Rogers, Harrison used to come to blows with Irish Catholics when he lectured on New York street corners on birth control. J. A. Rogers, "Hubert Harrison" (WPA Biography, 1939, SCRBC).

20. Wilfred Samuels, "Hubert Harrison," p. 32.

21. Elinor Des Verney Sinnette, *Arthur Alfonso Schomburg, Black Bibliophile and Collector* (Detroit: New York Public Library and Wayne State University Press, 1989), pp. 36, 126.

22. Richard B. Moore, "Africa Conscious Harlem," in John Henrik Clarke, *Harlem USA* (New York: Collier, 1964), pp. 37–38; Elinor Des Verney Sinnette, p. 86.

23. Hubert Harrison, "A Tender Point," in Hubert H. Harrison, *When Africa Awakes* (New York: Porro Press, 1920), p. 86.

24. J. A. Rogers, "Hubert Harrison"; *NYAN,* February 3, 1923.

25. According to the *Pittsburgh Courier,* December 31, 1927, Harrison was hired by Columbia as a lecturer on contemporary civilization in that year; Rogers, "Hubert Harrison"; McKay, A *Long Way from Home,* p. 113.

26. Harrison to Pickens, n.d., in Pickens Papers, SCRBC.

27. *Boston Chronicle,* December 31, 1927.

28. *Negro World,* December 31, 1927.

29. *Pittsburgh Courier,* December 31, 1927.

30. Anderson, *A. Philip Randolph: A Biographical Portrait,* p. 58.

31. Ibid., p. 61.

32. Ibid., p. 80. In 1917 Randolph and Owen became editors of the *Hotel Messenger* at the request of the Headwaiters and Sidewaiters Society, but were fired eight months later for exposing unfair practices within the Society. Two months later they launched their own monthly magazine, *The Messenger,* Anderson points out, with the financial backing of Lucille Randolph. Without her help, Anderson quotes Randolph as saying, "we could not have started the *Messenger.*" The *Messenger* became, even by the admission of its critics, one of the best-edited monthlies of the period.

33. Anderson quotes a survivor of the prewar (WWI) soapbox era, p. 78.

34. Quoted by Anderson, p. 78. Anderson also quotes a former associate of Randolph's in the Independent Political Council who "never knew him to do any work for a salary, but I never saw him without a starched collar, a carefully knotted tie, a white handkerchief in his breast pocket, and a blue serge suit that looked like he had just bought it from Brooks Brothers. It was his wife, of course. She had a good hairdressing business, and she was a sweet and motherly woman. He was lucky to have had a wife like that.

Only she could have put up with all those people he used to bring home from political meetings two, three times a week to talk till one, two, three o'clock in the mornings."

35. Anderson, Ibid. A major problem faced by Harlem radicals was the ability to finance their undertakings. Here their personal and public affiliations are important to understanding the social context in which they operated. After the loss of his post office job, Harrison apparently had personal financial problems in supporting his large family. Raising money to support his independent operations (after he cut all ties with the Socialists) was also a problem in his public undertakings. It was perhaps the Liberty League's inability to raise funds that led to its demise and, as some historians have suggested, its takeover by the UNIA's more capable financial networks. Randolph's debt to Lucille Randolph's successful hairdressing business was acknowledged by him on several occasions. Richard B. Moore's occupation as an elevator operator and later book dealer was apparently not sufficient to support a family *and* his far-ranging community activities. (See Turner and Turner, *Richard B. Moore,* p. 58). At times Ethelred Brown's earnings from his Socialist street meetings were his only income, desperately needed to support a family and an invalid wife.

36. Moore, "Afro-Americans and Radical Politics," p. 217 in Ibid. For an analysis of black Socialists' activities, see Foner, *American Socialism and Black Americans.*

37. Joyce Moore Turner, "From Barbados to Harlem," in Turner and Turner, *Richard B. Moore,* p. 30.

38. Ibid.

39. Ibid.

40. Ibid., p. 29.

41. Harrison, *When Africa Awakes,* pp. 9–10.

42. Harrison, *When Africa Awakes,* p. 63.

43. *New York Times,* May 31, 1917.

44. Ibid., May 27, 1917.

45. Ibid., June 7, 1917.

46. Ibid., July 5, 1917.

47. Ibid.

48. Harrison, *When Africa Awakes,* pp. 16–17.

49. Edwin C. Walker to Editor, *Crusader* I, no. 4 (December 1918), p. 31. Miller was actually the first black person ever nominated for Congress in New York. See Hill, *MGP* I, p. 345.

50. Frank Crosswaith, "The Newer Negro," *Vanguard Press* (July 1928). Clipping in Vertical File, SCRBC. Based on an interview with Richard B. Moore, Joyce Moore Turner has stated that Owen actually appealed for order when members of the crowd harangued and booed Roosevelt. His intent was to have Roosevelt finish his statement so that the Socialists could answer him. Turner and Turner, *Richard B. Moore,* p. 31.

51. Anderson, *A. Philip Randolph,* p. 95. *Messenger,* November 1920; Richard B. Moore, "Africa Conscious Harlem," *Freedomways* (Summer 1963), III, pp. 319–320.

52. *New York Age,* September 6, 1924; Richard B. Moore, "Afro-Americans and Radical Politics," in Turner and Turner, p. 217.

53. Hill, *MGP IV,* p. 688.

54. Hill, Ibid.

55. A friend of Briggs, Harry Haywood, a fellow Communist, noticed that he stuttered less when he was angry. On one occasion during a dispute with Garvey, who resisted Briggs's attempts to draw the UNIA into a more class-conscious political stance, the UNIA leader publicly denounced the fair-complexioned Briggs as "a white man trying to pass himself off as a Negro." Haywood recounts the following anecdote: "Friends told me that this account sent Briggs into such a rage that he mounted a soapbox at Harlem's 135th Street and Lenox Avenue and assailed Garvey for two hours without a stutter." Harry Haywood, *Black Bolshevik* (Chicago: Liberator Press, 1978), p. 127.

56. Theodore Vincent, *Black Power and the Garvey Movement* (San Francisco: Ramparts Press, 1971), p. 75. According to Vincent one ABB recruit, a Mr. White, read the *Crusader* and was so impressed that he walked all the way to New York City from South Carolina to join the movement.

57. *New York Times,* June 20, 1921.

58. Hill, *MGP* II, p. 40.

59. Hill, *MGP* I, "Account by W. A. Domingo of Marcus Garvey's St. Mark's Church Hall Lecture," pp. 191–192.

60. Anderson, *A. Philip Randolph,* p. 122.

61. James Weldon Johnson, *Black Manhattan* (1930. Reprint, New York: Atheneum, 1972), p. 253.

62. Clipping from "Bruce Grit" column in John E. Bruce papers, SCRBC.

63. *New York Age,* August 28, 1920. Morris and Powell escaped injury, but years later Ethelred Brown was not so lucky. In 1928 Brown, actually one of Garvey's milder critics, held a meeting at his church to give an "impartial assessment of the Garvey legacy" following the UNIA leader's deportation. At the session's opening, Brown began by presenting what he considered some of Garvey's weaknesses, whereupon a disappointed listener rose, approached the pulpit, clubbed the Reverend over the head with a blackjack, and quickly departed, leaving a black derby initialed P. H. as the only clue to his identity. *New York Age,* January 21, 1928.

64. Harry Haywood, *Black Bolshevik: Autobiography of an Afro-American Communist* (Chicago: Liberator Press, 1978), pp. 126–131.

65. *MGP VI,* p. 311; *NYAN,* June 26, 1929.

66. The *Harlem Liberator,* December 7, 14, and 21, 1929.

67. Haywood, *Black Bolshevik,* p. 145.

68. *NYAN,* March 2, 1935.

69. Negro Labor Committee Papers, Biographical Sketch of Frank Crosswaith, SCRBC; *NYAN,* March 2, 1935. In 1930 Crosswaith was also in demand by progressive church groups. The Students Literary and Debating League invited him to Brooklyn's Trinity Baptist Church. "So insistent have been the entreaties for Mr. Crosswaith to

speak since last he spoke under the auspices of the League . . . that it has actually taken on the form of a demand; therefore, in order not to disappoint the public the meeting was arranged by the officers of the club." *NYAN,* October 22, 1930.

70. *NYAN,* March 2, 1935.

71. *Boston Chronicle,* August 4, 1928.

72. Anderson, A. *Philip Randolph,* p. 154; see the Civic (August 1955), organ of the American Virgin Islands Civic Association, for more information on Totten.

73. Crosswaith, "The Newer Negro," *Vanguard,* July 1928.

74. *NYAN,* September 19, 1926.

75. *NYAN,* September 29, 1926.

76. A. Philip Randolph, "Free Speech in Harlem," *Messenger,* November 1926.

77. Williana J. Burroughs to Dear Friend, October 4, 1926, in Gumby Clipping Collection, Columbia University; Naison, *Communists in Harlem during the Depression,* p. 53.

78. Claude McKay, *Long Way from Home,* p. 224. A concern with pragmatic solutions and methods appears to have been at the core of other women's activism as well. Caribbean immigrant and radical Bonita Williams and southern migrant Audley Moore were "effective street speakers who could argue for Communist policies in the cadence of the Garvey movement and the church," notes historian Mark Naison. During the jobs campaign Bonita Williams led a "flying squad of black housewives . . . through the streets of Harlem demanding that butchers lower their prices by 25 percent." According to a *Daily Worker* account: "So great was the sense of power of the workers that when butchers agreed to cut prices, housewives jumped on tables in front of stores and tore down old price signs and put up new ones. . . . No store held out for more than five minutes after the pickets arrived." From *Daily Worker,* June 3, 1935, pp. 136, 149.

79. Audley Moore, interview, BWOHP (Schlesinger Library), p. 33.

80. Audley Moore, Ibid., p. 24. Powell had been involved in community activism previously, but Moore's account is interesting for its revelations about the strategy used by some women activists in selecting well-known ministers to "head" community-initiated movements.

81. Audley Moore, Ibid.

82. Wallace Thurman, "Odd Jobs in Harlem," typescript, Thurman Papers, James Weldon Johnson Collection, Yale University.

83. *NYAN,* August 8, 1928, p. 192. The writer Ivan Taylor was probably referring to men such as St. William Grant, a Garveyite who was involved in a number of violent clashes.

84. See Frank R. Crosswaith, "The Newer Negro," clipping dated July 1928, in Vertical File, SCRBC.

85. Pollard, "Harlem as Is," p. 132.

86. *NYAN,* November 3, 1937.

87. Sadie Hall, "Stepladder Speakers" (WPA Research Paper) SCRBC.

88. Tyrell Wilson, interview, March 7, 1978, Gordon Heights, Long Island, New York. Program of Testimonial Dinner in Honor of Tyrell S. Wilson, Sr.," May 1, 1971.

89. *New York News,* 1926. Clipping Gumby Collection

8

Denise Love Johnson

Black Neighborhood Formation in Poughkeepsie during the Great Migration, 1950–1970

The relocation of southern blacks to the North did not necessarily occasion lasting discontinuities in the newcomers' sense of identity. This is because of the manner in which such migration occurred—from specific sending points, as extended family or community cohorts, with frequent return visits to the South—and because it often resulted in the re-creation of southern black clusters in new northern neighborhoods. The particular nature of the migration process and neighborhood concentrations of southern black residents in the Hudson Valley reinforced a sense of black communal identity. Former geography student, Denise Love Johnson, sheds light on this process in her study of Poughkeepsie, New York, during the latter decades of the twentieth century Great Migration which transported millions of African Americans from the southern to the northern reaches of the country. Based on primary source research conducted in 1972, she focuses mainly on the period between 1950 and 1970 and emphasizes the importance of kinship and regional ties in cementing late twentieth century black neighborhood formation in Poughkeepsie.

A sizeable portion of the increase in the size of Poughkeepsie's black population between 1950 and 1970 resulted from black migration from the South. The new arrivals in The Queen City were not widely dispersed in their origins, they tended to come from a precise range of sending areas in the South. Migration was aided by shared family and personal connections. This resettlement process led to the expansion of existing black neighborhoods and the creation of new black clusters in Poughkeepsie.

According to tabulations of the United States Census of Population for the years 1950, 1960, and 1970, the black population of the City of Poughkeepsie expanded by a factor of more than six during this span of twenty years from

888 to 5,876. This increased black presence was accompanied, however, by a steady decrease in the size of the white population within the city limits from 41,023 to 32,029. Between 1960 and 1970 alone, the white population of the city diminished by 16% while the black population grew by 19%.[1] Such a rapid increase in the black population in such a short period of time is partly attributable to in-migration, but where did these newcomers originate? Although quantitative evidence from 1970 reveals that most Poughkeepsie blacks were born in New York State (usually within the City of Poughkeepsie or other parts of Dutchess County), it also indicated that the largest proportion of the persons that listed different states as their birthplace were from the South. In fact, 31% of the black populace (1,809 individuals) in Poughkeepsie in 1970 was born "down home." Also, 30 of the 80 people (38%) who responded to a questionnaire of my own design named the South as their birthplace.[2]

Migration fields from the South to Poughkeepsie were not equally important. Streams of movers to the Queen City came from particular areas in the South. In trying to pinpoint the specific states, counties, and cities of the southern region of the United States that constituted the migration fields to Poughkeepsie, three basic references were used: the relocation file of the Poughkeepsie Urban Renewal Agency (PURA), the city register of deaths from 1882–1972, and my questionnaire. These sources were augmented by interviews I conducted with Poughkeepsie residents, black and white. Calculations based on this data indicated several things concerning the migration from the South to Poughkeepsie. A total of 565 persons specified places of birth in the South. On a regional level, an overwhelming majority of black migrants came from the South Atlantic section of the United States that includes the states of Virginia, North Carolina, Georgia, South Carolina, Florida, Maryland, and West Virginia. More specifically, nearly 90% of this number or 509 individuals were from this section of the South. Of the states comprising the South Atlantic region, Virginia and North Carolina contributed the most significant number of migrants to the city. Nearly two-thirds, 64%, or 356 individuals hailed from these two states. These findings would agree with more general census statistics relating to New York State which show that, outside of movers from the immediate areas, most nonwhite migrants to the state were born in the South Atlantic region, specifically in Virginia and North Carolina. In terms of a migration pattern, these discoveries are also in compliance with the traditional tendency of the interregional migration of blacks to follow routes nearly due north from the state of origin.[3]

It is possible to further identify the migration field of blacks to Poughkeepsie based on the 565 records comprising the database here. More than half of these files (356) listed a person's birthplace by the particular county or city (town) subdivision within the appropriate state. An analysis of these particular places disclosed that the southern to northern movement of blacks in to Poughkeepsie was highly specific in its origins. This migration apparently "appear[ed] less as

[a] generalized flow and more as intricate webs of geographic connections between small areas" when it was mapped at large scales.[4] Moreover, findings ascertained by an examination of the localities within the five major source states of the South—Virginia, North Carolina, Georgia, South Carolina and Florida—revealed that, to either a greater or a lesser degree, the migration fields for all five states were distinguishable as networks of separate communities who shared an actual or perceived propinquity to one another, with a larger and more urban area at its node.[5]

Several very good examples of this phenomenon present themselves in the instances of migration from Virginia and North Carolina. In Virginia, by locating towns on a map, I found the major specific source areas to form concentric circles around Charlottesville, namely, Columbia, Scottsville, and Palmyra in the first ring, encompassing a 10–30-mile radius; Richmond, Cumberland, Lynchburg, Staunton, Orange, Madison, and Culpepper within a 30–60-mile radius; and Petersburg, about 80 miles from the city.[6]

The Rocky Mount area of North Carolina showed similar patterns of distinctiveness. This minor city was at the middle of a string of towns that served as the primary source area for Poughkeepsie migrants from that state—Whitakers, Scotland Neck, Enfield, Greenville, and Washington. Fayetteville, North Carolina, is part of another important migration center that includes the towns of Clinton, Roseboro, Magnolia, Garland, and Southern Pines. Further investigation shows that the "boundaries" of many of these fields are contiguous to one another, sometimes apparently crossing state lines and county lines. This multicounty focus of rural migration fields for larger cities has also been reported by other scholars.[7]

In Virginia, the mapping of migration fields at the single-county level was also significant, particularly for the counties of Culpepper, Orange, Madison, Fluvanna, and Cumberland. There is a probability that the distinctiveness of migration fields at the county level in this state is attributable to the earlier occurrence of migratory movement from Virginia. This is supportive of other studies that suggest that over time, the ties between the place of origin and place of destination extend areally into regionally distinctive migration fields.[8]

The regional specificity of the sending areas from the South—at the city/town subdivision level, the multicounty level, or the single-county level—to Poughkeepsie suggests the importance of interpersonal linkages in the migration process. Indeed, conversations with residents of the city and the results of a questionnaire survey disclosed the paramount importance of kinship and friendship contacts as migration facilitators. A majority of questionnaire respondents indicated that they had received the impetus to migrate because of relatives or friends who were already living in or had lived in Poughkeepsie. Twenty-one of them or 70% learned about Poughkeepsie from either relatives or friends. Fifteen people, exactly half of southern-born respondents, pointedly stated that the reason for coming to Poughkeepsie was because of relatives already living here. The persuasiveness of relatives' and friends' testimonies regarding Poughkeepsie's attractiveness may further be reflected in the fact that 24 people or 80% of the southern migrants indicated that they had no intentions of settling any place else before coming to Poughkeepsie. Results demonstrated that most people came with their families and at some later point were joined by other relatives, usually sisters, brothers, or cousins. These findings confirm a pattern of chain migration, a process whereby "prospective migrants learn of opportunities, are provided with transportation, and have initial accommodation and employment arranged by means of primary social relationships with previous migrants" among southern migrants to Poughkeepsie—a process which has been well documented nationally in numerous case-studies.[9]

If a chain may be employed as a metaphor for migration networks, so can a grapevine. Regarding opportunities in Poughkeepsie, a grapevine of information in the South spread over time from early roots in late nineteenth-century Virginia to shoots spreading as far south as Florida in the quarter century after World War II. Reading the city register of deaths (which covers an early migration period) and both the PURA files and the questionnaire results (which covers recent migrations) revealed that Virginia and North Carolina as migration fields for Poughkeepsie remained remarkably stable for a time span of just over a century, but that the migration fields also diffused southward to adjacent areas. The earliest fields were those comprising several major cities of Virginia—Richmond (1860), Charlottesville (1873), Norfolk (1883) and Lynchburg (1884). The information field about the promise of Poughkeepsie for blacks then apparently spread to the smaller counties and towns immediately surrounding Charlottesville (in Albemarle County)—namely to Nelson County (1889) and Fluvanna County (Columbia, Virginia—1895). From here it embraced the contiguous counties of Culpepper, Madison, and Orange, Virginia (1905, 1909 and 1912, respectively). These early Virginia source areas like Culpepper County fed migration to Poughkeepsie and continued to do through 1970, but the migration waves from Virginia steadily decreased in importance from the 1930s onward as North Carolina gained primacy as a sending area. North Carolina showed very slow growth as a field in the early years, but increased in its importance as a source of migrants from the 1930s to 1970. Significantly, the first area in North Carolina to supply an important number of migrants for Poughkeepsie was Murfreesboro, a town in close proximity to Norfolk, that is, on the North Carolina-Virginia border.[10] Additionally, in plotting the major eras of in-migration to the city over time, the migration field expanded areally in a progressively southerly direction beneath North Carolina. In fact, as one travels geographically from Virginia to Florida, indications are that each additional state becoming a sending area displayed few significant proportions of migrants at first, but then gradually increased the number of movers it sent to Poughkeepsie.[11] Based on the findings of previous research on the subject of migration, evidently the information field concerning Poughkeepsie crept southward like a grapevine.

Perhaps a much taken-for-granted aspect of migration is the season of the year in which people were prone to move. Information dealing with this question was primarily obtained from the questionnaire survey. Although results demonstrated that people migrated from the South to Poughkeepsie throughout the year, it was primarily in the summer and spring when most movement occurred. The most obvious reason for this is that the weather was nice at those times and was thus conducive to easy travel. The importance of good weather in timing the migration process is even greater when one considers that it was the car that apparently provided the major means of transportation for southern migrants to Poughkeepsie, as conversations with residents seemed to indicate. Travel was easier and "passe[d] in no time" when the weather was good. Also people had time to move in spring and summer months when school was not in session and/or when many were on vacation.[12]

The frequency with which black informants mentioned late summer as their time of migration to Poughkeepsie underscores the importance of a migration fueled by personal contacts. Typically during the Great Migration, migrants who returned to their southern hometowns for visits "looking prosperous and urbane" encouraged more migration from these original sending areas.[13] In the case of Poughkeepsie, a secondary Labor Day Movement of southern blacks to the Queen City developed as resettled migrants went back down South over the Labor Day weekend—the last big warm-weather holiday of the year—to their former homes, often in large, new cars they had recently procured, and returned to Poughkeepsie with kinfolk and friends. One lady aptly described this process saying: "They go home over the Labor Day weekend and come back with carloads." A man said: "If you really want to see a sight, just be on the turnpike Labor Day and see the cars with black folks driving at night and heading for the South. . . . On the return trip, the cars will be low to the ground, filled with people."[14]

The relative spontaneity of this secondary black migration pattern is a feature that should be noted in itself, but it is also a factor underscoring the significance of personal ties for blacks who moved to Poughkeepsie.[15] Television commercials often project the image of the large moving van with all of one's personal belongings; necessarily this would imply long planning and a considerable amount of forethought given when and how the change of residence takes place. But the apparent prevalence of journeys back to the southern place of origin in the Poughkeepsie case as evidenced in such processes as the Labor Day Movement suggest instead the suddenness of moves as black migrants quickly put together a few personal belongings to join their friends and relations on the return trek north. Most likely, this was possible because of the influence of kinship and personal relationships in the migration process. As in the case of migration to Chicago from the South, the movers "relied heavily on the word of such travelers."[16] These last-minute, secondary migrants apparently felt prepared. Since so many moves were among other relatives and friends, quick decisions to move were feasible. They felt they had dependable information about their destination. They had a ready, convenient, and affordable means of transportation to their destination. And once at their destination, the receiving family could be counted on as a resource offering shelter and initial material provisions, emotional support, and job contacts.[17] Lured from the South to Poughkeepsie by friends and relatives, traveling to Poughkeepsie in transportation provided by friends and relatives, and with the promise of aid in settling in Poughkeepsie from friends and relatives, black migrants often felt comfortable about a spur-of-the-moment decision to resettle.

Once in Poughkeepsie, where did southern black migrants locate? On the whole, research suggests that there was an overall similarity in the spatial distribution of black migrants, local black movers (namely, those already living in Poughkeepsie who relocated within the city during the period studied), and the total black population in the city. Migrants sought residences in all accessible areas of the city compatible with their actual or self-perceived economic and or social status, as did the rest of the black population and no areas of exclusive black migrant concentration appeared. An analysis of the commercial city directories, city registers of deaths, and my questionnaire survey underscored that migrants usually settled in the established zones of black occupancy. Black old-timers often rented out their houses that had been generations in their family to recent migrants to the area. In the early 1970s, many of these older black neighborhoods in Poughkeepsie were characterized by a high proportion of elderly people in their 70s and 80s who had been living in those locations for two, three, and four decades. Lower Main Street, for example, which contained nearly 30% of the city's senior citizens in 1961, was described as "a Negro ghetto." This area extended west of Market Street to the Hudson River, roughly from Mill Street on the north to Pine/Montgomery Street to the south.[18] Many migrants settled here in the 1950s and 1960s.

The reasons for this pattern of black migrant settlement are several. First, the mere presence of pre-existing centers of black population concentration is indicative of well known historical forces at work that nurtured residential segregation targeted against new black arrivals—racism, racial steering by realtors, and white homeowner resistance. Those black professionals recruited from the South to the Poughkeepsie-area International Business Machines (IBM) facilities in the 1950s and early 1960s, in fact, described a pattern of "rigid residential segregation" in Poughkeepsie and Dutchess County whereby even IBM neglected to provide them with the same residential relocating services they normally offered new white employees. A survey of Poughkeepsie renters done in 1967 revealed that "discrimination" and "no vacancy" accounted for 19% of all barriers to securing new apartments for black respondents; in contrast, these reasons among white respondents amounted to only 6% of their problems. Second, the pattern of chain migration contributed to the reinforcement of clustering into black residential areas. According to this process, people often lived close to or with their relatives or friends, and were not actually desirous of living outside of this family circle for social reasons. Third, the housing stock and arrangements in these established black areas—often deteriorating—apparently absorbed the southern black influx through the years studied here for the most part due to the low-income status of many migrants. Black professionals arriving in the area from the South at the same time confirmed that the city's long-standing black population was "trapped in decaying census tracts in the city." The 1967 housing survey of Poughkeepsie renters provided evidence of this reality in two ways. The top complaint to landlords from black respondents was that of poor plumbing. In fact, many of the rental units in this Lower Main Street section were cold-water flats requiring tenants to heat water, according to one newcomer from Florida whose family came to work the nearby farms across the river as migrant labor. Also, nearly 40% of black respondents, as opposed to only 15% of white respondents, indicated that they would like to live in public housing—a measure of deep financial need in the black community of renters. All these elements worked to maintain black residential areas within specific boundaries and to push those boundaries outward at their fringes in order to accommodate the press from a swelling population.[19]

Within these black residential clusters, black migrants linked easily to other blacks, and especially to their southern-born neighbors. The migrant-to-migrant bonds within these neighborhoods were strengthened by two additional developments. Some established black residents left the neighborhood to the migrants. Seeking new housing in areas outside the ghetto, they chose to vacate their homes and rent them to the newcomers. Also, within these black neighborhoods, migrants began to establish their own institutions in the city. New churches appeared. Two local historians found that "the Holiness-Pentecostal movement, which developed out of Methodism in the late nineteenth century, also stressed an emotionalism that appealed to many migrants, particularly during the Depression and post-war year." In Poughkeepsie, three new Holiness-Pentecostal churches were formed between 1950 and 1970—Holy Light Pentecostal Church (1952), Green Chapel Overcoming Church of God (1960), and Bethel Church of God in Christ (1966).[20]

Southern migrants also settled outside of already established black clusters in Poughkeepsie. In some cases new black neighborhoods appeared when certain established black areas could not accommodate the large press of new migrants. Also housing stock deterioration in many older black areas prompted spatial expansion to new locations in the city made available by the exodus of the white population. Following the Second World War, local whites increasingly occupied new housing in suburban developments, which accompanied the movement of industries like DeLaval Milk Separator Company and IBM outside of Poughkeepsie's city limits to surrounding areas within Dutchess County. My conversations with one subject revealed that her parents had bought the Poughkeepsie house in which she lived in 1973 back in 1921. They were the only black family on the block for years, with no major turnover of whites that resided on the block until the migration between 1940 and 1970.[21] This period was the one in which the influx of southern migrants to Poughkeepsie inflated the size of the local black population and the attrition in the white populace of the city began.

Spatial expansion of the black community in Poughkeepsie as a result of southern migration therefore seems to have taken place primarily through a moderately scaled form of residential succession. Rapid in-migration of blacks and the availability of additional housing for whites outside the city sowed the foundation for this pattern. After filling up established black neighborhoods, blacks moved into housing peripheral to places where they were already heavily concentrated. This process was supported by the limited income of many migrants, real estate market practices catering to antiblack prejudices, and the dynamics of chain migration that reinforced close-knit family and friend location patterns.[22]

Evidence suggests that federally funded urban renewal and housing projects in Poughkeepsie also accounted for other black residential clusters containing black migrants. The W. W. Smith public housing project, built in 1952 on the site of the old city dump is a case in point. Designed to meet the need for more low-income housing in the city, its planners tried to establish an occupancy ratio of 55% black and 45% white. A former member of the Poughkeepsie Housing Authority agency informed me that by 1962 this ratio had increased to about 60% black and 40% white. Because of the project, this area in 1973 had a black population concentration of between 75 to 90%.[23] The timing of this racial majority shift suggests that black in-migration from the South was an explanatory factor. Also, two overwhelmingly black-occupied federal housing projects were built in the Lower Main Street vicinity in the early 1970s. One was a high-rise development, Jefferson Towers, the result of the Jefferson Street Urban Renewal Project. Tubman Terrace, a low and moderate-income low rise was constructed in this area as well. Residents of housing that had to be demolished in this area had to be relocated in other sections of the city, particularly in Census Tract 2205, Enumeration District 91. One particular block picked up the largest share of persons relocated—the block bounded by Morgan, Winnikee, Cottage, and Mansion, which in 1970 stood at 90% black as compared with significantly smaller proportions in 1960.[24]

In these ways, steady black migration from the South into Poughkeepsie shaped black neighborhood formation between 1950 and 1970. Black migrants lent their numbers to enlarging and new black residential areas. Within these neighborhoods, the migrants connected to each other through personal relationships and the new social institutions they brought with them.

Notes

1. U.S. Bureau of the Census, *U.S. Census of Population: 1950,* Vol. II, *Characteristics of the Population,* Part 32, New York, Chapter B (Washington, D.C.: U.S. Government Printing Office, 1952), p. 95; U.S. Bureau of the Census, *U.S. Census of Population:* 1960. *General Population Characteristics, New York,* Final Report PC(1)—34B (Washington, D.C.: U.S. Government Printing Office, 1961), p. 91; U.S. Bureau of the Census, *U.S. Census of Population: 1970. General Population Characteristics, New York* (Washington, D.C.: U.S. Government Printing Office, 1971), pp. 70, 124.

2. U.S. Bureau of the Census, *U.S. Census of Population: 1970. General Social and Economics Characteristics, New York* (Washington, D.C.: U.S. Government Printing Office, 1972), p. 538; Lawrence H. Mamiya and Lorraine M. Roberts, "Invisible People, Untold Stories: A Historical Overview of the Black Community in Poughkeepsie," *Dutchess County Historical Society Year Book,* Vol. 72 (1987), pp. 85, 88–89; Denise Love Johnson, "Black Migration Patterns—A Case Study of the Origin and Development of the Black Population in the City of Poughkeepsie, New York," B.A. thesis, Department of Geology and Geography, Vassar College, 1973, pp. 22–23.

3. *U.S. Census of Population: 1960.* Special Report on "Mobility of the Population-State of Residence in 1960 by Division of Residence in 1955 and Division of Birth for Population 5 Years and Over, by Age, Color, and Sex" (Washington D.C.: U.S. Government Printing Office, 1963); Daniel M. Johnson and Rex R. Campbell, *Black Migration in America: A Social Demographic History* (Durham, N.C.: Duke University Press, 1981), pp. 127–129, 131, 160–161; Mamiya and Roberts, "Invisible People," p. 89.

4. James Allen, "Migration Fields of French Canadian Immigrants to Southern Maine," *Geographical Review,* Vol. 62 (July 1972): 366–383; Poughkeepsie Housing Authority Records (PHA Records), 1965–1976, Local History Room, Adriance Memorial Library, Poughkeepsie, N.Y.; Poughkeepsie Model Cities Proposal and Program (PMC Proposal and Program), 1965–1971, Local History Room, Adriance Memorial Library, Poughkeepsie, N.Y.; Poughkeepsie Urban Renewal Agency (PURA), Queen City Urban Renewal Project N.Y.A.-22, Neighborhood Development Program, First Year Action Proposal 1971–1972, Local History Room, Adriance Memorial Library, Poughkeepsie, N.Y.; Poughkeepsie Urban Renewal Agency (PURA), The Relocation Plan, Riverview Project 1-A-N.Y.R. 166, December 1965, Local History Room, Adriance Memorial Library, Poughkeepsie, N.Y.; Register of Deaths for the City of Poughkeepsie,

1882–1972, City Chamberlain and Office of Vital Statistics, Poughkeepsie, N.Y.; Johnson, "Black Migration," p. 23 and Appendix.

5. City Register of Deaths, 1882–1972; Johnson, "Black Migration," pp. 25–27. The "nearness" of areas was also a matter of how people perceived it in several interviews. By looking on the map, I would not have considered a few places like Greenville to be in close proximity to Rocky Mount. There is a standard saying people have about the southern idea of "down the road a piece" which is certainly applicable. Since the introduction of the automobile, places have been also brought closer together in terms of perceived distances.

6. Johnson, "Black Migration," p. 27.

7. Curtis C. Roseman, as cited in Allen, "Migration Fields of French Canadian Immigrants"; Johnson, "Black Migration," pp. 27–28.

8. Ibid.

9. Johnson, "Black Migration," pp. 32–34 and Appendix; John S. MacDonald and Leatrice D. MacDonald, "Chain Migration, Ethnic Neighborhood Formation and Social Networks," *Milbank Memorial Fund* 42 (1964): 82; Sidney Goldstein, "Migration: Dynamics of the American City," *American* Quarterly, Vol. 6 (Winter 1954), pp. 337–48; Earl Lewis, "Expectations, Economic Opportunities, and Life in the Industrial Age: Black Migration to Norfolk, Virginia 1890–1945" in Joe William Trotter, Jr., ed., *The Great Migration in Historical Perspective: New Dimensions of Race, Class, and Gender* (Bloomington, Indiana: Indiana University Press, 1991), pp. 24–25; Peter Gottlieb, "Rethinking the Great Migration: A Perspective from Pittsburgh" in Trotter, *The Great Migration,* pp. 72–73; Shirley Ann Moore, "Getting There, Being There: African American Migration to Richmond, California, 1910–1945" in Trotter, *The Great Migration,* pp. 108–109; James R. Grossman, *Land of Hope: Chicago, Black Southerners, and the Great Migration* (Chicago: University of Chicago Press, 1989), pp. 66–97; Carole Mark, *Farewell, We're Good and Gone: The Great Migration* (Bloomington, Indiana: Indiana University Press, 1989), pp. 20, 24–25; Myra B. Young Armstead, *"Seeking Our Fortune in the North": The African American Population of Sullivan County, New York from 1930 to 1980* (South Fallsburg, N.Y.: The Association for the Study of Afro-American Life and History, Sullivan County Chapter, 1998), pp. 8–9.

10. PURA, Queen City Urban Renewal Project N.Y.A.-22; PURA, The Relocation Plan N.Y.R 166; Register of Deaths: Johnson, "Black Migration," pp. 35–37. Much historical literature has traced early migration (during the late nineteenth century and early twentieth century) from Virginia and North Carolina to the involvement of these states' Piedmont region in a tobacco economy, the declining profitability of tobacco cultivation for smaller farmers, and the difficulties associated with work in tobacco processing plants in this area. As examples, see Jeffrey R. Kerr-Ritchie, *Freedpeople in the Tobacco South: Virginia, 1860–1900* (Chapel Hill: University of North Carolina Press, 1999), pp. 233–241; Anthony J. Badger, *Prosperity Road: The New Deal, Tobacco, and North Carolina* (Chapel Hill: University of North Carolina Press, 1980), pp. 200–204;

and Beverly W. Jones, "Race, Sex, and Class: Black Female Tobacco Workers in Durham, North Carolina, 1920–1940" in Claire Goldberg Moses and Heidi Hartmann, eds., *U.S. Women in Struggle: A Feminist Studies Anthology* (Urbana: University of Illinois Press, 1995), pp. 134–144.

11. Johnson, "Black Migration Patterns," p. 36.

12. Johnson, "Black Migration Patterns," pp. 37–38 and Appendix; see Gottlieb, "Re-thinking the Great Migration," pp. 72–73 for a discussion of the regularity of return trips South on the part of migrants.

13. Grossman, *Land of Hope*, p. 93.

14. Johnson, "Black Migration Patterns," p. 34.

15. See a discussion of such spontaneity in Grossman, *Land of Hope*, p. 102–103. Grossman argues that apparently "reckless," hasty departures from the South were often based on information regarding life in the North that the sudden movers had been considering for some time.

16. Grossman, *Land of Hope*, p. 102; Johnson, "Black Migration," pp. 38–39.

17. See Grossman, *Land of Hope*, p. 133, for a discussion of the immediate help provided by friends and relatives to black southern newcomers to Chicago.

18. *Polk's Poughkeepsie City Directory, 1950* (Boston: R. L. Polk and Co., Inc., 1950); *Polk's Poughkeepsie City Directory, 1956* (Boston: R. L. Polk and Co., Inc. 1956); *Polk's Poughkeepsie City Directory, 1957* (Boston: R. L. Polk and Co., Inc., 1957); *Polk's Poughkeepsie City Directory, 1958* (Boston: R. L. Polk and Co., Inc. 1958); *Polk's Poughkeepsie City Directory, 1959* (Boston: R. L. Polk and Co., Inc., 1959); *Polk's Poughkeepsie City Directory, 1960* (Boston: R. L. Polk and Co., Inc. 1960); *Polk's Poughkeepsie City Directory, 1961* (Boston: R. L. Polk and Co., Inc., 1961); *Polk's Poughkeepsie City Directory, 1962* (Boston: R. L. Polk and Co., Inc., 1962); *Polk's Poughkeepsie City Directory, 1964* (Boston: R. L. Polk and Co., Inc. 1964); *Polk's Poughkeepsie City Directory, 1965* (Boston: R. L. Polk and Co., Inc. 1965); *Polk's Poughkeepsie City Directory, 1967* (Boston: R. L. Polk and Co., Inc., 1967); *Polk's Poughkeepsie City Directory, 1968* (Boston: R. L. Polk and Co., Inc., 1968); *Polk's Poughkeepsie City Directory, 1970* (Boston: R. L. Polk and Co., Inc., 1970); *Polk's Poughkeepsie City Directory, 1971* (Boston: R. L. Polk and Co., Inc., 1971); *Polk's Poughkeepsie City Directory, 1972* (Boston: R. L. Polk and Co., Inc., 1972); City Register of Deaths; Johnson, "Black Migration," maps between pp. 53 and 54, p. 54; Harvey K. Flad, "A Time of Readjustment: Urban Renewal in Poughkeepsie, 1955–75," *Dutchess County Historical Society Year Book*, Vol. 72 (1987), p. 159; Patricia Jones, interview with Myra B. Young Armstead, 26 January 2002. A similar process of a black migrant influx into pre-existing black neighborhood's on Chicago's South Side is described in Grossman, *Land of Hope, pp.* 135–138.

19. Karl and Alma Taeuber, *Negroes in Cities* (Chicago: Aldine Publishing Company, 1965); Mamiya and Roberts, "Invisible People," p. 94; City of Poughkeepsie Planning Board, Rental Housing Survey, August 1967, Local History Room, Adriance Memorial Library, Poughkeepsie, N.Y.; Jones, interview with Armstead, 26 January

2002; Flad, "A Time of Readjustment," p. 159–160; Johnson, "Black Migration," pp. 48–51; Grossman, *Land of Hope,* pp. 135–138.

20. Johnson, "Black Migration," p. 54; Mamiya and Roberts, "Invisible People," pp. 91–92. See Armstead, *Seeking Our Fotune in the North,"* pp. 8, 28–29, and Grossman, *Land of Hope,* pp. 94–95 on new church formation by black migrants to northern communities.

21. PHA Records; PURA, Queen City Urban Renewal Project N.Y.A.-22; PURA,The Relocation Plan; Mamiya and Roberts, "Invisible People," p. 94; Johnson, "Black Migration," pp. 50–55.

22. Johnson, "Black Migration," pp. 52–53.

23. Johnson, "Black Migration," pp. 55–56.

24. Johnson, "Black Migration," pp. 56–57.

9

Bruce D. Haynes

Race and Class Politics in a Black Middle-Class Suburb

Class allegiances complicated the political identities of suburban blacks in the Hudson Valley. In his study of local political behavior in a black middle-class neighborhood in Yonkers, New York, sociologist Bruce Haynes found that these blacks have actively engaged in local politics since the 1920s, maintaining leverage in both the local Democratic and Republican Parties throughout the twentieth century. Still, the racial conservatism of the national Republican Party during the era of the Civil Rights Movement led these black suburbanites to shift party loyalties and to prefer Democratic national candidates after the 1960s. Even so, at the local level these black Yonkers residents resisted city efforts to place low-income housing within their community boundaries and opposed redistricting efforts that would have placed poor blacks within their electoral boundaries. As political actors, Yonkers's African American middle-class voters increasingly evinced a double-faceted black identity, aligning with most of the country's blacks in national elections, but sometimes at odds with many grassroots race leaders within their own city. Their special circumstances caused them to carve out a singular space within the political landscape—in line with their white neighbors over standard suburban concerns regarding property values but in step with poor blacks over issues of racial equality.

The middle-class black community of Nepperhan-Runyon Heights is nestled in the northeast section of Yonkers, New York, on the banks of the Hudson River, in the southwest corner of Westchester County, just north of New York

---

Adapted from *Red Lines, Black Spaces: The Politics of Race and Space in a Middle-Class Suburb,* by Bruce D. Haynes. Copyright © 2001 by Yale University Press. Reproduced by permission of Yale University Press.

City. Firmly established by the 1920s, today Runyon Heights is home to some 1,300 predominantly black residents. The formation of the community was predicated upon residents' stable jobs and access to suburban real estate that was isolated from poorer populations. The community's survival, however, depended upon strong community solidarity, including active participation in local politics. Though physically isolated, Nepperhaners were able to wield considerable leverage in local politics. A close examination of local political behavior reveals how political loyalties and voting patterns expressed residents' race and class interests.

Negotiating the Political Infrastructure

At the turn of the century, Yonkers was organized into a ward system characterized by a strong mayoral form of government. Under this system, the mayor controlled the budget and all administrative appointments; the approval of the City Council was not required.[1] At the time Nepperhan came into existence, the City of Yonkers was divided into 12 wards, each electing a representative to the City Council. Nepperhan was originally designated as a small portion of the large Third Election District in the Tenth Ward. In 1930, Nepperhan was reassigned to the Sixth Election District of the Tenth Ward, which made the district's political boundaries closely approximate those of the community. The change had only symbolic importance for political power in Runyon Heights because the community remained within the same ward. However, aligning the district with community boundaries did make it easier for local politicians to assess voting behavior in Nepperhan and helped to carve out the area as a Negro space.

After a controversy involving the former mayor, this system was abandoned in 1940 in favor of the council-manager style of government (sometimes known as the weak-mayor system), which remained in effect until 1991.[2] The city was still divided into 12 wards, each of which elected, by majority vote, a representative to the City Council. Both the mayor and the 12 ward representatives were elected for two-year terms. The only city-wide election was for the mayor, who served on the council as member-at-large. The mayor's primary responsibilities were to appoint members of the Board of Education, vote in the City Council, and act as official head of the City. The City Manager was the chief executive and administrative officer and was appointed by the council to oversee the budget and the appointment of administrative heads. Termination of the City Manager was decided by a majority vote of the Council. The new system shifted political power to the wards and ultimately to the city council representatives; the mayor maintained control of only the school system.

Though the Runyon Heights community was first established during the era of the strong mayor, it evolved primarily during the period of political organization characterized by strong wards and weak mayors. Even under the earlier system, political patronage through the wards was an integral part of Yonkers politics.

Until the 1980s, Yonkers continued the 12-ward weak-mayor system. Following the release of the 1980 federal census, a plan was adopted in 1983 to redistrict and switch to a seven-member City Council. Under this proposal, the city would be divided into four council districts, each comprising three wards, and each electing a council member. Three additional members would be elected at large, of whom the two who received the most votes would become the mayor and vice mayor. This plan was challenged by the local NAACP on the grounds that it virtually excluded minority representation on the City Council. The plan received widespread criticism from other local groups because it gerrymandered the large working-class black area of southwest Yonkers into a predominantly white council district, thereby weakening its influence on the Council. The plan also designated Runyon Heights as a small component of a district much larger than the old ward. In response to criticism, a new redistricting plan was ordered by the courts, and in 1985 elections were held temporarily using the old 12-member ward system. The first black council person, Joseph E. Burgess, Jr., was elected to represent the First Ward, an area inhabited by black working-class and poor residents on the City's west side. In 1987, the ward system was finally abandoned in favor of the seven-member City Council system. Instead of the 1983 proposal, which created only four council districts, the 1987 plan created six districts.

Under the six-district plan, each district elected a representative to the City Council, and the Mayor was elected at large. While this new plan maintained the homogeneity of the first predominantly "minority" working-class council district in the southwest downtown area, it also placed middle-class Runyon Heights in the predominantly white and Republican Sixth Council District. In fact, the majority of the Tenth Ward and all of the Fifth Ward became part of the Sixth Council District. Compared to the old ward system, the council district system divided the political geography into larger areas, thereby increasing the relative power of each council member but diminishing the impact of the middle-class Runyon vote.

From the community's outset in the 1920s, residents of Nepperhan were involved in local government and politics. The highly organized nature of the community ensured that they would quickly learn about issues facing them and their neighbors. While residents believed that contributing their financial and intellectual resources to civic and community organizations was essential to fostering and preserving the Nepperhan enclave, they also believed that active participation in local ward politics was a critical factor in community preservation.

Active participation in local affairs became a community norm. High levels of community organization led directly to high levels of political involvement. The Runyon Heights Democratic Club was formed in June 1933. By that time, the Republican Club of Nepperhan and the Phillis Wheatley Republican Club had already been established. Historically, the Tenth Ward Republican Club was a center of political influence in local politics; Nepperhan residents supported club activities.

Between the 1940s and the 1970s, even a trip to the barber or hairdresser could be a catalyst for political action in Nepperhan. Two Nepperhan-owned beauty salons along Saw Mill River and Tuckahoe Roads catered to local women. Men often frequented Trent's Place, a makeshift barbershop in the basement of a local resident's home. These establishments not only provided practical cosmetic services but also served as a gathering place for locals. One resident recalled: "Trents, it was a very political atmosphere. You know, when you went in, they talked about what was going on in the community."

Like other residential suburban populations, Nepperhaners made full use of the electoral system. An early characteristic of Nepperhan voting was that residents were issue-driven and tended to cross traditional party lines in casting their ballots. Locally, such independence gave them leverage in closely contended mayoral and ward races. But successful involvement in local politics meant more than voting; it meant getting involved in ward and club activities. Early Nepperhaners established a tradition of active involvement that has been continued by succeeding generations. Many residents are aware of the multiple strategies that have been employed to wield political influence in Yonkers and continue to socialize new community members into the practice. One 31-year-old male resident of eight years shared his understanding of the local political scene:

> What happens is, politicians count every vote, no matter which one it is, and fortunately for us, because of the education of the folks in the neighborhood, this is something that's been there way before my time. So people are smart enough to be on both sides of the playing field. We have a Republican leader of the Tenth Ward . . . and he has a lot of networks. And a lot of the folks that live in Runyon Heights either work for the city as employees . . . so they have a lot of political savvy. They know that you have to show up at the fund raisers, and all that other kind of stuff, and that's how that works, that people are able to make phone calls and do that. . . . And now it hits them twice, because is this going to be a problem with people of color, is this going to be a problem for the NAACP, . . . or is this a problem in the neighborhood, is this a problem for Runyon Heights? And we know how to use our leverage appropriately to get the things done.

He then explained the community's political philosophy.

> The community would survive without the different organizational levels, but they wouldn't survive if they did not participate politically. If they didn't participate politically they would get left out, as everyone does when you don't participate politically. That's been the general problem for our folks is that they vote and they vote one line. They vote Democratic, but they don't look at issues. I try to educate people, you don't have to vote Democratic. You vote for the person that does, that handles your issues best, that supports the things you're looking to support. And if that person is from the New Zimbabwe Party, then you vote for them. . . . Political support doesn't mean you voted for somebody. It meant who you worked for. Because they need foot soldiers, and all that stuff, going out there, priming the pump, talking to people, delivering whatever percentage of votes, because one vote, [Mayor] Nicholas Wascizco can tell you, he won by 12 votes.

Informal channels were equally important in addressing community concerns. As one resident explained: "You network, you work for the city, you know the right people, you talk to the right people. And if you do that properly, you'll get things done, because you'll be able to pick up the phone and talk to the right person. You see the appropriate person is not always the one that's in charge. The one that's appropriate may be the one that's sitting on the truck."

Yonkers has developed its own system of political patronage that is closely linked to residential life and interpersonal ties in the city. Many of the early Nepperhaners attended school with whites whose families became important players in local government and city administration. These ties have proved useful in navigating the bureaucracy at City Hall. Milton Holst, one of the most active members of the local voluntary association, the Runyon Heights Improvement Association (RHIA), is often called the "mayor" of Runyon Heights by local residents and public officials. Holst, president of the Tenth Ward Republican Club, explained how he first got involved during the 1960s by attending city hall meetings, planning board seminars, and participating in the clubhouses and party politics. He maintains that the local district leaders are the "first line of offense" in local political battles. One woman, a former district leader, explained why she got involved: ". . . By this time, I was beginning to get a little involved into politics. I had become the district leader, but prior to that I was attending a lot of political meetings. I was interested in Malcolm X who I knew and his words were the words that I felt and I felt that I could make a contribution in Runyon Heights."

These leaders, who have resided in the community since the late 1920s, represent an aging cohort of extremely active residents. Indeed, many oldtimers have expressed concern over the aging of its organizational base.

The Infusion of Race Politics in Yonkers

Though early residents supported both Democratic and Republican political clubs, initially Nepperhaners were predominantly Republican. Voter registration records reveal the early Republican leanings of the black population in Nepperhan.[3] In 1930,77% of the Nepperhan residents were registered Republicans.[4] This may reflect the traditional GOP commitment that many black Americans held following the Civil War, or it may have reflected a typically conservative suburban insularity. Since President Truman solidified the black vote through his civil rights campaign of 1948, black Americans have maintained a predominantly Democratic affiliation and have overwhelmingly voted for Democratic candidates both locally and nationally, save for a few local Republican enclaves.[5] Nepperhan remained supportive of the GOP ticket well into the 1960s. As we shall see, Nepperhan voting behavior is explained neither by Republican traditionalism nor by blind allegiance to post-New Deal Democratic party liberalism.

While the total number of registered Republicans in Nepperhan grew from 189 in 1930 to 223 in 1940, the percentage of Republicans actually fell, from 77% to 57%. Democrats entered the community at a rate of more than two to one. Nevertheless, the community remained predominantly Republican into the mid-1960s, a period when many black Americans had become solid supporters of the Democratic Party. In fact, in contrast to national trends in black voting behavior, the largest aggregate increase in the number of registered Republicans in Runyon Heights occurred between 1950 and 1960; 56 registered Republicans while only nine joined the Democrats. One woman explained, "When I registered to vote Republican, it was back in the Eisenhower years." Her comment echoes those of a number of older residents who claimed that they were "Eisenhower Republicans."

Within a decade the racial climate of the nation was reflected in local community registration patterns. Residents slowly began to turn away from the GOP; newer voters increasingly registered Democrat. Between 1960 and 1970, the percentage of Republicans declined by 11% while Democratic registration grew by 91%. Despite this trend, 41% of the voters remained Republican in 1970. During the 1970s, some older residents began shifting party affiliation and retreating from the GOP. The total number of voters declined by 14%, while Republican registration declined by 44%; the Democratic ranks dipped only slightly, by 8%. For the first time, the majority of voters were now registered Democrats.

The 1980s witnessed further erosion in Republican support. As of this writing there are only 99 registered Republicans, a meager 16% of the voters, the weakest Republican registration in the history of Nepperhan. Significantly, 11% of the voters are not currently affiliated with any party, while the Conservative party has seen a small growth of 2%.

The early pattern of heavy Republican registration begs the question: "Did Nepperhaners vote for Republican candidates?" Did residents follow the post-World War II middle-class pattern of Republican patronage typical of white suburbs, or did they support the Democratic Party, as much of black America has done since the 1930s? Our analysis suggests that Runyon Heights residents did both: they voted to protect their material interests as well as their racial group interests.

Republican sympathies reflected in party affiliation were also extended to residents' support for early GOP presidential candidates. While Republican registration reached a peak of 60% in 1960, 69% of the district actually voted for the Republican Eisenhower/Nixon ticket in 1956. In 1960, the Republican Nixon/Lodge ticket received 51% of the community's vote.

Until 1964, the Sixth Election District, namely, Runyon Heights, supported the GOP at roughly the same rate as the rest of Ward 10 and the City of Yonkers.[6] The 1964 presidential election brought an abrupt change to this pattern. Debates over the passage of the Civil Rights Act, the liberalization of the Democratic Party, and Republican intolerance on the question of race shifted Nepperhan voters' political support away from GOP candidates. Voters concluded overwhelmingly that the liberal agenda was in their interest. The conservative Goldwater and Miller, running on the GOP ticket, received 39% of the city's vote but only 9% of the community's vote. The Liberal/Democrats, Johnson and Humphrey, received 92% of the Nepperhan vote, but only 62% of the city's patronage. For the first time, the voting behavior of Runyon Heights residents deviated significantly from that of Yonkers residents in a national election.

This trend toward support of Democratic presidential candidates continued. In 1968, the Republican team of Nixon and Agnew did gain ground, capturing 17% of the Sixth District's vote, although this was a far cry from the 51% Nixon marshaled in 1960. The Liberal/Democratic team of Humphrey and Muskie still claimed 82% of the vote. During this period we can observe a lag between party affiliation and voter preference. Although at least 41% of the community was still registered Republican, many supported liberal candidates. Republicans continued to receive appreciable support in the Tenth Ward and in Yonkers, 49% and 48%, respectively.

The 1980 presidential election continued the pattern. The Conservative/Republican Reagan/Bush team received only 15% of the Sixth District's vote, while Democrats Carter and Mondale received 83%. For Nepperhan-Runyon Heights voters, middle-class suburban issues like crime, schools, taxes, and the quality of life were overshadowed by concern with trends in national policy on race. Despite the material interest of this middle-class suburb, residents have become increasingly liberal in their voting behavior since Goldwater transformed the GOP in 1964.

During the 1990s, race became a central issue in American politics, as conservatives attacked both social welfare policy and affirmative action, and charged that the liberalism of the 1960s created today's problems of unemployment, teen pregnancy, drug abuse, and youth violence. The conservative agenda, led by Speaker of the House Newt Gingrich and Senate Majority Leader Bob Dole, ushered in a new wave of attacks on liberal policies aimed at ending racial discrimination. Insisting that racial discrimination in America had been eradicated, the GOP proclaimed America a color-blind society. However, continued decline in GOP support by Runyon Heights residents suggests that the black middle-class did not buy into conservative rhetoric on race. In 1992, the Bush/Quayle presidential ticket received just 13% of the vote in District 6, the smallest percentage since Goldwater. Democratic support dipped slightly as well, as Clinton and Gore took 80% of the vote. Perot and his Reform Party picked up 5% of the district, and Lenore Fulani and The New Alliance Party mustered another percentage point. Republican support in Yonkers also slipped, from 58% in 1980 to 42% in 1992. In 1996, the incumbent Democrats secured an impressive 90% of the Runyon Heights vote but only 56% of the city's vote. Republicans claimed only 7% of District 6 votes, the smallest percentage in Runyon Heights history.

A comparison of residents' voting behavior and their political affiliation reveals an interesting paradox. The two roughly coincided until Goldwater's bid in 1964. The candidate's position on civil rights shifted the traditional platform of the GOP on race in America and instituted a color line in national party politics. Although more Republicans than Democrats actually supported the Kennedy-Johnson Civil Rights Act in 1964, Goldwater was one of only six Republican senators to vote against the bill. With this act, Republicans were no longer viewed by many blacks as the party of Lincoln and the free Negro. Goldwater's politics on the question of race actually pushed black suburban voters out of the GOP. Meanwhile, the conservative, racist southern wing of the Democratic Party gave way to a more liberal leadership and concomitant social agenda. Democratic presidential patronage in Runyon Heights quickly followed.[7]

Scholars have observed that Democratic support among the educated professional middle-class increased between 1972 and 1992, owing to liberal views on social issues such as abortion, civil rights, and women's roles.[8] Yet abandonment of the GOP began early in Runyon Heights. The shift can be attributed only partly to professionalization and liberalism. More importantly, it has been a response to the discourse on race in national politics. Black Nepperhaners responded to the GOP attack on the civil rights agenda by withdrawing their support.

While the 1980s brought a renewed racial discourse in national politics, local politics also took a decisively racial turn. The local crises over school and housing desegregation during the 1980s exacerbated local racial cleavages. As the GOP again became associated with an anticivil-rights agenda, Runyon Heights support for local Republicans eroded. In 1986, Yonkers was the site of a landmark ruling handed down by United States District Court Judge Leonard B. Sand on the housing and school desegregation suit brought by the United States and the local NAACP.[9] Judge Sand ruled that the City of Yonkers and its agencies had intentionally segregated blacks in both housing and public schools. Sand's decision ignited widespread white opposition, and the conservative interests of white homeowners were reflected in the political positions of local politicians. Though efforts to desegregate the schools were already undertaken by the more moderate school board, Republicans generally opposed compliance with Judge Sand's order to construct low-income housing in predominantly white areas; Democrats generally supported compliance.

Runyon Heights voting patterns reflected local community concerns. During the 1980s, residents increasingly supported policies that challenged racial discrimination and segregation in Yonkers. As minorities and the poor squared off with white homeowners over the court-ordered desegregation plan, Runyon residents responded to the racial and class polarization taking place in the city.

Former Republican Mayor Angelo Martinelli (1973–1977) had developed a reputation for supporting and encouraging the segregationist policies of the city and the school board during his tenure, even leading marches and demonstrations against desegregation in the late 1970s. He narrowly lost the mayoral bid in 1979 to Liberal Gerald Loehr, who won 51% of the city vote. Martinelli had a modest showing of 30% in District 6. He ran again in 1981, just as Yonkers's landmark desegregation lawsuit was under way. During this campaign, Martinelli shifted dramatically toward a less provincial political outlook. Claiming that his earlier position had been an error, he now encouraged settling the federal desegregation lawsuit and ultimately desegregating low-income housing and public schools in Yonkers. Whether desegregation was his aim or whether he simply assessed the city's slim chance of victory in the lawsuit, District 6 voters were unconvinced of his change of heart. Martinelli gained only one percentage point over the previous election, securing 31% of the vote. Even this modest showing is a curiosity given his former opposition to the desegregation plan.

In 1985, now positioned as a moderate, Martinelli was again elected mayor, gaining an astounding 66% of the vote in District 6. This was the strongest showing for a local Republican candidate since John Flynn received 51% of the vote in 1965. It is actually not a surprising figure since Martinelli's opponent, Bernie Spreckman, was a stark opponent of desegregation. In 1987, Martinelli lost the mayoral race to the late Nicholas Wascisko, another Democratic candidate who flirted with the segregationist idea of challenging the Court's decision. This time the vote was split, and Martinelli won a thin majority of Election District 6, with nearly 53% of the vote.

After the Court's 1986 ruling, the school board quickly moved to develop a magnet program to desegregate the schools; the school plan proceeded unencumbered. White homeowners, however, opposed the court's proposal to place predominantly black and Latino families in 200 units of low-income rental housing and 800 units of subsidized middle-income housing across the city. Local politician Jack O'Toole organized the Save Yonkers Federation, a group of white, largely middle-class homeowners from around the city who adamantly opposed public housing in their communities. While the group often claimed to be protecting their housing values and communities, public discussions often centered around the implied race of potential occupants. Community opposition to Negroes had a long tradition in Yonkers; in this case, class acted as a mask for underlying racial animosities.

Before long, however, Yonkers's stubborn resistance to the court-ordered housing plan would come to an end. After the City Council refused to develop a desegregation plan in 1988, Council Representatives Ed Fagan, Jr., Nicholas versus Longo, Henry Spallone, and Pete Chema were found in contempt of court. In September of that year, under threat of state intervention and fiscal bankruptcy, the council reluctantly voted to comply with the court order, though some members still vowed to oppose the judge. By 1989, Democratic mayoral candidate Nicholas Wascisko had shifted positions, as had Martinelli, and wanted the council to settle. Henry Spallone angered Runyon Heights residents during the campaign with his controversial rhetoric. Ironically, Spallone and the "Gang of Four" successfully challenged contempt fines levied against the individual representatives by Judge Sand. With renewed vigor they swore to fight on. In 1991, Pete Chema ran for Mayor on the GOP ticket, still vowing to direct, if not resist, the court order. In an unusual three-way race, Terence M. Zaleski won on the Democratic ticket with merely 36% of the vote. Martinelli, running on the Independent ticket, became the spoiler candidate, capturing 28% of the vote and crushing Chema's bid in the process. Still, Chema received a respectable 34% of the city vote. In District 6, he mustered only 9%, while Zaleski and Martinelli received 48% and 42%, respectively.

After the 1991 elections and the shift to the strong-mayor form of government, the City Council finally decided in April of 1992 to comply with the housing mandate. Their proposal, however, was ultimately rejected by the judge. Since then, the council has sought to comply with the judge's order, without upsetting their respective constituencies, in the hope of reclaiming the city's autonomy and future. In 1993, city officials finally complied with Sand's initial order to construct 200 units of scatter-site low-income rental housing, which has been built at seven sites across the city. By 1996, city officials had regained more control over the housing program and plans were made to assist predominantly black and Latino middle-income families in buying homes, while another 140 units of subsidized middle-income housing was constructed at four sites. In February, 1998, Judge Sand ruled that New York State was partly responsible for housing segregation patterns in southwest Yonkers, and the state agreed to pay Yonkers $16.4 million to finish the desegregation plan.

The Persistence of Class Politics

Solutions by city government to aid the black working class on the west side have often failed to benefit east side Nepperhaners. In one case, a working-class minority district was salvaged by redistricting at the expense of a weakened Runyon Heights voter block. This was not the first occasion. During the 1950s the local elementary school, School 1, was closed and Runyon children were bused to schools in other neighborhoods as a token effort to solve segregation in the public schools. In addition, Runyon Heights has been targeted on numerous occasions for desperately needed city public-housing projects, although the community successfully prevented all but one (the 48-unit Hall Court) from being constructed. In many ways, black working-class needs in Yonkers have often been met in the context of a political trade-off with Runyon Heights residents.

One political insider revealed how favoritism determined the political composition of District 6. The Republican-controlled City Council helped to maintain the political constituency of Ward Ten's long-time Republican incumbent Ed J. Fagan, Jr. When district lines were redrawn in 1987, rather than including a balance of Republicans and Democrats in the Sixth District, the district was weighted toward Republicans. The majority Republican City Council insured Fagan's political future. As it currently exists, the Sixth District is more white and more conservative than the Tenth Ward had been. Consequently, Fagan has remained in office.

The new system curtailed the influence of the Runyon vote in local elections. During the earlier ward system, Nepperhan carried critical swing votes in elections that were closely contested, particularly since Nepperhaners supported both Democrats and Republicans. A balance between Republicans and Democrats would have secured Runyon Heights's swing-vote status. Owing to the closeness of recent races, however, the Runyon vote remains a factor in local contests. The recent trend in declining voter turnout could eventually jeopardize this leverage. Residents are placed at a further disadvantage because council districts overlap with the old ward political divisions, thereby diminishing the influence of local ward leaders in local politics. Shifts in the political landscape could have consequences for Runyon Heights if the system of personal contacts in the old political machine is disrupted.

Race came to dominate the Yonkers political scene during the 1980s. The housing and schooling discrimination lawsuit, filed in the U.S. District Court in Manhattan in 1980 by the NAACP and Justice Department against the City of Yonkers, was the spark that ignited local racial tensions. City Council members nearly bankrupted the city by ignoring the federally mandated housing desegregation plan handed down by Judge Sand. Council Member Fagan at first supported compliance but soon became an outspoken opponent of the federal proposal. Council members finally conceded to the court order after hefty fines were levied against the city. The incident, which nearly crippled city finances, helped to shift the political winds in Yonkers. Voters moved to transfer real power back to the Mayor. In 1991, the strong-mayor form of government, abandoned in 1940, was revived. The new city government reinvested power in the Mayor's office and weakened City Council influence over administrative decisions. Under the new system, both the Mayor and the President of the City Council were elected at large; the remaining six districts elected representatives to the council. The 1993 redistricting plan, which had been based on the 1990 census reports, created a second "minority" council district on Yonkers' west side. The Second Council District included a portion of the former First District, but contained a predominantly Latino population.

The 1993 redistricting plan raised troubling issues for Runyon Heights. An initial proposal by the Puerto Rican Legal Defense Fund, in a bid to create the second minority district, elicited strong opposition from the Runyon Heights community. The proposal suggested collapsing the middle-class, east-side Runyon community and the predominantly black and working-class, First District on the west side into a single minority district. This plan would have politically segregated virtually the entire black population of Yonkers. The plan was strongly opposed by community members; as a result, Runyon Heights remained a part of the Sixth District. Residents feared that becoming part of a single minority district would not be in their best interests. The class interests of Nepperhaners would have been overshadowed by the needs of the much larger and poorer west side community. In political terms, their swing vote would no longer count in a predominantly Democratic area. The hoopla surrounding the proposal to subsume Runyon Heights voters into the First District hindered consideration by the community of the potential for diminished political influence resulting from the redistricting plan that was finally adopted. Seeking to protect their political autonomy and class interests, residents resisted racial homogenization but ultimately lost critical leverage in the local political landscape.

We have seen that the political influence Runyon Heights wielded in local elections was strengthened by supporting both major parties. From the 1930s to the mid-1960s, residents often split their votes in local council and mayoral contests. Until 1981, Nepperhan voting patterns were indistinguishable from those of their neighbors. In a sample of mayoral and council elections from 1935, 1939, 1945, 1957, 1965, 1969, and 1979, Nepperhaners supported both Republican and Democratic candidates at roughly equal levels as Ward Ten. Support was strong for GOP Tenth Ward candidates until the mid-1960s, when moderate Democrat Alfred Del Bello claimed 57% of the election district. By 1969, Democratic support had solidified. Del Bello claimed 63% of Election District 6 in his successful bid for Mayor, while Dominick Cuccia claimed 60% of the district in his successful bid for Councilman of Ward Ten. Even with slowly increasing Democratic support throughout the 1960s and 1970s, GOP candidates still collected a respectable 30% of the vote in District 6.

Runyon Heights residents have managed to resist housing in their area. Local residents hold paradoxical attitudes toward low-income housing, at times lending support through organizations like the NAACP and at times resisting through organizations like the RHIA. One resident explains. "I think we kind of felt that, look, we've done our responsibility, and we've made it work. A lot of people in the community were initially members of the projects (Hall Court). I think we kind of divorced ourselves from the issue [of low-income housing] in a sense. We realized that this was something the city should do, but in terms of pressing for it, I don't think we pressed very hard."

The dramatic impact of race and class on voting patterns in Runyon Heights is demonstrated by the 18-year career of Councilman Ed Fagan, Jr., long-time representative of Ward Ten and most recently of Council District 6. In his early years as Ward Ten representative, Fagan enjoyed a fair share of the votes in Election District 6. As he became more opposed to Judge Sand's housing desegregation order, voting patterns became polarized along racial lines. In 1979, as a newcomer to the political scene, Fagan received 58% of the votes in Ward Ten, but only 20% of the votes in Election District 6. By 1981, support for Ed Fagan in the Sixth election district had grown to 29% compared with 64% in the entire ward. His support had gradually risen among Runyon Heights residents, probably as a result of his having provided city services to the community. As one resident proclaimed, "Issues come and issues go, but services always stay. People always say, 'What have you done for me?'" Fagan clearly recognized his constituency, making regular visits to the community and appearing at community events. By 1985, he had regained 37% of the election district, in opposition to the future Save Yonkers Federation supporter John P. O'Toole, who ran on the Democratic ticket. Over time, Fagan's extremely conservative position began to chip away at his local support. In 1987, running for council representative of the newly formed 6th Council District, and just as he was approaching a standoff with Judge Sand, his support slid to 32% in the district. In the 1989 council race, his support dropped still further, to 18%, where it remained in 1991. The desegregation battle exacerbated racial cleavages in Yonkers and polarized the Runyon Heights vote. With the passing of the crisis, Fagan has slowly reestablished respectable support in District 6. In 1993 and 1995, he maintained his stronghold on the Council District, winning the elections with 55% and 50%; in District 6, he received a modest 21% and 34% of the votes, respectively.

Scholars have noted that African American political behavior is influenced by national politics and perceptions of group interests, yet little attention has been paid to how segregation and local policies have informed the construction of group interests.[10] Voting behavior in Nepperhan is motivated by neither knee-jerk racial nationalism nor blind adherence to Democratic liberalism. Residents have been careful to select candidates who have best represented their multifaceted interests. Until the late 1960s, residents were strong supporters of Republican candidates in national elections, while splitting their vote between the major parties in local elections. After the racial polarization in national political discourse in 1964, support for the GOP in presidential elections shifted. Race became a central concern to Runyon Heights voters. During the 1980s, a similar shift in the local political discourse placed race at the center of local contests. In general, support for the Democratic Party has paralleled the GOP's retreat from antidiscrimination policy. Consequently, voting patterns in Runyon Heights have become more homogeneous as residents have articulated their collective racial and material interests.

Notes

1. Arnold L. Steigman, "Mayor-Council Government: Yonkers, New York 1908–1939—A Study of Failure and Abandonment," Ph.D. diss., Graduate School of Public Administration, New York University, 1967, p. 69.

2. Steigman, "Mayor-Council Government," p. 11.

3. Westchester County Archives has maintained voter registration data beginning in 1929. No earlier records exist in the county.

4. Registration rolls were acquired from the Westchester County Board of Elections in White Plains, New York for the years 1930–1970. Between 1930 and 1960, political party affiliation was calculated by including only streets within the boundaries of Runyon Heights. These numbers, therefore, do not represent the entire district. After 1960, community boundaries were completely in line with the district boundary so that Election District 6 comprised only streets within the boundaries of Runyon Heights. For the years 1970 through 1992, the entire 6th district is used. However, in 1993, the southern portion of Bushed Avenue was gerrymandered into another election district in the 6th Council District.

5. Howard Schuman, Charlotte Steeh, and Lawrence Bobo, *Racial Attitudes in*

America: Trends and Interpretations (Cambridge: Harvard University Press, 1985), p. 17; Gerald David Jaynes and Robin M. Williams, *A Common Destiny: Blacks and American Society* (Washington, D.C.: National Academy Press, 1985), p. 216.

6. Election return data were acquired from the Westchester County Board of Elections, White Plains, New York.

7. Jaynes and Williams, *A Common Destiny,* p. 216.

8. Clem Brooks and Jeff Manza, "The Social and Ideological Bases of Middle-Class Political Realignment in the United States 1972–1992," *American Sociological Review,* Vol. 62, No. 2 (1997): 191–208.

9. See the decision of United States District Court Southern District of New York State: USA and Yonkers Branch of NAACP et al. versus Yonkers Board of Education, City of Yonkers, and Yonkers Community Development Agency, 80 CIV 6761 (LBS), 1985.

10. See Michael C. Dawson, *Behind the Mule: Race and Class in African American Politics* (Princeton: Princeton University Press, 1994).

10

Linda Pershing

Representations of Racial Identity in a Contemporary Pinkster Celebration

The record of black participation in public ceremonies, parades, and festivals can supply researchers with valuable clues for understanding black identity at any given historical moment. Black numerical representation and roles in such rituals provide a script revealing the nature of interracial relationships and changes in those relationships over time. Below, folklorist and anthropologist Linda Pershing reports on her observations of several Pinkster festivals she attended in the Hudson Valley during the mid-1990s. The contemporary celebrations presented a contrast to their late eighteenth- and early nineteenth-century versions, as documented in several other chapters in this volume. In Westchester County particularly, recent racial tensions in the region and nation as well as the race pride of event organizers made possible the assertion of a nationalist black identity through Pinkster revivals: Black storytellers and actors quite literally inserted a new text into the festivities as they conveyed celebratory stories of blacks and black culture in the region, the country, and Africa by print, by word, and by their presence in historical re-enactments. At the same time, the narrative criticized past racial injustices. The expression of this nationalist identity sought to affirm the persistent presence of African Americans in the valley.

> The United States suffers from a severe case of amnesia. In its obsessive quest to "construct the future," it tends to forget or erase the past. Fortunately, the so-called disenfranchised groups who don't feel part of this national project have been meticulously documenting their histories.

Reproduced by permission of the New York Folklore Society from *New York Folklore*, Vol. XXIV, Nos. 1–4, 1998, pp. 77–96.

—Guillermo Gómez-Peña, "The Other Vanguard," in Ivan Karp, Christine Mullen Kreamer, and Steven D. Lavine, eds., *Museums and Communities: the Politics of Public Culture* (Washington and London: Smithsonian Institution Press, 1992), pp. 65–75.

All history is a production—a deliberate selection, ordering, and evaluation of past events, experiences, and processes.
—Michael Wallace, "Visiting the Past: History Museums in the United States," *Radical History Review* 25 (1981): 63.

As they moved into colonial New York and New Jersey in the seventeenth century, Dutch settlers brought with them their tradition of Pinkster, a celebration of Pentecost and the arrival of springtime.[1] By the late 1700s, enslaved blacks also participated in the festivities, which included several days of dancing, parades, feasting, and the syncretization of African and Dutch rituals. Pinkster gradually became a festival in which slaves were the principle actors and organizers while local whites and Native Americans observed from the sidelines as spectators. In 1811 white officials in Albany, New York, voted to ban the holiday for fear that the public visibility and sense of autonomy it fostered among blacks might lead to slave revolts and rioting. Recently, some African Americans in the Hudson River Valley have reinvented the Pinkster festival as a celebration of cultural pride and racial identity. This chapter is an analysis of the cultural politics—particularly the processes of historical reformulation and resistance—which characterize a contemporary Pinkster festival in North Tarrytown, New York .[2]

My theoretical approach is based on the premise that cultural performances such as festivals and community celebrations may offer people a public forum for selectively creating and expressing their ideas about social identity. Alessandro Falassi has noted that "both the social function and the symbolic meaning of . . . festival are closely related to a series of overt values that the community recognizes as essential to its ideology and worldview, to its social identity, its historical continuity, and to its physical survival. . . ."[3] Arising out of local traditions and community histories, festivals often constitute dramatic presentations of contemporary ideologies that legitimize or advocate particular versions of the past.[4] Characterized by communicative strategies that Joan N. Radner defines as "coding" and James C. Scott describes as 'hidden transcripts," festivals and related events can enable people to comment upon how they have been—and how they want to be—defined within larger social and political contexts.[5]

In the annual Pinkster celebrations I observed, a range of subversive activities occurred that observers could have chosen to ignore or to interpret as innocent entertainment. Scott contends that expressive behaviors of this kind signal a type of resistance. He identifies these as hidden transcripts embedded in the public presentation of subordinate groups, behavioral messages that are usually repressed or omitted in the dominant historical record.[6] Rather than, or in addition to, emphasizing shared identities, community festivals may accentuate contrasts: between "insiders" and "outsiders," between the viewers and the organizers of the performance, or between the viewers and people or cultures on display. The Pinkster celebrations I discuss here simultaneously reaffirmed racial heritage in opposition to the dominant culture, reminded or informed a group of people about their collective past, and educated outsiders about a history they might otherwise have chosen to ignore or forget.

Frank Manning delineates four central features of cultural celebration in the modern world, features relevant to this study because they characterize the North Tarrytown Pinkster festival.[7] First, celebration involves the dramatic presentation of cultural symbols. Second, celebration offers entertainment. Third, it publicly enacts personal and collective meanings. Fourth, celebration is participatory and involves a specific constituency.[8] Drawing on the work of MacCannell, Bateson, Geertz, Turner, and Babcock,[9] Manning also notes that cultural celebrations often become symbolic battlefields for waging competitive struggles for power and social legitimization. Particularly significant for my purposes is Manning's observation that when the people who create or participate in celebration are in a socially subordinate position, "there is a tendency to emphasize the playful devices of negation, such as reversal, irony, and the juxtaposition of social forms."[10]

In their work on the politics of multiculturalism in cultural displays, Steven D. Lavine and Ivan Karp note that every exhibition, no matter what the subject matter, is shaped by the cultural assumptions and resources of the people who design it.[11] Cultural performances may range widely in their political functions, from reifying the existing social order, representing momentary rituals of rebellion, to expressing ongoing resistance to dominant social norms.[12] However, cultural performances are more than simply forms of entertainment, more than cathartic experiences, and more than didactic or persuasive formulation offered in a group setting.

They create and present versions of reality in which groups of people can take part, providing them with a springboard for continuing social action and relations.[13] Implicit notions of difference and inequality and contentious interpretations of the past are characteristic of festivals of this type, which may embellish conflict and ambiguity, rather than resolving or removing them. People sometimes use festivals to voice the ways in which their own experiences contradict dominant ideologies or official histories. This expressive strategy involves recognition of how one's own group is defined by the dominant culture and then resisting those definitions by offering alternative or oppositional accounts through carefully designed cultural performances.

I am suggesting that the Pinkster festival in North Tarrytown represents an effort by contemporary African Americans to validate and valorize their roles in U.S. life by taking what conventionally has been left on the margins of historical accounts and placing it in the center of social history. According to Scott, cultural performances that advance the social critique or alternative worldviews of a subordinate group often involve smuggling portions of a hidden transcript, suitably veiled to avoid reprisal or retribution, onto the public stage. Scott notes that "the often fugitive political conduct of subordinate groups" requires the cultural analyst to pay special attention to the contradictions, tensions, and circumscribed possibilities for expression that exist for oppressed groups in the face of power and dominance.[14] Hierarchical and oppressive social conditions may require that the members of a marginalized group adopt a strategic pose—usually a subordinate or deferential one—in the presence of the dominant group. Organizers of and performers in the North Tarrytown Pinkster festival found ways to resist dominant cultural forces through coding and parody, celebrating interpretations of the past and present that remind viewers of the legacy of racism and slavery.

Enslaved Africans arrived in the lower Hudson River Valley first under Dutch rule in the early 1600s and later under the British after 1664, when England officially acquired the area then known as New Netherlands. With its large slave market at the foot of Wall Street, New Amsterdam (now New York City) became an international port for slave traders and buyers. After the 1740s, merchants often sent their ships directly to the coasts of Africa to capture and export slaves. Before that time, traders shipped most of the blacks they enslaved to New York from British territories in the Caribbean (such as Barbados, Antigua, and Jamaica), other parts of North American (the British colonies of Maryland, Virginia, and the Carolinas), as well as from Curaçao, what later became Havana, and Brazil. The first federal census in 1790 listed the New York population of enslaved blacks at 21,324, less than 8,000 below Georgia's total of 29,264.[15] Indeed, enslaved blacks comprised over 20% of the total population in parts of New York and New Jersey, where throughout the eighteenth century the economy was more reliant on the labor of enslaved laborers than in any other regions in the North.[16]

It was not unusual for Northerners to publicly condemn the barbarities of slavery in the West Indies or the South while remaining indifferent to the continued existence of the institution in their midst. One example was John Jay, who served as Chief Justice of the United States and Governor of New York. For many years, Jay was President of the New York Manumission Society, although he actually owned five or more enslaved blacks.[17] In his 1991 analysis of slavery in New York, historian Shane White argues that although slavery in the northern states was in some ways different from slavery in the South, it was not necessarily milder.[18] Slaves in the New York area were often worse off than their southern counterparts: it was more difficult to keep their families together and to retain opportunities for an independent social and religious life. Northern ideology promoted the notion that the speedy adoption of white values and norms was both inevitable and beneficial for enslaved blacks. Forced cultural assimilation—combined with the fact that slave masters owned relatively fewer numbers of slaves and northern slavery was often characterized by a very high rate of turnover—was particularly disruptive for enslaved families. Although there were a few gentry who owned ten or more enslaved blacks, many whites owned two or three. Seldom were slave buyers interested in purchasing entire families, and most seemed to be untroubled by separating loved ones, including very young children from their mothers.[19] Many of the wealthiest merchants and landowners were Dutch, who in some areas constituted over 80% of the slaveholders who owned ten or more enslaved blacks. These men were influential in the establishment and promotion of northern slavery, voicing strong and long-lasting opposition to freeing slaves in rural New York.[20]

Pinkster is a festival that originated with the Dutch celebration of Pentecost *(Pingsterdag),* commemorating the descent of the Holy Spirit on the seventh Sunday after Easter. It also became a simultaneous celebration of spring and the planting season, a time when the Hudson River Valley comes alive with abundant greenery and blossoming trees and flowers. During the several days that followed Pentecost Sunday, Dutch immigrants in North America took a respite from their daily activities in order to attend church services, visit with one another, and enjoy communal food, drink, and music. Enslaved workers were usually relieved of their duties, making the festivities similar to the English Boxing Day, when servants were given a day off after the Christmas holiday.[21] Shane White has speculated that after the North American Revolution, the younger Dutch population gradually abandoned the celebration of Pinkster as a relic of the Old World that their ancestors left behind, while blacks played an increasing role in Pinkster festivities.[22] A. J. Williams-Myers, a scholar of African American history in the Hudson Valley, argues that Pinkster—as it was practiced in New York and New Jersey—also has roots in African religious traditions, including elements such as ". . . the installation of an African ruler, normally accompanied by drumming, dancing, and various games performed by the king's subjects; the 'first fruits ceremony' which was agricultural offerings of thanksgiving to the village chiefs just before harvest; a coming out ceremony for those youngsters newly received into adulthood. . . ; and/or the end of a long period of mourning after a funeral," followed by feasting, singing, dancing, and drinking.[23] Some time during the late 1700s or early 1800s, people of African descent appropriated a holiday that the Dutch were in the process of discarding and transformed it to meet their own needs.

There is more information available about the Pinkster activities in Albany, New York, than other Pinkster festivities in Long Island, New York City, along the lower Hudson Valley, or eastern New Jersey.[24] On "Pinkster Hill" Albany participants erected and decorated booths from which they sold a variety of foods and beverages. Performers built tents, arbors, and an amphitheater in which to entertain the crowds with their dancing, music, and other attractions. African slaves and their descendants incorporated the worship of the African god Totau through dance and playing the drum. In Albany, a black slave called King Charles personified Totau; he presided over the celebrations and was purported to be a descendant of Angolan royalty.[25] One chronicler described the titular patriarch as "tall, thin, and extremely agile," even at 70 years of age.[26] King Charles wore a scarlet coat with gold ornamentation, reminiscent of a "British brigadier of olden times," yellow buckskin clothes, black shoes with silver buckles, and a three-cornered hat. His reputation as a master drummer was renowned. After parading through the town with an entourage of dancers and musicians, King Charles made his royal appearance on Pinkster Hill.[27] As a heterogeneous crowd of blacks, whites, and Native Americans gathered, King Charles officially opened the festivities, enjoining the onlookers to commence with the celebration. One of King Charles's honorary duties included a tour of the festival grounds, during which he collected one shilling from every tent inhabited by blacks and two shillings from every tent occupied by whites. According to one chronicler, his authority was undisputed. If anyone refused to pay the fee, the King ordered that his or her tent be "instantly demolished."[28]

A range of entertaining activities occurred during the next three or four days and nights. Primary among them were dancing and sporting competitions, which often represented syncretizations of African and European cultures. Most significant was the reversal of roles by blacks and whites. Enslaved blacks became the central designers and performers in Pinkster celebrations; for a few brief days they were free from the control and domination of white slave owners, who, in turn, sometimes attended as spectators of the performances. Pinkster celebrations in Albany and elsewhere hit their peak in the early 1800s. By this time, Africans and African Americans had transformed the originally Dutch festival into a celebration that turned everyday social relations and racial stratification upside down.

The annual Pinkster celebrations that I observed from 1992–1995 in North Tarrytown, New York, represented an attempt to recreate the festival as it might have occurred in the mid-1700s in this region. The two-day event in May was sponsored by an organization called Historic Hudson Valley, a community-based educational society whose staff and volunteers engage in research and programs ". . . that seek to advance the knowledge, understanding and appreciation of the Hudson River Valley's historic, scenic, and cultural resources as a national treasure."[29] Entrepreneur and philanthropist John D. Rockefeller, Jr., assisted in creating and funding the organization, with a specific focus on preserving the history and culture of people who have lived along the Hudson

River. The society operates a museum and manages six historical sites in the lower Hudson Valley. One of the properties is Union Church of Pocantico Hills, famous for its stained glass windows by Henri Matisse and Marc Chagall. The other five are manors and mansions that belonged to influential white families during the 1700s and 1800s, including Sunnyside, the 1835 home of Washington Irving, the author of "The Legend of Sleepy Hollow" and "Rip Van Winkel." Another site owned by Historic Hudson Valley is Philipsburg Manor, named after the Dutch émigré Frederick Philipse. A carpenter and entrepreneur who came to North America in 1693, Philipse became one of the wealthiest men in the colonies.

Staff members of History Hudson Valley chose Philipsburg Manor as the location for the contemporary Pinkster festival. This site actually constitutes just the Upper Mills of the Philipsburg estate, representing only 25 out of Philipse's original 52,500 acres of property. Philipse's descendants sided with the British during the North American Revolution and fled to England at the conclusion of the war. The new government seized and partitioned the immense estate and sold parcels at auction to generate revenue. Rockefeller purchased and restored what remained of the manor site in 1940; it was opened to the public three years later. In 1951 the property became part of Sleepy Hollow Restorations, which was later renamed Historic Hudson Valley. After conducting research on the original site, architects, archeologists, and society staff worked together to restore the property to its 1720–1750 condition, a time when Frederick Philipse's son, Adolf, was the owner. The Upper Mills property now includes a restored three-story manor house, reconstructed and operational grist mill, reconstructed mill pond and wooden bridge, New World Dutch barn moved to this site from upstate New York, an Old Dutch Church built by slave labor in the seventeenth century, a reproduction of a tenant farmer's stone cottage, animal sheds (present-day employees raise chickens, cows, sheep, goats, and oxen), and assorted gardens, fields, and orchards. At one time, the Upper Mills also included several buildings that are no longer standing, such as a bake house, slave house, fowl house, two additional tenant farmsteads, and the original wooden barn.

Frederick and Adolf Philipse rarely lived at the upper mills, preferring instead to reside at a home in New Amsterdam. The upper mills was a working and trading site, located on a tributary known as the Pocantico River, which facilitated the movement of sloops and barges that could load and unload cargo at the upper mills wharf. The primary and most profitable crop was wheat, hence the importance of the grist mill. The Philipse family used tenant farmers and enslaved laborers (23 at the upper mill alone) to work the land that made them rich.

From 10:00 A.M. to 5:00 P.M. on the first or second weekend in May, the North Tarrytown Pinkster Festival offers storytelling, exhibition dancing, musical entertainment, and an educational slideshow. Each kind of performance typically occurred three times a day on a rotating schedule. On a grassy area inside the manor grounds, wooden stilts and long, thick tug-of-war ropes were available for anyone who cared to try them. At one booth during the 1992 festival, a woman who described her heritage as Mohican and Cherokee taught children how to make beaded jewelry while she told them how her ancestors once traded furs for beads, which they used to decorate their garments. Young girls dressed in colonial costumes wandered through the crowd selling, or "hawking," colored hard-boiled eggs, a practice described in nineteenth-century accounts of Pinkster. Freshly ground flour and delicious smelling baked goods were available for purchase inside the gristmill, where workers demonstrated how they processed flour on a daily basis. There were booths offering games and toys reminiscent or imitative of colonial pastimes, including wooden whistles, pop guns, tops, and flutes, rag dolls (available with either white or black faces), and three-cornered felt hats. The air was filled with the smell of such delicacies as roasted chicken, vegetable stew, spiced rice, black beans, and fried sweet potatoes, all cooking on a large outdoor grill fueled by split logs.

Radiah Harper Sumler, Director of Programs during the years of my fieldwork, explained to me that the Historic Hudson Valley staff had attempted to recreate—as nearly as was feasible given the limited historical record and funding available to them—an environment that replicated conditions of the mid-eighteenth century. She sent written information on Pinkster celebrations to each of the performers, asking them to adapt their performances to match the times and setting. A concern for historical accuracy was evident in the language, costume, and food that typified the festival. The African American storytellers assumed accents imitative of Caribbean- or African-born speakers. All performers and vendors wore colonial costumes appropriate to their role. In 1992 Historic Hudson Valley contracted with a local catering company called "My Belizean Gourmet" to provide and sell the food, under the condition that they would develop menu items that were available in the region during the 1700s. Drawing on the Albany Pinkster tradition, members of the African colonial dance troupe introduced their act by singing, "I hear King Charles' drummer calling/It won't stop 'til the sun is falling." The historical society's desire to reconstruct the past in the present was also evident in the architecture of Philipsburg Manor. In order to replace the original barn when it burned down, staff located a similar structure in Guilderland Center, New York, some 150 miles north. Workers hired by the society not only used eighteenth century tools to reframe and erect the newly acquired barn, but they also wore reproductions of eighteenth-century clothing while they did the construction work.[30]

The dyed eggs were hard-boiled in iron kettles that hung in the fireplace of the tenant farmer dwelling at Philipsburg. Rather than using commercial dyes, female volunteers in period costumes colored the eggs using extracts of plants that were grown on the manor during the 1700s. In the same building they dyed and spun yarn using eighteenth-century materials and technology. Other attempts to replicate Pinkster festivals of the eighteenth century included the central role given to the master drummer, embodied by a man known as Chief Bey. He demonstrated African and Caribbean drumming while talking to onlookers about the significance of drums in African Diaspora cultures. There were booths for selling food and wares. In addition, like the Pinkster festivals of centuries past, the event included the celebration of springtime. At Philipsburg Manor, there were newborn lambs, trees in bloom, and gardens sprouting. All of these combined to heighten the sense of new life and rebirth that historically characterized Pinkster celebrations.

Other elements of historic Pinkster festivals, as described in eighteenth- and nineteenth-century accounts, were noticeably lacking. There was no King Charles figure to preside over the festivities, although Program Director Radiah Sumler mentioned that Chief Bey, the oldest and most distinguished performer at the festival, symbolized King Charles for her. The North Tarrytown Pinkster event was much more rigidly controlled than were historic Pinkster celebrations. Each performance was carefully scheduled and listed in a printed program that visitors received when they entered the grounds. Missing were the revelry and abandon, sexualized dancing, and the tradition of King Charles demanding money from onlookers, no doubt because these would have offended the viewing public and patrons, on whose financial support the contemporary festival and the historical society depends.

As a researcher, I found the questions of ideology and racial identity that emerged throughout the event particularly intriguing. Driving through North Tarrytown, a Westchester County village with a 1990 population of 10,739, did not prepare me for the levels of contested meaning that I subsequently encountered. Situated on the east bank of the lower Hudson River Valley, not far from Yonkers, North Tarrytown appears to be a quiet, homogeneous, and charming suburban community. The main street is lined with American colonial architecture, large homes and well-preserved red brick buildings shaded by tall trees, and small specialty shops designed for well-to-do consumers—by all outward appearances a white, middle- or upper-middle-class enclave (in the 1990 census, 84.8% of the population identified their racial identity as white, and the median income was $48,295). In the spring, tulips bloom in the gardens of many homes and businesses, reminders of the Dutch influence that so strongly pervades the area. The Dutch colonial ambiance contrasted sharply with the Pinkster celebration at Philipsburg Manor, with its emphasis on the valuation of African American history in the region. As an observer, I soon became aware of the attempt to reconstruct or reenact the festival from the point of view of those who are most often omitted in U.S. social history, particularly people of African descent. Performers emphasized not the heritage of the Dutch and other Europeans who claimed this land as their own, but rather the lives, artistic practices, and cultural contributions of people whom slave traders brought here against their will and whom the white population forced to serve them.

The inversion was especially striking when contrasted to another Pinkster celebration that occurs in New York. To kick off the yearly festival in Albany, a group of people dressed in colonial Dutch costumes (including oversized wooden shoes) played at scrubbing a section of downtown State Street with soapy water and heavy wooden brooms, while amused television camera crews, reporters, city officials, and onlookers recorded and applauded their efforts. Two of the costumed participants carried a banner that read "The Dutch Settlers Society of Albany, 1624–1664." Standing to the side was a group of (identically dressed) contestants for Albany's Tulip Queen, chosen annually from among approximately a half dozen beautiful young women who compete for the title.[31] In the Albany festivities, the celebration of Dutch heritage is paramount, while the African roots of Pinkster have been rendered nearly invisible. The naming of the event highlights this shift in focus. The Albany celebration—including crowds of thousands who patronize the food and crafts booths and come to hear the music of popular local bands—is now known as the Tulip Festival (tulips bloom by the thousands at the festival site in Washington Park), conceptually underscoring the valuation of Dutch history and heritage.*

In contrast, the printed program that visitors received upon entering the North Tarrytown festival was decorated with an image of enslaved blacks, dancing during the holiday. Visitors saw from the outset that the primary emphasis was on the African, rather than the Dutch, celebration of Pinkster. Another flyer described Pinkster as "an African Dutch Festival," linguistically focusing the emphasis on the former. In 1992, among the six different forms of scheduled entertainment, only two were performed by whites: Linda Russell, who wore the lace and velvet clothing of the gentry, played the hammered dulcimer, and a group of white women and men demonstrated English Country Dancing. The English dancing seemed restrained when compared to that of the African Colonial Dancers, who even mimicked and satirized the English dancers as a part of their performance. As a regular component of their act, African American dancers watched their white counterparts perform. In their own performances immediately thereafter, they sarcastically mimicked the rigidity and formality of the white dances and then used English dance steps as a springboard from which to create their own much more energetic

---

*Editor's note: The contemporary Tulip Festival in Albany is a three-day event. One of those days is called Pinksterfest. See http://www.albanyevents.org/tulip_festival/index.cm/ (3 October 2002).

and expressive dance style, accompanied by African drums. The effect was to demonstrate not only that they could perform European-based dances, but also that they could improve on these performances by adding their own energy and cultural flair.

Other efforts to validate African American heritage included the performances of master drummer Chief Bey, who educated his audiences about African culture by explaining some of the features that distinguish African drumming. He exhorted his audience to "forget you're Americans for the time," and taught them a series of oral responses, which he instructed them to use as he chanted and beat out particular rhythms. Openly declaring the sophistication of drumming and the artistry of his own music, he commented, "it is very difficult, very hard to play." Chief Bey also used his stature as a performer to decry racism and its consequences by exhorting his audience, "We got to make beautiful music together. We've got to turn this thing around. White, black, red, yellow, or green. We've got to do it together." At the same time, he challenged Eurocentric assumptions with his observation that "African music is more harmonious than Western music," a statement that he slipped into his presentation among many other comments as a way of reaffirming the value and primacy of African cultural practices.

The African colonial dance troupe chose as their name the Children of Dahomey (after the African kingdom currently known as the Republic of Benin). Group leader Judith Samuel informed me that the dances they performed at the Pinkster festival were imitative of dances done by eighteenth-century slaves in the area, drawing on various national dances, work dances, and quadrilles from the African Diaspora. The dancers framed their performance with pointed reminders of cultural context and the history of racial oppression. Samuel introduced the troupe to the crowd by stating that although enslaved people certainly enjoyed Pinkster festivities, this celebration was not an everyday practice for them. Slavery was not fun, she reminded the audience, and the contemporary Pinkster festival would not give viewers a realistic understanding of what it was like to be enslaved. Samuel explained that the troupe members would be assuming the roles of first-generation Africans, who had been captured in their homelands and exported by slave traders. Imitating an African accent, a second dancer then introduced herself as "Sara of the Malagasy people, of Madagascar." She continued her narrative, "I was stolen when I was a little girl and brought here to be slave. I am not happy. I was sold from my parents, and I will never see my mother and father again."

As she began singing, she instructed the audience, about half of whom were African Americans, to join her in a melancholy refrain, "Work till the day is done," which they sang repeatedly. The four dancers played the roles of Philipsburg Manor slaves, two women and two men. Part of the story they enacted involved a father teaching his grown son how to play the drums, again reinforcing the centrality of drumming in African cultures. During a 1993 performance, a group of young African American children from the Tabernacle of Prayer Bible Institute in White Plains, New York, watched attentively as they saw and heard aspects of their own racial heritage publicly valorized in a multiracial setting. They were clearly captivated by what they saw, and most of them were eager to join in the dancing. Many other people in the crowd, such as myself, were exposed to an interpretation of a past about which they previously knew very little.

African American storytellers also performed at the festival, one to three each year, both women and men. All of them imitated African accents when they told their stories, adapting their grammar and diction to suggest they had taken on the personas of unschooled, enslaved Africans. Their material varied widely, but many of the stories they told referred to African life or cultures. Dylan Pritchett told African and African American stories that encouraged his listeners to consider moral dilemmas. He explained to me that he also attempts to teach African history and cultural values through his storytelling, particularly to audiences of children. Racial pride and the inversion of dominant cultural norms were central features in many of his tales.

While assuming a slave persona, Pritchett offered a political reading of a Biblical creation story during the 1993 Pinkster festival. In the beginning, according to Pritchett's rendition, God created Adam, and then he created Eve from Adam's rib:

> They was all Negroes. Weren't no white folks here in the beginning. No, not in the beginning. What happened was, Cain and Abel got arguing 'bout who was the handsomer. So Cain killed Abel. And God came down lookin for Abel, didn't see him nowhere, but he saw Cain. Cain was workin' in the field. And he said, "Cain, where art thy brother?" Cain was uppity, didn't even turn around. He said, "Am I my brother's keeper?" Lord said, "Cain, where art thy brother?" Cain said, "Am I my brother's keeper?" So God got hot then. God said, "CAIN, WHERE ART THY BROTHER?" And Cain turned around and saw that it was God. His hair went straight up, his face went pale. And that's where white men came from!

In the guise of a humorous punchline, Pritchett delivered a message about the primacy of black identity.[32] Pritchett later told me that he saw himself as a *griot,* drawing on the African tradition of an oral historian and storyteller whose role it is to educate his or her listeners about their cultural traditions. Senegalese storyteller D'Jimo Kouyate describes a griot as a combination of an oral historian, educator, and a cultural informant, noting that ". . . the griot's main intention is not to entertain but to teach the people to know themselves."[33] Pritchett clearly used his stories to teach values and to convey a sense of cultural and racial identity. At the end of a storytelling session during the 1992 festival, he exhorted his audience, "The importance of Pinkster is to remember."

In September 1992 Historic Hudson Valley sponsored their First Annual African American Heritage Awards, honoring five researchers, writers, and performers who have focused their work on African American culture and history in the region. The invitations to the award banquet noted that "in 1983 we uncovered an African presence specific to our sites that reflects the contribution made by enslaved Africans in the eighteenth century to the building of New York State through commerce and industry. At Historic Hudson Valley we are committed to continuous research and program development relating to these discoveries." A growing awareness of the multiple traditions of marginalized groups has affected the ways in which this historical society, like a growing number of other societies and museums, have broadened and redefined their work in cultural preservation and representation. An evolving sense of diversity among racial, ethnic, and cultural groups in the United States has the potential to become a major force for change in the theoretical directions that museum professionals and community-based social historians pursue in the future.

Two factors have dramatically affected this reorientation. First, among an increasing number of people there is the recognition that many cultural groups previously overlooked by historians and scholars are no longer willing to accept their "invisible" status. Second, immigration has altered the composition of many communities across the country. African Americans, who now exceed 30 million in number, are more recognized, even among whites, as important social and political forces. . . . Moreover, currently a full one-quarter of the annual growth in the U.S. population is the result of immigration, and the majority of these immigrants are people of color and non-Europeans.[34]

Historic Hudson Valley's efforts to recreate a Pinkster festival that centers on the experiences of African Americans exemplifies attempts by historical societies and museums to encourage the participation of people of color both as audiences and performers of significant traditions that have been eradicated or forgotten. In her essay in an anthology entitled *Museums and Communities: The Politics of Public Culture,* Fath Davis Ruffins[35] delineates some of the ways in which African American museums have been involved in attempts to combat racist interpretations of history by reconstructing self-identities and building knowledge about heritage and accomplishments that seldom are known or recognized. She notes that as museums and historical societies begin with and center on African American experiences, they shift the focus of public attention from the dominant Euro-American historical record to a broader and deeper understanding of the past. When this occurs, cultural events such as the Pinkster festival have the potential to become vehicles for social change, speaking to African Americans through expressive forms familiar to them and educating others by exposing them to alternative ways of understanding the world.

The history of class stratification and economic inequality also influenced the Pinkster festival design. The North Tarrytown celebration accentuated the lives and activities of the slaves and tenant farmers, the latter represented by the English Country Dancers, the women who dyed and spun yarn in the tenant farm house, and various laborers who tended the livestock, worked in the grist mill, and staffed the booths. With the exception of a walk-through tour of the manor house and, possibly, one woman's performances on the hammered dulcimer, the cultural practices of the wealthy landowners were altogether absent from the North Tarrytown festivals. Instead, the celebrations focused on the slaves and working poor, as they did at the height of Pinkster festivities during the late eighteenth and early nineteenth centuries. This was doubly ironic given that the North Tarrytown Pinkster festival was reenacted on the grounds of a manor owned by one of the wealthiest white landowners in the colonies, whose estate and artifacts were preserved precisely because of his wealth and social privilege.

Issues of gender also caught my eye at the Philipsburg Manor celebrations.[36] Despite the fact that there was little written about them, it would have been surprising had black women been absent from or uninvolved in historic Pinkster celebrations. Chronicles suggest that enslaved women were centrally involved in the historical celebration. The Pinkster Ode, a lengthy poetic tribute written in 1803, noted that while the master drummer performed, "vocal sounds were readily taken up and as oft repeated by the female portion of the spectators not otherwise engaged in the exercises of the scene, accompanied by the beating of time with their ungloved hands," and they sang and celebrated along with men.[37] In his insightful analysis of Hudson Valley social history, A. J. Williams-Myers delineates the diversity of roles that enslaved African and African American women maintained while working in homes, farms and manors, and in the cities. Williams-Myers clearly demonstrates how the financial security and prosperity of white society depended in large measure upon these women's unpaid labor. In cooking, housekeeping, washing clothes, caring for their owners' children, manufacturing textiles, gardening, tending to animals and livestock, planting and harvesting crops, and a wide array of other tasks, enslaved women were central to the social organization and economic prosperity of New York.[38]

I noticed an unusual sense of gender balance in the structure and presentation of the contemporary Pinkster festival in North Tarrytown. In 1992, for example, women were in charge of staging the festival and leading both the

African Colonial and the English Country Dance Troupes. Two of the three storytellers were women. Women cooked, and they dyed and spun yarn. Men were the drummers, and they were members of both dance troupes. One of the storytellers was a man, and men worked on the manor grounds as millers, cooks on the open grill, and as livestock caretakers.

Although it was never directly mentioned or emphasized, women were responsible for much that occurred at the contemporary North Tarrytown festivals. They had major roles in organizing the festivities and performing for the crowds. Primary among them was Director of Programs Radiah Harper Sumler, who commented to me that during the first four years of the contemporary festival at Philipsburg Manor, the event was a celebration by whites of Euro-American colonial history. Sumler began her work with Historic Hudson Valley in 1988, building on the initial efforts of her predecessor, Renee Friedman. Sumler, an African American social historian, soon cultivated contacts and resources in African American as well as Native American communities in the region, working to make the annual Pinkster festival a more multiracial event. She noted that more African Americans now attend this event than any other sponsored by the historical society.[39]

Conclusion

In their discussion of the complexities of representation in multicultural societies, Arjun Appadurai and Carol A. Breckenridge remind us that heritage is a profoundly political issue, that museums and historical societies interested in portraying social histories and traditions are immersed in political issues. They note that prioritizing, presenting, viewing, and experiencing cultural heritage are problematic processes that must be negotiated on many levels.[40] Historic Hudson Valley, like other historical societies and museums, is involved in the business of conceptualizing and displaying cultural practices from the past in ways that shape our thinking about the cultural politics of the present. Artist Guillermo Gómez-Peña, in writing about the politics of public culture and historical representation, contends that the decision *not* to reproduce the dominant cultural record, but rather to resist it, often leads to the celebration of the lives, stories, and artistic expression of people who have been defined as the Other.[41] Regeneration of the Pinkster festival suggests that staff members and performers were acutely aware of the need to problematize and negotiate dominant interpretations of the past by offering differing or contested versions to a contemporary audience.

The Pinkster tradition of the late eighteenth and early nineteenth centuries infused an originally European holiday with cultural memories of Africa. African Americans redefined the festival, eventually appropriating control over its form and content. Starting in the late 1780s, just as Pinkster celebrations by enslaved blacks were reaching their peak, the number of runaway slaves increased dramatically, both reflecting and contributing to the increasing restlessness of the black population in the North after the Revolutionary War. Enslaved blacks and slaveholders in New York heard news of slave revolts in places like Saint Dominique, the West Indies, and Virginia. In the 1790s and early 1800s a new mood of assertiveness arose among northern blacks, and incidents of arson, assaults on white slaveholders, and small-scale rioting by blacks became more frequent.[42] Historian Williams-Myers suggests that just prior to U.S. involvement in the War of 1812, whites were becoming increasingly suspicious that blacks supported the cause of the enemy.[43] In 1811 a slave revolt in Louisiana foreshadowed uprisings throughout the country. Citing a history of "boisterous rioting and drunkenness" by Pinkster participants, the Albany Common Council passed a city ordinance in 1811 banning future Pinkster celebrations. In reflecting on the impact that Pinkster and other African American cultural events may have had on the history of New York State, Shane White observes that Pinkster foreshadowed the ways in which blacks

> . . . largely through their own efforts, hastened the death of slavery, broadening the scope of the emancipation program and moving forward by a number of years the more limited and leisurely timetable put in place by the state legislature. Although under the New York legislation slaves born before 1799 were not to be freed until July 4, 1827, all but the most recalcitrant slave owners had come to some sort of arrangement with their slaves well before this date. Again, one is impressed with the ability of these slaves to sense the indecisiveness of their masters and to convert a local practice into an effective vehicle for attaining freedom.[44]

Contemporary Pinkster celebrations in North Tarrytown have been shaped by their own set of social and historical circumstance. Program Director Radiah Sumler was acutely aware of racism and racial tensions in the world around her as she organized the festival. In my May 1993 interview with her, she mentioned recent violent incidents between African Americans and whites in nearby Ossining, Mount Vernon, and New Rochelle, where the percentage of African Americans and racial tensions are higher than in North Tarrytown. And just a few weeks earlier, she commented, race riots in Los Angeles threatened to destroy the inner city there. In this context, the reappropriation and adaptation of Pinkster acquired added meaning. Sumler's efforts, and those of other organizers and performers, represented an attempt to reclaim and redefine African American cultural history in a society shaped by racism.

Notes

1. Shane White, "Pinkster: Afro-Dutch Syncretization in New York City and the Hudson Valley," *Journal of American Folklore* 102:403 (Jan—Mar. 1989): 68.

2. My analysis is based on my observations of Pinkster festivals I attended in North Tarrytown, New York, during the weekends of May 9–10, 1992; May 8–9, 1993; May 7–8, 1994, and May 13–14, 1995.

3. Alessandro Falassi, "Festival: Definition and Morphology"; in *Time Out of Time: Essays on the Festival,* ed. by Alessandro Falassi (Albuquerque: University of New Mexico Press, 1987), p. 2.

4. Robert Dirks, *The Black Saturnalia: Conflict and its Ritual Expression on British West Indian Slave Plantations* (Gainesville: University of Florida Press, 1987), p. 2.

5. See Juan Newton Radner, ed., *Feminist Messages: Coding in Women's Folk Culture* (Urbana and Chicago: University of Illinois Press, 1993) and James Scott, *Domination and the Arts of Resistance: Hidden Transcripts* (New Haven: Yale Univ. Press, 1990) and *Weapons of the Weak: Everyday Forms of Peasant Resistance* (New Haven: Yale Univ. Press, 1985).

6. Scott, *Domination and the Arts of Resistance,* p. 19.

7. Frank Manning, "Cosmos arid Chaos: Celebration in the Modern World," in *The Celebration of Society: Perspectives of Contemporary Cultural Performance,* ed. by Frank E. Manning (Bowling Green, Ohio: Bowling Green University Popular Press, 1983), p. 14.

8. Ibid., p. 4.

9. See Barbara A. Babcock, ed., *The Reversible World: Symbolic Inversion in Art and Society* (Ithaca and London: Cornell University Press, 1978); Gregory Bateson, *Naven: A Survey of Fete Problems Suggested by a Composite Picture of the Culture of a New Guinea Tribe Drawn from Three Points of View,* 2d ed. (Palo Alto, California: Stanford University Press, 1958); Clifford Geertz, *The Interpretation of Cultures; Selected Essays* (New York: Basic Books, 1973); MacCannell, Dean, *The Tourist* (1976; reprint, New York: Schocken Books, 1989); and Victor Turner, *Dramas, Fields, and Metaphors; Symbolic Action in Human Society* (Ithaca, New York: Cornell University Press, 1974) and *Schism and Continuity in an African Society: A Study of Ndembu Village Life* (Manchester, England: Manchester University Press, 1957).

10. Manning, "Cosmos and Chaos," p. 7.

11. Steven D. Lavine and Ivan Karp, "Introduction: Museums and Multiculturalism," in *Exhibiting Cultures: The Poetics and Politics of Museum Display,* Ivan Karp and Steven D. Lavine, eds. (Washington and London: Smithsonian Institution Press, 1991), p. 1.

12. Robert H. Lavenda, "Festivals and the Creation of Public Culture: Whose Voice(s)?" in *Museums and Communities: The Politics of Public Culture,* Ivan Karp, Christine Mullen Kreamer, and Steven D. Lavine, eds. (Washington and London: Smithsonian Institution Press, 1992), p. 101.

13. John J. MacAloon, "Introduction: Cultural Performances, Culture Theory," in *Rite, Drama, Festival, Spectacle: Rehearsals Toward a Theory of Cultural Performance,* ed. by John J. MacAloon (Philadelphia: Institute for the Study of Human Issues, 1983), pp. 1–2.

14. Scott, *Domination and the Arts of Resistance,* p. xii.

15. A. J. Williams-Myers, "The African Presence in the Hudson River Valley: The Defining of Relationships Between the Masters and the Slaves," *Afro-Americans its New York Life and History* 12: 1 (1988): 3.

16. Shane White, *Somewhat More Independent: The End of Slavery in New York City, 1770–1810* (Athens and London: University of Georgia Press, 1991), p. 16. In his study of slavery in New York City, White noted that "the ratio of slaveholding to non-slaveholding households effectively highlights the striking involvement of whites from this region in the institution of slavery. There were proportionately more households containing slaves in New York's hinterland than in the whole of any southern state."

17. Ibid., p. 86.

18. See Williams-Myers, "The African Presence in the Hudson River Valley" for a description of the climate of fear and violence that often characterized slavery in New York.

19. White, *Somewhat More Independent,* pp. 88–90.

20. Ibid., pp. 21, 55. The activist and abolitionist Sojourner Truth began her life as an enslaved black in Ulster County, New York. Born in the late 1700s, she was given the name Isabella Baumfree by her Dutch master. See Gloria I. Joseph, "Sojourner Truth: Archetypal Black Feminist," in *Wild Women in the Whirlwind: Afro-American Culture and the Contemporary Literary Renaissance,* Joanne M. Braxton and Andrée Nicola McLaughlin, eds. (New Brunswick, New Jersey: Rutgers University Press, 1990), p. 35.

21. White, "Pinkster: Afro-Dutch Syncretization," p. 68.

22. White, *Somewhat More Independent,* p. 103.

23. A. J. Williams-Myers, "Pinkster Carnival: Africanisms in the Hudson River Valley," *Afro-Americans its New York Life and History* 9 (1985): 9. In contrast, see Shane White,

"Pinkster in Albany, 1803: A Contemporary Description," *New York History* 70: 2 (1989): 193, for his argument that, although influenced by African features, the Pinkster celebrations of black slaves were antecedents and adaptations of festivals of misrule, or the world-turned-upside-down festivals, that characterized early modern Europe.

24. See Sterling Stuckey, *Slave Culture: Nationalist Theory and the Foundations of Black America* (New York and Oxford: Oxford University Press, 1987); White, "Pinkster in Albany," "Pinkster: Afro-Dutch Syncretization;" and *Somewhat More Independent;* and Williams-Myers, "Pinkster Carnival," A Portrait *of* Eve: Towards a Social History *of Black Women* in the Hudson River Valley (New Paltz, New York: Center for the Study of the African Presence in the Hudson River Valley, 1987), and "The Arduous Journey: The African American Presence in the Hudson-Mohawk Region," in *The African American Presence in New York State History: Four Regional History Surveys*

(Albany: State University of New York, The New York African American Institute, 1989), pp. 19–50.

25. Williams-Myers, "The African Presence in the Hudson River Valley," p. 9.

26. White, "Pinkster Afro-Dutch Syncretization," p. 70.

27. Williams-Myers, "Pinkster Carnival: Africanisms in the Hudson River Valley," pp. 10–11.

28. White, "Pinkster: Afro-Dutch Syncretization," p. 68.

29. *Friends of Historic Hudson Valley,* brochure, n.d.

30. Exhibition entitled "Preserving New York," Philipsburg Manor Museum, 1993.

31. Winifred Yu, "Tulip Queen Finalists Selected," *Albany Times Union,* 2 May 1994, B-3. All seven of the 1994 Tulip Queen finalists were white women between the ages of 18 and 23. The contestants, who must be residents of Albany or the surrounding townships, vie for the title, a cash prize of $1,500, and the chance to appear at city and civic events during a one-year reign.

32. Pritchett's rendition of this tale offers a significant contrast to related stories that depict either the creation of blacks as an accident by God, or the creation of blacks as secondary or peripheral to the creation of whites (see, for example, "In the Beginning" and "Why the Nigger is So Messed Up" in Daryl Cumber Dance, *Shuckin' and Jivin': Folklore from Contemporary Black Americans* (Bloomington, Indiana, 1987), pp. 7–8.)

33. D'Jimo Kouyate, "The Role of the Griot," in *Talk That Talk: An Anthology of African American Storytelling,* Linda Goss and Marian E. Barnes, eds. (New York: Simon and Schuster, 1989), p. 180.

34. Edmund Barry Gaither, "'Hey! That's Mine': Thoughts on Pluralism and American Museums," in *Museums and Communities: The Politics of Public Culture,* Ivan Karp, Christine Mullen Kreamer, and Steven D. Lavine, eds. (Washington and London: Smithsonian Institution Press, 1992).

35. Fath Davis Ruffins, "Mythos, Memory, and History: African American Preservation Efforts, 1820–1990," in *Museums and Communities: The Politics of Public Culture,* Ivan Karp, Christine Mullen Kreamer, and Steven D. Lavine, eds. (Washington and London: Smithsonian Institution Press, 1992), pp. 506–611.

36. For a broader analysis of women's roles in the North Tarrytown Pinkster festival, see Linda Pershing, "'You Can't Do That, You're the Wrong Race!': African American Women Storytellers at a Contemporary Festival," *Women and Language* 14: 1 (1996): 57–63.

37. White, "Pinkster: Afro-Dutch Syncretization," p. 73. I would speculate that eighteenth- and nineteenth-century observers wrote so little about women's roles in Pinkster festivities because they were men, most of them white men, who due to their own gender biases and racial bigotry, either did not see or could not appreciate the participation of black women.

38. Williams-Myers, "The African Presence in the Hudson River Valley," pp. 81–98.

39. Radiah Harper Sumler, interview with author, 10 May 1992.

40. Arjun Appadurai, "Museums Are Good to Think: Heritage on View in India," in

Museums and Communities: The Politics of Public Culture, Ivan Karp, Christine Mullen Kreamer, and Steven D. Lavine, eds. (Washington and London: Smithsonian Institution Press, 1992), p. 37.

41. Guillermo Gómez-Peña, "The Other Vanguard," in *Museums and Communities: The Politics of Public Culture,* Ivan Karp, Christine Mullen Kreamer, and Steven D. Lavine, eds. (Washington and London: Smithsonian Institution Press, 1992), pp. 65–75.

42. White, *Somewhat More Independent,* p. 145.

43. Williams- Myers, "Pinkster Carnival," p. 16.

44. White, *Somewhat More Independent,* p. 111.

11

Paul Stoller

Spaces, Places, and Fields

The Politics of West African Trading in New York City's Informal Economy

In the following chapter on the Harlem street vendors' controversy of the mid-1990s, anthropologist Paul Stoller permits a glimpse into the multiplex of contemporary black identities in the Hudson Valley, especially as influenced by the immigration of West African merchants from Senegal, Mali, and Niger to Manhattan during the last decade. Assorted West African ethnic, religious, national, and trade identities jostled against each other and alongside fragmented African American political, religious, and economic identities to make for a melange of competing transnational alliances in the struggle for access to market space. West African merchants disagreed among themselves over the likely effects of Mayor Rudolph Giuliani's decision to move their operating venue from 125th Street to 116th Street. African American businesses on 125th Street differed over whether their competing businesses would suffer or improve if West African merchants were forced to relocate. Black American Muslims—varied between the Nation of Islam and the Masjid Malcolm Shabazz—both proclaimed support for the vendors; yet only the latter offered alternative space to the street retailers, and many Muslims among them rejected the former as a genuine representation of their faith. A formal neighborhood and economic development organization endorsed the change. Other outside black activists seized the opportunity to gain political capital by opposing the move as an attack on traditional black self-help through race entrepreneurship. In all these maneuvers, what was at stake was the identity of blacks as honest, hard-working business people, with all groups claiming legitimacy for their vision and practice.

The "field" in anthropology is becoming a dizzying array of crosscutting transnational spaces within zones of multiple contestation. Consider the kaleidoscopic forces that converged in mid-October 1994 on New York City's 125th Street, the cultural crossroads of Harlem. A loosely organized "union" of African American vendors and West African traders from Senegal, Mali, Niger, and the Gambia (the 125th Street Vendors Association) threatened to shut down 125th Street if Mayor Giuliani made good on his campaign promise to disperse the African market from Harlem's main thoroughfare. Although the union is supported by the Nation of Islam, whose ministers preach versions of Islamic purity and African American self-sufficiency, some members of the union dislike and distrust Louis Farrakhan. Many of the West African traders wonder how such a man can call himself a Muslim.

The vendors are also supported by the Reverend Al Sharpton, who uses his particular orientation to Christianity to articulate his solidarity with hard-working African and African American people. After the market's dispersal, Sharpton was arrested for selling Bibles. Then there are the supportive Asian and African American shop owners on 125th Street who think that the crowds brought in by the African market are good for business. There are, of course, just as many Asian and African American shop owners who think the presence of the vendors is bad for business. They say that the vendors are disrespectful, dirty, and engage in unfair business practices.

Like the Nation of Islam, the Masjid Malcolm Shabazz (the religious organization founded by Malcolm X) promotes Islamic austerity and African American self-sufficiency. But the Masjid promotes a plan to regulate the vendors, suggesting that the unregulated 125th Street market be moved nine blocks south of the shopping district to their regulated and city-sanctioned site at 116th Street and Lenox Avenue, a commercially depressed space. They want to charge the vendors a $100 vending registration fee, which would make them "legal," as well as rents of $7 per day. In exchange, they would monitor the market's cleanliness and security.

This idea is endorsed by the Harlem Business Alliance and the Harlem Urban Development Corporation. Both organizations promote economic ties to West Africa but do not like the cluttered, unregulated presence of an open-air African market on Harlem's major business boulevard. Such a presence may well be intolerable, for it suggests spatially that Harlem's economic renaissance is but an illusion. Harlem's elected officials, who have vested interests in economic development, also support the 125th Street crackdown and the Masjid's "generous offer." The Masjid Malcolm Shabazz's plan is also welcomed warmly by the Giuliani administration. And why not? The plan co-opts a generally revered African American religious institution and provides a peaceful alternative to the violent racial confrontation that no mayor would want. At the same time, city hall would receive 30% of the revenues that the Masjid collects, meaning that it would collect taxes from previously unlicensed and untaxed vendors. In exchange, city hall would police the market and clean the streets regularly. The plan also provides positive political payoffs for the Giuliani administration. Giuliani could say that he is keeping his political promises. Police Commissioner Bratton could say he is following through on his promise to enforce city regulations, which, as we shall see, are at odds with the practices of an informal economy.

Most of the West African traders, who say that their market reinvigorated the economy of 125th Street, are seemingly powerless pawns in the "chessboard" of New York City's political and cultural discourse. And yet they, like the exceedingly diverse African American community in Harlem, construct complex discourses of their own. The Senegalese, for example, have been in New York City since 1982 and are well represented among the West African traders in Harlem. Some Senegalese, most notably those well established in various businesses, support the market's move to 116th Street. Many Senegalese street vendors, however, oppose the mayor's crackdown. These differences are exacerbated by ethnic, regional, and religious differences. Senegalese from the Casamance, the south, are less likely to be tied into northern economic and religious networks that are controlled by majority peoples (Wolof, Serere). Many of the Senegalese in New York City, moreover, are also devotees of the Mourid Sufi order, which, according to street vendors from Mali and Niger, had invested capital in the Masjid Malcolm Shabazz, giving the Masjid's market plan a putative behind-the-scenes Senegalese connection. Vendors from Mali reacted to the market's dispersal with pragmatic resignation. Although they all wanted to remain at the African market, they refused to march with the 125th Street Vendors Association on October 17. Some of them decided to pay $100 to register at the Masjid's 116th Street market; others, who blamed the African market's demise on the Senegalese, refused to pay money to people who wanted to ruin their trading businesses. Several recently arrived people from Niger, however, marched in the vendors' October 17 demonstration. Most of the more established traders from Niger did not participate, even though they wanted to remain on 125th Street. Thinking that the cost of trading on Canal Street—as much as $2,500 a month to rent storefront shelf space—would be too expensive, some of them agreed to move their operations to 116th Street; others refused to do so. The Nigeriens angrily blamed the market's demise on the greed of the African American community, for which they have little respect and much distrust.

Market Space in Harlem

New York City, October 15, 1994. Two bowtied men in black suits hawk Nation of Islam pamphlets and sell bean pies on the northeast corner of 125th Street and Lenox Avenue, the commercial crossroads of Harlem. People stream along the sidewalks. The intersection is choked with traffic: buses transport people to appointments uptown and downtown, fleets of large delivery trucks make their rounds, late-model cars blare rap music as they pass through, and older and more silent clunkers feature hand-lettered signs that say "livery" or "taxi." These gas-guzzlers are gypsy cabs, the main substitute for taxis in the poorer neighborhoods of New York City; their drivers discharge and pick up fares at 125th and Lenox.

The crowds thicken considerably, however, on the west side of Lenox Avenue at 125th Street, the site of the African market. From a distance, the market is a collage of parked vans, aluminum tables, incense smoke, and brilliantly colored and patterned imported cloth. People saunter through this space, pausing here to chat, there to bargain and perhaps buy strips of brightly colored homespun Ghanaian kenti cloth, Kenyan baskets, leather bags from Niger, Meccan incense, West African trade beads, or Tuareg silver jewelry. They might also select from assortments of "trademarked" American T-shirts, sunglasses, handbags, and baseball caps, almost all of which are manufactured in export processing zones outside the United States.

At first glance the African market appears to be a mass of disorganization. Sidewalks seem cluttered with vendors' tables. To an outsider, chaos seems to govern where or what a vendor might sell. But first impressions are misleading, for the space of the African market is indeed organized, albeit informally.

Such informal organization is the hallmark of markets throughout West Africa. Like the market in Harlem, the movement of goods and people through open-market space in West Africa also appears chaotic to outsiders—at least initially. It is well known, however, that the space of most West African markets is often, if not always, apportioned and regulated through informal mechanisms.[1] In those markets, members of the same ethnic group or small village cluster and sell the same kind of merchandise. In the larger Songhay/Zarma markets in the republic of Niger, for example, Fulani herders sell cattle, milk, and butter; Hausa people butcher and sell meat; Yorubas from Nigeria sell pots, pans, and hardware; and Songhay/Zarma people sell grain and spices—all from informally designated spaces.

The story of markets in West Africa entails much sociological and religious complexity. The lure of trade and markets spurred the medieval spread of Islam from North to West Africa.[2] The attraction of centralized urban markets also sparked much urban migration throughout West African history.[3]

The over 100 years' history of migration—long and short-term—of Songhay and Hausa from Niger to the Guinea Coast is a case in point.[4] In the political arena, Islam provided the context for the construction of specific religious identities (Quadiriyya, Tijaniyya, Muridiyya, Hammalliya, Wahhabiyya) that have continuously fragmented local, regional, and state social relations in West Africa (see Brenner 1993).[5] No matter the extent of frictions generated by this religious fragmentation, it has not usually interfered with trade. As Emmanuel Gregoire wrote in his study of Islam and identity among Hausas in Niger, "A marabout explained, `You can do business with anybody; what's important is to earn a profit.' Another went even further: `Money has no smell, and you can, indeed, do business with non-Muslims, with Christians for example.'"[6]

This rich and complex set of traditions and practices influences the attitudes and behaviors of West African traders at the African market in Harlem. In terms of the spatial allocation of market tables, the 125th Street space is organized like many West African markets, though more by country of origin than by ethnic identity. Malians, for example, are the principal cloth merchants. They sell from tables and stalls along both sides of the wide Lenox Avenue sidewalk. Pockets of Malians can also be found along the north sidewalk of 125th Street. Senegalese and Gambians occupy the northwestern corner of 125th and Lenox, where they sell trade beads, incense, leather bracelets decorated with cowrie shells, and earrings and rings, also decorated with cowrie shells. Walking farther west on 125th Street, one passes some African Americans selling religious books, including the *Koran*. One bookseller hawks Afrocentric titles as well as cassettes. He displays the books on two tables. Videos, including lectures by Ivan Van Sertima, an Afrocentric historian, are shown on a television set on the roof of the vendor's parked car—a complex articulation of multiple ideologies in the space of 50 feet.

Farther west on the north side of 125th Street, one approaches the Carver State Bank and the vendor space occupied by men from Niger. Some of these vendors sell handbags from Korea; others hawk straw hats from China or straw bags from Kenya. One man offers woven bags from Turkey and leather bags from Niger. Another Nigerien sells sunglasses from Chinatown in the summer and pirated videos in the winter. In order to test the quality of the videos, he has a television and video playback machine wired to a car battery underneath his vending table.[7] Other Nigeriens sell baseball caps with the insignias of professional and college sports teams. Other caps, T-shirts, and sweatshirts are inscribed with trademarked social messages from Spike Lee or with such trademarked names as Hugo Boss, Karl Kani, or Timberland. Into this cultural kaleidoscope, West African street merchants bring trading traditions that are profoundly shaped by Islam. Indeed, for West African traders, "money has no smell" on the sidewalks of Harlem, and these merchants have no regrets about selling copies of the latest "ethnic" chic. As one trader admitted, "We will sell anything to anyone, even drug dealers who have lots of cash. We don't believe in drugs or drug dealing, but we are in business, are we not?"[8]

Moving ever westward, one approaches the Adam Clayton Powell State Office Building. Here are Senegalese selling sunglasses—including Ray Bans—dolls, and jewelry. A vendor from Uganda sells print reproductions of batiks. Toward the corner of 125th Street and 7th Avenue, Jamaicans sell what the West African vendors call "wood"—statues carved in Africa.[9] Much of this "wood" is carved in the parodic image of West African colonial officials; this ubiquitous type of African art (known as the "colon") has become economically viable, perhaps because it accords well with contemporary mainstream tastes for colonial nostalgia. In Harlem, the dreadlocked men from the Caribbean, situated among closely cropped West Africans, sell "authentic" images of Africa to African American shoppers whose urge to buy "wood" is compelled by long-standing notions of African pride, most of which are incomprehensible to the Africans "represented" by the statuettes. Ironically, such incomprehensibility charges the market with energy.

Unlike West African markets, none of these "national" spaces in Harlem is purely national.[10] A few African American vendors can be found among the Malians, Senegalese, and Nigeriens. Several Malians sell from tables among the Nigeriens. Small clusters of Senegalese sit next to Jamaicans. No "national" space is inviolable at the African market.

Such informality gives this open-air market an easy, festive air. Double-decker buses from Apple Tours bring camera packing Europeans to "shoot" the African market—from a safe distance. Swarms of shoppers move freely up and down the sidewalks, looking at bags, touching print fabrics, trying on straw hats or jewelry. Their movement through space is constrained only by the presence of other shoppers and by Senegalese women selling African food from shopping carts.

The vendors talk freely to shoppers in American English of varying degrees of sophistication, influenced by local African American idioms. Prices are fairly rigid for baseball caps, scarves, and gloves. They are less so for African merchandise, for which many shoppers bargain. Refusing to bargain or buy, some of the shoppers complain about high prices.[11]

Among themselves the traders converse in English, French, and a variety of West African languages, enjoying the banter that comes with periodic lulls in trading. During their afternoon prayers, the vendors look after one another's merchandise—informal protection against the ever present threat of theft.

Although the vendors at the African market occasionally violate any number of minor city regulations and trademark and copyright statutes, the police are subdued. Their primary preoccupation, it seems, is to enforce parking regulations, especially along 125th Street. Otherwise they tend to leave the vendors alone. The easy, festive openness of the African market, however, came to an abrupt end on October 17, 1994, when Mayor Giuliani ordered it closed.

A Brief History of the African Market

Although African Americans have a long history of vending on the streets of Harlem, the first West African vendors did not migrate uptown until 1990.[12] A Senegalese art dealer claims to be the first African to vend on 125th Street.[13] He was soon joined by other Senegalese, Malians, and Nigeriens. Gradually, the African character of the 125th Street market became more and more dominant.

Prior to 1990, the primary practitioners of informal street trading in New York City were Senegalese men vending from tables set up along midtown Manhattan sidewalks. Given the regulatory difficulties of obtaining a vending license in New York City, the majority of the Senegalese conducted unlicensed operations.[14] By 1985, scores of Senegalese had set up tables in front of some of Manhattan's most expensive retail space on Fifth Avenue. Such a cluttered, informal third-world space in a first-world setting soon proved intolerable to the Fifth Avenue Merchants Association. Headed by Donald Trump, the association urged city hall to crack down on unlicensed vendors.

Following the "cleanup," Senegalese vendors relocated to less precious spaces in Midtown such as Lexington Avenue, 42nd Street near Grand Central Station, and 34th Street near Times Square. They also worked in teams to protect themselves from the authorities and petty criminals. One person would sell goods at his table while his compatriot partners would post themselves on corners as lookouts. Another compatriot would serve as the bank, holding money safely away from the trade site. In this way, Midtown side streets became Senegalese turf.

As more and more Senegalese arrived in New York City, the vending territory expanded north to 86th Street on the East Side and south to 14th Street in Greenwich Village and Canal Street in Lower Manhattan. In some areas the Senegalese replaced vending tables with attaché cases filled with Rolex and other "high-end" watches. The vendor would stand on a Midtown corner with his attaché case open for casual inspection. A man with an attaché case—even an open one—in Midtown blends in with first world spatial surroundings. Besides, he had his lookouts across the street and his money holder at midblock. This strategy made these vendors more mobile and less visible. It also demonstrates how the Senegalese confounded mainstream American spatial assumptions—to their own economic advantage.

By 1990 the Senegalese had a lock on informal vending space in most of Manhattan. Backed by the considerable financial power of the Mourids, a Muslim Sufi brotherhood in Senegal to which the vast majority of Senegalese vendors belonged, they soon became the aristocracy of African merchants in New York.[15] When merchants from Mali and Niger immigrated to New York City in 1990, the Senegalese had already saturated the lucrative Midtown markets, compelling them to set up their tables along 125th Street in Harlem.

As West African vendors trickled into Harlem between 1990 and 1992, the African market grew, extending west from the corners of 125th and Lenox to 125th and Adam Clayton Powell Boulevard. Although vendors reported that business was only fair during the week, on weekends the market swelled with shoppers. By 1992, the African Market had become one of New York City's tourist attractions. "Before we brought African things here," said one vendor from Niger, "125th [Street] was deserted. No one came here. People were afraid of little bandits and drugs. When we came here we brought crowds and tourists. We revitalized 125th Street."[16]

The growth and success of the market brought with it a bevy of political problems in New York City. Like the Fifth Avenue Merchants Association, the Harlem Business Alliance lobbied the Dinkins administration to disperse the "illegal" vendors. With the support of Harlem's elected officials (federal, state, and city), the administration decided, albeit reluctantly, to enforce the city's vending ordinances. The enforcement plan proved to be a dismal failure. In protest against Dinkins's decision, the 125th Street Vendors Association, comprised of African American and West African street merchants, staged a demonstration that shut down 125th Street for one day. Although the police voiced their willingness to disperse the protesters, Dinkins, fearing the violent consequences of a police–vendor confrontation, backed down. The market continued to grow following Dinkins's capitulation. In March of 1993, vendors reported hearing rumors about the imminent dispersal of the market. "We hear these things all the time," one merchant said. "But we are not worried. Last time they tried to shut us down, we shut down all of 125th Street. They will leave us alone."[17] Most of the vendors I talked with seemed more worried about the effect of cold weather on sales than the effect of city hall's regulatory enforcement. Rumors nonetheless persisted throughout the spring and into the summer of 1993.

On August 19,1993, bureaucrats from the New York City Department of Business Services distributed the following letter to the vendors on 125th Street.

> Dear Vendor:
>
> The New York City Department of Business Services with assistance from the 125th Street Local Development Corporation, the Harlem Business Alliance, Community Board #10, the 125th Street Vendors Association, and members of the business and street vendor communities have been working together to improve business conditions on 125th Street.

> You should be aware that the law currently prohibits almost every form of street vending that now exists on 125th Street. This is why we are now proposing to establish an open air market for street vendors on 126th Street between Adam Clayton Powell Blvd. to St. Nicholas Avenue as a way to provide an alternative legal site for vendors. We will also work with the vendors currently at Malcolm X Blvd. from 125th to 126th Streets on a plan to legally remain at this site. This solution is being presented to you as a way to provide a legitimate place for you to conduct your business.
>
> In order for you to participate in this program, you should fill out the vendor registration form and mail it to the New York City Department of Business Services, 110 William Street, New York, NY 10038, Attention: Intragovernmental Business Affairs Division. This information will be used for vendor identification cards, to determine the exact location of street vendor spaces and other requirements for the street vendor market.
>
> We appreciate your cooperation and assistance to make the 126th Street alternative site a success. Thank you for your time and attention.[18]

The form requested the following information: name, address, telephone number, the nature of goods sold, and the number of tables used for vending. Many vendors provided the requested information; some furnished false names, addresses, and phone numbers; others simply refused to comply with the request for information.

In the end it didn't matter whether the vendors complied with Department of Business Service's request, for city hall solved the problem of unlicensed vending on 125th Street the usual way—by doing nothing substantive. City hall held meetings with the concerned parties: the 125th Street Local Development Corporation, the Harlem Business Alliance, and the 125th Street Vendors Association. People vented their frustrations, and city hall scheduled additional meetings, which led to more vented frustrations, more meetings. Meanwhile, the African market continued to grow. Despite these ongoing negotiations, all parties knew that nothing would be resolved until after the mayoral election in November 1993. "When Dinkins was a teenager," one vendor told us, "he peddled on the streets of Harlem. He will not deny us our living."[19]

Closing Spaces

In November 1993 Mayor Dinkins lost his reelection bid to Rudolph Giuliani, the Reagan-appointed former U.S. Attorney for New York City. One strong reason for Giuliani's victory was his pledge to make New York more "livable," by which he meant crime-free. Considering this seemingly insurmountable pledge, Giuliani's choice of William J. Bratton as Police Commissioner became his most important and politically significant appointment. Prior to his appointment, Bratton had secured his reputation by successfully policing Boston. In concert with Giuliani's views, Bratton believed in consistent and energetic enforcement of regulations. This belief meant that one polices a city from the bottom up—through the enforcement of minor regulatory infractions that sometimes causes minor headaches for citizens. Such enforcement, according to Bratton's theory, compels people to believe that there is some semblance of law and order in the streets. In this way one begins to order the perceived chaotic urban clutter and make the city more livable.

Soon after his appointment, Bratton presented a detailed outline of his pragmatic philosophy of law enforcement to the press. He spoke about the presence of "squeegee men" in Manhattan. These men, mostly unemployed African Americans who are unlicensed by city hall, approach motorists stuck in Manhattan traffic and propose to wash their windshields for a modest fee. In some instances they wash windshields without the consent of motorists and aggressively demand money. Although such unregulated activity hardly constitutes a major law enforcement problem, it is a nuisance in Commissioner Bratton's universe of meaning. By eradicating the nuisance, following Bratton's logic, one takes a small but significant step toward making New York City a better place to live—at least for those who commute into Manhattan.[20]

Commissioner Bratton's proclamation can be read as a declaration of war against the informal economy of New York City, in which the exchange of goods and services is unregulated by the state.[21]Participants in informal economies, which have grown exponentially since 1980, would include:

> The parent who purchases day care service without filling out social security forms, the unlicensed gypsy cab driver who serves poor neighborhoods, the craftsperson building furniture in an area not zoned for manufacturing activity, the immigrant woman reading pap smears or sewing teddy bears in a poorly lit suburban garage, and the unlicensed African street vendor.[22]

To enforce overlooked city regulations, then, is to crack down on the informal economy.

Early talk from Giuliani and Bratton led to much speculation among West African vendors on 125th Street. Would Giuliani act quickly to close down a market that was in gross violation of New York City ordinances?

As it turned out, the beginning of the Giuliani administration did not mean the immediate end of the African market. In fact, the market expanded in February and March of 1994, usually a slow season. Reeling from pervasive political instability as well as the World Bank's January 1994 decision to devalue the West African franc (CFA), new waves of West African immigrants arrived in New York looking for commercial opportunities. They quickly found places for themselves at the African market. According to some Harlemites quoted in the New York Times, as many as 1,000 vendors might line the sidewalks of 125th Street on some weekends.[23] In the spring of 1994, more rumors swept down the 125th Street sidewalks: Commissioner Bratton was organizing an imminent police action; Mayor Giuliani would soon issue an order to relocate the vendors to 126th Street and St. Nicholas Avenue. Some of the vendors reacted to these rumors with anger. "I will never move from here. No one will go over there to buy our goods."[24] Others reacted with the equanimity of pragmatic Muslim traders. "We are here to do business. If they decide to move us, we will go. We will be all right wherever they send us. We are here to make money, not to cause trouble."[25]

In July 1994, the Masjid Malcolm Shabazz erected a large sign on an abandoned lot on the northeast corner of 116th Street and Lenox Avenue. It read, "Coming Soon, Masjid Malcolm Shabazz International Plaza." The sign listed the following sponsors: the Masjid Malcolm Shabazz, the Harlem Business Alliance, the 125th Street Local Development Corporation, Community Board #10, and the 125th Street Vendors Association.

Soon after the appearance of the 116th Street sign, members of the 125th Street Vendors Association circulated a flyer that denied their sponsorship of the International Plaza. The flyer stated that one of the former officers of the 125th Street Vendors Association was guilty of misrepresentation. When I asked the vendors from Niger about this political bickering, they said that it was not uncommon for African Americans to play politics.[26]

As business leaders and elected officials of Harlem lobbied the mayor to remove the street vendors from 125th Street, rumors of an imminent police action circulated through the market. Most African vendors believed that the city would eventually evict them, but not until after the summer.[27] Meanwhile, the battle lines had been drawn. Federal, state, and city elected officials from Harlem joined forces with the Masjid Malcolm Shabazz, the Harlem business community, and the Giuliani administration, political groups with very different agendas. They suggested moving the vendors to the proposed site of the Masjid Malcolm Shabazz International Plaza on 116th Street and Lenox Avenue. Led by Morris Powell and backed by Louis Farrakhan's Nation of Islam and the Reverend Al Sharpton, the 125th Street Vendors Association, a loosely organized group of some 500 African American and West African street vendors, vehemently opposed this plan.[28]

Making good on one of his campaign promises, Mayor Giuliani said that as of October 17, 1994, street vending would no longer be allowed on 125th Street. Several days before October 17, the Department of Business Services of the City of New York circulated the following notice, written in English, Spanish, and French, to the shoppers on 125th Street.

> TO ALL SHOPPERS ON 125TH STREET:
>
> If you patronize the street vendors who sell on 125th Street and its immediate vicinity, then this notice is for you. Beginning Monday, October 17, 1994, street vending will no longer be allowed on 125th Street and its immediate vicinity.
>
> That's why we want you to know that as of that date (October 17, 1994) all of the street vendors carrying your favorite goods will be operating from two new markets at the corners of 116th Street and Lenox and 117th Street and Lenox. The new markets are only a few blocks away and they offer many conveniences and advantages over 125th Street.
>
> For instance:
>
> - the markets will be cleaner.
> - the vendors will be more organized.
> - because of the markets, there will be less over-crowded sidewalks on 125th Street.
> - less overcrowded sidewalks should help reduce the opportunity for crime and the dangers posed to your safety.
> - you can shop in an environment of relative comfort. You can buy your usual goods from the same vendors at no more than the usual prices.
>
> So please, beginning October 17, 1994, bear in mind where your vendors whom you've always patronized will be at new markets on 116th and 117th Streets and Lenox Avenue; sponsored by the Malcolm Shabazz Masjid. Your vendors in their new location need you now more than ever! Help make them a success.[29]

I took a copy of this notice and showed it to several West African vendors. They scoffed at city hall's plan. One vendor theorized that the shoppers would never frequent the 116th Street market. "It's too far away [from the shopping district], and there is nothing there except crack houses and thieves. I will never go there."[30] Other vendors took a more circumspect attitude. A Malian vendor said that the move to 116th Street was nothing more than a plot to profit the Masjid Malcolm Shabazz and its putative Senegalese cohorts. "The Senegalese see this move as a way to crush the other West African competition and make much money for themselves."[31] On 125th Street vendors did not pay for their spaces, which meant that the city of New York did not receive tax revenues from them—the very definition of informal economic enterprise. Under the plan sponsored by the Giuliani administration and the Masjid Malcolm

Shabazz, the vendors would pay a flat fee of $100 to register legally. They would also pay a fee of $7 per day for their spaces, each of which would be marked by painted lines and numbers. City hall agreed to take only 30% of these revenues, leaving 70% to the Masjid Malcolm Shabazz.[32]

Two days before Mayor Giuliani's police action, West African vendors speculated about the plans that the Masjid Malcolm Shabazz had for them. All the vendors I talked with suggested that the 116th Street site was temporary. "We'll be there for only one year," one vendor predicted. "By that time, the Masjid will have gotten enough money to build a new mosque on the site. What will happen to us then?"[33] This view was underscored by Lance Shabazz, who on October 17 told Jonathan Hicks of *The New York Times* that the Masjid would build a mosque at the 116th Street site. "So this [the open-air market at 116th Street] is just a temporary arrangement. . . . When the new mosque is built, what's going to happen to the vendors then? I don't think the city has considered any of this."[34]

On the eve of Mayor Giuliani's police action, Morris Powell, head of the 125th Street Vendors Association, was defiant, saying that his members planned to stay put "even if they bring in the National Guard. We're not going anywhere."[35] For their part, the New York Police Department seemed determined to control the public order by maintaining a high profile. "We're going to have a sufficient contingent to make sure that public safety is maintained," Assistant Chief of Police Wilbur Chapman told the *New York Post*.[36] Police also mentioned that vendors who defied the mayor's order to leave 125th Street might face arrest and fines as high as $1,000.

Meanwhile, an ad hoc group known as the Concerned People for the Development of Harlem, which did not identify its membership, underscored the issue of race in the politics of the African market. They circulated a flyer that put Asian and white store owners on notice.

> If we are not allowed to do business among our own people . . . then we're not going to allow any other non-black entity to continue to exploit our consumer market. If our children don't eat we will make damn sure your children don't eat off our people's spending power.[37]

The imminence of police action prompted many West African vendors to speculate about their economic future in New York City. For several days they had been meeting among themselves to discuss their options. Some of them vowed to march in the streets to protest Mayor Giuliani's decision. Others took a wait-and-see attitude. Perhaps the market at 116th Street would work out—if only temporarily. Still other West Africans thought of economic alternatives. One man said he would move his business to Canal Street in Lower Manhattan. Another said that he would seek a work authorization card and move to Greensboro, North Carolina, to find work in a factory. Most of the vendors I talked with expressed a kind of cynical resignation. "We have no power here. What is our choice? We do not want trouble. We will make the best of a bad situation."[38]

Policing Space

October 17, 1994. There are no vendors on the street. They have been replaced by fleets of blue paddy wagons and police vans. Men dressed in suits walk along the sidewalks, talking into their walkie-talkies. The clatter of hoofs announces the arrival of a contingent of mounted police. Young men and women with press IDs walk stiffly up and down the street, taking photos and writing notes. Older Harlemites walk the scene carrying their own video cameras and notebooks. One man says that he wants to make sure that the police action is properly documented.

At 10:00 A.M. the police block off 125th Street and Lenox Avenue. Shortly thereafter a group of demonstrating vendors, mostly African Americans, begin their march down 125th Street. Carrying the tricolored Garveyite flag, which symbolizes the group's "nationalist" ideology, they chant: "No food, no peace." Considering the throngs of street vendors on 125th Street, the number of demonstrators seems slim—perhaps 150. They are literally surrounded by police in vans, in paddy wagons, on foot, on horseback. The demonstrators form a core, which the police seal off. Encircled by the police, the demonstrators move slowly down 125th Street. "No food, no peace." Although most of the demonstrators seem to be African Americans, a few West Africans join in.

The demonstrators gather on the plaza of the Adam Clayton Powell Building. Morris Powell, short, gray, and formless in his military fatigues, stands on a platform to speak. He is wearing a kenti cloth hat and beads. A motley group gathers around him: vendors, a few Korean and Japanese tourists, a smattering of white civil servants, and people from the neighborhood, many of them older African Americans who carry still and video cameras.

Mr. Powell begins to speak and immediately injects the issue of race into his discourse. "We will not move," he said. "We have a right to be here. We must stop the move of whites to take over 125th Street." Another speaker talks of police racism and brutality. He says there is a conspiracy to rob African Americans of their own self-determination. He says the cops are nothing less than the Gestapo and that Mayor Giuliani is a disgrace. A woman stands up to speak. She, too, talks about the realities of racism in America, saying that African Americans need to feed their own children before letting others feed their children with the dollars of African Americans.

Someone gives Mr. Powell a bullhorn. He asks the demonstrators to begin marching in an orderly fashion. Soon thereafter, Mr. Powell is arrested for the unauthorized use of a bullhorn. Police arrest 21 other demonstrators, some of whom had knocked down barriers and confronted store owners.

After the rally and arrests, the crowd disperses, but the police remain in force, strolling the sidewalks. Except for fast food restaurants, all the businesses along 125th Street are shuttered. After his arrest, Mr. Powell vows to continue to boycott "non-black owned stores."[39] On the other side, Chief of Patrol Louis Anemone says, "We'll be here forever, if necessary."[40]

Following the rally, I talked with some of the West African vendors. Many of them did not leave their apartments on the morning of October 17. One man from Niger, who sells handbags, sees the crackdown in purely economic terms. He pooh-poohs the racial discourse of African American politics in Harlem, suggesting that the crackdown on 125th Street devolved from the Masjid Malcolm Shabazz's economic interests. Indeed, if the Masjid received weekly rents from 400 vendors, it would significantly increase the religious organization's revenues. "Why should I pay them $9 [*sic*] per day and a $100 license fee so they can collect money to build a mosque? I refuse to go there."[41] This same Nigerien suggests that the Masjid Malcolm Shabazz International Plaza would be an absolute failure. "Just see how many people show up there today."

Boycotted Space

As promised, the 125th Street Vendors Association attempted to boycott businesses on 125th Street owned and run by nonblacks. Supported by the Nation of Islam, the Reverend Al Sharpton, and Khalid Muhammed, the vendors set up picket lines in front of these businesses. On October 18, police arrested Reverend Al Sharpton for illegally selling Bibles on 125th Street. On subsequent days, picketers lambasted black shoppers for frequenting white- and Asian-owned stores. Perhaps many of the shoppers grasped the irony that at least some of the picketers missed: the forces behind the crackdown had less to do with racial politics than with economic incentive. Consider the commentary of E. R. Shipp in the *New York Daily News*.

> This week, picketers—egged on by the likes of Khalid Muhammed—are spending their days outside stores they say are owned by whites and Koreans, shouting slogans like "Close 'em down" and berating anyone who insists on shopping rather than acceding to their boycott.
>
> They miss the point: It's not just whites and Koreans who want to bring some semblance of order to the chaos on 125th St., Harlem's main commercial strip. Indeed, it's downright insulting when Powell and his

> ilk ignore the fact that black business, civic and political leaders have been after the mayor—from Koch to Dinkins to Giuliani—to do something about the situation. Giuliani took his sweet time, but he's finally listening to responsible Harlemites.[42]

Writing in the *New York Amsterdam News,* Abiola Sinclair took a position more moderate than either Morris Powell or E. R. Shipp. Sinclair has bought from both black and Asian store owners as well as street vendors. She supports the right of the vendors to be on 125th Street, but believes they should be regulated.

> My position is they should be regulated. Not in front of bus stops, hydrants, etc. Not blocking the sidewalk to the extent that people can't pass by. They should also be ticketed for keeping a dirty space. I've seen Africans and African Americans set up in the morning, leave the spot dirty, and they pay it no attention. They leave it that way or worse. Those large concrete tubs were meant for flowers not trash.[43]

Such official talk about order as opposed to chaos, cleanliness as opposed to clutter, and regulation as opposed to informality partially recapitulates the mainstream discourse of the Fifth Avenue Merchants Association in their successful attempt to clear Midtown of Senegalese "clutter" in 1985. Such discourse seeks to replace third-world chaos, filth, and informality with first-world order, cleanliness, and regulation.

Given the diversity of political opinion, racial ideology, and spatial preferences about the dispersal of the African market, it was hardly surprising that the boycott had mixed results. Four days after the police action, Commissioner William J. Bratton visited 125th Street and said that he was pleased that the picketing vendors had not denied shoppers access to stores. He vowed to maintain the considerable police presence as long as necessary and said—to counter charges of police racism—that similar vending regulations would be enforced in other parts of the city. "It's getting cold," he said. "I believe nature will end up controlling the situation."[44]

By the fourth day of the 125th Street boycott, the number of picketers had dwindled, the vendors had gone, the crowds had left. Even though the police profile was still high, their behavior remained low key.

The 125th Street Vendors Association's boycott of nonblack-owned businesses petered out in less than a week. Many forces worked against its success. First, many Harlemites, who felt that the informal market had disrupted commerce on 125th Street, supported the dispersal of the street vendors from 125th Street. Even those like Abiola Sinclair, who supported the vendors, believed that they should be spatially regulated. And like many other Harlemites, Sinclair disagreed with a logic that connected the mayoral crackdown to the boycott of nonblack-owned businesses. Second, the vendors, like anyone in New York City, needed income. Some of them, including many West Africans, relocated their unlicensed operations to other parts of the city, including Canal Street, Chambers Street, and 14th Street between 6th and 5th Avenues. The great majority of people I knew from 125th Street, however, rented stalls at the new Harlem market on 116th Street and Lenox Avenue run by the Masjid Malcolm Shabazz.

Space, Power, and Multiple Positionings

The cultural and political significance of space has a long history in anthropology. For theorists such as Levi-Strauss, spatial relations replicate dual social orders.[45] For others, space constitutes a kind of text that unlocks the mysteries of social meaning. Indeed, most anthropological analyses of space assume the isomorphism of space, place, and culture—all logically arranged on a homogeneous "field" of social relations. However, for authors such as Akhil Gupta and James Ferguson, "the fiction of cultures as discrete, object-like phenomena occupying discrete spaces becomes implausible for those who inhabit borderlands."[46] They might have also included participants in informal economies in such transnational spaces as the African market on 125th Street. Such a transnational space has

> . . . rendered any strictly bounded sense of community or locality obsolete. At the same time it has enabled the creation of forms of solidarity and identity that do not rest on the appropriation of space where contiguity and face-to-face contact are paramount.[48]

The static notion of space is rendered superfluous by what David Harvey (1989) called the "condition of postmodernity," which has given rise to the implosion of space and time, the explosion of mass migration, and the erosion of national boundaries. It is no longer unusual to see men from rural West African villages in Harlem, hawking T-shirts emblazoned with Malcolm's "X."[48] They transformed the 125th Street corridor into the African market. "The ability of people to confound the established spatial orders, either through physical movement or through their own conceptual and political acts of reimagination, means that space and place can never be given."[49]

As we have seen, at the African market the political, cultural, and religious intentionalities of West Africans, African Americans, local elected officials, and local government bodies are articulated in a variety of conflicting spatial practices and ideologies. In New York City, many third-world spatial, social, and religious practices, which are themselves inextricably interconnected, have taken *place* in spaces zoned "first world"—all of which creates spatial arenas of multiple contestation and struggle. . . .

Notes

This chapter is based upon fieldwork in Harlem that began in July 1992 and has continued to the present as part of an ongoing project, "Transnationalism in Local Context," that is being conducted with Rosemary J. Coombe and sponsored by the National Science Foundation (Global Perspectives on Sociolegal Studies). Fieldwork in Harlem has been supported by generous grants from West Chester University and the Wenner-Gren Foundation for Anthropological Research. First and foremost I thank West African vendors who have graciously made me a member of their North American network. For their critical readings of earlier versions of the manuscript I thank Rosemary J. Coombe, Nelson Keith, Susan Ruddick, and Jasmin Tahmaseb McConatha. I am particularly grateful to Alma Gottlieb, Neil Lazarus, and an anonymous reviewer for their comments on the manuscript. All the names of the West African traders have been changed to protect their identities.

1. See Paul Bohannan, ed., *Markets in Africa* (Evanston, Illinois: Northwestern University Press, 1962; Gracia Clark, *Onions Are My Husband: Survival and Accumulation by West African Market Women* (Chicago: University of Chicago Press, 1994), pp.186–188.

2. Emmanuel Gregroire, "Islam and the Identity of Merchants in Maradi (Niger)" in Louis Brenner, ed., *Muslim Identity and Social Change in Sub-Saharan Africa* (Bloomington: Indiana University Press, 1993), p. 107; I. M. Lewis, *Islam in Tropical Africa* (Bloomington: Indiana University Press, 1980), pp. 15–19.

3. See Samar Amin, ed., *Modern Migrations in West Africa* (London: Oxford University Press, 1971); Joseph Gugler and William Flanagan, *Urbanization and Social Change in West Africa* (Cambridge: Cambridge University Press, 1978).

4. See Thomas Painter, "From Warriors to Migrants: Critical perspectives on Early Migrations Among the Zarma of Niger," *Africa* 58 (1): 87–100; Jean Rouch, "Migrations au Ghana," *Journal de la Societé des Africanistes* 26 (1–2): 33–196; Paul Stoller, *The Cinematic Griot: The Ethnography of Jean Rouch* (Chicago: University of Chicago Press, 1992).

5. The Quadiriyya, Tijaniyya, Hammalliya, and Muridiyya all represent important Sufi brotherhoods in West Africa. The Wahhabiyyas are antimystical and reject Sufi practices. Differences among all of these sects have prompted political schism and turmoil in West Africa. The Mourids are an important political force in contemporary Senegal. Their transnational economic networks have become increasingly important in Europe and especially New York City (see Louis Brenner, ed., *Muslim Identity and Social*

Change in Sub-Saharan Africa [Bloomington: Indiana University Press, 1993]; Victoria Ebin, "Commerciants et missionaires: Une confrerie museimane senegalaise à New York," *Hommes et migrations* 1132: 25–31). For more detailed information on the Mourids, see Conor Cruise O'Brien, *The Mourids* (Oxford: Clarendon Press, 1971).

6. Gregroire, "Islam and the Identity of Merchants," p. 113.

7. Indeed, on July 8, 1994, a major ring of video pirates was busted in White Plains, but this did not disrupt the supply of pirated videos on 125th Street. See *New York Times* 1994. Whether the New York mafia actually is involved in video pirating is an open question.

8. See Soumann Sido, interview by author, 17 December 1994.

9. See Christopher Steiner, *African Art in Transition* (London: Cabridge University Press, 1993) and Lucien Taylor, Ilisa Barbash, and Christopher Steiner, *In and Out of Africa* (Berkeley: University of California Media Extension, 1992).

10. See Rouch, "Migrations au Ghana."

11. Economic anthropologists have been describing trading networks and market systems for decades, detailing and analyzing various exchange discourses. See Karl Polanyi's classic, *The Great Transformation: The Political and Economic Origins of Our Time* (Boston: Beacon Press, 1957) as well as the detailed market descriptions of Bronislaw Malinowski's and Julio de la Fuente's *Malinowski in Mexico: The Economics of a Mexican Market System* (London: Routledge and Kegan Paul, 1982). This piece has been about the symbolic and political ramifications of spatial practices in one market. In future publications I hope to describe the dynamics of buying and selling in several of New York City's transnational markets.

12. Daniel Bluestone, "The Pushcart Evil: Peddlers, Merchants and New York City's Streets, 1880–1940," *Journal of Urban History,* Vol: 18, No. 1 (1991): 68–92; Claude McKay, *Harlem: Negro Metropolis* (New York: Dutton, 1940); Gilbert Osofsky, *Harlem, The Making of a Ghetto: A History of Negro New York, 1900–1920* (New York: Harper and Row, 1971); Deborah Thomas, "The Removal of Vendors from Harlem as a Social Drama: Illuminating Economic and Racial Ideologies in an Age of Global Capitalist Restructuring," unpublished manuscript, n.d.

13. Karim Seyni, interview by author, 18 July 1993.

14. See Rosemary J. Coombe and Paul Stoller, "X Marks the Spot: The Ambiguities of African Trading in the Commerce of the Black Public Sphere," *Public Culture,* Vol. 7, No. 1 (1994): 249–275; Victoria Ebin and Rose Lake, "Camelots a New York: Respionniers de l'immigration senegalaise," *Hommes et migrations* 1160 (1992): 32–37.

15. The Mourids, a Sufi brotherhood headquartered in Touba City, Senegal, were founded by Cheik Ahamadou Bamba in 1898. French colonial officials found the brotherhood a threat to the established order and expelled Ahamadou Bamba from Senegal to Mauritania and then to France. During his exile, the size of the brotherhood swelled, and the group is today a major political and economic force in Senegal. An offshoot of the Tijani brotherhood, Mouridism stresses that the pathway to salvation is through hard work and trade. Accordingly, the brotherhood acquired vast tracks of land, used for

groundnut cultivation, and sent its devotees overseas—to France and the United States—to earn hard currency to send back to the confreres in Senegal. For more detailed information, see O'Brien, *The Mourids*. The vast majority of female street vendors in New York City are Senegalese women, mostly married, who are known in West Africa for their independence and commercial spirit. Since 1992 I've met only three women from Mali who are vendors and none from Niger. See Coombe and Stoller, "X Marks the Spot" and Ebin and Lake, "Camelots a New York."

16. Amadou Adamou, interview by author, 15 October 1994.

17. Salif Maiga, interview by author, 18 July 1993.

18. Files of the author.

19. Issifi Harouna, interview by author, 18 July 1993. Harouna also suggested that Dinkins, being a black man, would be afraid to adopt a policy that would incite a racial conflict. When he announced his plan to disband the 125th Street market in 1992, Mayor Dinkins revealed that as a youth in Harlem he, too, had been a peddler. See Deborah Sontag, "To Illegal Street Vendors, American Dream Needs Work, Not License, *New York Times,* 14 June 1993, p. A12.

20. Michael T. Kauman, "Squeegees and Hope: New Peril. Men Who Wash Car Windows on Street Targeted by William Bratton," *New York Times* 8 December 1993, pp. A18, B5.

21. Manuel Castells and Alejandro Portes, "World Underneath: The Origins, Dynamics, and Effects of the Informal Economy" in Manuel Castells and Alejandro Portes, eds., *The Informal Economy* (Baltimore: Johns Hopkins University Press, 1989), pp. 11–17.

22. See Coombe and Stoller, "X Marks the Spot," pp. 253–254; Saskia Sassen, *The Global City* (Princeton: Princeton University Press, 1991).

23. Jonathan Hicks, "Vendors' Ouster and Boycott Divide Harlem," *New York Times* 23 October 1994, pp. A1, A43.

24. Amanda Adamou, interview by author, 19 August 1994. Indeed, economic activity along 116th and Lenox is depressed, due in part to the presence of many burned-out buildings and the absence of commercial establishments.

25. Issifi Harouna, interview by author, 19 August 1994.

26. Harouna, interview with author, 19 August 1994; Abdou Karimoun, interview by author, 19 August 1994.

27. Adamou, interview by author, 19 August 1994.

28. The key political groups supporting the mayoral crackdown constitute the Harlem business and political establishment. They included Community Board #10, the local governing council of central Harlem and its chairwoman Barbara Askins (who is also executive director of the 125th Street Business Improvement District [BID]), the Harlem Urban Development Corporation (which was set up in 1971 by Governor Nelson Rockefeller to attract commercial development and spur new housing in depressed areas of Harlem), and nearly all of Harlem's city and state elected officials. Even though the Masjid Malcolm Shabazz, established after Malcolm X's disassociation from the

Nation of Islam, is not part of the Harlem business and political establishment, it too supported the mayoral crackdown. The Masjid stresses fidelity to Sunni Islam. Headed by devotees of Malcolm Shabazz, they, as landlords, stood to profit substantially from the move of the market to 116th Street.

Those opposed to Giuliani's decision included the loosely organized 125th Street Vendors Association, which came into existence when Mayor Dinkins attempted to shut down the Harlem market in 1992. Headed by Morris Powell, who has been a street vendor in Harlem for more than 30 years, the Association's estimated membership of 500 vendors consists mostly of African American merchants but also includes a contingent of West Africans. Members are asked to pay a fee of $20 a month to finance a newsletter and promote peddling. Powell has long been an advocate of the self-determination of black people in Harlem and has long been at odds with the Harlem business and political establishment. Powell's organization was supported by the Nation of Islam, which also supports African American self-determination in Harlem. Such self-determination is also a theme espoused by the Reverend Al Sharpton, who has unsuccessfully run for political office in New York State. For more detailed information on Morris Powell, see Dan Barry and Jonathan P. Hicks, "Protestor is Caught in Fatal Fire's Glare: New Look at Harsh Message," *New York Times* 15 December 1995, pp. B1, B4. One could say that social class seems to be a significant political determinant in this case. For other analyses of the African market's demise, see Thomas, "The Removal of Vendors From Harlem" and Sharon Zukin, *The Cultures of Cities* (Oxford: Blackwell, 1995), pp. 230–247.

29. Files of the author.

30. Issifi Harouna, interview by author, 15 October 1994.

31. Soulay Younoussa, interview by author, 15 October 1994.

32. Harouna, interview by author, 15 October 1994; Jonathan Hicks, "Police Move Illegal Vendors From Harlem Thoroughfare," *New York Times* 18 October 1994, p. B3; Abdou Karimoun, interview by author, 15 October 1994.

33. Chaibou Anzura, interview by author, 15 October 1994.

34. Hicks, "Police Move Illegal Vendors."

35. Christopher Policano, "Showdown Today on Rudy Plan to Evict Harlem Vendors," *New York Post* 17 October 1994, p. 2.

36. Policano, "Showdown Today."

37. Ibid.

38. Adamou, interview by author, 15 October 1994.

39. Christopher Policano, "22 Busted in Melee at Vendors' March," *New York Post* 18 October 1994, p. 9.

40. Policano, "22 Busted in Melee."

41. Issifi Harouna, interview by author, 17 October 1994.

42. E. R. Shipp, "Cool It, Face Facts in Harlem," *New York Daily News,* 19 October 1994, p. 15.

43. Abiola Sinclair, "Boycott of 125th Street?," *New York Amsterdam News,* 15 October 1994, p. B1.

44. Alan Finder, "Bratton Joins Watch Over Harlem Boycott," *New York Times* 21 October 1994, p. B1.

45. See Claude Levi-Strauss, *Structural Anthropology* (Garden City, New York: Doubleday, 1966).

46. Akhil Gupta and James Ferguson, "Beyond 'Culture': Space, Identity and the Politics of Difference," *Cultural Anthropology* 7 (1992): 6–24.

47. Gupta and Ferguson, "Beyond 'Culture,'" p. 9.

48. See Coombe and Stoller, "X Marks the Spot."

49. See Gupta and Ferguson, "Beyond 'Culture,'" p. 17 and Paul Stoller, *The Taste of Ethnographic Things* (Philadelphia: University of Pennsylvania Press, 1989).

12

Sherri-Ann P. Butterfield

Something in Between

Locating Identity among Second-Generation West Indians in New York City

The Hudson Valley, especially New York City, has received many black Caribbean newcomers as part of the post-1965 immigration to the United States. These new arrivals, particularly those of the second generation, face identity and assimilation issues that both resemble and differ from those experienced by previous generations of European immigrants and their descendants in the area. Sherri-Ann Butterfield investigates identity formation among contemporary second-generation West Indian residents in New York City and uncovers the ways in which they negotiate a course between race and ethnicity, and how that course is influenced by a number of factors, including parental expectations, black nationalist leanings, cultural affinities, assessments by whites, and shifting levels of acceptance among African Americans.

Introduction

The growth of nonwhite voluntary immigrants to the United States since the revision of the federal immigration laws in 1965 has led to new understandings of racial and ethnic groups within American society. Contemporary society recognizes that "Latino" no longer denotes just Cubans, Mexicans, and Puerto Ricans; it also includes Dominicans, Colombians, Peruvians, and Ecuadorians. "Asian" encompasses Vietnamese, Cambodians, and Laotians, along with Chinese, Japanese, and Koreans. And "black" refers not only to African Americans, but also to people from the Caribbean and Africa as well. As the largest immigration flow in the nation's history, these populations challenge previous immigration theories of assimilation and inclusion that were constructed in reference to early twentieth-century European immigrants and their children at the turn of the century. Unlike the early European immigration, this relatively recent wave of immigrants is mostly comprised of people who have migrated voluntarily and who are racially defined in the United States. Given this influx of racial and ethnic immigrants, the question then becomes: is the process of assimilation for nonwhite immigrants and their children similar to that of earlier white immigrants? Or does their racial and ethnic group affiliation overdetermine the choices and constraints they will face?

A substantial amount of research on the identities and affiliations of contemporary immigrants from the Caribbean, Asia, and South America addresses these issues for first-generation immigrants. Paths taken by first-generation immigrants can be characterized as somewhat governed by language barriers, residential segregation, and the arrangement of existing support networks in the receiving country. Their children, however, will experience a far more complex array of constraints and opportunities than their parents. For the most part they will know English, they will attend public schools and even universities, and they will be more likely to cross over into diverse areas of the urban landscape. Will these children simply become "American," or, are there more complex processes at work? This chapter attempts to address part of this story—the formation of a racial and ethnic identity among second-generation West Indians.

While there has been considerable research on the identities of West Indian immigrants, with the exception of Tekle Woldemikael and Mary C. Waters, there has been very little research on the racial and ethnic identities of their children.[1] In fact, until recently, scholarly work on all the children of post-1965 immigrants was largely speculative.[2] However, in the last few years, an emerging body of work has sought to extrapolate future adult patterns of incorporation from the experiences of second-generation youth.[3] What is problematic is that all these studies focus on adolescents—a population at an unstable developmental stage, thus only allowing researchers to examine the beginning of their racial and ethnic identity formation process.

In addition, one of the major struggles in studying second-generation immigrants is that social scientists do not fully comprehend the social and cultural contexts in which identity formation takes place. Second-generation West Indians have the option to either maintain an independent and cultural identity—as Jamaicans, Trinidadians, Guyanese, and others, they may identify as blacks, or have some combination thereof.[4] Additionally, the West Indian second-generation immigrants may adopt a particular ethnic identity in one context or circumstance, and still another in another context or at a different stage in their life course.

This chapter is most concerned with the contexts in which ethnic identity is contested and negotiated. While we know that ethnic identity is not inherited or fixed, but variable, situational, and contextual, researchers do not know the *process* of ethnic identity construction.[5] Do second-generation West Indians who adopt an ethnic identity do so because of their racial identity, or in spite of it?

Moreover, the shifting demographics of New York City communities, as well as the intense degree to which different racial and ethnic groups share public space, provide a landscape in which the process of identity formation can be problematized. Specifically, the presence of a large African American community in New York City (and surrounding areas) strongly influences second-generation identity formation. It is simply not a matter of choosing between a racial and ethnic identity, but a process in which the concept of "blackness" is given new meaning. Similar to the racial classification of "white" which encompasses Italians, Russians, and the Irish, we must acknowledge that the term "black" also incorporates multiple ethnic groups. As such, I argue that the broadening definition of "blackness" is being played out in New York culture where it is just as common to hear reggae and Latin music on street corners as it is to hear rap and pop music. Quite simply, New York City provides individuals with more options and more space for creativity when constructing their own identities. In essence, this research seeks to illuminate how racial and ethnic identity are constructed in particular contexts and within an urban landscape for second-generation immigrant adults.

This chapter then, will do five things: (1) provide an overview of earlier theoretical approaches to assimilation; (2) discuss the importance of New York City as a site for identity development; (3) outline the institutional mechanisms that impacted identity construction among the second generation; (4) identify the ways in which Caribbean immigration has fostered a diasporic identity among black ethnic groups in New York; and (5) point to some of the implications of a diasporic understanding of race.

Research Methods and Objectives

The findings of this chapter emerged from an analysis of structured, open-ended interviews with 65 second-generation West Indian immigrants between the ages of 20 and 32.[6] This age category was chosen because 32 was the oldest a child born to post-1965 immigrants could have been at the time of the study, while the lower age was selected in order to capture those who had come into full adulthood and thus are the primary agents responsible for their own lives (younger respondents may still rely on parents or guardians). This age category also encompasses individuals who, although still young, have experienced socioeconomic advantages and/or disadvantages via the labor market.[7]

The respondents were selected by a modified snowball sampling approach, which began with my ties to the West Indian community through friends, acquaintances, and community organizers. My contacts resided and worked throughout metropolitan New York (which in addition to New York City included Long Island and northeastern New Jersey), and as such, provided me access to second generationers from all over New York. I was introduced to a large number of my respondents via this West Indian network, but I was also approached by some people after they learned about the project from peers who had already been interviewed.

My sample was selected based on age, gender, country of origin, and later, borough in which the respondent resided, with my sampling strategy shifting as I tried to ensure that no relevant categories were missed. For instance, I began targeting West Indian male respondents when I realized that my sample was becoming skewed to women (the sample is almost evenly split with 35 female respondents and 30 male respondents).

All of the respondents in the study reside in four of the five boroughs of New York City—Brooklyn, Bronx, Manhattan, and Queens. Consistent with the literature on the residential patterns of West Indians in New York the majority of the respondents reside in Brooklyn and Queens.[8]

The interview schedule included questions about racial and ethnic self-identification; the composition and structure of social networks; the incorporation of ethnicity into household life; the negotiation of ethnic boundaries. The length of the interview averaged 2 hours and 15 minutes in length, with the longest interview lasting five hours (in two meetings) and the shortest being one hour. The location of the interviews varied as they took place in the respondents' homes, their place of employment, coffee shops/diners, parks, fast-food restaurants, among other locations—wherever it was convenient for the respondent.[9]

Concepts and Measures Employed

The major analytic thrust of this chapter is to demonstrate the complexity of racial and ethnic identity formation. In addition, this project also seeks to provide a more inclusive understanding of ethnic identity and the adaptation process among black immigrants in the United States. However, before I can undertake this task, I must first offer some clarification of some of the concepts and measures that were utilized during the course of the data collection.

First, and foremost, this study aims to highlight the limitations of the prevalent usage of the terms "race" and "ethnicity" among scholars and the wider American community. Within social science literature, there is a problematic tendency to treat race and ethnicity as if they are interchangeable social categories.[10] While the conflation of these two concepts may have proven useful for the study of white ethnic groups, I posit that this has detrimental affects on the study of contemporary immigrant groups. "Race" and "ethnicity" for white ethnics are considered to be the normative path of all immigrant groups, while ignoring the obvious and startling differences between whites and immigrants of color. Accordingly, this study treats "race" and "ethnicity" as two distinct concepts. "Race" is defined as socially constructed distinctions drawn from physical appearance, while "ethnicity" is operationalized in terms of distinctions based on national origin, language, religion, food, and other cultural markers.[11]

I define "West Indian" to include all people not of Asian ancestry descended from those born in the Anglophone Caribbean: the 13 Caricom member nations (including the mainland countries of Guyana and Belize), the Caribbean British colonies, and the Dutch Caribbean islands where people speak English and are descendants of immigrants from the British West Indies. This sample also includes English-speaking Panamanians, as a significant number of West Indians reside in Panama.[12] However, it does not include those from the Hispanic Caribbean and Haiti, as they speak different languages and were not part of the British colonial empire. "Second-generation" West Indians were identified as those for whom at least one parent is from the West Indies.[13]

Theoretical Approaches to Immigrant Assimilation

The Straight Line Assimilation Model

The term "assimilation" has had various meanings within the discipline of sociology and American popular discourse.[14] Early twentieth-century sociologists often disagreed on the degree to which (mainly European) immigrants would come to share American values and norms, or in fact change American society, and tended to assume (and the continued use of "assimilation" within current American society still assumes) that incorporation into the dominant society means adopting the *culture* of the dominant society, and that that culture was correlated with upward mobility.

This model is highly problematic for the children of contemporary immigrants as it suggests that each succeeding generation will become more similar to the general native-born population in the United States.[15] Generation has thus been a key term in assessing the assimilation of different ethnic groups in American society.[16] While this depiction of socioeconomic mobility was generally true of the various European immigrant groups, it is important to note that there were differences in the pace of assimilation across the groups. For instance, authors such as Richard Alba and Stanley Lieberson both suggest that East European Jews achieved social mobility by the second generation, while it took Italian immigrants and their descendants several generations to reach parity with native-born whites of American parentage.[17]

These findings assume that for European immigrants, time spent in the United States explains success because the immigrants acquire the language skills, educational credentials, and general cultural knowledge, morals, and values needed to compete (and co-exist) with native-born white Americans. Researchers have frequently argued that second-generation immigrants often "do better" than those born to native-born Americans, and attribute this success to the fact that the immigrants instill a drive and achievement orientation in their children that is not present in native-born Americans.

One of the earliest and detailed discussions of identity and the experience of the second generation is Warner and Srole's study of ethnic groups in New Haven.[18] Warner and Srole describe a generational march of ethnic groups from initial residential and occupational segregation and poverty to residential, occupational, and identity integration and Americanization.[19] The authors put forth a model that suggests that the second generation first learns an immigrant culture in the home and then encounters the more highly valued American native culture in the schools, their peer groups, and the mass media. They then internalize American culture and identity and reject their parents' culture and identity as foreigners.

This model's central assumptions may have been true for generational change among white ethnic groups; however, these assumptions most certainly do not hold for the children of contemporary immigrants. Warner and Srole, and other early twentieth-century immigration scholars, assumed that immigrant children would absorb a self-reliant, individualistic, middle class "American culture," that by adopting, would lead to upward mobility. This model ignores the possibility that *retaining* immigrant culture might provide access to networks that facilitate upward mobility.[20] Additionally, the concept of straight line assimilation mistakenly assumes that American culture remains untouched or unaffected by the presence of large numbers of immigrants. For example, it is important to recognize that while the Irish and the Jews are often considered as having "assimilated" to American culture, they vastly changed the culture and social structures of numerous American cities at the turn of the century, particularly Boston and New York.

It is the misassumption that immigrants do not impact the societies they enter that this chapter is most concerned with. For many of today's second generation, and I would argue, even for those at the turn of the twentieth century, they are not entering a monolithic American society which over time comes to define their "Americanness." Rather, the children of contemporary immigrants impact, and are impacted by, the cities and contexts in which they live their daily lives. Particularly in a place like New York City, which has always prided itself on its ethnic diversity, how can the second generation help but to redefine New York City culture while at the same time seeking to define themselves?

In addition, Warner and Srole assume that being "American" has a higher status than immigrant culture. While this may be the case for some immigrant groups, for many of today's second generation, this model is antithetical to their experiences and belief systems. For the second generation, experiences with racism, prejudice, and discrimination teach them that they are the "unmeltable" Americans—people who by definition of their phenotype get defined out of what it means to be "American."[21]

In other words, for immigrants of color, the idea of assimilation gets turned on its head—they can only assimilate into a racialized American society which may facilitate downward mobility rather than upward. For example, if West Indian immigrants lose their ethnic distinctiveness, they become indistinguishable from African Americans, thereby making their American experience not necessarily higher than their home country experiences. They are coming from societies where, for the most part, they constitute the racial majority, where blacks are in positions of leadership and authority, and the ascription of a minority status is perceived as at step down.[22]

In fact, it is the severe racial discrimination and inequality experienced by African Americans that has led some first-generation West Indians to resist assimilation by engaging in a distancing of themselves from native-born blacks, even though they are constrained from doing so by virtue of their phenotype.[23] However, for second-generation West Indians who are raised primarily with (and treated as) African Americans as their peer group, what assimilation choices do they have, if any?

Contemporary Theories of Immigrant Adaptation

Several speculative theories describing the experiences of becoming American emerged after numerous scholars realized that the straight line assimilation model was not necessarily applicable to the post-1965 immigrants and their children.[24] These works stress the multiple and contradictory paths that can be followed by second-generation children. Some may achieve socioeconomic success while retaining strong ethnic attachments and identities, while others assimilate to American subcultures with limited socioeconomic mobility.

Herbert Gans outlines several possible scenarios for the socioeconomic and social integration of the post-1965 second generation. He speculates that the children of contemporary immigrants could face socioeconomic decline relative to their parents' positions due to the fact that the children might refuse to accept the low-level, low-pay jobs that employ their parents. Another possibility is that the youth who do not "become American" and adopt the negative attitudes toward school, opportunity, hard work, and "the American Dream" that their American peers have adopted, but rather stay tied to their parents' ethnic community and values, will end up doing better.[25]

Based on research conducted with second-generation youth in Miami and San Diego, Portes and Zhou make a similar argument. They introduce the model of "segmented assimilation" in explaining the outcomes of the different groups of second-generation youth. The authors argue that the mode of incorporation of the first generation creates differential opportunities and cultural and social capital in the form of ethnic jobs, networks, and values that create differential pulls on the allegiances of the second generation. For those immigrant groups who face extreme discrimination, reactive ethnicity emerges in the first generation. The model asserts that those in the second generation whose parental generation lacks the degree of social capital to provide opportunities and protection for them are likely to develop an "adversarial stance" that American minorities such as poor African Americans and Latinos hold toward the dominant white society. This adversarial stance stresses that discrimination in the United States is very strong and devalues education as a vehicle of advancement. Portes and Zhou emphasize that the adversarial stance of this peer culture directly contradicts the immigrant parents' expectations of upward mobility and educational success for their offspring. The second generation that ally themselves with America's racial minority groups will most likely be at risk of downward social mobility.[26]

These ideas greatly inform the work of Mary Waters who seeks to explain and understand the experiences of second-generation West Indian youths in New York City. Waters specifically explores the racial and ethnic identities adopted by these youths. In her study, Waters found three types of identities among the second generation—a black American identity, an ethnic or hyphenated national origin identity, and an immigrant identity. "These different identities are related to different perceptions and understandings of race relations and of opportunities in the United States." She found that those in the second generation who identify as West Indians tend to see more opportunities and rewards for individual effort and initiative, while those who identify as black Americans tend to see more racial discrimination and limits to opportunities for blacks in the United States. Thus, Waters suggests that assimilation to America for the second-generation black immigrant is complicated by race and class and their interaction, with upwardly mobile second-generation youths maintaining ethnic ties to their parents' national origins and with poor inner city youths assimilating to the black American peer culture that surrounds them.[27]

Using data he collected in Evanston, Illinois, in the 1970s, Tekle Woldemikael found that the Haitian second generation mostly identified as American blacks. He found that while first-generation Haitians stressed their differences from American blacks, the second generation experienced pressure from African American students to adopt to the way they spoke, dressed, and acted.[28]

This chapter aims to contribute to, and problematize previous research by not only examining the racial and ethnic identity of adults rather than youth, but also by suggesting that the adult second generation do not view themselves as having to choose one identity over the other, but as a hybridization of both their racial and ethnic selves. For the second generation West Indian adults in this study, New York City provides a context in which they can embrace their multiple identities while maintaining close ties to other racial and ethnic groups, particularly African Americans and Latinos.

New York as a Site for Identity Development

Urban centers, such as New York City, serve as critical sites of the drawing and redrawing of racial lines. New York in the last few decades has absorbed a large number of immigrants from around the world and a very high percentage of the nation's West Indian immigrants. New York draws a disproportionately large share of non-Latino and Latino immigrants. For instance, among immigrants arriving in the 1980s, 45% of all Jamaican immigrants live in New York, as do 49% of all Trinidadians, 61% of all Barbadians, and 70% of all Guyanese.[29] In 1990 there were 417, 506 non-Latino foreign-born blacks in New York City, 23% on the city's non-Latino black population. The West Indian ancestry population in the city grew at a rapid rate, from 172,192 in 1980 to 391,744 in 1990, an increase of 127.5%. By 1996 it was estimated that 35.1% of the city's black households was headed by a foreign-born person with the vast majority from the Caribbean.[30]

Though the second generation is not clearly "taught" their racial and ethnic identity in the same way that they are taught history and math in school, New York City provides a venue by which they acquire some version "of the rules of racial classification" and of their own racial and ethnic identity.[31] As I will show, not only does only the racial and ethnic geography of New York City teach many racial lessons, but social institutions such as schools and family also serve as a source of racial and ethnic information, a location (and means) for interracial interaction, and a means of both affirming and challenging previous racial attitudes and understandings.[32] Is it easier for the second generation to articulate an ethnic identity because there are so many West Indians living in the city? Do they develop an ethnic identity that also incorporates their relations with ethnic neighbors who can be Dominicans, Puerto Ricans, Chinese, Koreans, native-born whites, African Americans, among others? Or does the multitude of ethnicities in New York lead the second generation to simply identify as "black" as a way of simplifying matters?

In the 30 years since the Hart-Cellar reform in 1965, which effectively lifted the restrictions for immigration to the United States, the state has experienced major demographic transformations, transformations that may, in fact, affect the country as a whole over the next several decades.[33] New York City's massive immigrant influx during the past several decades has brought racial and ethnic issues to the forefront of many residents' minds. In addition, or in some cases, as a consequence, race and ethnicity *and* immigration have played major roles in popular, political, and legal struggles in the state over the past several years (for example, the Abner Louima beating, the shootings of Amadou Diallo and Patrick Dorismond, their subsequent trials, and racial profiling.)[34] After California, New York leads the nation in social, economic, and political trends, and manages to do so in the nation's second most diverse context. Due to the sending countries of contemporary immigrants, New York's racial and ethnic dynamics do not occur in the usual black/white dichotomy that typifies the frequent discourse on racial issues.[35] In a national context in which this kind of diversity is likely to characterize racial and ethnic encounters in the coming decades, New York provides a unique setting in which to begin to study such multiple group/intergroup dynamics today.

The boroughs of New York City offer a compelling setting because of their bounded geographic size, their substantial racial and ethnic diversity, and their relative racial and ethnic integration.[36] Even though the boroughs are not that small in size, their many racial and ethnic groups are not as geographically separate from one another as they are in other cities in New York State. Due to the residential segregation of many groups of color from white communities, many of New York City's racial and ethnic groups provide a context of extensive interracial and interethnic interaction among groups of color.

I contend that racial/ethnic make-up of the population of the area in which second-generation West Indians reside played a significant role in the construction and negotiation of their racial and ethnic identity. The residential segregation of ethnic and racial communities in urban areas led many social scientists to assume (and rightfully so), that there is very little interaction across racial and ethnic lines. However, New York City presents a unique case in the fact that there is an extensive transportation system that allows people access to virtually all parts of the city. The majority of respondents talked of having constant interactions with blacks, but also with other ethnic immigrant groups in New York City. More often than not, this interaction took the form of dance clubs, parades, and festivals around the city. Numerous people spoke of their exposure to other cultures as integral parts of their identity development. For example, Steve greatly appreciated his ability to be several different ethnicities all in the same day if he wanted,

> Alright, I can start off in Flatbush with the Jamaicans, jump on a train to Bensonhurst and hang with the Italians . . . I might not *want* to, but I could

> . . . then get on a train to Flushing, hang with the Asians and get some food, take another train to Harlem and hang with the African Americans on 125th Street, keep taking the train uptown to the Heights and hang out with the Dominicans and dance some salsa real quick, and then go to the Bronx and get some good pasteles from the Boricuas up there . . . you can't get that anywhere else. And I ain't really done a good job . . . I forgot all about the Jews. . . (26-year-old Jamaican)

The intense degree to which various racial and ethnic groups share public space facilitates an awareness and knowledge of different cultures. Particularly within the last decade, this transmittal of cultures and ethnicity has become evident within the ways the second generation construct their own identities.

Identity Construction among the Second Generation

While all the respondents identified as black, West Indian, and American, the interviews suggest that the racial and ethnic identity construction among second-generation West Indians was (as continues to be) an extremely complex matter. However, there were key social institutional milieus that had a significant impact on the identities of the respondents: familial relationships, educational experiences, and neighborhood interactions.[37]

Familial Relationships

For many of the respondents in this study, relationships with their family (immediate and extended), served to reinforce their sense of ethnic identity, while at the same time downplaying their racial one. First-generation immigrant family members would often distance themselves from African Americans, stating that they were "superior" to them. They often tried to stress to their children that African Americans did not have the same values as West Indians, and thus the respondents should be careful not to "act" like "them" by engaging in any wrongdoing—from being disrespectful to violent acts. Steve stated,

> My parents were just like the white people, blaming African Americans for everything that went wrong. If kids were hanging out on the corner, then my mom would say that they must be American[38] 'cause West Indians would not allow their kids to hang out like that. . . . If someone had killed somebody else on the news and they showed a picture of a black person, my family would always assume that it was an African American . . . like West Indians don't commit murder . . . please!

Another respondent recalled,

> My grandmother always told me about how lazy Americans were when I was little. She would always say that you would never find any West Indians on welfare, because West Indians didn't believe in it . . . they worked for their money. When I would tell her that not all Americans were on welfare, and that many of them had their own money, she would say that they were probably of West Indian heritage! Its too bad that grandma isn't alive now, because there are plenty of West Indians on welfare now. I wonder what she would think about that . . . would she call them lazy? I don't think so. . . . (Joan)

While many of the respondents spoke of their family's negative attitudes and treatment of African Americans, they also talked of how the family stressed the importance of education because of their ethnic *and* racial identity:

> My parents would often act like it didn't matter that I was black or not, that I could do whatever I wanted. They never tried to limit me, but they did remind me that I would have to be twenty times better than white people if I wanted to get anywhere. . . . So, while we weren't caught up with being black, my family did acknowledge that we were black and would talk about it. They just didn't want us to be seen like African Americans. . . . (Demali)

Educational Experiences

It is important to note that while family members were preaching the ills of being considered "African American," many of their children were attending school with African Americans. Having daily contact with a population that their parents denigrated served to send the respondents into an identity tailspin. Many of the second generation found it difficult to associate with their peer group of African Americans and then have to go home to their family's negative attitudes:

> I hung out with my friends all day at school and we would have a great time. Then I would go home and someone in the house would say something stupid like Americans don't value education. Are you kidding me? Who was I in class with the whole time? . . . The problem is that anytime that I said anything, I would end up in an argument with my family, or they would say that I didn't know what I was talking about. So after a while I didn't say anything . . . it wasn't worth the drama. . . . (Alecia)

School also became a source of great stress and emotional upheaval for the second generation in that it was in school where they first learned what their "blackness" meant. Many respondents spoke of their mistreatment at the hands of teachers and other school personnel, talking specifically about being left back a grade because of their accent, being ignored when trying to participate in class. Alana commented,

> I loved learning in school, but I hated actually having to deal with the teachers and stuff there. For the first few couple of months in the fourth grade, I remember that my teacher was convinced that I was cheating on my tests because she thought that no one could get all the answers right all the time. But she only worried about me, and only moved my seat right near her. She never paid any attention to the white kids in class, and they cheated all the time. . . why was I singled out? Can black girls not get good grades?

It was in school that some of the respondents realized that their parents were not the only ones who could be prejudiced—they often got teased by their African American peers for their accents and style of dress. Elementary and junior high school in particular was particularly oppressive for the West Indians as they tried to negotiate their parents, teachers, and peers while maintaining some semblance of self. The struggle of trying to deal with home and school often became an unbearable burden to the second generation,

> It wasn't worth it, my African American friends kept asking me if I thought that I was better than them. My parents kept telling me that I *was* better than African Americans. It was just too much. . . . No one understood, and I was tired of trying to explain. It was easier just to be black, not African American, just black . . . you know? (Winston)

Experiences with identity during the period of junior high and high school were most clearly put forth by Keisha, who said that she spent that time, ". . . *being black by day, and being West Indian by night*." She continued,

> I was in no position to make anyone mad at me for being one thing or another. I had to live with my parents, but I also wanted to fit in school, so what was I supposed to do? So, I spoke with my accent with my parents, and didn't when I was hanging out with my friends. I used to feel guilty about switching, but now I don't. I am *both* after all. . . .

The most dramatic change in identity for the second generation occurred in college. For those who went, college presented West Indians with the opportunity to recreate themselves in ways that were most comfortable for them. As many of them enrolled in the City University of New York (CUNY) educational system, they encountered other second-generation immigrants from multiple countries. Through the exposure to other ethnicities, as well as a critical mass of other West Indians, the second generation found the first opportunity to celebrate the dual parts of their identity. The feeling of not completely belonging in either in an immigrant or American world was found to be a phenomenon of other second-generation immigrants. Sharon commented,

> I got to Brooklyn College, and I almost lost my mind. There were so many other Caribbeans there, African Americans, Puerto Ricans, other Latinos, and whites. I mean, even the white people there were immigrants. Meeting all those people and getting to know them showed me that I was not as different as high school had made me feel. There were plenty of people just like me who didn't really fit in anywhere except with each other. Even though we were from different countries, we had similar experiences with family and friends . . . who knew that my best friend would be a Boricua that I met in college?

College was seen as a microcosm of the city in which the second generation had lived in most of their lives, but might not necessarily had been exposed to:

> I knew there were a lot of Puerto Ricans in New York City. All you got to do is go to the Puerto Rican Day parade in Manhattan to see them . . . but I didn't realize that so many of them lived in Queens. . . . damn, I got to LaGuardia Community College and you would have thought that they had taken over the city. . . . After a while it was cool though . . . I realized that they were just like me. We all like hip-hop and good food, so we all real cool now. I go with them to Nell's on Wednesday night, and they go with me and my other friends on Thursday night.[39]

Important to note is that those West Indians who left New York City to attend college often attended predominantly white schools, yet still felt the same kinds of "freedom" in their identity constructions as those who attended the predominantly minority CUNY system.[40] They also encountered a number of West Indians within the black college community and felt that they had entered a space that was conducive to their multiple identities:

> There were all these people from the Caribbean when I got to school. I could not believe it! Who knew that an Ivy League school would have so many immigrant children in it. I was barely expecting to see other black people much less those from the island. I was a member of the

> Black Student Union as well as the Caribbean Club, and no one thought that that was strange. The Caribbean Club . . . it taught me a lot about the Caribbean that I didn't know . . . for example, I didn't know anything about Montserrat until I got to college.

Neighborhood Interactions

For many of the second-generation West Indians, their experiences within their neighborhood, coupled with their familial and school interactions, all contributed to very trying times in their lives. The typical experience for the second-generation immigrants was that their parents arrived in the United States and chose to live near friends and family who came before them—and thus ended up living in West Indian neighborhoods. For many of the second generation I spoke with, their parents entered the United States in the late 1960s or 1970s under a worker's permit or a visitor's visa with sponsorship from a friend or family member.[41] After living with friends, family, or their actual sponsor, many West Indian immigrants went on to buy or rent homes in predominantly white areas. And these moves were not met without difficulty:

> . . . [A]nd they talk about how different the North is from the South? You couldn't tell when I was growing up. When we moved into the Heights [Cambria Heights] we used to get chased home all the time by the white kids. My parents had to drive us to school for a long time because the bus driver would refuse to pick us up. . . . I mean, we would watch it pull up in front of the white people's houses, but when the bus got to our block, it would just pass us on by. At first my parents thought that we were making up stories, but then they saw for themselves and ended up taking us to school. I wanted them to complain to the school, but they were afraid of starting trouble. Our nearest relatives were back in Brooklyn, and what could they do for us from there if something went down? I learned to fight early because I refused to get beat up, particularly by no white kids! (Lisa)

Another respondent recalled:

> I'm sorry. My parents could pretend all they wanted that we were different from African Americans, but who would believe you? Sure as hell not the white people that were in Bed-Stuy [Bedford-Stuyvesant] when we moved in! They couldn't tell the difference between who was West Indian or African American, and they didn't care. All they saw was black and that was enough for them. People would call us "niggers" to our

> faces and try to spit on us when we walked down the street. I remember that my mother would always tell me and my brother and sister to ignore them and just keep walking . . . that we had manners and they did not. One day when I was about ten, I told her that there had only been one Martin Luther King, Jr., and I was not him . . . of course she beat me for being smart with her, but I just wanted her to know that I had limits to how much I was going to take from those kids. . . . (Derrick)

Not surprisingly, these neighborhoods did not stay predominantly white for very long. Over the years, there has been increasing ethnic and racial complexity in neighborhoods throughout the region: more and more neighborhoods contain multiple groups; fewer are homogeneous. In this sense, growing integration seems to be the master trend at the neighborhood level. However, at the same time, there is a cross-cutting trend: the growth of all minority neighborhoods, occupied by blacks and/or Latinos. These two trends have a direct impact on constructions of identity for the second generation. Respondents spoke about how the composition of the neighborhood in which they resided provided different contexts for identity choices that they made over the course of their lives. Specifically, the predominance of West Indians and other ethnic groups such as Latinos in the neighborhood led them to identify ethnically, while when they were a racial minority or resided in a predominantly African American neighborhood, they tended to identify racially.

These findings on racial/ethnic diversity support many of the sentiments expressed by the respondents, particularly the younger half of the sample. Several people commented on having much more interactions with Latinos, Puerto Ricans in particular, than some of the older respondents in the study:[42]

> I was surprised when I saw some Spanish people around this neighborhood a couple of years ago, but now they are everywhere. My best friend is a Boricua who lives two doors down from me.[43] At first I thought that there might be some problems with the old heads who live here, but everything is cool. We all hang out, go to parties and clubs together, and all that stuff. I taught Angie about making Roti, and she taught me how to make Pasteles.[44] (Lorna)

Overall in New York's cities, blacks are largely segregated from whites and reside mostly in areas which they are the numerically dominant, if not the exclusive, group. However, with the influx of numerous other Caribbean groups into previously predominantly black neighborhoods, there is bound to be increasing changes in the identity development and may require new ways for thinking about "ethnicity" more generally.

Identities of the Second Generation

For the second generation with whom I spoke, they all saw themselves as having a separate identity from the African American community. The respondents had specific ideas about what constituted being "African American," and they most often did not see themselves as fitting into that identity. Sheila stated,

> Being African American means that you have a specific cultural background, just as being Basian [Barbadian] has a particular culture to it. African Americans have a general understanding of their migrant experiences the same way that we generally know of ours. . . . I mean, we can all trace our slave history to Africa, but African Americans can also trace their family history to down South somewhere, and I can trace mine back to the Caribbean. They know grits, hamhocks, and pigs' feet, and we know about cornmeal porridge, tripe, and oxtail. . . . I mean, we all black, but we're not all the same . . . cause everybody different from the straight-up Africans.

Like Sheila, many of the respondents regarded African Americans as an ethnic group as opposed to a racial group, so most people stated that they would not identify as both African American and West Indian. They did not see this as a method of "distancing" themselves from African Americans, but acknowledging the different histories of the black groups in the United States. Winston commented,

> When I got to high school and learned about the Civil Rights Movement, I was very self-conscious that I didn't know much about it before I started the class. All my African Americans friends had some knowledge about it, and some of their parents had participated in the marches. I remember being impressed by that fact and them just sort of brushing it off as normal. They would want to know why I didn't know anything and I would tell them it was because my parents missed most of it by coming to this country in 1972. I always felt like I missed something really important to my history as a black person in this country. My parents always reminded that we had our own history too, it was just different. . . . So when my African American friends say that they do not have an ethnicity, I tell them that yeah, they do, we just don't talk about it right. We are all black, but we are *not* all African American with everything that goes along with it. . . . There is still a Southern culture that I am still trying to learn about in the same way that they are learning about the history of the Caribbean. . . .

While the second generation argues that they are not "African American" in the sense that it is an ethnic group, they also find that they don't fit into the strict category of "West Indian" either:

> I know that I like to think of myself as Jamaican, but if you ask my family who lives in Jamaica, or even my parents, they would tell you that I am an American. I go to Jamaica every summer for months at a time, speak the language, dance to the music, but I always get accused of not being a *true* dread. I never *had* to live there except when I was first born, and I have never been poor they way they are, and . . . I realize that my family is right about me when they use a phrase that I don't recognize, or talk about food that only grows in Jamaica that I haven't eaten before. . . . (Carmen)

Contrary to the social science identity categories of West Indian and African American, the second generation does not see themselves as one identity or the other, but rather something in between the West Indian and black American:

> My family tells me that I am not Guyanese because I did not grow up there. But I am not African American either. I mean . . . I grew up differently than my African American friends. Their parents were not as strict as mine, I had to work harder in school because my parents were not accepting less than an A . . . not that my African American friends' parents didn't care about their grades, but there was this sense of . . . I don't know urgency with my parents? . . . after leaving everything that they had even known, we could not let them down . . . I don't know, it's still hard to explain. I just know that my life has been different from my parents *and* my African American friends. No one knows what its like having to decide everyday when and where I can be West Indian, Guyanese, or black. Well, I shouldn't say that . . . because I am black everyday, I don't really have a choice. . . . (Precious)

Precious and many other West Indians detailed their struggle of trying to exist in between two cultural experiences while retaining a commitment to both their racial and ethnic identities. Their phenotype frequently defined how they were treated in society; however, when West Indians spoke of their experiences between the two worlds, they often used African Americans as a reference point:

> Come on man, I know that white people just see me as another nigga on the street . . . ready to shoot you in the front, back, upside down and all around, and then get away with it like nothing.[45] When you ask me

> about how I identify, I think about if you mean when I am hanging with my West Indian family and friends, or my African American friends . . . cause I think about them first. I mean, I don't hang out with white people, so I don't give a rat's ass what they think. But, I do care what my African American brothers think about me. They are the ones that I roll with on a daily basis. . . . But sometimes it is hard being with them. They don't understand why I saw or do certain stuff because they are not from the islands. And I don't know . . . I don't call myself an African American . . . not because I don't like them or because I think that I'm better than them . . . it's just . . . that's not what I am . . . and what I am is a Jamaican from Maypen.[46]

Based on the interviews with the respondents, it became quite clear that the New York City context played a major role in their process of identity formation as black ethnics. I contend that the landscape of New York City facilitates this kind of identity construction and can lead to coalition building among ethnic groups that have not previously been explored in the social science literature. Thus, I move to examining how the transference of a West Indian culture manages to redefine what is considered New York culture.

From Marginalized to Mainstream

"You don't understand, it wasn't cool to be West Indian growing up the way it is NOW . . ."

This was the sentiment of numerous respondents during the course of the study. After spending significant periods of their childhood questioning the saliency of their ethnic identity in an effort to "go along to get along," the second generation realized in their adult lives that not only can they claim their racial and ethnic identities simultaneously, but being West Indian is now also "en vogue" in New York City. They all referred to what they saw as the adoption of West Indian culture and music into mainstream New York City life by people of all races and ethnic groups:

> There are few New York black clubs that you can go to where they do not play dance hall . . . actually they will have one whole floor for reggae, with hip-hop and slow jams on other floors. The first time I saw that, I was like, what the hell? When did y'all decide that it was okay to dance to the "boat people's" music? I almost passed out . . . cause now West Indians can't even get into their own clubs . . . they're always packed with whites and whoever else acting like it ain't nothing but a thing. . . . (Donovan)

> How did they go from laughing at the way we spoke to trying to speak like us? I am still tripping about what is going on here in New York. Who decided that it was the "in-thing" to be West Indian . . . and better yet, who told people to listen? (Patrice)

> I went to a club the other day and there were Asian kids who had taken over the dance hall floor. First, I felt old because they looked really young, and then I thought, what are they doing here? And how y'all going to take over? Only in New York can it be cool for Vietnamese kids to dominate a reggae room. . . . (Everald)

None of the respondents could pinpoint when New York City style included West Indian speech and music, but they were all amused by the change. Some attributed the change to the fact that there are more West Indians in New York City than ever before, but does that account for the cultural shift? Some saw the production of the "Caribbean Rhythms" show on Black Entertainment Television (BET) as the first sign that they were becoming a powerful voice not just in New York City, but also across the country.[47] Donna stated,

> The first time I saw "Caribbean Rhythms" I wondered how long it was going to last. I mean, damn, they only used to play it on Saturday nights at like three o'clock in the morning. Who's going to see that? Then they kept moving it, moving it, until it was shown during primetime. That's when I knew we had made it. Someone at BET was smart enough to know that there was a large audience for that kind of music. . . . Black people are international, why isn't anyone trying to show the diversity of our people? Or would that mean that we would have to change how we think about black people in general?

The increased interest in West Indian culture could also be seen in attendance in annual West Indians parades. Several respondents noted that many of the people who frequent the Labor Day parade on Eastern Parkway are non-West Indians who are there for the food, the floats, and the music. Some even commented that how Caribana, the West Indian parade held in Toronto, Canada, is increasingly becoming less West Indian and more everyone else. Donna was completely perplexed, *how did they even KNOW about Caribana? It's not like it's publicized a whole lot. But the last two times I went I had to make sure that I was at the right place there were so many white people there. . . .*

The inclusion of West Indian culture and music into the mainstream is not just some accident—many pop culture icons have also "outed" their ethnicity to the public. In addition to rock star Lenny Kravitz, the widely popular Haitian

Wyclef Jean and his success with the rap group "The Fugees," rap impresarios Queen Latifah, Busta Rhymes, and the late Biggie Smalls all acknowledged and celebrate(d) their ethnic backgrounds. Several of the respondents commented that this a just another commodification of an ethnic culture by the mainstream, similar to the advent of the hip-hop culture:

> Someone told these people that there was money to be made if you had a West Indian accent. We used to get beat up for that shit in elementary school, and now people are making loot off it? When they have the experiences that I have had growing up in this country, in this city, then they can be Jamaican all they want. When someone strip searches you in the Gap for supposedly stealing as well as in JFK airport for allegedly bringing in drugs, then you can talk all the shit you want about "being down" with the struggle for blacks and immigrants in this country. . . . I know that all them fools are [the pop stars mentioned above] bredren, but come on man, when did they let the masses know? *After* they blew the hell up. So I'm still suspect of their motives for "outing" themselves. After all, they trying to make bank too, just like everybody else. . . . (Michael)

> If you think that these people are out here dancing to reggae music and eating beef patties because they *like* West Indians, you are sadly mistaken. It's just because the music is cool and the food tastes good, and for some reason it's cool to be Jamaican, not West Indian, just Jamaican, cause that's all they know . . . bet no one can even tell where St. Lucia is on the map . . . anyway, every culture at some point gets adopted as the "in" thing . . . remember what Madonna did to the East Indians in one of her CDs? . . . and this so-called Latin explosion? Weren't the Latinos always there? Anyway, that's all that's happening here, after they can't make any more money off us, they'll go back to treating us like shit again. (Demali)

While Michael, Demali, and several others were clearly skeptical of the motives behind the current mainstreaming of West Indian culture, others were slightly more positive and optimistic about the potential for broader recognition:

> If you get someone like Busta Rhymes out there talking about his West Indian parentage, then that's a good thing. He is a great example of someone who clearly identifies as black. I know that most people think of him as African American, but his very presence symbolizes how far we have come as West Indians. . . . We are not the ignored group any longer. . . . (Jason)

> Only in New York do you know that at least one major star got to be from the Caribbean. . . . People outside of New York didn't know that Biggie was Jamaican, but we did. He's probably not a good example though, since he was a mad drug dealer before he blew up as a rapper, but still, he was holding it down, representing for all the West Indians in New York. Wasn't nobody telling him that he couldn't talk about how he grew up differently from some of his African American friends cause his mother was Jamaican. He used to talk about it all the time in the hood and that was okay . . . yeah, that was aight, too bad he got shot and died, who knew what he could done about getting our experiences out there. . . . (Carol)

For some of the second-generation respondents, these "outings" of rap and pop stars and the mainstreaming of West Indian culture indicates that it is possible to exist in both worlds as a black and as a West Indian. It is not a question of distancing from others, but acknowledging and celebrating difference within the black community.

Several of the second-generation West Indians reported that the wearing of dreadlocks or "dreds" by both African Americans and a few whites is another example of the diffusion of West Indian culture to popular culture or "the mainstream." Sheila stated,

> I remember when dreds were seen as dirty, and that only something the Rastafarians would do to their hair. But now everyone's wearing dreds as if it was always popular and the "in thing" to do.

The concentrations of West Indians in central Brooklyn, southeast Queens, northern Bronx, and in the upper West side of Manhattan accounts for the prevalence of West Indian stores such as food markets and restaurants. However, this does not account for why African Americans within, and outside of, those same areas also frequent those businesses. Colwick commented,

> I remember when my American friends would make fun of what I brought to school for lunch. Now?! Now, everyone wants what my mother has been making for years. What's the big fascination all of a sudden? This stuff has always been there.

It is important to note that this transmittal of culture is bi-directional. Respondents spoke of being as connected to Hip-Hop and R&B culture, as they are to West Indian culture:

> I can go from dancing to Bob Marley and Beenie Man one minute to Jay-Z and Lauryn Hill in the next. (Michael)

Others found it problematic to think of Hip-Hop and Dance Hall as separate entities,

> [W]hy you acting like if they not one and the same? Dance Hall is Hip-Hop and vice-versa. We all black people ain't we? *All* of it is black culture, just different pieces of it.

Implications of a Diasporic Understanding of Race

The majority of the scholarship on ethnic adaptation employs a bi-modal framework that engages one of two opposing outcomes—either complete abandonment of ethnic identity for an American one or a complete rejection of American identity. This chapter sought to illuminate the fact that the experiences of second-generation West Indian immigrants, and even the general black immigrant population, does not conform to such rigid and simplistic notions of ethnic identity. Like Richard Alba, Frederick Barth, and Mary Waters, I find that the meanings of ethnic identity are shaped through the nature of interpersonal and intergroup relations and the social context.[48] For the second-generation respondents in this study, ethnic identity was treated as a dynamic process that is negotiated and renegotiated in different social contexts and at different stages of their life course.[49]

The current movement of anti-immigration, racial backlash, globalizing economy, and steady if not increasing inequality all necessarily shape how people understand who they are, where they fit in relation to others, and what is going on in the world. This is not a unidirectional process, however. How people understand the world and their place in it necessarily affects how they operate and thus shapes the world in which they live. Identity formation is thus a consequence of, and contributor to, the social world in which second-generation immigrants live in the space of New York City.

Numerous social scientists and nonacademics have argued that the significance of race continues to be one of the most pressing problems in American society. If this is truly the case, then there is a dramatic need for a more substantial and nuanced understanding of the way race functions in relation to people's everyday lives. Conveniently, the recent influx of large numbers of nonwhite immigrants and their incorporation into U.S. society, or lack thereof, provides us with another mechanism by which to study racial phenomena. Specifically, I contend that examining the lives of black immigrants will reveal how phenotype can lead an ethnic group (such as West Indians, African immigrants) to become defined solely by their racial classification, forcing them to make some important decisions around how they self-identify.

The emergent significance of black ethnicity in the post-Civil Rights Movements era demonstrates that we can longer think of race as the definitive characteristic of all blacks in the United States. Just as the pan-ethnic category "Asian" encompasses numerous nationalities, it should be recognized that "black" is also an umbrella term for various ethnicities and cultures. Over the past few years while scholars were fervently arguing about whether people should be allowed to check off more than one box for their "race" on the 2000 census, no one considered what the sole box of "Black/African American/Negro" would mean to blacks filling out the census. I heard repeatedly from those in the West Indian population that they had no idea what to check off because while they saw themselves as "Black," they were by no means a "Negro." They also often complained of the categories for ethnicity that other racial groups were able to choose from (such as Korean or Japanese), yet they had no choice at all. What does this say about how race and ethnicity are constructed in American society? The aim of this chapter is to demonstrate that ethnic identity is not salient just for members of some racialized groups, but all of them.

Notes

1. See Bonnett, Aubrey. "West Indians in the United States of America: Some Theoretical and Practical Considerations" in Aubrey Bonnett and G. L. Watson, eds., *Emerging Perspectives on the Black Diaspora* (Lanham, Maryland: University Press of America, 1990); Roy S. Bryce-LaPorte, "New York City and the New Caribbean Immigration: A Contextual Statement," in Constance R. Sutton and Elsa M. Cheney, eds., *Caribbean Life in New York City: Sociocultural Dimensions* (New York: Center for Migration Studies, 1987); Nancy Foner, "Race and Color: Jamaican Migrants in London and New York City," *International Migration Review,* Vol. 19: 708–727; Nancy Foner, "The Jamaicans: Race and Ethnicity among Migrants in New York City" in Nancy Foner, ed., *New Immigrants in New York* (New York: Columbia University Press, 1987); Nancy Foner, "Ideology and Social Practice in the Jamaican Diaspora," Working Paper #65, Russell Sage Foundation, 1994; Ira Reid, *The Negro Immigrant: His Background Characteristics and Social Adjustment, 1899–1937* (New York: Columbia University Press, 1939); Philip Kasinitz, *Caribbean New York: Black Immigrants and the Politics of Race* (Ithaca, New York: Cornell University Press, 1992); Constance R. Sutton and S. Makiesky, "Migration and West Indian Racial and Ethnic Consciousness," in Helen Safa and Brian DuToit, eds., *Migration and Development: Implications for Ethnic Identity and Political Conflict* (Paris: Mouton and Co., 1975); Milton Vickerman, "The Response of West Indians to African Americans: Distancing and Identification," in Rutledge Dennis, ed., *Research in Race and Ethnic Relations,* Vol. 7. (Greenwich, Connecticut, JAI Press,

1994); Milton Vickerman, *Crosscurrents: West Indian Immigrants and Race* (New York: Oxford University Press, 1999); Tekle Woldemikael, "Black Ethnics: A Case Study of Haitian Immigrants," *New England Journal of Black Studies,* Vol. 5: 15–30; Tekle Woldemikael, *Becoming Black American: Haitians and American Institutions in Evanston, Illinois* (New York: AMS Press, 1989); Mary C. Waters, "Ethnic and Racial Identities of Second-Generation Black Immigrants in New York City," *International Migration Review,* Vol. 28 (4): 795–820; Mary C. Waters, *Black Identities: West Indian Immigrant Dreams and American Realities* (Cambridge: Harvard University Press, 1999).

2. This was due to the fact that the post-1965 second generation population had yet to come of age by which researchers could explore their racial and ethnic identities.

3. See Patricia Fernandez-Kelly and Robert Schauffler, "Divided Fates: Immigrant Children in a Restructured U.S. Economy," *International Migration Review,* Vol. 28: 662–668; Margaret A. Gibson, *Accommodation Without Assimilation* (Ithaca: Cornell University Press, 1989); Alejandro Portes and Min Zhou, "The New Second Generation: Segmented Assimilation and Its Variants," *The Annals of the American Academy of Political and Social Science,* Vol. 530: 74–97; Ruben Rumbaut, "The Crucible Within: Ethnic Identity, Self-Esteem, and Segmented Assimilation Among Children of Immigrants," *International Migration Review* Vol. 28 (4): 748–794; Ruben Rumbaut, "The New Californians: Comparative Research Findings on the Educational Progress of Immigrant Children" in Ruben Rumbaut and Wayne Cornelius, eds., *California's Immigrant Children: Theory Research, and Implications for Educational Policy* (La Jolla, California: Center for U.S. Mexican Studies, University of California, San Diego, 1995); Ruben Rumbaut, "Origins and Destinies: Immigration, Race, and Ethnicity in Contemporary America" in Silvia Pedraza and Ruben Rumbaut, eds., *Origins and Destinies: Immigration, Race, and Ethnicity in America* (Belmont: Wadsworth Publishing, 1996); Ruben Rumbaut, "Ties that Bind: Immigration and Immigrant Families in the United States" in Alan Booth, Ann C. Crouter, and Nancy Landale, eds., *Immigration and the Family: Research and Policy on U.S. Immigrants* (Mahwah, New Jersey: Lawrence Erlbaum Associates, Publishers: 1997); Min Zhou and Carl Bankston III, "Social Capital and the Adaptation of the Second Generation: The Case of Vietnamese Youth in New Orleans," *International Migration Review,* Vol. 28(4): 775–799; Min Zhou and Carl Bankston III, *Growing Up American: The Adaptation of Vietnamese Adolescents in the United States* (New York: Russell Sage Foundation, 1998).

4. See Reid, *The Negro Immigrant;* Waters, "Ethnic and Racial Identities"; Waters, *Black Identities;* Foner, "The Jamaicans;" Alejandro Portes and Dag MacLeod, "What Shall I Call Myself?: Hispanic Identity Formation in the Second Generation," *Ethnic and Racial Studies,* Vol. 19 (3): 523–547; Portes and Zhou, "The New Second Generation;" Alejandro Portes and Dag MacLeod, "Educational Progress of Children of Immigrants: The Roles of Class, Ethnicity and School Context," *Sociology of Education,* Vol. 69 (October 1996): 255–275.

5. See Frederick Barth, ed., *Ethnic Groups and Boundaries: The Social Organiza-*

tion of Culture Difference (Boston: Little, Brown, and Co., 1969); Richard Jenkins, *Social Identity* (London, Routledge, 1996); Joane Nagel, "Constructing Ethnicity: Creating and Recreating Ethnic Identity and Culture," *Social Problems,* Vol. 41: 152–176.

6. Most of the fieldwork for the project that produced these data was conducted during the 1998–1999 academic year. Thus, all references to age pertain to that time period. The larger objective of this research was to document the respondents' constructions of their racial and ethnic identities, paying specific attention to how they implicated race, class, and gender in their views and experiences (see Sherri-Ann Butterfield, "Big Tings a Gwaan: Constructions of Racial and Ethnic Identity Among Second Generation West Indian Immigrants," Ph.D. dissertation, University of Michigan, 2001). Prior to eliciting their comments on this topic, I attempted in my interviews to capture a specific sense of the life histories and contemporary experiences of the second generation. The interviews concentrated on self-identification at different stages through the life course, including past and present interactions with social institutions (family, schools, churches, formal and informal peer institutions, labor market, law enforcement, and others).

7. The lower age bracket of 20 was also chosen as it was my intention to reach second-generation West Indians who had completed high school and had some experience in the workforce.

8. See Foner, "Race and Color"; Foner, "The Jamaicans;" Kasinitz, *Caribbean New York;* Sutton and Makiesky, "Migration and West Indian Racial and Ethnic Consciousness"; Waters, "Ethnic and Racial Identities"; Waters, *Black Identities.* The respondents in the study specifically reside in central Brooklyn, Northern Bronx, the upper West side of Manhattan (mainly Harlem), and southeast Queens.

9. Regardless of the location, I interviewed each of the respondents in a one-on-one interactive format. In addition to the interviews, for the larger project I also conducted ethnographies at two different sites, Brooklyn and Queens, during the 1998–1999 academic year. In both cases I used a small business in the neighborhood—a hair salon and a farmer's market—as a mechanism for meeting and talking to people that I otherwise would not be able to capture via interviews. Despite the richness of the ethnographic material, the data presented here are derived mainly from the interviews conducted.

10. See Marilyn Halter, *Between Race and Ethnicity: Cape Verdean American Immigrants, 1860–1965* (Urbana: University of Illinois Press, 1993); Michael Omi and Howard Winant, *Racial Formation in the United States: From the 1960's to the 1990's* (New York: Routledge, 1994); Milton Gordon, *Assimilation in American Life: The Role of Race, Religion, and National Origins* (New York: Oxford University Press, 1964); John Higham, *Strangers in the Land: Patterns of American Nativism, 1860–1925* (Urbana: University of Illinois Press, 1970).

11. The examination of ethnic identity and its significance for second-generation West Indian immigrants entails looking at the ways in which they define themselves; how these identities influence their social behavior, networks, and attitudes; and how they define the membership boundaries of their group (see Barth, *Ethnic Groups and*

Boundaries; Nagel, "Constructing Ethnicity"; Mary C. Waters, *Ethnic Options: Choosing Identities in America* [Berkeley: University of California Press, 1990]). In the larger study, the salience of ethnic identity is also evaluated with measures used in other studies such as: preference for and use of home country language/style of speech, patronage with co-ethnics, church membership, or religious affiliation, participation in voluntary organizations, and participation in events and activities sponsored by such organizations (see Richard Alba, ed., *Ethnicity and Race in the U.S.A.: Toward the Twenty-First Century* [Boston: Routledge and Kegan Paul, 1985]); Nagel, "Constructing Ethnicity"; Waters, *Ethnic Options*). In addition to these traditional measures, I also considered the degree to which the respondents listen to West Indian music, read West Indian books and/or newspapers, and participate/attend in city-wide West Indian activities (such as the annual Eastern Parkway celebration in Brooklyn on Labor Day—see Kasinitz, *Caribbean New York*).

12. Almost half of the Panamanian immigrants to the United States are of Jamaican descent (see Waters, *Black Identities*).

13. The sample also includes people who are what Ruben Rumbaut (see his "The Agony of Exile: A Comparative Study of Indochinese Refugee Adults and Children" in F. Ahearn, Jr., and J. Athey, eds., *Refugee Children: Theory, Research and Services* [Baltimore: Johns Hopkins University Press, 1991]) described as the "1.5 generation"—children born abroad but educated and socialized primarily in the United States (arriving in the United States before the age of 12). Rumbaut contends that these children straddle both worlds—their home country and the United States—but are fully part of neither. While I recognize that there can be important differences between children of the 1.5 and second generation, particularly in their physical and psychological developmental stages, in their socialization process in the family, the school, and the society at large, as well as the orientation of their homeland, it is important to note that none of the 1.5 respondents in the sample arrived in the United States past the age of ten.

14. See Gordon, *Assimilation in American Life.*

15. "Contemporary immigrants" refers to those arriving in the United States post-1965.

16. See Gordon, *Assimilation in American Life;* Charles Hirschman, "America's Melting Pot Reconsidered," *Annual Review of Sociology,* Vol. 9 (1983): 397–423; Stanley Lieberson, *A Piece of the Pie: Blacks and White Immigrants Since 1880* (Berkeley: University of California Press, 1980); Stanley Lieberson and Mary C. Waters, *From Many Strands: Ethnic and Racial Groups in Contemporary America* (New York: Russell Sage Foundation, 1988); Joel Perlmann, *Ethnic Differences: Schooling and Social Structure among the Irish, Jews, and Blacks in an American City, 1888–1935* (New York: Cambridge University Press, 1988); Waters, *Ethnic Options.*

17. See Alba, *Ethnicity and Race in the U.S.A.;* Lieberson, *A Piece of the Pie.*

18. See W. Lloyd Warner and Leo Srole, *The Social System of American Ethnic Groups* (New Haven: Yale University Press, 1945).

19. John Mollenkopf, Philip Kasinitz, and Mary Waters, "The Immigrant Second

Generation in Metropolitan New York," Research Proposal to the Russell Sage Foundation, 1995.

20. See Ivan Light, *Ethnic Enterprise in America: Business and Welfare Among Chinese, Japanese, and Blacks* (Berkeley: University of California Press, 1972; Portes and Zhou, "The New Second Generation"; Waters, "Ethnic and Racial Identities"; Zhou and Bankston, *Growing Up American*).

21. In his *Unmeltable Ethnics: Politics and Culture in American Life* (New Brunswick, New Jersey: Transaction, 1972), Michael Novak first coined the term "unmeltable ethnics" in his discussion of the plight of lower-middle-class whites and white southern European ethnics within American society. I, however, am using the same term to convey the idea that by continuing to engage in racist and discriminatory behavior, American society treats immigrant groups of color as the "unmeltable ethnics."

22. See Michel Laguerre, *American Odyssey: Haitians in New York City* (Ithaca: Cornell University Press, 1984).

23. See Foner, "The Jamaicans"; Foner, "Ideology and Social Practice in the Jamaican Diaspora"; Halter, *Between Race and Ethnicity;* Kasinitz, *Caribbean New York;* Vickerman, "The Response of West Indians to African Americans"; Vickerman, *Crosscurrents;* Waters, "Ethnic and Racial Identities"; Waters, *Ethnic Options;* Woldemikael, *Becoming Black American.*

24. See Herbert Gans, "Second Generation Decline: Scenarios for the Economic and Ethnic Futures of the Post-1965 American Immigrants," *Ethnic and Racial Studies,* Vol. 15 (2): 173–192; Joel Perlmann and Roger Waldinger, "Second Generation Decline?: Immigrant Children Past and Present—A Reconsideration," *International Migration Review,* Vol. 31 (4): 893–922; Portes and Zhou, "The New Second Generation."

25. Gans, "Second Generation Decline."

26. Portes an Zhou, "The New Second Generation."

27. Waters, "Ethnic and Racial Identities"; Waters, *Black Identities.*

28. Woldemikael, *Becoming Black.*

29. See Joseph Salvo and Ronald Ortiz, *The Newest New Yorkers: An Analysis of Immigration into New York City during the 1980s* (New York: Department of City Planning, 1992).

30. See Waters, *Black Identities.*

31. Omi and Winant, *Racial Formation in the United States,* p. 60.

32. Included in the institution of schools are school personnel such as teachers, guidance counselors, and school administrators.

33. Along with the demographic changes that have occurred in California over the past several decades, in the next few decades, the Eastern *and* Western seaboards of the United States will significantly alter the composition of America's major and minority racial and ethnic groups. In fact, the 2000 Census reports that immigration is the leading cause of the increase in population in the major U.S. cities. Those areas that did not experience large-scale immigration actually saw a decrease in population size. William Frey states, "New York is a prototypical case of a place where if not for immigration, it

would not be the vibrant city that it is. The lifeblood of the cities and hope for the cities is continued immigration" (*Washington Post,* 16 March 2001).

34. With the exception of racial profiling, all of the cases involving the beatings and shootings of New York residents involved black immigrants.

35. For example, see work by John Mollenkopf and Manuel Castells, eds., *Dual City: Restructuring New York* (New York: Russell Sage Foundation, 1991) and others on the multi-racial politics in the boroughs of New York City.

36. Below the borough level, all geographic names are pseudonyms, introduced to help protect the confidentiality of the research sites.

37. Due to the preliminary condition of the data, I am purposely not including a discussion on the second generation's experiences within the labor market and how it may affect their identity construction.

38. For many first-generation West Indians, "American" refers to African Americans, as a way of differentiating between the two groups.

39. Nell's is a nightclub in New York City that plays Latin music on Wednesday nights and Reggae/Dance Hall music on Thursday nights.

40. Often the West Indians who left New York City still attended colleges that were not that far from the city. In fact, none of the respondents attended a college more than five hours away from New York City by car. Similar to the process of choosing a high school, West Indian parents often demanded that their children stay in New York City for college. Once again, they assumed that their children would be "safer" and "do better" if they remained at home. For the respondents who attended school outside of New York, they remarked how it was either school personnel, a family member, or a friend that would impress upon the parents to discuss the merits of leaving home for college.

41. During the 1960s and 1970s, many West Indians entered the United States with what was referred to as a "Visitor's Visa." This allowed them to stay in the country for a set period of time, usually two to three weeks. These visas were only issued if someone with American residence decided to sponsor the individual, thereby taking responsibility for the immigrant and could be held accountable if something should go awry. For many of the people I spoke with, they, or their parents came over on a Visitor's Visa and "just never went back." The immigrants achieved residency by finding employment before Immigration and Naturalization Services (INS) could send them back to their home countries. Despite using creative ways in order to obtain residency, many West Indians did not recognize (or would admit) that for a period of time they were "illegal immigrants." Interestingly, they did not feel that that terminology referred to them, but some "other people"—like "the people from Cuba and Haiti who come over on boats," as one man pointedly stated.

42. Interestingly, when I asked the older respondents about their interactions with other racial and ethnic groups, several people talked about the presence of white Latinos in their neighborhoods when the immigrant family initially moved in. The second generation remarked that the Latino parents also discriminated against them by not allowing their children to hang out with the West Indian kids. (This appeared especially prevalent

in the Queens neighborhoods.) Based on these remarks, it is clear that black immigrant children found themselves discriminated against by majority *and* minority groups.

43. "Boricua" is a slang term that refers to Puerto Ricans.

44. "Roti" and "Pasteles" are Trinidadian and Puerto Rican dishes, respectively.

45. This interview took place after the African immigrant, Amadou Diallo, was fatally shot 41 times by New York City police officers. Though the verdict in the trial had not been decided at the time, the respondent correctly predicted the outcome.

46. Maypen is a province in the country of Jamaica.

47. "Caribbean Rhythms" was a show hosted by a Jamaican woman that visited different Caribbean islands and showed music videos from various Caribbean groups.

48. Alba, *Ethnicity and Race in the U.S.A.;* Barth, *Ethnic Groups and Boundaries;* Waters, *Ethnic Options.*

49. Nagel, "Constructing Ethnicity."

Andrew A. Beveridge and Michael McMenemy

Appendix

The Black Presence in the Hudson River Valley, 1790 to 2000: A Demographic Overview

A demographic overview of the black population of the Hudson River Valley confirms their presence and persistence in the area from the founding of the United States through the present. This brief study paints a general picture of black settlement patterns through 22 censuses, starting in 1790—the first year such population counts were taken in the United States. Our tabulations end in 2000 regarding variables for which these latest data are available. The numbers reveal a fluid population that has undergone demographic change even as the entire Hudson River Valley has experienced transformations in its place in the nation.

We have examined a 24-county expanse of land adjacent to the east and west of the Hudson River in New York and New Jersey. This area stretches from New York City and parts of northeastern New Jersey all the way north to the Canadian border (see small illustration, Figure A1). We have placed these 24 counties into five regions, but our analysis is mostly focused on the southernmost four of these regions in which the majority of blacks in the Hudson River Valley have lived and which the chapters in this collection address (see large illustration, Figure A1). The first area we have identified is what we call the "Mouth of the Valley" or the "Valley Mouth." This area includes the Bronx, Manhattan, Queens, and Brooklyn, as well as Hudson and Essex counties in New Jersey. At times, this first region, because it is easily the most urban and most populous regarding blacks, is compared in our analysis to the three regions immediately and successively north. Just above the Valley Mouth is an area we have dubbed the "South Hudson," which includes Westchester and Rockland counties in New York, and Bergen and Passaic counties

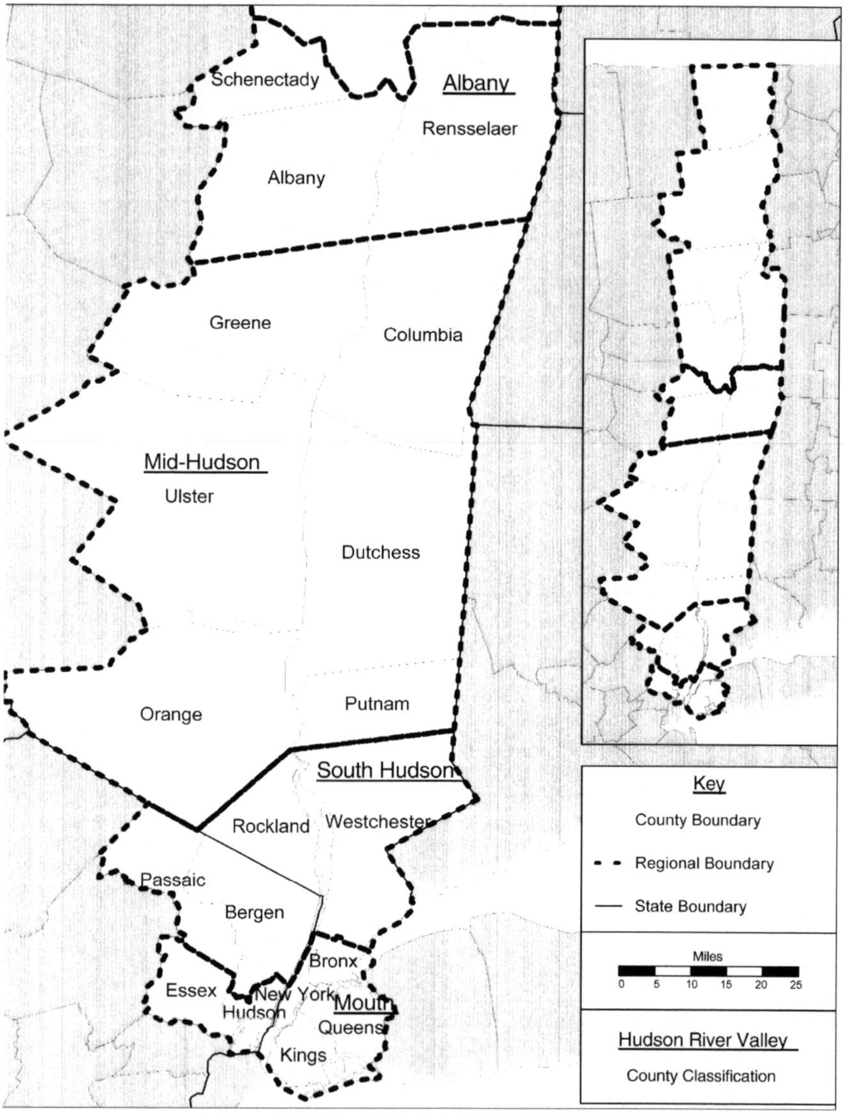

Figure A1. Hudson Valley Counties and Regions, 1790–2000 (Historical Composite).

in New Jersey. Passaic does not have any access to the Hudson River today, but for decades in the past, it was part of Bergen County, which has the Hudson River running along its eastern border. The six counties of Orange, Putnam, Dutchess, Ulster, Greene, and Columbia make up an area we call the "Mid-Hudson." North of these is the "Albany Region," including Albany, Schenectady, and Rensselaer counties. The six counties stretching to the Canadian border make up our "North Hudson" region. These include Saratoga, Washington, Warren, Essex, and Clinton counties. This area was never highly developed. It now exists mainly as a tourist center and, to some extent, as a bedroom community for Albany.[1]

We used two sources of data, both derived from the U.S. censuses from 1790 to 2000, for this project. The first is published tabulations from the census as compiled by the Inter-University Consortium for Political and Social Research.[2] These include population totals and totals for blacks for each decade. The second source was samples of census returns themselves, as coded from the raw schedules by various researchers. These are called Public Use Micro-data Samples (PUMS). More specifically, we used Integrated Public Use Micro-data Samples (IPUMS) from a demographic project at the University of Minnesota. The IPUMS data preserve all of the original census-collected information, while trying to put it into as common a format as possible. The tabulated data were used to get a comprehensive picture of black settlement from 1790 to 2000, while the IPUMS data were used to look at the status of the black population from 1850 to 1990 regarding urbanity, birthplace, literacy, education, and occupation.[3]

The literature on settlement patterns of blacks offers some guidance to the present study. There has been considerable work done on The Great Migration, a redistribution of blacks from the South to major metropolitan areas especially in the North.[4] Additional research has been conducted that examines the trend toward increased rates of suburbanization among blacks, particularly during the 1960s, 1970s, and 1980s.[5] However, none of these works, with the exception of Faustine Jones's *Black Americans and the City: A Historical Survey* attempt to sketch the migration patterns of a people for any period of more than a few decades, nor do they focus on a specific region. The availability of the data resources touched upon above makes this analysis possible.

Changing Regional Settlement Patterns in the Hudson River Valley

Table A1 documents that the proportion of blacks living in the Hudson River Valley declined in the nineteenth century but increased in the twentieth century.

Table A1 *Black and Total Population in Hudson River Valley, 1790–2000*

	1790	1800	1810	1820	1830	1840	1850	1860	1870	1880	1890
North Hudson											
% Black	0.52%	1.09%	4.07%	1.08%	0.87%	0.76%	0.66%	0.65%	0.66%	0.66%	0.61%
Blacks	81	750	3,866	1,177	1,149	1,117	1,176	1,259	1,324	1,411	1,292
Persons	15,692	68,571	94,915	109,217	131,741	146,846	178,790	192,971	200,678	213,618	210,708
Albany Region											
% Black	5.12%	4.91%	4.01%	3.03%	2.55%	1.99%	1.39%	1.02%	0.81%	0.84%	0.73%
Blacks	3,893	3,164	3,256	2,766	2,935	2,914	2,601	2,237	2,046	2,469	2,338
Persons	75,980	64,485	81,171	91,350	115,291	146,239	186,696	220,220	253,948	293,756	318,863
Mid-Hudson											
% Black	6.81%	6.24%	5.63%	4.95%	4.29%	3.81%	3.15%	2.73%	2.44%	2.41%	2.08%
Blacks	8,217	9,352	9,249	9,471	9,219	8,983	8,364	8,154	8,131	8,408	7,397
Persons	120,619	149,891	164,212	191,356	214,902	235,482	265,858	298,184	333,314	349,046	355,419
South Hudson											
% Black	11.67%	11.01%	10.07%	8.58%	7.39%	5.82%	4.43%	2.92%	2.38%	2.63%	2.28%
Blacks	4,267	5,387	5,503	5,121	5,044	5,275	4,982	5,041	5,548	6,369	7,609
Persons	36,579	48,937	54,633	59,653	68,256	90,618	112,519	172,602	233,099	242,324	334,206
Valley Area North of Mouth											
% Black	6.61%	5.62%	5.54%	4.10%	3.46%	2.95%	2.30%	1.89%	1.67%	1.70%	1.53%
Blacks	16,458	18,653	21,874	18,535	18,347	18,289	17,123	16,691	17,049	18,657	18,636
Persons	248,870	331,884	394,931	451,576	530,190	619,185	743,863	883,977	1,021,039	1,098,744	1,219,196

Table A1 *Black and Total Population in Hudson River Valley, 1790–2000 (continued)*

	1790	1800	1810	1820	1830	1840	1850	1860	1870	1880	1890
Mouth of Hudson											
% Black	13.26%	12.20%	11.15%	9.57%	7.39%	5.61%	3.07%	1.78%	1.53%	1.71%%	1.59%
Blacks	9,478	12,856	16,726	17,913	21,248	24,971	24,168	23,370	26,105	38,999	47,803
Persons	71,458	105,391	149,996	187,205	287,495	444,751	787,034	1,311,749	1,708,922	2,274,241	3,013,131
Total Valley											
% Black	8.10%	7.21%	7.08%	5.71%	4.84%	4.07%	2.70%	1.82%	1.58%	1.71%	1.57%
Blacks	25,936	31,509	38,600	36,448	39,595	43,260	41,291	40,061	43,154	57,656	66,439
Persons	320,328	437,275	544,927	638,781	817,685	1,063,936	1,530,897	2,195,726	2,729,961	3,372,985	4,232,327

Table A1 *Black and Total Population in Hudson River Valley, 1790–2000 (continued)*

	1900	1910	1920	1930	1940	1950	1960	1970	1980	1990	2000
North Hudson											
% Black	0.62%	0.56%	0.53%	0.69%	0.87%	0.89%	1.45%	1.35%	1.32%	1.99%	2.07%
Blacks	1,325	1,252	1,132	1,551	2,058	2,229	4,201	4,473	5,029	8,476	9,182
Persons	214,793	223,606	212,359	224,616	236,551	249,926	289,596	331,371	380,334	426,011	443,725
Albany Region											
% Black	0.71%	0.60%	0.65%	0.89%	1.04%	1.71%	2.77%	3.78%	4.70%	6.04%	8.49%
Blacks	2,356	2,308	2,636	4,060	4,840	8,782	15,747	22,654	27,638	36,121	50,394
Persons	334,120	384,177	408,598	456,755	465,643	514,490	568,407	599,107	587,821	597,617	593,658
Mid-Hudson											
% Black	2.40%	2.42%	1.95%	2.34%	2.89%	3.20%	4.42%	5.07%	5.17%	5.84%	6.97%
Blacks	8,694	9,280	7,048	9,299	12,540	15,144	26,060	36,758	43,482	54,491	70,173
Persons	362,427	383,968	362,098	397,169	433,617	473,891	588,962	725,445	840,357	933,561	1,006,300
South Hudson											
% Black	2.61%	2.37%	2.23%	3.18%	3.73%	4.11%	5.18%	6.99%	8.89%	9.95%	10.24%
Blacks	11,908	16,216	19,195	39,725	51,045	65,434	110,377	173,262	215,045	240,985	264,603
Persons	456,198	683,832	859,861	1,247,652	1,366,818	1,591,324	2,132,567	2,480,106	2,419,099	2,421,389	2,583,379

Table A1 *Black and Total Population in Hudson River Valley, 1790–2000 (continued)*

	1900	1910	1920	1930	1940	1950	1960	1970	1980	1990	2000
Valley Area North of Mouth											
% Black	1.78%	1.73%	1.63%	2.35%	2.82%	3.24%	4.37%	5.73%	6.89%	7.77%	8.52%
Blacks	24,283	29,056	30,011	54,635	70,483	91,589	156,385	237,147	291,194	340,073	394,352
Persons	1,367,538	1,675,583	1,842,916	2,326,192	2,502,629	2,829,631	3,579,532	4,136,029	4,227,611	4,378,578	4,627,062
Mouth of Hudson											
% Black	1.86%	2.02%	2.79%	4.84%	6.16%	9.41%	14.30%	21.85%	26.39%	27.06%	25.99%
Blacks	76,592	115,834	189,275	401,336	539,970	870,323	1,300,321	1,991,075	2,145,211	2,312,337	2,330,813
Persons	4,115,282	5,731,031	6,784,760	8,296,343	8,769,934	9,253,788	9,094,272	9,111,572	8,127,606	8,545,518	8,967,158
Total Valley											
% Black	1.84%	1.97%	2.54%	4.29%	5.42%	7.97%	11.49%	16.82%	19.72%	20.52%	20.05%
Blacks	100,875	144,890	219,286	455,971	610,453	961,912	1,456,706	2,228,222	2,436,405	2,652,410	2,725,165
Persons	5,482,820	7,406,614	8,627,676	10,622,535	11,272,563	12,083,419	12,673,804	13,247,601	12,355,217	12,924,096	13,594,220

Source: ICPSR, Historical Data, as enhanced by Michael Haines; U.S. Census Bureau, USA Counties; U.S. Census Bureau, Census 2000; Ruggles and Sobek and Associates, *IPUMS*.

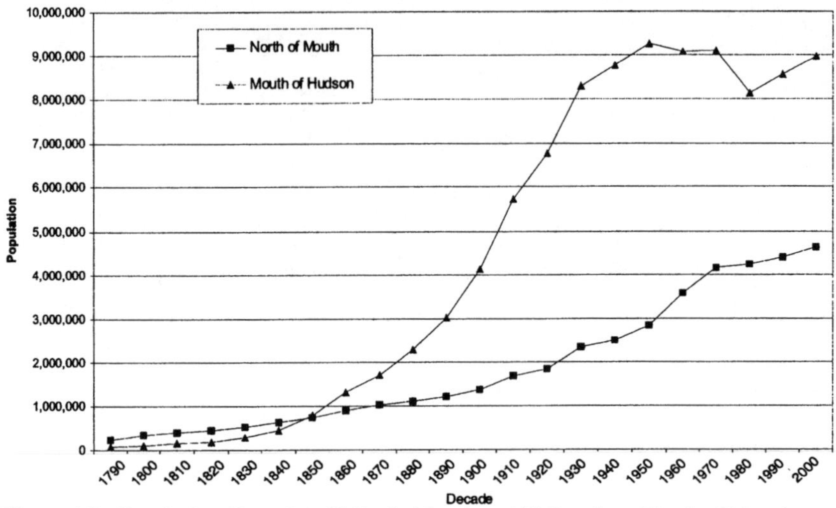

Figure A2. Population Growth in Valley's Mouth and Valley Area North of Mouth, 1790–2000.

Source: Inter-university Consortium for Political and Social Research (ICPSR), *Historical Demographic, Economic, and Social Data: The United States, 1790–1970* [computer file] (Ann Arbor, Michigan: Inter-university Consortium for Political and Social Research [producer and distributor, Summer 2001], Department of Economics, Colgate University, Hamilton, New York; U.S. Department of Commerce, U.S. Census Bureau, Economic and Statistics Administration, *USA Counties* 1998 [cd-rom], Issued May 1999; U.S. Census Bureau, *Census 2000 Profiles of General Demographic Characteristics: New York* (http://www.census.gov/Press-Release/www/2001/demoprofile.html); Steven Ruggles and Matthew Sobek and Associates, *Integrated Public Use Microdata Series: Version 2.0* (Minneapolis: Historical Census Projects, University of Minnesota, 1997, http://www.ipums.umn.edu).

Although the absolute number of blacks in the Hudson River Valley grew from 25,936 in 1790 to 66,439 100 years later, the total proportion of blacks slid steadily during the nineteenth century from its 1790 figure of 8.1% down to 1.6% in 1890. A reverse pattern occurred in the twentieth century as the black percentage of the valley's total population inched up from 1.8% in 1900 to 20.1% in 2000; these proportions stood in relation to a total black population of 100,875 in 1900 and 2,725,165 in 2000.

When these totals are disaggregated by region, several demographic trends are revealed. Not surprisingly, the Valley Mouth exceeded all other regions in the number of blacks it contained during the entire period (see Table A1 and Figures A2 and A3). Interestingly, however, from 1850 until the years following World War I, the suburban/rural South Hudson and Mid-Hudson claimed a greater proportion of blacks than did the New York City area (see Table A1). In

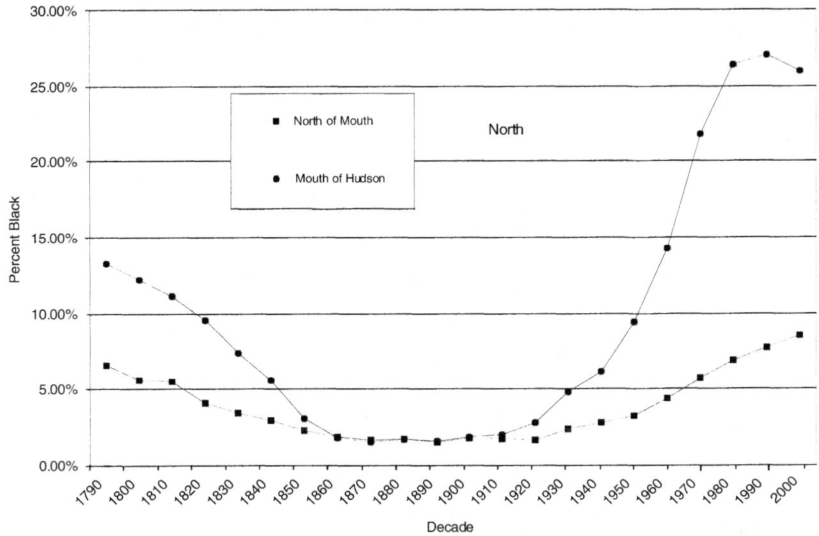

Figure A3. Percentage Black in Valley's Mouth and Valley Area North of Mouth 1790–2000.

Source: ICPSR, *Historical Data,* as enhanced by Michael Haines; U.S. Census Bureau, *USA Counties;* U.S. Census Bureau, *Census 2000;* Ruggles and Sobek and Associates, *IPUMS.*

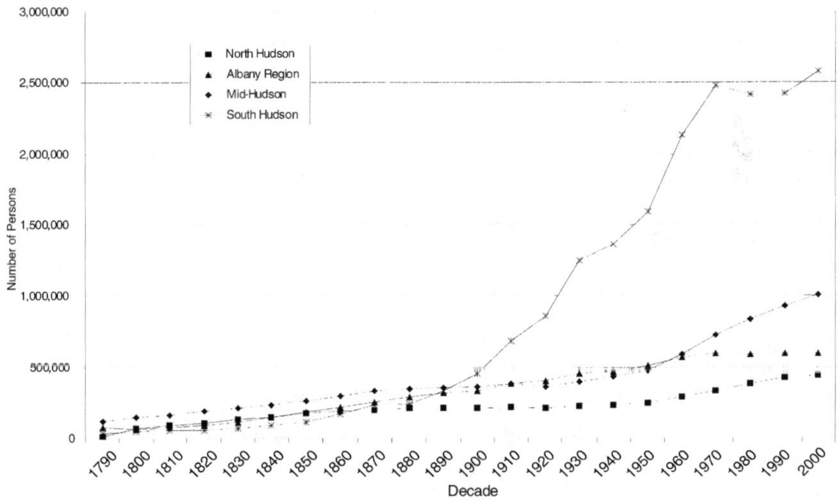

Figure A4. Population Growth by Valley Regions North of Valley Mouth, 1790–2000.

Source: ICPSR, *Historical Data,* as enhanced by Michael Haines; U.S. Census Bureau, *USA Counties;* U.S. Census Bureau, *Census 2000;* Ruggels and Sobek and Associates, *IPUMS.*

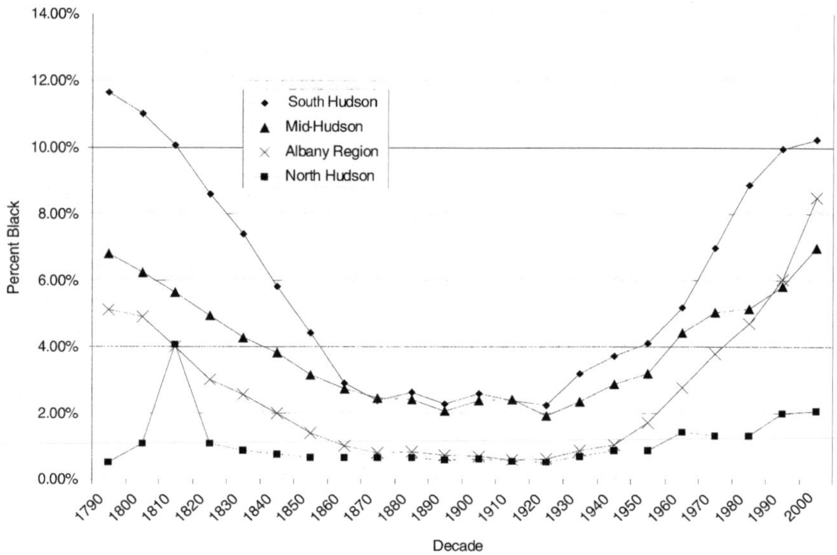

Figure A5. Percentage Black by Valley Regions North of Valley Mouth 1790–2000.
Source: ICPSR, *Historical Data,* as enhanced by Michael Haines; U.S. Census Bureau, *USA Counties;* U.S. Census Bureau, *Census 2000;* Ruggles and Sobek and Associates, *IPUMS.*

other words, although blacks in these two regions were less numerous than they were in the immediate vicinity of New York City during the late nineteenth and early twentieth century, they were a more salient presence than elsewhere in the valley at the same time. As Figure A4 shows, the growth of population in the areas north of the Valley Mouth was steady, except that growth was very rapid after 1900 in the South Hudson area.

Throughout the entire 210 years, the black population dipped and climbed at about the same rates in the South Hudson, Mid-Hudson, and Albany regions (see Figure A5). However, of these three regions, the Mid-Hudson, Albany, and South Hudson regions claimed the greatest number of blacks in descending order until 1890. Still, judging by proportional representation, blacks were most noticeable in the South Hudson, Mid-Hudson, and Albany regions in descending order (see Table A1 and Figure A5). During the twentieth century, with rare exception only, the closer a region to the Valley Mouth, the larger its total and proportionate black population. Thus, except for a few antebellum years, among all valley regions north of the Mouth of the Valley, the North Hudson claimed the smallest number and proportion of blacks for most of the period (see Table A1 and Figure A5).

Rural-UrbanShifts

Beginning in 1850, when data are first available, up through 1990, black and nonblack settlement patterns in terms of rural and urban location in the Mouth of the Valley were almost identical.[6] In 1850 about 80% of all blacks and nonblacks lived in urban settings, which is defined as any place with at least 2,500 people. By 1910, virtually all blacks and nonblacks in the Mouth of the Valley were urban. In the four regions north of the mouth, however, blacks and nonblacks followed very different trends. Very few of either group were urban in 1850 as was true of most Americans at this time. For blacks, it was a mere 5.5% and for nonblacks 15.8%. But urbanization increased generally in the nation during the late nineteenth and early twentieth centuries, with the Northeast leading the way. Not surprisingly then, by 1880, both blacks and nonblacks in the Hudson River Valley were about 40% urban, but by 1920, blacks were over 80% urban, while nonblacks stood at about 70% urban. By 1990, the last year for which we have data, virtually all blacks, but only four-fifths of the nonblacks have settled in urban areas. Plainly, in recent times, blacks are much more urban than nonblacks. This is directly related to the patterns identified by many demographers of nonblack rapid settlement in so-called nonmetropolitan areas during the late twentieth century. At the same time, more and more blacks are in places that formerly would be considered suburban.[7]

Changes in Birthplace

The shift in source of the black population in the Hudson River Valley can be discerned by noting the shift in the birthplaces of blacks. Figure A6 presents data for the entire region for the period 1850 to 1990. As that figure shows, in 1850, 1870, and 1880 the vast majority (over three-quarters) of blacks were born in New York or New Jersey. A small proportion was born in the southern United States, a few in the West Indies, and a small proportion came from elsewhere. But by 1910, over half the blacks in the Hudson River Valley were born in the South, and only about one-third in New York and New Jersey. The Great Migration had started and continued throughout the period until a downturn in 1970. (Unfortunately, comparable data do not exist for 1940, 1950, or 1960.) By 1970 about one-half were born in New York or New Jersey and about one-quarter were born in the South. By 1990 about one-sixth were born in Caribbean countries, one-fifth in the South, and over half in New York and New Jersey.

These general patterns of black birthplace hold true even when the more populous Mouth of the Valley is compared to valley regions to its north. As a major national and international metropole, the New York City-based Mouth,

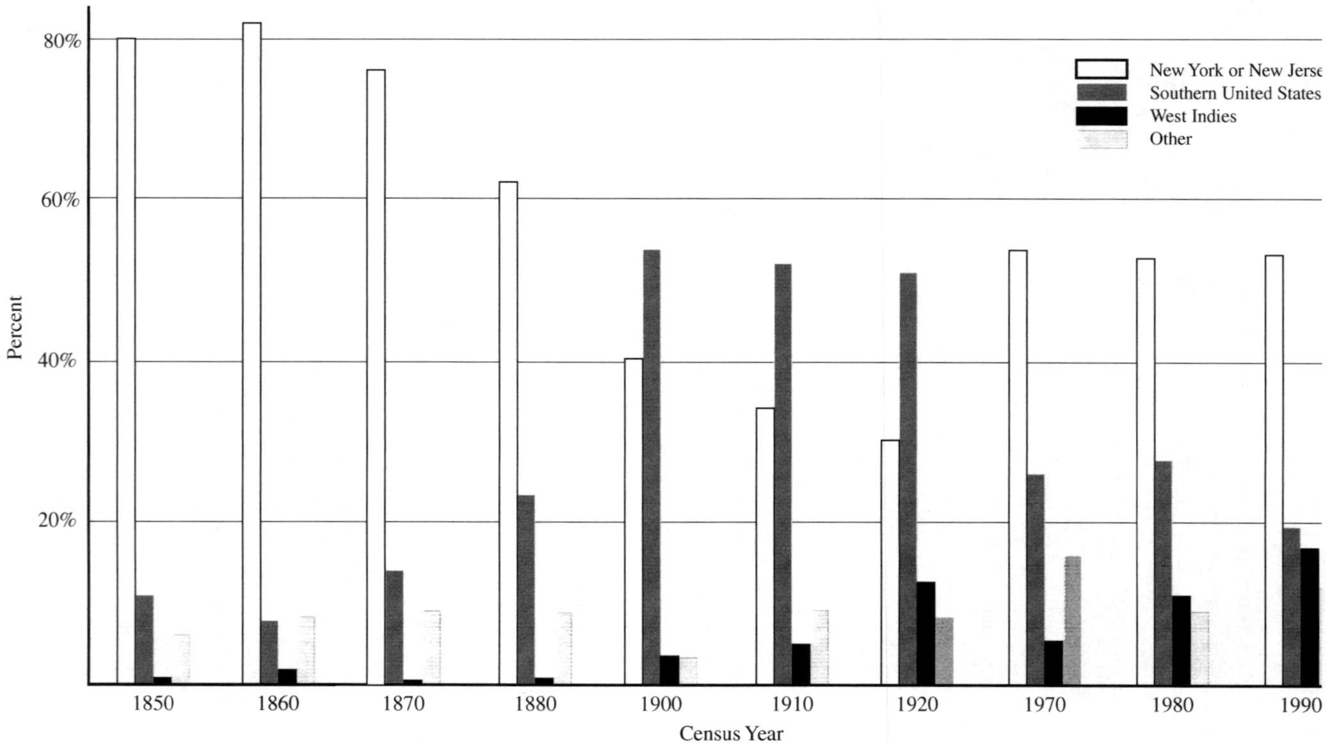

Figure A6. Place of Birth, Blacks in the Hudson River Valley. *Source:* ICPSR, *Historical Data,* as enhanced by Michael Haines; U.S. Census Bureau, *USA Counties;* U.S. Census Bureau, *Census 2000;* Ruggles and Sobek and Associates, *IPUMS.*

however, drew a larger nonlocal black population and did so earlier on. In the Mouth of the Valley in 1850, 73% of blacks reported being born in New York or New Jersey, but only 51% of nonblacks were born in those two states. For blacks, about 18% were born in the southern part of the United States, while a handful were from the West Indies. Considering the area North of the Mouth, the percentage from New York and New Jersey was predominant until 1900. As in the Mouth, the proportion from the South soared by 1900 to over 50%. By late in the twentieth century, the percentage born in New York and New Jersey began to rise again, but there was a substantial presence from the Caribbean.

In summary, the black presence in the Hudson River Valley first was furnished largely by blacks born in the area. After the beginning of the twentieth century, southern blacks began to join those born nearby. More recently, a substantial number of Caribbean-born blacks arrived. The latter group continues to grow. These immigrants were joined by a rise in black newcomers from Africa and elsewhere in the African diaspora—noticeable from 1970 to the present. Therefore, the origins of blacks in the Hudson River Valley changed in major ways during the 140 years for which we have data.

Occupational, Literacy, and Educational Changes

To document the changing role of the blacks in the Valley, information on their changing occupational patterns was examined. Though there was some divergence of patterns in the Valley Mouth and the region to the North, because of the potential number of occupations and the relatively small sample sizes overall trends will be considered. In 1850, about 50% of blacks were employed as laborers, about 5% as semi-skilled operatives, 21% in services (not including private services such as a maid, a cook), about 13% in farming occupations, and 8% in private services (see Table A2). In the sample, no blacks were found in professional, managerial, clerical, or sales positions, and only 4% were working in craft occupations. For nonblacks, things were much different. Only 15% were laborers, 15% were semi-skilled operatives, 2% were in services (not including private services), 1% were in private service, and 23% were in farming. For nonblacks 3% were in professional occupations, 7% in managerial fields, 6% in sales, but 26% in craft occupations.

By 1910, the occupational situation of blacks had radically altered. Laborers accounted for only 13%, down from about half, but 42% of employed blacks were now in private service. Very small percentages were now in professional, managerial, clerical, sales, or craft fields, but 20% were now semi-skilled operatives, partly as a reflection of growing levels of industrialization in the region. Still in all, the major change in occupations held by blacks was

Table A2 *Occupational Distribution of Blacks and Non-Blacks in Hudson River Valley, 1850 to 1990*

Non-Blacks						Blacks					
1850	1880	1910	1940	1970	1990	1850	1880	1910	1940	1970	1990
Professional											
14,054	52,852	181,869	514,641	1,031,385	1,369,480	0	100	2,518	12,798	97,052	240,292
3.3%	2.9%	5.6%	9.3%	16.5%	23.0%	0.0%	0.2%	2.8%	4.0%	9.3%	15.4%
Managerial											
30,726	108,022	346,097	532,285	477,855	806,919	0	600	2,520	6,898	23,935	103,238
7.2%	5.9%	10.6%	9.6%	7.6%	13.6%	0.0%	1.2%	2.8%	2.2%	2.3%	6.6%
Clerical											
2,627	51,888	332,490	933,630	1,629,319	1,273,288	0	199	1,512	14,392	250,783	433,219
0.6%	2.8%	10.2%	16.9%	26.1%	21.4%	0.0%	0.4%	1.7%	4.5%	24.0%	27.8%
Sales											
25,484	86,188	238,056	460,117	519,018	438,119	0	300	755	5,848	37,305	61,761
6.0%	4.7%	7.3%	8.3%	8.3%	7.4%	0.0%	0.6%	0.8%	1.8%	3.6%	4.0%
Craft											
109,346	225,737	540,827	762,258	631,487	488,710	404	300	3,274	17,871	83,026	103,841
25.7%	12.2%	16.6%	13.8%	10.1%	8.2%	3.9%	0.6%	3.7%	5.6%	8.0%	6.7%
Armed Forces											
1,920	4,791	5,542	22,425	31,749	16,026	0	0	0	1,010	4,555	5,018
0.5%	0.3%	0.2%	0.4%	0.5%	0.3%	0.0%	0.0%	0.0%	0.3%	0.4%	0.3%

Table A2 *Occupational Distribution of Blacks and Non-Blacks in Hudson River Valley, 1850 to 1990 (continued)*

Non-Blacks						Blacks					
1850	1880	1910	1940	1970	1990	1850	1880	1910	1940	1970	1990
Operatives											
65,082	331,180	796,959	1,144,312	989,708	572,213	505	7,186	9,319	53,222	234,480	173,503
15.3%	18.0%	24.4%	20.7%	15.8%	9.6%	4.9%	14.8%	10.4%	16.8%	22.5%	11.1%
Services											
9,707	45,882	188,170	498,155	651,436	726,254	2,123	9,883	18,390	54,091	189,688	345,805
(Not Private)											
2.3%	2.5%	5.8%	9.0%	10.4%	12.2%	20.6%	20.3%	20.5%	17.1%	18.2%	22.2%
Laborers											
63,296	703,966	305,804	398,263	214,826	207,113	5,153	14,666	12,089	53,548	56,178	72,819
14.9%	38.2%	9.4%	7.2%	3.4%	3.5%	50.0%	30.2%	13.5%	16.9%	5.4%	4.7%
Farm											
98,035	105,942	112,587	96,391	26,290	16,484	1,316	1,997	1,763	2,685	3,004	1,743
23.1%	5.7%	3.5%	1.7%	0.4%	0.3%	12.8%	4.1%	2.0%	0.8%	0.3%	0.1%
Private Service											
4,854	126,503	212,116	162,999	48,623	30,483	810	13,372	37,534	94,268	63,398	19,026
1.1%	6.9%	6.5%	2.9%	0.8%	0.5%	7.9%	27.5%	41.9%	29.8%	6.1%	1.2%
Total (Weighted)											
425,131	1,842,951	3,260,517	5,525,476	6,251,693	5,945,089	10,311	48,603	89,674	316,631	1,043,402	1,560,265

Source: ICPSR, Historical Data, as enhanced by Michael Haines; U.S. Census Bureau, *USA Counties;* U.S. Census Bureau, *Census 2000;* Ruggles and Sobek and Associates, *IPUMS*.

the switch from laborer to private service. For nonblacks, there were some gains in professional, managerial, sales, and semi-skilled operatives. There was a major decline in farm occupations from 23% to 3%. These percentages are in Table A2.

Through the twentieth century, the occupational structure of the blacks and nonblacks began to converge as equal employment opportunities became available to blacks. By 1990, as shown in Table A2, blacks had begun to bridge the gap in professional and managerial occupations. Few blacks continued in private service and virtually none in farming. Instead, a greater percentage of blacks than whites were employed in clerical positions. Blacks were almost twice as likely as whites to be working in the service sector, 22% versus 12%. As throughout the United States, blacks shifted from relatively menial occupations in the nineteenth and early twentieth centuries to more mainstream occupations by the end of the twentieth century.[8] Nonetheless, substantial gaps remain in terms of the occupational attainment of blacks compared to others in the Hudson River Valley.

The course of literacy and then education for blacks in the Valley follows that of occupation. In 1850, only two-thirds of blacks in the Mouth and about 55% North of the Mouth reported that they were fully literate. Compare this to the 93% of nonblacks in both areas, who indicated that they were fully literate. By 1920, the last census for which literacy data exist, 98% of the blacks in the Valley Mouth and 92% North of the Mouth report that they are fully literate. The proportion literate in the Valley Mouth is higher than that for nonblacks, which report a literacy rate of 93%. This is undoubtedly due to the high proportion of European immigrants in the Valley Mouth at this time. North of the Mouth, the figure for nonblacks is 96%.

The census began to collect information of educational attainment in 1940. Though the area that can be used for 1940 and 1950 is somewhat larger than the Valley as we have been defining it, the rapidly growing educational attainment of blacks as well as nonblacks is striking. In 1940, just 13% of blacks had completed high school, and only 2% had completed college. For nonblacks, the figures are much greater, 24% completing high school and 6% completing college. By 1990, the figures for blacks are 12% completing college and 73% completing high school. Compare this to 78% of nonblacks completing high school, but 27% have completed college. Though the educational gap has closed for high school, it remains large and significant for college.

Conclusion

Our brief demographic portrait of blacks in the Hudson River Valley makes several points plain. The black presence in the Valley can be founded in the earliest population counts of the American republic. Despite this early presence, there was only very slow growth of blacks in the area during the nineteenth century. Blacks in the Valley became more literate, yet they were relegated to menial occupations. First, they worked primarily as laborers. Then many went into private service. It was only with the later part of the twentieth century that blacks began to move in large numbers into the entire range of occupations. This may be due to the fact that in the middle of the twentieth century, black levels of education began to rapidly improve, and many new opportunities opened for blacks based upon the Civil Rights Acts of the 1960s.[9] The large growth of the black population in the Valley, which began with the Great Migration from the South and which continues to the present day, reflects these new opportunities. Now settlers from the Caribbean, Africa, and elsewhere are adding to the black population, which is now about one-fifth of the total population of the area.

In sum, the black presence in the Hudson River Valley both reflects and contributes to the wider trends affecting the black population in the United States. These include migration from the South, increased urbanization, increased education, and increased occupational attainment. One should expect that the black presence will continue to grow and the black contributions to Valley life, always important, will become even more prominent.

Notes

1. It should be noted that the physical boundaries of several Hudson River Valley counties changed during the 210-year period examined here. As examples, Putnam County was set apart from Westchester County in 1812; Passaic County, as noted above, was carved from Bergen County in 1837; and the Bronx was absorbed by New York County (Manhattan) in two stages in 1874 and 1895, and then made into a borough of the city in 1898. When such changes occurred, we did our best to assign the units to the general areas described.

2. We used so-called ICPSR Study 3 enhanced by Michael Haines to include all tabulations available at the county level from 1790 through 1990. For 2000, we used the recently released 2000 Census. See Inter-university Consortium for Political and Social Research, *Historical, Demographic, Economic, and Social Data: The United States, 1790–1970* [Computer file] (Ann Arbor, Michigan: Inter-university Consortium for Political and Social Research [producer and distributor], 1975).

3. One should always allow some margin of error for census tabulations regarding all populations, and for blacks in particular, for several reasons. First, the census was tabulated by hand and then, in the late nineteenth through the mid-twentieth centuries, using punch cards. Second, there is the issue of the historical undercount of minority and poor populations who live in areas deemed undesirable by or whose mobility makes

them elusive to enumerators. In addition, census definitions of blacks constantly changed during this period. Through 1880, black was considered a reply to the census query about "color." Thus, it was possible for people of light, Caucasian-like complexion who were partly of African ancestry to be regarded as "white." In 1890 and after, the notion of "race" became important on the census and this category replaced "color" on the questionnaire. Indeed, for the 1890 census, various definitions of octoroon, quadroon, mulatto, and Negro were used. In the early twentieth century, the census adopted the so-called "one-drop" rule whereby anyone with any trace of African ancestry was classified as black. Even with the one-drop rule, some people were hard to classify. In 2000, the Office of Management and Budget mandated that census responses from persons identifying themselves with more than one race be allowed. Still, only a small proportion of census respondents chose this option. For purposes of standardizing the count of race, as it is generally understood today, the United States Justice Department has promulgated a rule on "how to count," which is effectively a generalization of the one-drop rule for all minorities.

4. Faustine C. Jones, "Black Americans and the City: A Historical Survey," *Journal of Negro Education,* Vol. 42, No. 3 (Summer 1973), pp. 261–282; George W. Groh, *The Black Migration: The Journey to Urban America* (New York: Weybright and Talley, 1972); Arna Bontemps and Jack Conroy, *They Seek a City* (New York: Doubleday, Doran and Co., 1945).

5. William H. Frey, "Mover Destination Selectivity and the Changing Suburbanization of Metropolitan Whites and Blacks," *Demography,* Vol. 22, No. 2 (May 1985), pp. 223–243; Scott J. South and Kyle Crowder, "Residential Mobility Between Cities and Suburbs: Race, Suburbanization, and Back-to-the City Moves," *Demography,* Vol. 34, No. 4 (November 1997), pp. 525–538.

6. Information about rural and urban residence, birthplace, occupation, literacy, and education were derived from the Integrated Public Micro-Data Samples (IPUMS). See Steven Ruggles and Matthew Sobek and Associates, *Integrated Public Use Microdata Series: Version 2.0* (Minneapolis: Historical Census Projects, University of Minnesota, 1997), *http://www.ipums.umm.edu.* Data exist for samples of Census Records for 1850, 1860, 1870, 1880, 1900, 1910, and 1920, where complete location, including county are recorded. For these years, the areas used are the Mouth of the Valley and North of the Mouth. Census records from 1890 were destroyed in a fire. Data from 1930 are not yet publicly available. For the years 1940 through 1990, the samples have much less information on location. For 1970, 1980, and 1990 the areas are broadly comparable to the Mouth of the Valley, and North of the Mouth. For 1940 and 1950, a larger area comparable to the whole Valley was constructed. For 1960, no comparable areas could be created. The 2000 data with this information have yet to be released.

7. See Frey, "Mover Destination Selectivity" and South and Crowder, "Residential Mobility."

8. See Reynolds Farley, *The NewAmerican Reality: Who We Are, How We Got Here, Where We Are Going* (New York: Russell Sage Foundation, 1996).

9. See Farley, *The New American Reality.*

Contributors

Aileen B. Agnew received her doctorate from the University of New Hampshire. She has taught as an adjunct at the University of Southern Maine and the University of Maine at Farmington, and currently is an independent historian. She is also a trained public archeologist who has served as executive director for the Maine Center for Archeological Studies and for Maine Citizens for Historic Preservation.

Myra B. Young Armstead is Professor of History at Bard College where she chairs the Multiethnic Studies program and co-chairs the American Studies Program. Her teaching and research interests are in U.S. urban history, African American and African diasporic history, women's history, and labor history. She has published *"Lord, Please Don't Take Me in August": African Americans in Newport and Saratoga Springs, 1870–1930* and is currently conducting research on black Pentecostalism in the United States.

Andrew A. Beveridge is Associate Professor of Sociology and Director of the M.A. in Applied Social Research Program at Queens College, City University of New York. He is engaged in a number of projects and has published widely concerning demographic trends and change. He also serves as a demographic consultant for *The New York Times,* and has testified on demographic issues in numerous civil rights cases.

Sherri-Ann P. Butterfield, the child of Jamaican parents, was born and raised in New York City. She recently received her Ph.D. in Sociology from the University of Michigan and now teaches at Rutgers University. Her general research interests are race and ethnicity, immigration in the United States and internationally), and urban studies. Building on her dissertation and fieldwork in England, her new project is a comparison of second-generation West Indian immigrant experience in New York City and London.

Joan H. Geismar began practicing as an urban archaeologist in the New York metropolitan area in 1981, when she received her doctorate in Anthropology from Columbia University. She has extensive experience in documenting the history of sites in the New York metropolitan area through archival research and in-ground exploration. Among her publications are *The Archaeology of Social Disintegration in Skunk Hollow, a Nineteenth–Century Rural Black Community* and numerous scholarly popular journals.

Michael E. Groth is Associate Professor of History at Wells College. He has lectured extensively throughout New York State on slavery and freedom in Dutchess County in public and academic forums, including those funded or sponsored by the National Endowment for the Humanities, the New York Council for the Humanities, and the Conference on New York State History. He has published on this subject as well as in *New York History* and *Hudson Valley Regional Review.*

Bruce D. Haynes is Assistant Professor of Sociology at the University of California at Davis. His interests include racial identity formation, suburbanization, and community organization. He has recently published *Red Lines, Black Spaces: The Politics of Race and Space in a Black Middle-Class Suburb,* and is currently writing a book about Jews of African descent in the United States.

Graham Russell Hodges is Professor of American History at Colgate University where he specializes in teaching U.S. colonial history. He is the author of *Root and Branch: African Americans in New York and East Jersey, 1613–1863* and of many other books on early New York and African Americans. His current projects include a study of cabdrivers in New York City and of David Ruggles.

Denise Love Johnson (1951–2001) graduated from Vassar College where, as a student majoring in geography, she completed a senior thesis in 1973 on African American migration to Poughkeepsie from the South. From 1973 to 1977, she served as a faculty member in the history department at Poughkeepsie High School and established its African American Studies program. She worked as a marketing consultant, corporate trainer, and college instructor in business management and information technology.

Michael McMenemy, who lives in Middletown, New York, received his B.A. in Sociology from the State University of New York at New Paltz and M.A. in applied social research from Queens College—The City University of New York. He has now begun a career in social research.

Linda Pershing serves as Director of the Women's Studies program at California State University at San Marcos. A folklorist and anthropologist by training, her scholarship focuses on the politics of gender, ethnicity, race, and class in everyday cultural expression. Prior to her current position, she was an associate professor in the Department of Women's Studies at the State University of New York, Albany, and Director of Academics for the University of Redlands's San Diego Regional Programs.

Edythe Ann Quinn is Associate Professor of History at Hartwick College. Her book, *The Hills in the Mid-Nineteenth Century: The History of a Rural Afro-American Community in Westchester County, New York,* was crucial in successful historical preservation efforts to include *The Hills* cemetery in the National Register of Historic Sites.

Paul Stoller is Professor of Anthropology at West Chester University of Pennsylvania. For over two decades, he has conducted research among Sonhay-speaking populations in Niger and New York City. His research interests include Africa, ethnographic film, anthropology of religion, and the culture of cities. He currently co-edits the Contemporary Ethnography series for the University of Pennsylvania Press.

Irma Watkins-Owens is Associate Professor of History and Chair of the African American Studies Department at Fordham University. Her teaching and research interests include African American history, ethnic history, and the history of women of color.

Index